NEW ZEALAND'S
BEST TRIPS

26 AMAZING ROAD TRIPS

This edition written and researched by

**Brett Atkinson,
Sarah Bennett, Lee Slater**

SYMBOLS IN THIS BOOK

✓	Top Tips	📖	History & Culture	📷	Essential Photo
🔗	Link Your Trips	👫	Family	🏃	Walking Tour
⬤	Tips from Locals	🍷	Food & Drink	✖	Eating
↱	Trip Detour	🌳	Outdoors	🛏	Sleeping

☎ Telephone Number	@ Internet Access	✚ Family-Friendly
⊙ Opening Hours	🛜 Wi-Fi Access	
P Parking	🥗 Vegetarian Selection	
❄ Air-Conditioning		
	🏊 Swimming Pool	

MAP LEGEND

Routes
- ▬▬ Trip Route
- ▬▬ Trip Detour
- ▬▬ Linked Trip
- ▬▬ Walk Route
- ▬▬ Tollway
- Freeway
- Primary
- Secondary
- Tertiary
- Lane
- Unsealed Road
- ⁘⁘ Plaza/Mall
- ⁙⁙⁙ Steps
-)꞉꞉꞉(Tunnel
- ══ Pedestrian Overpass
- --- Walk Track/Path

Boundaries
- --- International
- --- State/Province
- ⌐⌐ Cliff
- ⌐⌐ Wall

Population
- ✪ Capital (National)
- ◉ Capital (State/Province)
- ● City/Large Town
- ● Town/Village

Transport
- ✈ Airport
- ⊕ Cable Car/Funicular
- P Parking
- ⊕ Train/Railway
- ⊕ Tram
- Ⓜ Underground Train Station

Trips
- 1 Trip Numbers
- 9 Trip Stop
- 🏃 Walking tour
- ↱ Trip Detour

Route Markers
- E44 E-road network
- M100 National network

Hydrography
- River/Creek
- Intermittent River
- Swamp/Mangrove
- Canal
- Water
- Dry/Salt/Intermittent Lake
- Glacier

Areas
- Beach
- Cemetery (Christian)
- Cemetery (Other)
- Park
- Forest
- Urban Area
- Sportsground

CONTENTS

Auckland &
the North
p32

Rotorua &
the Central
North Island
p84

Wellington
& the East
Coast
p132

Marlborough
& Nelson
p160

Canterbury
& the West
Coast
p202

Queenstown
& the South
p288

Contents cont.

DRIVING IN NEW ZEALAND 348

Classic Trips

Look out for the Classic Trips stamp on our favorite routes in this book.

Matamata Rolling green hills of Middle Earth (Trip 7)

WELCOME TO
NEW ZEALAND

It's hard to imagine a better country for a road trip. New Zealand's two main islands serve up a feast of mountain landscapes, sublime forests, sweeping beaches and remote fiords, and many of these places are easily reached by scenic highways and quiet country roads. Come and see NZ at your own pace, with the freedom to explore its many hidden corners.

The 26 trips in this book will help you plan the ultimate NZ adventure – whether you want to laze on Abel Tasman beaches, tour Marlborough's wineries, see Rotorua's steaming volcanic wonders or tick bungy jumping off your bucket list in Queenstown.

These trips are stacked to the max with memorable adventures and stunning scenery along the way, so settle on your start point and get planning. And if you've only got time for one journey, make it one of our nine Classic Trips, which transport you to the very best of NZ. Turn the page for more.

→

NEW ZEALAND
Classic Trips

What Is a Classic Trip?

All the trips in this book show you the best of New Zealand, but we've chosen nine as our all-time favourites. These are our Classic Trips – the ones that lead you to the best of the iconic sights, the top activities and the unique New Zealand experiences. Turn the page to see the map, and look out for the Classic Trip stamp throughout the book.

22 Milford Sound Majesty
Thrilling Queenstown offers breathtaking adventures amid stunning scenery. (p293)

21 Southern Alps Circuit
Lake Tekapo forms a serene surround for the Church of the Good Shepherd. (p270)

1 Northland & the Bay of Islands World-class diving in the crystal-clear water of the Poor Knights Islands. (p37)

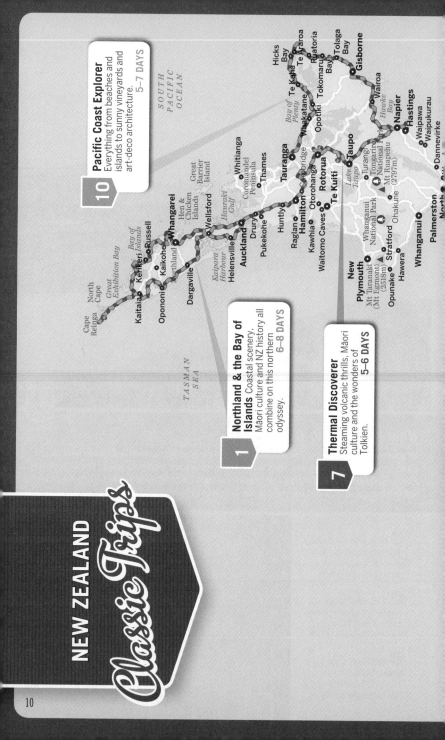

NEW ZEALAND
Classic Trips

SOUTH PACIFIC OCEAN

TASMAN SEA

10 Pacific Coast Explorer
Everything from beaches and islands to sunny vineyards and art-deco architecture.
5–7 DAYS

1 Northland & the Bay of Islands Coastal scenery, Māori culture and NZ history all combine on this northern odyssey. **6–8 DAYS**

7 Thermal Discoverer
Steaming volcanic thrills, Māori culture and the wonders of Tolkien. **5–6 DAYS**

Cape Reinga
North Cape
Great Exhibition Bay
Kaitaia
Kerikeri
Russell
Bay of Islands
Opononi
Kaikohe
Northland
Dargaville
Kaipara Harbour
Helensville
Wellsford
Hauraki Gulf
Hen & Chicken Islands
Great Barrier Island
Whangarei
Auckland
Drury
Pukekohe
Huntly
Hamilton
Cambridge
Raglan
Kawhia
Otorohanga
Waitomo Caves
Te Kuiti
Coromandel Peninsula
Whitianga
Thames
Tauranga
Bay of Plenty
Rotorua
Whakatane
Opotiki
Te Kaha
Hicks Bay
Te Araroa
Tokomaru Bay
Tolaga Bay
Ruatoria
Gisborne
Turangi
Lake Taupo
Taupo
Tongariro National Park
Mt Ruapehu (2797m)
Wairoa
Hawke Bay
Napier
Hastings
Waipawa
Waipukurau
Dannevirke
New Plymouth
Mt Taranaki (Mt Egmont) (2518m)
Opunake
Stratford
Hawera
Ohakune
Whanganui National Park
Whanganui
Palmerston North

10

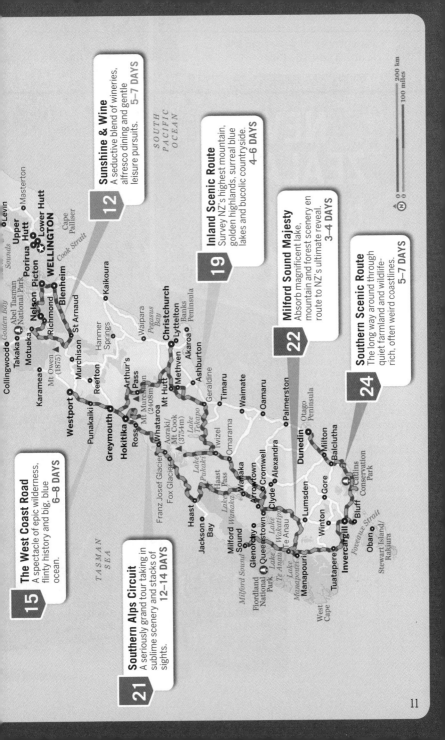

15 The West Coast Road
A spectacle of epic wilderness, flinty history and big, blue ocean. **6–8 DAYS**

21 Southern Alps Circuit
A seriously grand tour taking in sublime scenery and stacks of sights. **12–14 DAYS**

12 Sunshine & Wine
A seductive blend of wineries, alfresco dining and gentle leisure pursuits. **5–7 DAYS**

19 Inland Scenic Route
Survey NZ's highest mountain, golden highlands, surreal blue lakes and bucolic countryside. **4–6 DAYS**

22 Milford Sound Majesty
Absorb magnificent lake, mountain and forest scenery en route to NZ's ultimate reveal. **3–4 DAYS**

24 Southern Scenic Route
The long way around through quiet farmland and wildlife-rich, often weird coastlines. **5–7 DAYS**

200 km
100 miles

New Zealand's best sights and experiences, and the road trips that will take you there.

NEW ZEALAND
HIGHLIGHTS

★

Bay of Islands

History, culture and marine adventures combine on **Trip 1: Northland & the Bay of Islands**. Amble amid colonial history around genteel Russell, before cruising around the islands. At the Waitangi Treaty Grounds, modern New Zealand echoes amid warm Māori welcomes and cultural performances, and the new Museum of Waitangi presents the story of the 1840 agreement underpinning this country's past, present and future.

Trip

Bay of Islands Waitangi Treaty Grounds, Paihia

Queenstown Rafting on the Shotover River

Akaroa & Banks Peninsula

French-flavoured Akaroa bends around a pretty harbour on Banks Peninsula, with the world's rarest dolphin frolicking offshore. The Summit Rd above snakes around the rim of an ancient volcano while winding detours lead to hidden bays. Take **Trip 26: East Coast Express** to discover surprises on land and sea.

Trip

Queenstown

Queenstown may be the birthplace of bungy jumping, but there's way more to this place than leaping off a bridge attached to a rubber band. Against a backdrop of jagged mountains and a snake-shaped lake, travellers on **Trip 23: Central Otago Explorer** can hike, bike, raft or ride a ridiculously fun luge, then dine in cosmopolitan restaurants or party in some of NZ's best bars.

Trips

Rotorua

Infused with the aroma of sulphur, Rotorua's geothermal activity is central to its identity. Amid the steaming geysers and boiling mud pools of Whakarewarewa and Te Puia, traditional Māori culture is showcased proudly, and the nearby Redwoods forest is a verdant haven for walking and mountain biking. **Trip 7: Thermal Discoverer** will take you to other volcanic wonders nearby.

Trip

Rotorua Lady Knox Geyser, Wai-O-Tapu Thermal Wonderland

BEST ROADS FOR DRIVING

- -

SH35 (Pacific Coast Hwy) Negotiate the North Island's remote East Cape. **Trip**

- -

SH6 (Fox Glacier to Haast) Cop eyefuls of lake, ocean and rainforest scenery. **Trips** 15 21

- -

SH73 (Arthur's Pass) A neck-cricking journey crossing the Southern Alps. **Trips** 17 18

- -

SH8 (Inland Scenic Rte) Skirt the mountains and traverse the Mackenzie Country. **Trips** 19 21

- -

SH94 (Te Anau–Milford Hwy) A mountain and lake wonderland ending with a huge reveal. **Trip** 22

The West Coast

Hemmed in by the Tasman Sea and the Southern Alps, this long, skinny region is wild all the way. **Trip 15: The West Coast Road** runs its length, from Oparara's arches within Kahurangi National Park, to Jackson Bay on the edge of World Heritage wilderness. In between are wonders such as Punakaiki Rocks and the glaciers, Franz Josef and Fox.

Trips 14 15 17 21

Milford Sound Cruising on Milford Sound

Milford Sound

Fingers crossed you'll drive **Trip 22: Milford Sound Majesty** during clear weather when its collage of verdant cliffs, pointy peaks and cobalt waters is at its best. More likely though is the classic Fiordland scenario of mist and rain, with Mitre Peak revealed slowly through the atmospheric haze. But no matter: more water means better waterfalls, so either way you win.

Trip 22

BEST NATIONAL PARKS

- -

Fiordland World Heritage–listed wilderness – the world the way it used to be.

Trips 22 24

- -

Aoraki/Mt Cook New Zealand's highest mountain along with glaciers, tarns and alpine gardens. **Trips 19 20 21**

- -

Abel Tasman Sublime beaches and lush coastal forest.

Trips 12 13

- -

Tongariro Excellent hiking and biking amid volcanic scenery.

Trips 6 8

FIDSEY / GETTY IMAGES ©

Central Plateau Emerald Lakes along the Tongariro Alpine Crossing

Waiheke Island Man O' War vineyard

Central Plateau

The North Island's central heart is defined by the three volcanic peaks of Ruapehu, Tongariro and Ngauruhoe. On **Trip 6: Tongariro National Park Loop** take time out to tackle the Tongariro Alpine Crossing – one of the world's finest one-day hikes – or base yourself in National Park Village or Ohakune for mountain biking adventures.

Trips 6 8

Mackenzie Country

Home to such major sights as Lake Tekapo and Aoraki/Mt Cook, the Mackenzie Country is the star of **Trip 19: Inland Scenic Route**. This high-country basin – ringed by mountain ranges and infilled with golden tussock and surreal blue lakes – offers plenty of action, too, including tramping, biking, horse trekking, scenic flights and stargazing.

Trips 19 20 21

Waiheke Island

The welcome sign reads 'Slow Down. You're Here', and most visitors quickly oblige. Rural roads meander to sophisticated vineyard restaurants with stellar views back to Auckland, and Waiheke's more bohemian recent past echoes in art galleries and craft shops. On **Trip 4: Waiheke Island Escape**, set a course for beautiful Man O' War Bay.

Trip 4

Kaikoura

First settled by Māori with their taste for seafood, Kaikoura (meaning 'to eat crayfish') is a great spot for both consuming and communing with marine life. Crayfish is still king, but on fishing tours you can hook into other edible wonders of the deep. Whales, dolphins and seals are definitely off the menu, but on **Trip 11: Kaikoura Coast** you can take a boat tour or flight to see them.

Trips

Waitomo Caves

On **Trip 8: Waves & Caves to Whanganui**, get out from behind the wheel to descend into NZ's spectacular underworld. Go with the flow with on a relaxed guided tour through the Waitomo Glowworm Caves – the highlight is an ethereally silent boat ride on an underground river – or up the excitement level by tubing, abseiling and zip-lining amid the subterranean Stygian gloom.

Trip

(left) **Kaikoura** Sperm whale

(below) **The Catlins** Cathedral Cave

The Catlins

Unknown territory even for many New Zealanders, the rugged Catlin's coast is a diverse and interesting procession of isolated bays and coves, dramatic landforms such as waterfalls, caves and blowholes, and opportunities to swim or surf with dolphins at Curio Bay and walk to windswept Slope Point, the southernmost tip of the South Island. See it all for yourself on **Trip 24: Southern Scenic Route**.

Trip

BEST WINERIES

Man O' War Located in a beautiful Waiheke Island cove. **Trip** 4

Mission Estate NZ's oldest winery, established near Napier in 1851. **Trip** 10

Peregrine Impressive Central Otago wine matched with stunning architecture. **Trip** 23

Pegasus Bay Have lunch on the lawn with luscious Waipara wines. **Trip** 11

IF YOU LIKE...

Te Paki Recreation Reserve Giant dunes (Trip 1)

Coastal Scenery

A small country this may be, but New Zealand's 14,000-kilometre coastline is the world's tenth-longest. Many remote stretches are accessible only by boat, but quiet highways and back roads trace the country's edges with detours to salt-laden surprises.

1 Northland & the Bay of Islands Journey around tree-fringed coves, sleepy harbours and giant dunes.

3 Coromandel Peninsula Relax under Cathedral Cove's giant arch and explore a marine reserve by boat.

11 Kaikoura Coast Explore Queen Charlotte Sound and encounter Kaikoura's marine life.

15 The West Coast Road The big, blue ocean is a frequent companion on this long, wild route.

Outdoor Adventures

Thirteen national parks and countless other reserves offer endless scope for adventure. Outings range from easy walks or tough tramps, to kayaking in marine reserves and rafting down tumbling rivers.

6 Tongariro National Park Loop Hike the Alpine Crossing and bike the Old Coach Rd.

13 Tasman & Golden Bays Swim at beautiful beaches and hike Abel Tasman and other coastal walks.

19 Inland Scenic Route Hike, bike and kayak around Aoraki/Mt Cook National Park and beyond.

21 Southern Alps Circuit The adventures around these mountains could spin this trip out for months.

Food & Drink

Given NZ's world-class vineyards and dairy industry, you can't go wrong with wine and cheese to start. Continue with grass-fed beef, seafood, game and fresh produce, plus artisan goodies from kimchi to chocolate. Whether you self-cater or dine out like mad, expect local and seasonal specialities.

4 Waiheke Island Escape Enjoy world-renowned wines in relaxed alfresco vineyard settings.

9 North Island Southern Loop Bohemian eateries and hip beer bars in NZ's cool capital.

12 Sunshine & Wine Fill your days with vineyard lunches, farmers markets and roadside fruit stalls.

23 Central Otago Explorer NZ's answer to Burgundy, with food and views to rival it.

Rotorua Traditional Māori culture (Trip 7)

History

New Zealand's short history doesn't lack for good yarns and drama. From Māori *pa* (fortified village) sites and Captain Cook's landfalls, to pioneer industries such as whaling, gold mining and timber milling, expect monuments to hardship and heroism.

1 Northland & the Bay of Islands Explore the crucible of modern NZ history at the Waitangi Treaty Grounds.

3 Coromandel Peninsula Understand this region's shining, nugget-filled past at Waihi's superb Gold Discovery Centre.

15 The West Coast Road Atmospheric pioneer towns and rusty mining relics have many a story to tell.

25 Otago Heritage Trail Delve into NZ's flinty beginnings on a trip through big-sky country.

Mountains

Innumerable *maunga* (mountains) provide a backdrop to every NZ road trip, from the near-perfect volcanic cones of the North Island's Taranaki and Ngauruhoe, to the South Island's jagged spine – the unforgettable Southern Alps.

5 Taranaki Wanderer A leisurely coastal route through verdant farmland around conical Mt Taranaki.

19 Inland Scenic Route Sidle around foothills, over mountain passes and up to the foot of NZ's highest peak.

21 Southern Alps Circuit See the South Island's spine from all angles including two dramatic Alps' passes.

22 Milford Sound Majesty Absorb magnificent mountain and lakeland scenery en route to an unforgettable peak reveal.

Art & Culture

New Zealand is riddled with museums, galleries, architectural centres and other arts hubs, with changing programs and performances de rigueur. Artistic and cultural energy pulses far beyond their walls, particularly on city streets and in *marae* (Māori meeting places).

5 Taranaki Wanderer Feel New Plymouth's zizz at the Len Lye Centre and Govett-Brewster Art Gallery.

7 Thermal Discoverer Showcased through culture and cuisine, Rotorua is a heartland of NZ's proud Māori people.

10 Pacific Coast Explorer Napier's 1930's art deco architecture is an elegant time capsule of design.

26 East Coast Express Stop for settler history, steampunk, edgy art and an exuberant sculpture garden.

NEED TO KNOW

MOBILE PHONES
European phones work on New Zealand's networks; most American or Japanese phones won't. Use roaming or a local pre-paid SIM card.

INTERNET ACCESS
Wi-fi is available in most decent size towns and cities; sometimes free, sometimes hideously expensive. Internet cafes are few.

FUEL
Unleaded fuel (petrol, aka gasoline) is available from service stations across NZ, although be prepared in remote locations where there may be 100km between stations. Prices don't vary too much: per-litre costs at the time of research were around $1.80.

HIRE CARS
Ace Rental Cars (www.acerentalcars.co.nz)

Apex Rentals (www.apexrentals.co.nz)

Go Rentals (www.gorentals.co.nz)

IMPORTANT NUMBERS
Country code ☏ 64

Emergencies ☏ 111

Climate

Auckland
GO Feb–Apr

Rotorua
GO Oct–Dec

Wellington
GO Dec–Feb

Christchurch
GO Jan–Mar

Queenstown
GO Jun–Aug

When to Go

High Season (Dec–Feb)
» Summer: busy beaches, outdoor explorations, festivals and sporting events.

» Big-city accommodation prices rise.

» High season in ski towns and resorts is winter (June to August).

Shoulder Season (Mar–Apr & Sep–Nov)
» Prime travelling time: fine weather, short queues, kids in school and warm(ish) ocean.

» Long evenings sipping Kiwi wines and craft beers.

Low Season (May–Aug)
» Head for the slopes of the Southern Alps for some brilliant southern-hemisphere skiing.

» Few crowds, good accommodation deals and a seat in any restaurant.

» Warm-weather beach towns may be half asleep.

Daily Costs

Budget: Less than $150
» Dorm beds or campsites: $25–38 per night

» Main course in a budget eatery: less than $15

Midrange: $150–$250
» Double room in a midrange hotel/motel: $120–200

» Main course in a midrange restaurant: $15–32

» Hire a car: from $30 per day

Top End: More than $250
» Double room in a top-end hotel: from $200

» Three-course meal in a classy restaurant: $80

» Scenic flight: from $210

Eating

Restaurants From cheap 'n' cheerful, to world-class showcasing NZ's top-notch ingredients.

Cafes Freshly roasted coffee, expert baristas, brunch-mad and family friendly.

Pubs & Bars All serve some kind of food, good and bad!

Vegetarians Well catered for, especially in cities and ethnic restaurants.

Price indicators for average cost of a main course:

$	less than $15
$$	$15–32
$$$	more than $32

Sleeping

Motels Most towns have decent, low-rise, midrange motels.

Holiday Parks Myriad options from tent sites to family units.

Hostels From party zones to family-friendly 'flashpackers'.

Hotels Range from small-town pubs to slick global-chain operations.

Price indicators for double room with bathroom in high season:

$	less than $120
$$	$120–200
$$$	more than $200

Arriving in New Zealand

Auckland International Airport
Rental Cars Major companies have desks at airport.

Buses Airbus Express buses run into the city every 10 to 30 minutes, 24 hours; door-to-door shuttles run 24 hours.

Taxis To city centre around $75 (45 minutes).

Wellington Airport
Rental Cars Major companies have desks at airport.

Buses Airport Flyer buses run to the city every 10 to 20 minutes from 6.30am to 9.30pm; door-to-door shuttles run 24 hours.

Taxis To city centre around $30 (20 minutes).

Christchurch Airport
Rental Cars Major companies have desks at airport.

Buses Metro Red Bus (Nos 3 and 29) runs regularly into the city from 6.30am to 11pm; door-to-door shuttles run 24 hours.

Taxis To city centre around $50 (20 minutes).

Money

ATMs are available in all cities and most towns. Credit cards are accepted almost universally, although not American Express or Diners Club.

Tipping

Optional, but 10% for great service goes down well.

Useful Websites

Lonely Planet (www.lonelyplanet.com/new-zealand) Destination information, bookings, traveller forum and more.

100% Pure New Zealand (www.newzealand.com) Official tourism site.

Department of Conservation (www.doc.govt.nz) Essential information on national parks and reserves.

Te Ara (www.teara.govt.nz) Online NZ encyclopedia.

For more, see Driving in New Zealand (p348).

CITY GUIDE

Auckland Auckland Harbour Bridge and Waitemata Harbour

AUCKLAND

Arrayed around two natural harbours, Auckland celebrates a maritime vibe with waterfront restaurants and bars, and exciting ways to explore nearby islands and beaches. Observe Auckland's ocean-fringed horizons from the Sky Tower, head to Waiheke Island for a vineyard lunch, or learn about Kiwi culture at the Auckland Museum.

Getting Around

Auckland traffic is busy and parking expensive, so use the Link bus network instead. The Red City Link ($1) shuttles around the city centre, while the Green Inner Link ($2.50) services SkyCity, Ponsonby and the Auckland Museum.

Parking

Street parking options and car parks dot the city centre, costing up to $13 per hour. Park at the Wynyard Quarter car park (entrance on Beaumont St), where the first hour is free and each additional hour is $2. From there catch the City Link bus.

Where to Eat

Head to the harbour-front Wynyard Quarter for good restaurants. The nearby Britomart Precinct features eateries in repurposed heritage warehouses, and Ponsonby Central is a laneside collection of restaurants and cafes.

Where to Stay

Hotels dot central Auckland, while B&Bs in inner suburbs, including Ponsonby, Parnell and Mt Eden, are convenient bases for public transport and in close proximity to good eating and drinking.

Useful Websites

Tourist Information (www.aucklandnz.com) Sights, accommodation, restaurants and events.

The Denizen (www.thedenizen.co.nz) The city's best recently opened cafes, bars and restaurants.

Lonely Planet (www.lonelyplanet.com/new-zealand/auckland) Lonely Planet's city guide.

Trips Through Auckland `1` `2` `4` `7` `8`

Wellington Wellington Harbour at dusk

WELLINGTON

New Zealand's pint-sized capital is a beauty, draped around bushy hillsides encircling a freshly whipped harbour. There are hilltop lookouts, golden sand on the promenade and spectacular craggy shorelines on its southern coast. The centre is buoyed by museums, galleries and boutiques, and enlivened by modish coffee, foodie and craft beer scenes.

Getting Around

Wellington is one of the world's most compact capitals, and most central attractions are within easy walking distance. Regular bus services (www.metlink. org.nz) criss-cross the city centre and service all suburbs.

Parking

Central Wellington has many one-way streets; finding on-street parking ($1.50 to $4 per hour) can be difficult during the day and on busy weekends. Park outside the centre using a coupon (available from shops and service stations; first two hours free), then walk into the city.

Where to Eat

Cuba St has restaurants and cafes channelling a bohemian urban vibe, while the Courtenay Pl area – especially the Mt Victoria end – features some of the city's best eateries. Also worth exploring are the lanes off Dixon St.

Where to Stay

Wellington is a compact city, with many centrally located accommodation options within easy walking distance to attractions and restaurants. Being a hub for government and business, the city often has good accommodation discounts at weekends.

Useful Websites

Tourist Information (www. wellingtonnz.com) Sights, accommodation, restaurants and events.

Craft Beer Capital (www. craftbeercapital.com) 'Now Pouring' tap lists and a Wellington craft beer map.

Trips Through Wellington 9

Christchurch New Regent Street

CHRISTCHURCH

Christchurch is a vibrant city in transition, coping creatively with the aftermath of the 2010 and 2011 earthquakes. The city centre is graced by numerous notable arts institutions, the stunning Botanic Gardens and Hagley Park. Inner-city streets conceal art projects, pocket gardens and dynamic businesses repopulating the thinned-out cityscape.

Getting Around

Christchurch's flat topography and gridlike structure make getting around on foot or by bike a breeze. The extensive bus network (www.metroinfo. co.nz) is a cheap and convenient way of reaching the city's suburban attractions.

Parking

All-day parking is available throughout the city centre ($2 to $3.10 per hour), although road works and one-way systems may test your patience.

Where to Eat

While many cafes and restaurants still occupy the suburbs they fled to after the earthquakes – particularly around Addington, Riccarton, Merivale and Sumner – many new places are springing up in the CBD. Expect plenty of high quality, exciting surprises, especially around Victoria St.

Where to Stay

As the rebuild progresses, more beds (for all budgets) are becoming available in the city centre and its inner fringes. If you're camping or touring in a campervan there are decent holiday parks within 20 minutes' drive of the city centre.

Useful Websites

Tourist Information (www. christchurchnz.com) Sights, accommodation, restaurants and events.

Neat Places (www.neatplaces. co.nz) Authoritative local blogger's views on the best of Christchurch.

Trips Through Christchurch

11 16 17 18 19 21 26

Queenstown Lake Wakatipu seen from the Remarkables

QUEENSTOWN

Framed by mountains and the meandering coves of Lake Wakatipu, Queenstown is a right show-off. It wears its 'Global Adventure Capital' crown with pride. The town's bamboozling array of adrenalised activities is bolstered by cosmopolitan restaurants galore, and excellent vineyards nearby. Boredom is definitely off the menu.

Getting Around

Queenstown's compact town centre is easy to navigate on foot with the mountains and lakes allowing visitors to find their bearings. Connectabus (www.connectabus.com) has various colour-coded routes, reaching the suburbs and as far as Arrowtown.

Parking

There's plenty of cheap parking around the town but securing a space during busy times can be frustrating, especially near the lakefront. The Queenstown Lakes District Council website (www.qldc.govt.nz) shows car-park locations.

Where to Eat

The town centre is peppered with busy eateries. Many target the tourist dollar, but dig a little deeper and you'll discover local favourites covering a wide range of international cuisines. Reservations are recommended for the more popular places.

Where to Stay

Queenstown has endless accommodation options, but midpriced rooms are hard to come by. Hostels, however, are extremely competitive, and there are a couple of great holiday parks for campervanners. Places book out and prices rocket during the peak summer (Christmas to

February) and ski (June to September) seasons; book well in advance.

Useful Websites

Tourist Information (www.queenstownnz.co.nz) Official Queenstown tourism website.

Queenstown i-SITE (www.queenstownisite.co.nz) Queenstown visitor information centre.

Trips Through Queenstown `19` `21` `22` `23`

NEW ZEALAND
BY REGION

With world-famous landscapes and relatively little traffic, New Zealand is an absolute dream for a driving tour. To make things easy, we've divided the country into six regions and suggested a few top trips to get you on your way.

Marlborough & Nelson (p160)

Get the holiday vibe in coastal hotspots such as Kaikoura, the Marlborough Sounds and Abel Tasman; keep your picnic set at the ready to indulge in delicious local produce and world-class wines.

Watch whales and albatrosses on Trip 11

Blend sunshine and wine on Trip 12

Queenstown & the South (p288)

The country's adventure capital is a striking starting point for road trips taking in some of the country's most celebrated landscapes – from the golden-hued schist country of Central Otago to Fiordland's ancient forests.

See majestic Milford Sound on Trip 22

Take the long way round on Trip 24

Auckland & the North (p32)

New Zealand's most cosmopolitan city lies at the heart of this diverse region featuring the Bay of Islands' Māori and colonial history, the rugged surf beaches of Auckland's west coast, and the emerging gourmet food scene around Matakana.

Discover superb beaches on Trip 3

Linger over local wines on Trip 4

Rotorua & the Central North Island (p84)

Rugged alpine scenery and the impressive natural energy of the North Island's geothermal heart sit alongside active adventure and an insight into Māori culture.

Take to two wheels on Trip 6

Experience immense volcanic power on Trip 7

Canterbury & the West Coast (p202)

Drive through and around the Southern Alps to explore two starkly contrasting regions. Our trips dish up everything from swimming with seals to hiking amid snowy peaks to cycling through ancient rainforest.

Explore the wild West Coast on Trip 15

Tour the alps on Trip 21

Wellington & the East Coast (p132)

Look forward to remote coastal lighthouses, world-renowned wines, stellar beaches and fascinating islands, plus the hip coffee- and craft beer–fuelled urban buzz of Wellington.

Journey to an island sanctuary on Trip 9

Immerse yourself in art deco on Trip 10

Auckland & the North Trips

RELUCTANTLY LEAVE AUCKLAND'S HARBOUR-FRINGED URBAN CHARMS and chart a path north to sleepy harbours, compact coves and destinations etched into this young nation's heritage.

The Bay of Islands combines natural beauty with Māori and colonial history and further north is windswept and spiritual Cape Reinga. The upper west coast of the New Zealand's North Island is less developed, but equally spectacular and Auckland is the perfect base for journeys combining fine wine, farmers markets, and local wildlife.

Just a short drive away, the stunning Coromandel Peninsula is fringed by some of NZ's finest beaches and most spectacular coastal road trips.

Cape Reinga New Zealand's northernmost point (Trip 1)
ABI28L / GETTY IMAGES ©

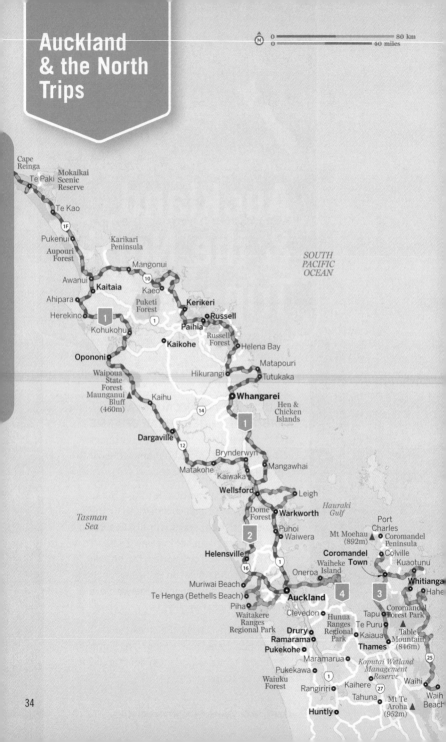

80 km
40 miles

Cape Reinga
Te Paki
Mokaikai Scenic Reserve
Te Kao

SOUTH PACIFIC OCEAN

1F
Pukenui
Karikari Peninsula
Aupouri Forest
Mangonui
Awanui
10
Kaitaia
Ahipara
Kaeo
Herekino
Puketi Forest
Kerikeri
1
Russell
Kohukohu
Paihia
Opononi
Kaikohe
Russell Forest
Helena Bay
Matapouri
Waipoua State Forest
Maunganui Bluff (460m)
Hikurangi
Tutukaka
Kaihu
14
Whangarei
Hen & Chicken Islands
1
Dargaville
12
Brynderwyn
Matakohe
Mangawhai
Kaiwaka
Wellsford
Leigh
Dome Forest
Warkworth
Hauraki Gulf
Port Charles
2
Puhoi
Waiwera
Mt Moehau (892m)
Coromandel Peninsula
Helensville
Colville
Coromandel Town
Kuaotunu
16
Waiheke Island
Whitianga
Muriwai Beach
Oneroa
4
Hahe
Te Henga (Bethells Beach)
3
Piha
1
Auckland
Coromandel Forest Park
Tasman Sea
Waitakere Ranges Regional Park
Clevedon
Tapu
Te Puru
Table Mountain (846m)
Drury
Hunua Ranges Regional Park
Ramarama
Kaiaua
Thames
Pukekohe
Maramarua
25
Pukekawa
Koputai Wetland Management Reserve
Waiuku Forest
1
Waihi
Waihi Beach
Rangiriri
27
Kaihere
Tahuna
Mt Te Aroha (952m)
Huntly

Te Paki Recreation Reserve Giant sand dunes

Classic Trip

1 Northland & the Bay of Islands 6–8 days
Coastal scenery, Māori culture and NZ history all combine on this northern odyssey. (p36)

2 East & West Coast Explorer 3 days
Vineyards, rugged surf beaches and a fascinating marine reserve. (p52)

3 Coromandel Peninsula 4–5 days
Spectacular coastal roads lead to brilliant beaches and fresh seafood. (p62)

4 Waiheke Island Escape 2 days
Great eating, superb wine and active adventures on Aucklanders' favourite island. (p74)

✔ **DON'T MISS**

Te Paki Recreation Reserve
Sandboard down the giant dunes on the fringes of Northland's famed Ninety Mile Beach on Trip **1**

Kawakawa's Hundertwasser toilets
NZ's most colourful conveniences were designed by Friedensreich Hundertwasser. Spend a penny on Trip **1**

Muriwai's gannet colony
Catch avian action high above this wild West Auckland surf beach. Brilliant ocean views on Trip **2**

Opito & Otama
Follow unsealed roads to these beautiful and spectacular Coromandel beaches on Trip **3**

Hauraki Rail Trail
Catch a heritage train before a gentle cycle through the Karangahake Gorge. It's full steam ahead on Trip **3**

Cape Reinga Lighthouse Crashing waves as the Tasman Sea meets the Pacific Ocean

Northland & the Bay of Islands

1

Embark on this diverse northern adventure showcasing New Zealand's Māori and colonial history amid a backdrop of sparkling beaches, soaring forests and hidden harbours.

TRIP HIGHLIGHTS

559 km

Cape Reinga
Leaving point for souls to the spiritual Māori homeland

313 km

Paihia
Boat trips and the historic Waitangi Treaty Grounds

194 km

Tutukaka
Departure point for the spectacular Poor Knights Islands

Awanui

Opononi Hikurangi

787 km

Waipoua State Forest
Pay homage to giant centuries-old kauri trees

Wellsford

Auckland **START/ FINISH**

6–8 DAYS
1057KM /
658 MILES

GREAT FOR...

BEST TIME TO GO
February to April offers the best weather, but try and avoid the busy Easter period

ESSENTIAL PHOTO
The iconic Cape Reinga Lighthouse

BEST FOR FAMILIES
Sandboarding down the North's giant dunes

37

Classic Trip

1

Northland & the Bay of Islands

Known as the 'Winterless North', the traditionally milder weather of this area is only one good reason to venture north of Auckland. The Bay of Islands combines Russell's heritage charm with boat cruises and marine adventures leaving from busy Paihia, and further north the attractions become even more remote and spectacular, leading all the way to the very top of the North Island at Cape Reinga.

① Auckland

Framed by two harbours, NZ's most cosmopolitan city spreads vibrantly across a narrow coastal isthmus. Explore Auckland's ocean-going personality at the New Zealand Maritime Museum (p83), or shoot the breeze on a sailing adventure on a genuine America's Cup yacht with **Explore** (☏0800 397 567; www.explorenz. co.nz; Viaduct Harbour). Other waterborne options include a ferry across the Waitemata harbour to the heritage Edwardian and Victorian architecture of the seaside suburb of **Devonport**, or a sea-kayaking excursion to **Rangitoto island**, a forested volcanic cone. Back on land, try our walking tour (p82), or for the best view of Rangitoto, stroll along **Takapuna Beach** on Auckland's North Shore or ride a bike around the bays along **Tamaki Drive**.

The Drive » For the first leg of 104km, depart across the Auckland Harbour Bridge heading north on SH1. North of Warkworth, turn into Wayby

Map

```
N  0 _____ 40 km
   0 _____ 20 miles
```

SOUTH PACIFIC OCEAN

p48 Karikari Peninsula
oubtless Bay
Hihi
aipa
⑨ Mangonui
Whangaroa Harbour
Matauri Bay
⑩
Puketi Forest Kaeo
Omahuta Forest
① Kerikeri ⑧
⑦ ⑥ Russell
Paihia Okiato
Russell Forest
Kawakawa
⑫ Rawene
Kaikohe
⑬ Opononi
Waipoua State Forest ⑭
Maunganui Bluff (460m) ⑫
Dargaville
Baylys Beach
p44
Whakapara
Hikurangi Ngunguru
Wairua River ①
④ Whangarei
⑤ Tutukaka
Matapouri
Cape Brett
Poor Knights Islands
Helena Bay
Hen & Chicken Islands
Ruakaka
Uretiti Bream Bay
Waipu ③ ③ Mangawhai Heads ②
Brynderwyn
Mangawhai
Matakohe ⑮
Kaipara Harbour
Wellsford ②
Pouto Warkworth
North Head Dome Forest ⑯
South Head
Woodhill Forest
Helensville Waiwera
Waimauku
Muriwai Beach
Te Henga (Bethells Beach)
Auckland ①
START/FINISH p82 ⑦

Valley Rd continuing on to Mangawhai Heads. Pay tolls for the Northern Gateway Toll Road on SH1 online at www.nzta.govt.nz.

② Mangawhai Heads

Mangawhai village lies on a horseshoe-shaped harbour, but it's Mangawhai Heads, 5km further on, that's really special. A narrow sandspit stretches for kilometres to form the harbour's south head, sheltering a **seabird sanctuary**. There's an excellent surf beach, best viewed while traversing the **Mangawhai Cliff Top Walkway**. Starting at Mangawhai Heads, this walking track (around two to three hours) offers extensive views of the ocean and the coast. Make sure you time it right to return down the beach at low tide. Other attractions around

LINK YOUR TRIP

2 East & West Coast Explorer

Explore to the northeast and northwest of NZ's biggest city, Auckland.

7 Thermal Discoverer

From Auckland, head south through the North Island's volcanic centre.

39

Mangawhai include **vineyards** and **olive groves**, and the **Mangawhai Museum** (📞09-431 4645; www.mangawhai-museum.org. nz; Molesworth Dr; adult/child $12/3; ⏰10am-4pm). Check out the roof shaped like a stingray. There's also a sun-drenched museum cafe here.

✗ p50

The Drive ›› From Mangawhai Heads continue along Cove Rd to Waipu Cove (around 13km).

This is a very pretty rural and coastal route away from the busier main roads. During summer, Langs Beach en route is enlivened the scarlet blooms of the pohutukawa, often dubbed 'NZ's Christmas tree'.

- - - - - - - - - - - - - - - -

③ Waipu

The arcing beach at **Waipu Cove** looks out to Bream Bay. On the near horizon, islands include the **Hen and Chickens**. Waipu Cove is excellent for swimming – and body surfing if there are good waves – and there are shaded spots for a picnic. A further 8km along a coastal road,

NGĀTI TARARA

As you're travelling around the north you might notice the preponderance of road names ending in '-ich'. As the sign leading into Kaitaia proclaims, 'haere mai, dobro došli and welcome' to one of the more peculiar ethnic conjunctions in the country.

From the end of the 19th century, men from the Dalmatian coast of what is now Croatia started arriving in NZ looking for work. Many ended up in Northland's gum fields. Pākehā society wasn't particularly welcoming to the new immigrants, particularly during WWI, as they were on Austrian passports. Not so the small Māori communities of the north. Here they found an echo of Dalmatian village life, with its emphasis on extended family and hospitality, not to mention a shared history of injustice at the hands of colonial powers.

The Māori jokingly named them Tarara, as their rapid conversation in their native tongue sounded like 'ta-ra-ra-ra-ra' to Māori ears. Many Croatian men married local *wahine* (women), founding clans that have given several of today's famous Māori their Croatian surnames, like singer Margaret Urlich and former All Black Frano Botica. You'll find large Tarara communities in the Far North, Dargaville and West Auckland.

Waipu is a sleepy village with excellent cafes that comes to life on summer weekends. The area was originally colonised by Scottish settlers – via Nova Scotia in Canada – who arrived between 1853 and 1860. The **Waipu Museum** (📞09-432 0746; www.waipumuseum. co.nz; 36 The Centre; adult/child $8/3; ⏰10am-4.30pm) tells their story, and on 1 January, Waipu's annual **Highland Games** (www. waipugames.co.nz; adult/child $15/5; ⏰1 Jan) celebrate heather-infused events including caber tossing and Scottish dancing. Here's your chance to discover your inner Caledonian.

The Drive ›› Rejoin SH1 from Waipu via Nova Scotia Dr, and continue north to Whangarei (39km). En route, Ruakaka and Uretiti offer excellent beaches, and the imposing profile of Marsden Point announces the entrance to Whangarei Harbour.

- - - - - - - - - - - - - - - -

④ Whangarei

Northland's only city has a thriving local art scene, and an attractive riverside area with excellent museums. Explore **Clapham's Clocks** (📞09-438 3993; www.claphams clocks.com; Town Basin; adult/child $10/4; ⏰9am-5pm) where more than 1400 ticking, gonging and cuckooing timepieces fill the **National Clock Museum** in Town Basin. This harbourside area is also a good place for shopping and stores selling local arts and crafts include **Burning Issues** (☏09-438 3108; www.burningissues gallery.co.nz; Town Basin; ⊗10am-5pm) and the **Bach** (☏09-438 2787; www. thebach.gallery; Town Basin; ⊗9.30am-4.30pm). A 1904 Māori portrait by artist CF Goldie is a treasure of the adjacent **Whangarei Art Museum** (☏09-430 4240; www.whangareiart museum.co.nz; The Hub, Town Basin; admission by donation; ⊗10am-4pm) and more contemporary art features at the **Quarry Arts Centre** (☏09-438 1215; www.quarryarts.org; 21 Selwyn Ave; ⊗9.30am-4.30pm), a raffish village of artists' studios and cooperative galleries. Around 5km west of Whangarei, **Kiwi North** (☏09-438 9630; www.kiwinorth.co.nz; 500 SH14, Maunu; adult/ child $15/5; ⊗10am-4pm) combines a museum displaying Māori and colonial artefacts with a kiwi house.

✗ p50

The Drive » Depart Whangarei via Bank St, Mill St and Ngunguru Rd to Tutukaka (30km). Worthy short stops include Whangarei Falls, a spectacular 26m-high cascade 6km from Town Basin, and Ngunguru, a sleepy estuary settlement just before Tutukaka.

TRIP HIGHLIGHT

5 **Tutukaka**

Bursting with yachts, dive crews and game-fishing charter boats,

MARINE RICHES AT THE POOR KNIGHTS

Established in 1981, the Poor Knights marine reserve is rated as one of the world's top-10 diving spots. The islands are bathed in a subtropical current from the Coral Sea, so varieties of tropical and subtropical fish not seen in other NZ waters can be observed here. The waters are clear, with no sediment or pollution problems. The 40m to 60m underwater cliffs drop steeply to the sandy bottom and are a labyrinth of archways, caves, tunnels and fissures that attract a wide variety of sponges and colourful underwater vegetation. Schooling fish, eels and rays are common (including manta rays in season).

The two main volcanic islands, **Tawhiti Rahi** and **Aorangi**, were home to the Ngāi Wai tribe, but since a raiding-party massacre by the Te Hikutu tribe in 1825, the islands have been *tapu* (forbidden). Even today the public is barred from the islands, in order to protect their pristine environment. Not only do tuatara (reptile) and Butler's shearwater (pelagic seabird) breed here, but there are unique species of flora, such as the Poor Knights lily.

To explore the Poor Knights underwater, contact **Dive! Tutukaka** (☏0800 288 882; www.diving.co.nz; Marina Rd; 2 dives incl gear $269). For non-divers, they also offer the **Perfect Day Ocean Cruise** including snorkelling, kayaking paddle boarding, and sightings of dolphins (usually) and whales (occasionally). Cruises run from November to May.

the **marina** at Tutukaka presents opportunities to explore the stunning above- and below-water scenery in the surrounding area. Many travellers are here to go diving at the **Poor Knights Islands**, but the underwater thrills are also accessible for snorkelling fans. Surfing lessons are available from **O'Neill Surf Academy** (☏09-434 3843; www. oneillsurfacademy.co.nz; 66 Te Maika Rd, Ngunguru; 2hr lesson from $75, one-day option

$125), and one of the best local walks is a blissful 20-minute coastal stroll from **Matapouri** to the compact cove at nearby **Whale Bay**.

✗ p50

The Drive » Allow two hours for this 106km leg. Leaving Tutukaka and heading north, the coastal road veers inland before reaching the coast again at Matapouri. From Matapouri, continue west to SH1 at Hikurangi. Head north on SH1, and turn right into Russell Rd just before Whakapara.

Classic Trip

DOUG PEARSON / GETTY IMAGES ©

GRANT ROONEY PREMIUM / ALAMY STOCK PHOTO ©

WHY THIS IS A CLASSIC TRIP
BRETT ATKINSON, WRITER

The oft-present coastline is this journey's defining feature. Secondary highways off busy SH1 combine for ongoing glimpses of beautiful bays and coves, often negotiating winding routes to showcase sleepy anchorages like the Whangaroa or Hokianga Harbours. All the while, the intersecting stories of Māori and colonial settlers conspire to provide a fascinating heritage counterpoint essential to understanding NZ history.

Top: Whale Bay, near Tutukaka
Left: Surfer at Waipu Cove
Right: Māori meeting house, Waitangi Treaty Grounds, Paihia

Featuring coastal scenery, this winding road – take care – continues via Helena Bay to Russell.

---

6 Russell

Once known as 'the hellhole of the Pacific', Russell is a historic town with cafes and genteel B&Bs. Russell was originally Kororareka, a fortified Ngāpuhi village. In the early 19th century the local Māori tribe permitted it to become NZ's first European settlement. It quickly attracted roughnecks like fleeing convicts, whalers and drunken sailors, and in 1835, Charles Darwin described it as full of 'the refuse of society'. After the signing of the Treaty of Waitangi in 1840, nearby Okiato was the country's temporary capital before the capital was moved to Auckland in 1841. Okiato, then known as Russell, was abandoned, and the name Russell eventually replaced Kororareka. Historical highlights now include **Pompallier Mission** (☏09-403 9015; www.pompallier.co.nz; The Strand; tours adult/child $10/ free; ☺10am-4pm), an 1842 Catholic mission house, and **Christ Church** (1836), NZ's oldest church.

✕ ⊨ p50

The Drive » It's about 8km to Okiato. A car ferry (car/motorcycle/passenger $11/5.50/1) – cash payment

Classic Trip

only and buy tickets on board – crosses regularly from Okiato to Opua (5km from Paihia).

TRIP HIGHLIGHT

➐ Paihia

Connected to Russell by passenger ferries across a narrow harbour, Paihia is more energetic than its sleepier sibling. Motels and backpacker hostels are crammed during summer holidays, and Paihia's waterfront hosts maritime excursions including island sight-seeing, dolphin-watching and sailing. A coastal road meanders 3km to the **Waitangi Treaty Grounds** (☎09-402 7437; www.waitangi.org.nz; 1 Tau Henare Dr; adult/child $40/20; ⊙9am-5pm Mar-24 Dec, 9am-6pm 26 Dec-Feb). Occupying a headland draped in lawns and forest, this is NZ's most important historic site. On 6 February 1840, the first 43 of more than 500 Māori chiefs signed the Treaty of Waitangi with the British Crown. Admission to the Treaty Grounds includes guided tours, Māori cultural performances and entry to the **Museum of Waitangi**, a showcase of the treaty in NZ's past, present and future.

✗ p50

The Drive ›› From Paihia, continue on SH11 (Black Bridge Rd) to Kerikeri, a meandering 24km route through citrus orchards. Around 4km from Paihia, the spectacular Haruru Falls can be reached by turning off Puketona Rd onto Haruru Falls Rd.

➑ Kerikeri

Famous for its oranges, Kerikeri also produces kiwifruit, vegetables and wine. It's also increasingly popular with retirees and hosts some of the Northland's best restaurants. A snapshot of early Māori and Pākehā (European New Zealander) interaction is offered by a cluster of historic sites centred on Kerikeri's picturesque river basin. Dating from 1836, the **Stone Store** (☎09-407 9236; www.historic.org.nz; 246 Kerikeri Rd; ⊙10am-4pm) is NZ's oldest stone building, and tours depart from here for the nearby **Mission House** (www.historic.org.nz; tours

---

↱ DETOUR: KAWAKAWA

Start: ➐ Paihia

Located 17km south of Paihia on SH11, Kawakawa is just an ordinary Kiwi town, but the public toilets (60 Gillies St) are anything but. They were designed by Austrian-born artist and eco-architect Friedensreich Hundertwasser, who lived near Kawakawa in an isolated house without electricity from 1973 until his death in 2000. The most photographed toilets in NZ are typical Hundertwasser – lots of organic wavy lines decorated with ceramic mosaics and brightly coloured bottles, and with grass and plants on the roof. Other examples of his work can be seen in Vienna and Osaka.

Kawakawa also has a railway line running down the main street. Take a 45-minute spin pulled by **Gabriel the Steam Engine** (☎09-404 0684; www.bayofislandsvintagerailway.org.nz; adult/child $20/5; ⊙10.45am, noon, 1.15pm, 2.30pm Fri-Sun, daily school holidays). South of town, a signpost from SH1 points to **Kawiti Glowworm Caves** (☎09-404 0583; www.kawiticaves.co.nz; 49 Waiomio Rd; adult/child $20/10; ⊙8.30am-4.30pm) (around 5km). Explore the insect-illuminated caverns with a 30-minute subterranean tour. Guided tours only.

If you're travelling from Okiato to Opua on the car ferry, Kawakawa is 12km south of the Opua ferry landing on SH11.

LOCAL KNOWLEDGE:
KERIKERI COTTAGE INDUSTRIES

You'd be forgiven for thinking that everyone in Kerikeri is involved in some small-scale artisanal enterprise, as the bombardment of craft shops on the way into town attests.

While Northland isn't known for its wine, a handful of vineyards are doing their best to change that. The little-known red grape chambourcin has proved particularly suited to the region's subtropical humidity, along with pinotage and syrah.

Look out for the *Art & Craft Trail* and *Wine Trail* brochures. Here are our tasty recommendations.

Kerikeri Farmers Market (www.boifm.org.nz; Hobson Ave; ⊗8.30am-noon Sun) From gourmet sausages to limoncello.

Old Packhouse Market (☑09-401 9588; www.theoldpackhousemarket.co.nz; 505 Kerikeri Rd; ⊗8am-1.30pm Sat) Combines a farmers market with great breakfasts.

Get Fudged & Keriblue Ceramics (☑09-407 1111; www.keriblueceramics.co.nz; 560 Kerikeri Rd; ⊗9am-5pm) An unusual pairing of ceramics and big, decadent slabs of fudge.

Makana Confections (☑09-407 6800; www.makana.co.nz; 504 Kerikeri Rd; ⊗9am-5.30pm) Artisanal chocolate factory with lots of sampling.

Marsden Estate (☑09-407 9398; www.marsdenestate.co.nz; 56 Wiroa Rd; ⊗10am-5pm) Excellent wine and lunch on the deck.

Ake Ake (☑09-407 8230; www.akeakevineyard.co.nz; 165 Waimate North Rd; tastings $5; ⊗cellar door 10am-4.30pm, restaurant noon-3pm & 6-9pm Mon-Sat, noon-3pm Sun, reduced hours outside summer) Wine tastings are free with lunch or purchase of wine, and the restaurant is one of Northland's best.

Cottle Hill (☑09-407 5203; www.cottlehill.co.nz; Cottle Hill Dr; tastings $5, free with purchase; ⊗10am-5.30pm Nov-Mar, 10am-5pm Wed-Sun Apr-Oct) Wine and port.

Byrne Northland Wines (Fat Pig Wine Cellar; ☑09-407 3113; www.byrnewine.com/wordpress; 177 Puketotara Rd; ⊗11am-7pm) Excellent viognier and rosé.

$10) NZ's oldest surviving building, dating from 1822. There's an ongoing campaign to have the area recognised as a Unesco World Heritage Site.

✕ ⊨ p51

The Drive » From Kerikeri, head north on SH10, turning east to Matauri Bay Rd to complete a stunning 41km loop back to SH10 just north of Kaeo. This coastal road takes in Matauri Bay, Tauranga Bay and the expansive Whangaroa Harbour. Back on SH10, continue 30km north to Mangonui, 90km from Kerikeri, and Doubtless Bay.

- - - - - - - - - - - -

❾ Mangonui

Doubtless Bay gets its name from an entry in Captain James Cook's logbook, where he wrote that the body of water was 'doubtless a bay'. The main centre, Mangonui ('Big Shark'), retains a fishing-port ambience, and cafes and galleries fill its historic waterfront buildings. They were constructed when Mangonui was a centre of the whaling industry (1792-1850) and exported flax, kauri timber and gum. At Hihi, 15km northeast of Mangonui, the **Butler Point Whaling Museum** (☑0800 687 386;

www.butlerpoint.co.nz;
Marchant Rd, Hihi; adult/child
$20/5; ⏱ by appointment)
showcases these earlier
days. The nearby settle-
ments of Coopers Beach,
Cable Bay and Taipa are
all pockets of beachside
gentrification and well-
tanned retirees with golf
habits.

✗ p51

The Drive ≫ This leg is 132km.
From Mangonui, drive west on
SH10 to rejoin SH1 at Awanui.
From Awanui head to NZ's
northernmost point, Cape
Reinga. An interesting stop is at
the Nga-Tapuwae-o-te-Mangai
Māori Ratana temple at Te Kao,
58km north of Awanui. Look
out for the two green-and-white
domed towers.

TRIP HIGHLIGHT

⑩ Cape Reinga

The waters off the
windswept **Cape Reinga
Lighthouse** (a rolling
1km walk from the
car park), is where the
Tasman Sea and Pacific
Ocean meet, crashing
into waves up to 10m
high in stormy weather.
Māori consider Cape
Reinga (Te Rerenga-
Wairua) the jumping-off
point for souls as they
depart on the journey to
their spiritual home-
land. Out of respect to
the most sacred site of
Māori people, refrain

from eating or drinking
anywhere in the area.
Around 16km south of
Cape Reinga on SH1, a
road leads west for 4km
to the **Te Paki Recreation
Reserve**. During sum-
mer, **Ahikaa Adventures**
(🕿09-409 8228; www.
ahikaa-adventures.co.nz; tours
$50-190) rent sandboards
to toboggan down the
reserve's giant dunes.

The Drive ≫ It is possible to
drive down Ninety Mile Beach,
but every year several tourists
– and their rental cars – get
hopelessly stuck in the sand.
Either join a 4WD bus tour or
drive south to Kaitaia from
Cape Reinga on SH1 (111km)
and continue 13km west to
Ahipara on the Ahipara Rd.

⑪ Ahipara

All good things must
come to an end, and
Ninety Mile Beach
does at this relaxed Far
North beach town. A few
holiday mansions have
snuck in, but mostly it's
just the locals keep-
ing it real with visiting
surfers. The area is
known for its huge sand
dunes and massive gum
field where 2000 people
once worked. Adventure
activities are popular on
the dunes above Ahipara
and further around
the Tauroa Peninsula.
**Ahipara Adventure
Centre** (🕿09-409 2055;
www.ahiparaadventure.co.nz;
15 Takahe St) can hook you
up with sand toboggans,
surfboards, mountain
bikes, blokarts for sand

yachting and quad bikes,
and Ahipara-based **NZ
Surf Bros** (🕿09-945
7276, 021 252 7078; www.
nzsurfbros.com; c/o 90 Mile
Beach Ahipara Holiday Park;
surf lessons $60-120) offer
surfing lessons.

✗ 🛏 p51

The Drive ≫ From Ahipara,
drive 64km through the
verdant Herekino forest to the
sleepy harbour settlement of
Kohukohu. Around 4km past
Kohukohu, a car ferry (car/
campervan/motorcycle/
passenger $20/40/5/2)
crosses the Hokianga Harbour
to Rawene. Payment is cash
only and the ferry leaves
Kohukohu on the hour from
8am to 8pm.

⑫ Rawene

During the height of the
kauri industry Kohukohu
was a busy town with
a sawmill, shipyard,
two newspapers and
banks. These days it's
a very quiet harbour
backwater dotted with
well-preserved heritage
buildings. Have a coffee
and one of NZ's best pies
at the local cafe, before
catching the ferry across
the harbour to Rawene.
Founded as NZ's third
European settlement,
a number of historic
buildings (including six
churches) remain from a
time when the harbour
was considerably busier
than it is now. Informa-
tion boards outline a
heritage trail of the main
sights. Built in the bus-
tling 1860s by a trader,

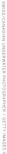

Poor Knights Islands Stingray

Classic Trip

stately **Clendon House** ([☎]09-405 7874; www. historic.org.nz; Clendon Esplanade; adult/child $10/free; [🕙]10am-4pm Sun May-Oct, Sat & Sun Nov-Apr) is now managed by the New Zealand Historic Places Trust. A few browse-worthy **art galleries** fill other historic buildings.

The Drive » After crossing on the vehicle from Kohukohu

to Rawene, another winding road and scenic road travels 20km to reach Opononi, near the entrance of the Hokianga Harbour.

- - - - - - - -

⑬ Opononi & Omapere

The twin settlements of Opononi and Omapere lie on the south head of Hokianga Harbour. Views are dominated by mountainous sand dunes across the water at North Head. During summer, the **Hokianga Express** ([☎]021 405 872,

09-405 8872; per tour $27; [🕙]10am-2pm summer) departs from Opononi Jetty, and travellers can sandboard down a 30m slope. Body boards are provided and bookings are essential. Starting at the car park at the end of Signal Station Rd – right off SH12 at the top of the hill leaving **Omapere** – the **Arai te Uru Heritage Walk** (30 minutes return) follows the cliffs and passes through manuka scrub before continuing to the Hokianga's southern headland. At

---

↱ DETOUR: KARIKARI PENINSULA

Start: ❾ **Mangonui**

Around 9km west of Taipa on SH10, head north on Inland Rd to explore the Karikari Peninsula. The oddly shaped peninsula bends into a near-perfect right angle. The result is beaches facing north, south, east and west in close proximity. This unique set-up makes Karikari Peninsula one of the world's best spots for kiteboarding, or at least that's the opinion of the experienced crew at **Airzone Kitesurfing School** ([☎]021 202 7949; www.kitesurfnz.com; 1-/2-/3-day course $195/350/485). Learners get to hone their skills on flat water before heading to the surf.

Despite its natural assets, the peninsula is blissfully undeveloped, with farmers well outnumbering tourist operators. Sun-kissed highlights include **Tokerau Beach**, a long, sandy stretch on the western edge of Doubtless Bay. Neighbouring **Whatuwhiwhi** is smaller and more built-up, facing back across the bay. **Maitai Bay**, with its tiny twin coves, is the loveliest of them all, at the lonely end of the peninsula down an unsealed road. It's a great sheltered spot for swimming. **Rangiputa** faces west at the elbow of the peninsula; the pure white sand and crystal-clear sheltered waters come straight from a Pacific Island daydream. A turn-off on the road to Rangiputa takes you to remote **Puheke Beach**, a long, windswept stretch of snow-white sand dunes forming Karikari's northern edge.

Eating opportunities are limited so stock up for a beachside picnic in Mangonui, or stop in at **Karikari Estate** ([☎]09-408 7222; www.karikariestate.co.nz; Maitai Bay Rd; tastings $15; [🕙]11am-4pm Oct-Apr, pizza evenings from 5pm late Dec-Feb). This impressive vineyard produces acclaimed red wines and has a cafe attached (mains and platters $16 to $40). During the peak of summer, good pizza is served in the cafe.

Count on 80km for a return trip from Mangonui to the Karikari Peninsula.

the headland are the remains of an old **signal station** built to assist ships making the treacherous passage into the harbour.

🛏 p51

The Drive ≫ Climbing south out of Omapere – don't miss the spectacular views back across the harbour – SH12 continues to the Waipoua State Forest – a meandering journey of around 20km.

TRIP HIGHLIGHT

⑭ Waipoua State Forest

This superb forest sanctuary – proclaimed in 1952 after public pressure – is the largest remnant of the once-extensive kauri forests of northern NZ. The forest road (SH12) stretches for 18km and passes huge trees. Near the northern end of the park stands mighty **Tane Mahuta**, named for the Māori forest god. At 51.5m high with a 13.8m girth, he's the largest kauri alive, and has been growing for between 1200 and 2000 years. Stop at the **Waipoua Forest Visitor Centre** (☎09-439 6445; www.teroroa.iwi.nz/visit-waipoua; 1 Waipoua River Rd; ⏰9am-6.30pm summer, 9am-4pm winter) for an exhibition on the forests, guided tours, flax-weaving lessons, and a cafe. You can also plant your own kauri tree, complete with GPS co-ordinates. Other massive trees to discover include **Te Matua Ngahere** and the **Four Sisters**.

🛏 p51

The Drive ≫ From the Waipoua Forest Visitor Centre, it's 107km on SH12 – via the riverine town of Dargaville – to Matakohe. Around 4km north of Dargaville, Baylys Coast Rd runs 9km west to Baylys Beach, a wild surf beach.

---

⑮ Matakohe

Apart from the rural charms of this village, the key reason for visiting Matakohe is the superb **Kauri Museum** (☎09-431 7417; www.kaurimuseum.com; 5 Church Rd; adult/child $25/8; ⏰9am-5pm). The giant cross-sections of trees are astounding, but the entire timber industry is brought to life through video kiosks, artefacts, fabulous furniture and marquetry, and reproductions of a pioneer sawmill, boarding house, gumdigger's hut and Victorian home. The Gum Room holds a weird and wonderful collection of kauri gum, the amber substance that can be carved, sculpted and polished to a jewel-like quality. The museum shop stocks mementoes crafted from kauri wood and gum.

The Drive ≫ From Matakohe, travel east on SH12 to join SH1 again at Brynderwyn. Drive south to Wellsford and then take SH16 for the scenic route southwest back to Auckland (163km in total from Matakohe). From Wellsford to Auckland on SH16 is around 110km, taking in views of Kaipara Harbour and West Auckland's vineyards.

Classic Trip

Eating & Sleeping

Auckland ❶

🍴 Mekong Baby   Southeast Asian €€

(☎09-360 1113; www.mekongbaby.com; 262 Ponsonby Rd, Ponsonby; mains $26-32; ◷noon-midnight Tue-Sun) This stylish and buzzing restaurant and bar offers excellent Southeast Asian flavours, mainly from Vietnam, Cambodia and Laos. Try the Madurese goat curry.

For more places to eat and stay in Auckland see p60.

Mangawhai Heads ❷

🍴 Wood Street Freehouse   Cafe $$

(☎09-431 4051; www.facebook.com/woodstfreehouse; 12 Wood St, Mangawhai Heads; mains $16-22, shared plates $11-14; ◷noon-late Mon-Fri, from 10am Sat & Sun) Craft beer has arrived in Mangawhai at this buzzing cafe, including beers from local Northland brewers such as Schippers and the Sawmill Brewery. Excellent food includes burgers, gourmet pizzas and shared plates – the truffle and parmesan fries are addictive – and from Friday to Sunday fresh local oysters from Wood Street's raw bar are best devoured on the sunny deck.

Whangarei ❹

🍴 à Deco   Modern NZ €€€

(☎09-459 4957; www.facebook.com/adeco.restaurant; 70 Kamo Rd; mains $37-42; ◷noon-3pm Fri, 6pm-late Tue-Sat) Northland's best restaurant offers an inventive menu that prominently features local produce, including plenty of seafood. Art-deco fans will adore the setting – a wonderfully curvaceous marine-style villa with original fixtures. To get here, head north on Bank St and veer left into Kamo Rd. Bookings recommended.

Tutukaka ❺

🍴 Schnappa Rock   Cafe €€

(☎09-434 3774; www.schnapparock.co.nz; cnr Marina Rd & Marlin Pl; breakfast & lunch $13-29, dinner $27-35, bar snacks $8-19; ◷8am-late, closed Sun night Jun-Sep) Filled with expectant divers in the morning and those capping off their Perfect Days in the evening, this cafe-restaurant-bar is often buzzing. Top NZ bands sometimes play on summer weekends.

Russell ❻

🍴 Gables   Modern NZ €€

(☎09-403 7670; www.thegablesrestaurant.co.nz; 19 The Strand; lunch $23-29, dinner $27-34; ◷noon-3pm Fri-Mon, from 6pm Thu-Mon) Serving an imaginative take on Kiwi classics (lamb, venison, seafood), the Gables occupies an 1847 building on the waterfront, built using whale vertebrae as foundations. Ask for a table by the windows for maritime views and look forward to local produce, including oysters and cheese. Cocktails are summery and there's a decent selection of NZ beer and wine.

🛏 Hananui Lodge & Apartments   Motel €€€

(☎09-403 7875; www.hananui.co.nz; 4 York St; units $150-270; 🛜) Choose between sparkling motel-style units in the trim waterside lodge or apartments in the newer block across the road. Pick of the bunch are the upstairs waterfront units with views straight over the beach.

Paihia ❼

🍴 El Cafe   Cafe, South American €

(☎09-402 7637; www.facebook.com/elcafepaihia; 2 Kings Rd; snacks & mains $5-15; ◷8am-4pm Tue-Thu, to 9.30pm Fri-Sun; 🛜)

Excellent Chilean-owned cafe with the best coffee in town and terrific breakfast burritos, tacos and baked-egg dishes, such as spicy Huevos Rancheros. Say *hola* to owner Javier for us. His Cuban pulled-pork sandwich is truly a wonderful thing. The fruit smoothies are also great on a warm Bay of Islands day.

Kerikeri ⑧

✖ Food at Wharepuke   Cafe €€

(☎09-407 8936; www.foodatwharepuke. co.nz; 190 Kerikeri Rd; breakfast $14-22, lunch & dinner $24-39; ☺10am-10.30pm Tue-Sun) With one foot in Europe, the other in Thailand, and its head in the lush vegetation of Wharepuke Subtropical Gardens, this is Kerikeri's most unusual and inspired eatery. On Friday nights it serves popular Thai banquets (three courses $47.50), while on Sunday afternoons it often hosts live jazz. Adjacent is the interesting Wharepuke Print Studio & Gallery.

⌂ Bed of Roses   B&B €€€

(☎09-407 4666; www.bedofroses.co.nz; 165 Kerikeri Rd; r $295-475; 🛜) It's all petals and no thorns at this stylish B&B, furnished with French antiques, luxe linens and comfy beds. The house has an art-deco ambience and awesome views.

Mangonui ⑨

✖ Little Kitchen on the Bay   Cafe €€

(☎09-406 1644; www.facebook.com/ littlekitchennz; 1/78 Waterfront Dr, Mangonui; breakfast & lunch $8-14, shared plates $13-16; ☺7.30am-3pm Mon-Wed, to 9.30pm Thu & Fri, 8am-3pm Sat & Sun) Our favourite Doubtless Bay eatery is this cute spot just across from the harbour. During the day the sun-drenched interior has Mangonui's best coffee, excellent counter food and good mains – try the terrific burger. On Thursday and Friday nights the emphasis shifts to wine, craft beer, and shared plates such as pork empanadas and Swiss cheese and beef sliders.

Ahipara ⑪

✖ North Drift Cafe   Cafe €€

(☎09-409 4093; www.facebook.com/ northdriftcafe; 3 Ahipara Rd; mains $12-29; ☺7am-3pm Mon-Wed, 7am-3pm & 5pm-late Thu-Sun) Ahipara's best coffee and a hip relaxed atmosphere both feature at this cafe with a spacious and sunny deck. Brunch and lunch standouts include the zucchini-and-corn fritters and the giant green-lipped mussels in a green curry sauce, and over summer it's a top spot for a few beers and dinner specials, such as NZ lamb crusted with Mediterranean-style dukkah.

⌂ Endless Summer Lodge   Hostel €

(☎09-409 4181; www.endlesssummer.co.nz; 245 Foreshore Rd; dm $34, d $78-92; @🛜) Across from the beach, this superb kauri villa (1880) has been beautifully restored and converted into an exceptional hostel. There's no TV, which encourages bonding around the long table and wood-fired pizza oven on the vine-covered back terrace. Body boards and sandboards can be borrowed and surfboards can be hired.

Opononi & Omapere ⑬

⌂ Kokohuia Lodge   B&B €€€

(☎021 779 927; www.kokohuialodge.co.nz; 101 Kokohuia Rd, Omapere; d $295-320; 🛜) Luxury and sustainable, ecofriendly practices combine at this B&B, nestled in regenerating native bush high above the silvery dune-fringed expanse of the Hokianga Harbour. Solar energy and organic and free-range produce all feature, but there's no trade-off for luxury in the modern and stylish accommodation.

Waipoua State Forest ⑭

⌂ Waipoua Lodge   B&B €€€

(☎09-439 0422; www.waipoualodge.co.nz; SH12; d incl breakfast $585; 🛜) This fine old villa at the southern edge of the forest has four luxurious, spacious suites, which were originally the stables, the woolshed and the calf-rearing pen. Decadent dinners ($80) are available.

Muriwai Gannets come to nest at this wild West Auckland surf beach

East & West Coast Explorer

2

From Auckland, embark on a circular route north of the city to uncover secluded and spectacular beaches, sophisticated vineyard restaurants, and a menu of family-friendly activities.

81 km

Goat Island
A marine reserve packed with underwater life

4

● Wellsford

3

Warkworth ●

66 km

Matakana
Vineyards, a farmers market and a local arts scene

● Helensville

● Kumeu

START/ FINISH
● Auckland

6

9

Muriwai
Gannets nest above this sprawling black sand surf beach

Piha
Lion Rock stands sentinel at this West Coast beach

200 km

275 km

3 DAYS
317KM / 197 MILES

GREAT FOR...

BEST TIME TO GO
February to April for leisurely vineyard lunches

ESSENTIAL PHOTO
Piha's Lion Rock from high above the beach

BEST FOR FAMILIES
Viewing the underwater spectacle at Goat Island

2 East & West Coast Explorer

The proud residents of Auckland are a lucky bunch, and this trip takes in some of their favourite day-escapes from the energy and bustle of the city. Plan your route to be slightly more leisurely, and enjoy a few days blending virtue and vice by combining fine wine, beer and local markets, with coastal bush walks, beaches and active adventure.

❶ Auckland

Before heading off on a journey where food, wine and markets are tasty features, explore the culinary scene of New Zealand's most diverse and cosmopolitan city. The best farmers market is at **La Cigale** (☎09-366 9361; www.lacigale.co.nz; 69 St Georges Bay Rd, Parnell; cafe $8-18, bistro $12-22; ⊗market 9am-1.30pm Sat & Sun, cafe 9am-4pm Mon-Fri, to 2pm Sat & Sun, bistro 6pm-late Wed-Fri), where stalls are laden with local goodies on Saturday and Sunday morning. Many of the stalls are run by recent arrivals contributing to Auckland's irresistible ethnic collage. On Wednesday evenings La Cigale becomes a food-truck stop, while on Thursdays and Fridays the space is converted into a quirky evening bistro serving simple rustic dishes. For a small-group city tour, including market visits, craft beer pubs, artisan producers and loads of tastings, hook up with the crew at **Big Foody** (☎021 481 177, 0800 366 386; www.thebigfoody.com; per person $125-185), or take our walking tour (p82).

✕ ⌂ p60

The Drive ›› Head north on SH1 and turn left to Puhoi after the spectacular Johnstone Hills tunnels. Pay tolls ($2.30) for the Northern Gateway Toll Road on SH1 online at www.nzta.govt. nz. The total distance of this leg is 43km.

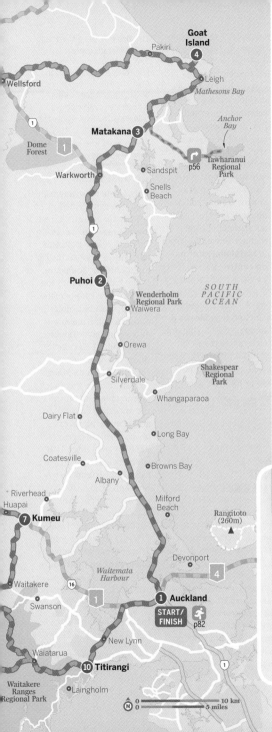

2 Puhoi

Forget dingy cafes and earnest poets – this quaint riverside village is a slice of the real Bohemia. In 1863, around 200 German-speaking immigrants from the present-day Czech Republic settled in what was then dense bush. The **Bohemian Museum** (☑09-422 0852; www.puhoihistoricalsociety.org.nz; Puhoi Rd; adult/child $3.50/free; ☺noon-3pm Sat & Sun, daily Jan-Easter) tells the story of the hardship and perseverance of these original pioneers. Raise a glass to their endeavour and endurance at the character-filled **Puhoi Pub** (☑09-422 0812; www.puhoipub.com; 5 Saleyards Rd; ☺10am-10pm Mon-Sat, to 8pm Sun). **Puhoi River Canoe Hire** (☑09-422 0891; www.puhoirivercanoes.co.nz; 84 Puhoi Rd) rents kayaks and Canadian canoes, either

LINK YOUR TRIP

1 Northland & the Bay of Islands

New Zealand's Māori and colonial history unfold to the north along both coasts.

4 Waiheke Island Escape

Use Auckland as a base for more stellar beaches and vineyard restaurants.

by the hour (kayak/canoe $25/50), or for an excellent 8km downstream journey from the village to Wenderholm Regional Park (single/double kayak $50/100, including return transport). Bookings are essential.

 p60

The Drive » Continue north on SH1 and turn right just after Warkworth to negotiate wine country and pretty coastal coves to Matakana, 25km from Puhoi.

TRIP HIGHLIGHT

3 Matakana

Around 15 years ago, Matakana was a rural village with a handful of heritage buildings and an old-fashioned country pub. Now its stylish wine bars and cafes are a weekend destination for daytripping Aucklanders. An excellent Saturday morning **farmers market**

(www.matakanavillage.co.nz; Matakana Sq, 2 Matakana Valley Rd; ⏰8am-1pm Sat) is held in a shaded riverside location, and the area's boutique wineries are becoming renowned for pinot gris, merlot, syrah and a host of obscure varietals. Local vineyards are detailed in the free *Matakana Coast Wine Country* (www.matakanacoast.com) and *Matakana Wine Trail* (www.matakanawine.com) brochures, available from the **Matakana information centre** (☎09-422 7433; www.matakanainfo.org.nz; 2 Matakana Valley Rd; ⏰10am-1pm). A local arts scene is anchored by **Morris & James** (☎09-422 7116; www.morrisandjames.co.nz; 48 Tongue Farm Rd; ⏰9am-5pm), a well-established potters' workshop.

⚔ 🛏 p60

DETOUR: TAWHARANUI REGIONAL PARK

Start: 4 Matakana

Around 1.5km northeast of Matakana en route to Leigh and Goat Island, turn right on Takatu Rd to follow a partly unsealed route for around 14km to **Tawharanui Regional Park** (☎09-366 2000; http://regionalparks.aucklandcouncil.govt.nz/tawharanui; 1181 Takatu Rd), a 588-hectare reserve at the end of a peninsula. This special place is an open sanctuary for native birds, protected by a pest-proof fence, while the northern coast is a marine park (bring a snorkel). There are plenty of **walking tracks** (1½ to four hours) but the main attraction is **Anchor Bay**, one of the region's finest white-sand beaches.

The Drive » Leave Matakana on Leigh Rd and continue through the seaside village of Leigh before turning right into Goat Island Rd. Twelve km north of Matakana, Mathesons Bay is a secluded cove with good swimming. The total distance to Goat Island is 16km.

TRIP HIGHLIGHT

4 Goat Island

This 547-hectare aquatic area was established in 1975 as the country's first **marine reserve** (www.doc.govt.nz; Goat Island Rd), and has now developed into a giant outdoor aquarium. Wade knee-deep into the water to see snapper (the big fish with blue dots and fins), blue maomao and stripy parore swimming around. Excellent interpretive panels explain the area's Māori significance (it was the landing place of one of the ancestral canoes) and provide pictures of the species you're likely to encounter. Hire snorkels and wetsuits from **Goat Island Dive & Snorkel** (☎09-422 6925; www.goatislanddive.co.nz; 142a Pakiri Rd; snorkel set hire adult/child $25/18, incl wetsuit $38/26) in Leigh or join a 45-minute boat trip with **Glass Bottom Boat Tours** (☎09-422 6334; www.glassbottomboat.co.nz; Goat Island Rd; adult/child $28/15).

The Drive » Continue to Wellsford (34km) before taking SH16 to meander another 57km southwest through farmland and past Kaipara Harbour to Helensville.

⑤ Helensville

Heritage buildings, antique shops and cafes make village-like Helensville a good whistle-stop for those negotiating SH16. Energetic and relaxing activities also combine for an interesting destination that's perfect for adventurous families. At the **Woodhill Mountain Bike Park** (📱027 278 0969; www.bikepark.co.nz; Restall Rd, Woodhill; adult/child $8/6, bike hire from $30; ⏰8am-5.30pm Thu-Tue, 8am-10pm Wed) 14km south of Helensville, challenging tracks (including jumps and beams) career through the Woodhill Forest, and at **Tree Adventures** (📱0800 827 926; www.treeadventures.co.nz; Restall Rd, Woodhill; ropes courses $17-42; ⏰10am-5pm Sat & Sun) high-ropes courses include swinging logs, climbing nets and a flying fox. Nearby **Parakai Springs** (📱09-420 8998; www.parakaisprings.co.nz; 150 Parkhurst Rd; adult/child $22/11; ⏰10am-9pm) has thermally heated swimming pools, private spas, and a couple of hydroslides.

The Drive » Continue south on SH16 to Waimauku (17km) and turn right for the 8km to Muriwai. Look forward to rolling pastures dotted with sheep, followed by a winding drive through the forest.

💬 **LOCAL KNOWLEDGE: THE WILD WEST COAST**

Peter Hillary, Mountaineer & Explorer
My family grew up loving Auckland's wild west coast, where the Tasman Sea pounds the black-sand beaches and black-back gulls ride the westerlies. Our family has walked and explored and lived out here for nearly a century and this is also where we came to grieve after my mother and sister were killed in 1975, where the invigorating salty air and the marvellous wild vistas to the Tasman Sea worked like a balm for our broken hearts. My father [Sir Edmund Hillary] would come here to dream up and then prepare for new expeditional challenges. It seemed the right sort of environment for someone like him: not a passive coastline, but active and exciting, with huge cliffs, crashing waves, thick bush and a tantalising far-away horizon.

TRIP HIGHLIGHT

⑥ Muriwai

A black-sand surf beach, Muriwai features the Takapu Refuge **gannet colony**, which is spread over the southern headland and outlying rock stacks. Viewing platforms get you close enough to watch (and smell) these fascinating seabirds. Every August hundreds of adult birds return to this spot to hook up with their regular partners and get busy in spectacular (and noisy) displays of courting. The net result is a single chick per season; December and January are the best times to see them testing their wings before embarking on an impressive odyssey to Australia. Nearby, two short tracks wind through beautiful native bush to a **lookout** that offers views along the 60km length of the beach. Note this wild beach is only safe for swimming when patrolled. Always swim between the flags.

The Drive » Return to SH16 and turn right to Kumeu. Orchards and vineyards feature along this 16km route, and it's a good area to buy fresh fruit.

---

⑦ Kumeu

West Auckland's main wine-producing area still has some vineyards owned by the original Croatian families who kick-started NZ's wine industry. The fancy eateries that have mushroomed in recent years have done little to dint the relaxed farmland feel to the region, but everything to encourage an afternoon's indulgence on the way back from the beach or the hot pools. Most cellars offer free tastings. Top vineyards include **Coopers Creek** (☎09-412 8560; www.coopers creek.co.nz; 601 SH16, Huapai; ⏰10.30am-5.30pm), **Kumeu River** (☎09-412 8415; www.kumeuriver.co.nz; 550 SH16; ⏰9am-4.30pm Mon-Fri, 11am-4.30pm Sat) and **Soljans Estate** (☎09-412 5858; www.soljans.co.nz; 366 SH16; ⏰tastings 9am-5pm, cafe 10am-3pm). **Hallertau** (☎09-412 5555; www.haller tau.co.nz; 1171 Coatesville–Riverhead Hwy, Riverhead; ⏰11am-midnight), at nearby **Riverhead**, is an excellent craft brewery also with very good food.

KAREL LORIER / ALAMY STOCK PHOTO ©

🍴 p61

The Drive » Depart Kumeu on Waitakere Rd and turn right into Bethells Rd after 10km. It's 12km further to Te Henga (Bethells Beach).

- - - - - - - - - - - - - - -

❽ Te Henga (Bethells Beach)

Breathtaking Bethells Beach is a raw, black-sand beach with surf, windswept dunes and walks, such as the popular one over giant sand dunes to **Lake Wainamu** (starting near the bridge on the approach to the beach). If you're keen to stay the night at this rugged and beautiful spot, enquire about glamping at the Bethells Cafe.

🍴 🛏 p61

The Drive » Leave Bethells Beach on Bethells Rd which veers into Te Henga Rd. Around 11km from Bethells Beach turn right into Scenic Dr and follow this winding bush-clad route before turning back towards the coast onto Piha Rd. This leg is 37km in total.

- - - - - - - - - - - - - - -

TRIP HIGHLIGHT

❾ Piha

This beautifully rugged, black-sand beach has long been a favourite for Aucklanders for day trips, teenage weekend roadies, or family holidays. Although Piha is popular, it's also incredibly dan-gerous with wild surf and strong undercurrents. Always swim between the flags, where lifeguards can see if you get into trouble. Near the centre of the beach is **Lion Rock** (101m), whose 'mane' glows golden in the evening light. It's actually the eroded core of an ancient volcano and a Māori *pa* (fortified village) site. A path at the southern end of the beach leads to great lookouts. At low tide you can walk south along the beach and watch the surf shooting through a ravine in another large rock known as **The Camel**.

Matakana Stall at the Matakana Farmers Market

🍴 🛏 p61

The Drive » Piha Rd leads back into Scenic Dr which continues through West Auckland suburbs to Titirangi, 25km from Piha.

- - - - - - - - - - - - - - -

🔟 Titirangi

This little village marks the end of Auckland's suburban sprawl and is a good place to spot all manner of Westie stereotypes over a coffee, wine or cold beer. Once home to NZ's greatest modern painter, Colin McCahon, there remains an artsy feel to the place. It's a mark of the esteem in which Colin McCahon is held that the **house** (📞09-817 7200; www.mc cahonhouse.org.nz; 67 Otitori Bay Rd, French Bay; $5; ⏰1-4pm Wed-Sun) he lived and painted in during the 1950s has been opened to the public as a mini-museum. The swish pad next door is temporary home to the artist lucky enough to win the McCahon Arts Residence. More art is on display at the **Te Uru Waitakere Contemporary Gallery** (📞09-817 8087; www.teuru.org.nz; 420 Titirangi Rd; ⏰10am-4.30pm), an excellent modern gallery housed in the former Hotel Titirangi (1930) on the edge of the village. Titirangi means 'Fringe of Heaven' – an apt name given its proximity to the verdant Waitakere Ranges.

🍴 p61

The Drive » From Titirangi, continue through the west Auckland suburbs of New Lynn and Avondale to rejoin the motorway (SH16) back to central Auckland, 17km from Titirangi, at Waterview.

Eating & Sleeping

Auckland ❶

✖ Street Food Collective   Fast Food $

(%021 206 4503; www.thestreetfoodcollective.
co.nz; Rear, 130 Ponsonby Rd, Grey Lynn; dishes
$5-15; ☺11am-3pm & 5-10pm) A great concept
this: 14 different food trucks take turns to
occupy four spots in a courtyard accessed from
a narrow back lane running between Richmond
Rd and Mackelvie St (look for the wrought-iron
gates). The roster's posted online and there's a
separate bar truck, too.

✖ Beirut   Lebanese $$

(☎09-367 6882; www.beirut.co.nz; 85 Fort St;
mains $26-29; ☺7am-late Mon-Fri, 5pm-late
Sat) Sacking curtains and industrial decor
don't necessarily scream out Lebanese, but the
sophisticated, punchy flavours bursting from
the plates at this wonderful new restaurant
certainly do. The cocktails are nearly as
exciting as the food – and that's saying
something.

▦ Great Ponsonby
Arthotel   B&B $$$

(☎09-376 5989; www.greatpons.co.nz; 30
Ponsonby Tce, Ponsonby; r $250-400; P🐾🗭)
In a quiet cul-de-sac near Ponsonby Rd,
this deceptively spacious Victorian villa has
gregarious hosts, impressive sustainability
practices and great breakfasts. Studio
apartments open onto an attractive rear
courtyard. Rates include breakfast.

For more places to eat and stay in Auckland
see p50.

Puhoi ❷

✖ Puhoi Valley   Cafe $$

(☎09-422 0670; www.puhoivalley.co.nz;
275 Ahuroa Rd; mains $15-22; ☺10am-4pm)
Renowned across NZ, Puhoi Valley cheese
features heavily on the menu of this upmarket
cheese shop and cafe, set blissfully alongside a
lake, fountain and children's playground. In the
summer there's music on the lawn, perfect with
a gourmet ice cream.

Matakana ❸

✖ Charlie's Gelato
Garden   Ice Cream $

(☎09-422 7942; www.charliesgelato.co.nz;
17 Sharp Rd; ice cream $4-6, pizza slice/whole
$5/18; ☺9am-5pm Nov-Mar, 10am-4pm Fri-Sun
Apr-Oct) Superb sorbet and gelato made from
fresh fruit and interesting ingredients – try the
liquorice or ginger-beer flavours – and excellent
wood-fired pizzas during summer from Friday
to Sunday.

✖ Mahurangi River Winery
& Restaurant   Modern NZ $$

(☎09-425 0306; www.mahurangiriver.co.nz;
162 Hamilton Rd; mains $28-34; ☺11am-4pm
Thu-Mon) Expansive vineyard views partner
with a relaxed ambience and savvy food at this
rural spot off Sandspit Rd.

✖ The Matakana   Pub Food $$

(☎09-422 7518; www.matakana.co.nz; 11
Matakana Valley Rd; mains $17-25; ☺noon-
12.30am) Following a trendy makeover,
Matakana's heritage pub now features quirky
decor, Matakana wines and craft beers, and
decent bistro food including local Mahurangi
oysters. Occasional DJs and live acts enliven
the cool outdoor space.

▦ BeauRegard
Accommodation   Cottage $$

(☎021 803 378; www.beauregard.co.nz; 603
Matakana Rd; d incl breakfast $150-190; 🐾🗭)
Sitting in rural surroundings, a 4km drive
from Matakana village, these three one-
bedroom self-contained cottages are the ideal
stylish haven for exploring the beaches and
vineyards of the surrounding area. Each of the
cottages has a Gallic name – Bel-Air, Voltaire
or Bastille – and the French–Kiwi hosts have
plenty of ideas for tasty discoveries at local
markets and restaurants.

Kumeu ❼

✕ Tasting Shed — Tapas $$

(☏09-412 6454; www.thetastingshed.co.nz; 609 SH16, Huapai; dishes $14-26; ⊙4-10pm Wed & Thu, noon-11pm Fri-Sun) Complementing its rural aspect with rustic chic decor, this slick eatery conjures up delicious dishes designed to be shared. It's not strictly tapas, as the menu strays from Spain, and appropriates flavours from Asia, the Middle East, Croatia, Serbia, Italy and France.

Te Henga (Bethells Beach) ❽

✕ Bethells Cafe — Burgers, Pizza $

(☏09-810 9387; www.facebook.com/thebethellscafe; Bethells Beach car park; mains $12-17; ⊙5.30-9.30pm Fri, 10am-6pm Sat & Sun Nov-May, 10am-6pm Sun Jun-Oct) Less a cafe and more a food truck with an awning, the Bethells Cafe does a roaring trade in burgers (beef and vegetarian), pizza, cakes and coffee. On Friday nights it's pretty much the perfect Kiwi beach scene, with live musicians entertaining the adults while the kids surf the sand dunes. Enquire about glamping opportunities nearby.

🛏 Wainamu Luxury Tents — B&B $$$

(☏022 384 0500, 09-810 9387; www.facebook.com/wainamu; Bethells Beach; d $250; ⊙Oct-Jun) Inspired by safari tents from Botswana and Māori whare (houses), these very comfortable tents combine quiet rural locations, recycled timber construction, and a luxurious 'glamping' vibe. Cooking is done on barbecues, lighting from gas lamps and candles is both practical and romantic, and outdoor baths also enhance the whole experience. Free-range eggs, fresh-baked bread and muesli are combined in DIY breakfast packs.

Piha ❾

✕ Piha Cafe — Cafe $$

(☏09-812 8808; www.pihacafe.com; 20 Seaview Rd; mains $14-27; ⊙8.30am-3.30pm Mon-Wed, to 10pm Thu-Sat, to 5pm Sun) Big-city standards mesh seamlessly with sand-between-toes informality at this attractive ecofriendly cafe. Cooked breakfasts and crispy pizzas provide sustenance for a hard day's surfing. After the waves, head back for a cold beverage on the deck.

🛏 Black Sands Lodge — Apartment $$

(☏021 969 924; www.pihabeach.co.nz; Beach Valley Rd; cabin $160, apt $220-260; 🛜) These two modern conjoined apartments with private decks match their prime location with appealing touches, such as stereos and DVD players. The cabin is kitted out in a 1950s Kiwiana bach style and shares a bathroom with the main house. Bikes and wi-fi are free for guests, and in-room massage and lavish dinners can be arranged on request.

🛏 Piha Beachstay – Jandal Palace — Hostel $

(☏09-812 8381; www.pihabeachstay.co.nz; 38 Glenesk Rd; dm/s $35/70, d $120, without bathroom $80; @🛜) Attractive and ecofriendly, this wood-and-glass lodge has extremely smart facilities. It's 1km from the beach but there's a little stream at the bottom of the property and bushwalks nearby. In winter an open fire warms the large communal lounge.

Titirangi ❿

✕ Hardware Cafe — Cafe $$

(☏09-817 5059; www.hardwarecafe.org.nz; 404 Titirangi Rd; brunch $10-18, dinner $18-28; ⊙6am-4.30pm Sun-Tue, to late Wed-Sat) This popular licensed cafe serves cooked breakfasts and lunches, along with tempting counter food.

Cathedral Cove Gigantic stone formations dot two sparkling coves

Coromandel Peninsula

Meandering coastal roads weave a magical path on this journey around the compact but colourful Coromandel Peninsula. Visit in January for the crimson splash of pohutukawa blossoms.

TRIP HIGHLIGHTS

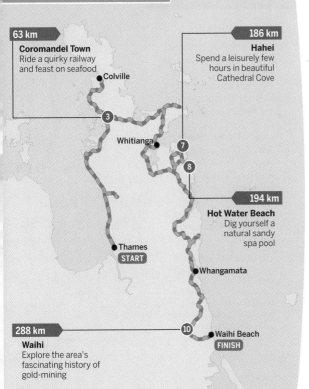

63 km
Coromandel Town
Ride a quirky railway and feast on seafood
● Colville

186 km
Hahei
Spend a leisurely few hours in beautiful Cathedral Cove

● Whitianga

194 km
Hot Water Beach
Dig yourself a natural sandy spa pool

● Thames
START

● Whangamata

288 km
Waihi
Explore the area's fascinating history of gold-mining

● Waihi Beach
FINISH

**4–5 DAYS
299KM /
186 MILES**

GREAT FOR...

BEST TIME TO GO

November to April, but try to avoid school holidays, Christmas and Easter

ESSENTIAL PHOTO

The graceful and spectacular arch of Cathedral Cove

BEST FOR BEACHES

The beautiful sandy arc of Opito

63

3 Coromandel Peninsula

A favourite holiday spot for residents of nearby Auckland and Hamilton, the Coromandel Peninsula packs attractions aplenty into its beach-fringed coastline. The legacy of a gold-mining past lingers in the heritage streets of Thames, Coromandel Town and Waihi, and natural attractions like Cathedral Cove and Hot Water Beach combine with exciting and diverse opportunities to explore and get active around a stunning marine-scape.

❶ Thames

Heritage wooden buildings from the 19th-century gold rush still dominate Thames – especially in the stately shopfronts along Pollen St – but grizzly prospectors have long been replaced by laid-back locals. Learn about the area's gold-flecked history at the **Goldmine Experience** (☎07-868 8514; www.goldmine-experience.co.nz; cnr Moanataiari Rd & Pollen St; adult/child $15/5; ☺10am-4pm daily Jan-Mar, to 1pm Sat & Sun Apr, May & Sep-Dec) – including watching a giant stamper battery effortlessly crush rock – and

at the interesting **School of Mines & Mineralogical Museum** (☎07-868 6227; www.historicplaces.org.nz; 101 Cochrane St; adult/child $10/free; ☺11am-3pm Wed-Sun Mar-Dec, daily Jan & Feb). The weekly **Thames Market** (☎07-868 9841; Pollen St, Grahamstown; ☺8am-noon Sat) is packed with local arts and crafts, and Thames is also a good base for tramping or canyoning in the nearby **Kauaeranga Valley**.

The Drive ❯❯ Heading north up the Coromandel Peninsula's west coast, narrow SH25 meanders past pretty bays. At Tapu, 20km north of Thames, turn inland for 6km on a mainly sealed road to the Rapaura Water Gardens.

② Rapaura Water Gardens

Beautifully located in a verdant stand of native forest, the **Rapaura Water Gardens** (☏07-868 4821; www.rapaurawatergardens.co.nz; 586 Tapu-Coroglen Rd; adult/child \$15/6; ◷9am-5pm) are a relaxing combination of water, greenery and art. Lily ponds, compact bridges and sculptures crafted from punga (a fern native to New Zealand) all blend at this soothing diversion from SH25, and there's also a very good cafe here.

The Drive » Rejoin SH25 at Tapu and continue north for 35km to Coromandel Town. Look forward to stunning coastal views, especially as you drop down off the winding hill road for the final drive into town.

LINK YOUR TRIP

7 Thermal Discoverer

Waihi Beach is 103km from Hamilton linking to this journey through the North Island's volcanic centre.

10 Pacific Coast Explorer

Continue south from Waihi Beach to Tauranga (55km) and around the East Coast.

LAURIE NOBLE / GETTY IMAGES ©

TRIP HIGHLIGHT

❸ Coromandel Town

Crammed with heritage buildings, Coromandel Town is a thoroughly quaint little place. Its natty cafes, interesting art stores, excellent sleeping options and delicious smoked mussels could keep you here longer than you expected. The **Driving Creek Railway & Potteries** (☎07-866 8703; www.drivingcreekrailway.co.nz; 380 Driving Creek Rd; adult/child $35/13; ⊙10.15am & 2pm, additional times in summer) was a lifelong labour of love for its conservationist owner, well-known potter, the late Barry Brickell. This unique train runs up steep grades, across four trestle bridges, along two spirals and a double switchback, and through two tunnels, finishing at the 'Eye-full Tower'. The one-hour trip passes artworks and regenerating native forest – more than 17,000 natives have been planted, including 9000 kauri trees. Booking ahead is recommended in summer.

✖ ⌖ p72

The Drive » Leave Coromandel Town on Kapanga Rd, the settlement's sleepy main drag. Kapanga Rd leads into Rings Rd and then into Colville Rd. From Coromandel Town to Colville is around 27km, a stunning route negotiating beautiful beaches including Oamaru Bay and Amodeo Bay.

❹ Colville

The tiny settlement of Colville is a remote rural community fringed by a muddy bay and framed by rolling green pastures. If you're continuing on the unsealed roads of Far North Coromandel, the Colville General Store is your last stop for both petrol and organic food. Wise travellers should plan ahead for both. Around 1km south of Colville, the **Mahamudra Centre** (☎07-866 6851; www.mahamudra.org.nz; RD4, Main Rd, Colville; campsite/dm/s/tw $18/28/50/80) is a serene Tibetan Buddhist retreat with a stupa, meditation hall and regular meditation courses. It offers simple accommodation in a park-like setting. Visiting is not possible if a retreat is scheduled, so phone ahead to check.

✖ p72

The Drive » Return south from Colville and turn east onto SH25 around 500m south of Coromandel Town. En route to Kuaotunu (52km from Colville), a turnoff at Te Rerenga after 15km leads to Whangapoua (6km). From there is a walking track (one hour return) to New

Hot Water Beach Dig your own spa pool

Chums Beach, regarded as one of NZ's finest beaches.

❺ Kuaotunu

Located at the end of a sweeping beach – with views of the Mercury Islands on the near horizon – Kuaotunu is an interesting holiday village with a fine **cafe and art gallery**, and access on scenic unsealed roads to the nearby beaches of **Otama** and **Opito**. Departing Kuaotunu by Blackjack Rd, Otama is 3.5km away and reached by a winding road over a spectacular headland. Dunes fringe the sandy arc of the beach, and a further 6km on lies Opito, more populated but arguably even more spectacular. Both beaches are good for a swim before you return to Kuaotunu.

✖️ 🛏 p72

The Drive ❱❱ From Kuaotunu it's an easy 15km drive on SH25 to Whitianga. The view coming down off the final hill towards Whitianga's Buffalo Beach is spectacular.

❻ Whitianga

Whitianga's big attractions are the sandy beaches of **Mercury Bay**, and diving, boating and kayaking in the nearby **Te Whanganui-A-Hei Marine Reserve**. The pretty harbour is also a base for game fishing, especially marlin and tuna between January and March. North of the harbour, **Buffalo Beach** stretches along Mercury Bay, and the town is a magnet for holidaymakers throughout summer. The legendary Polynesian seafarer Kupe is believed to have landed near here around AD 950, and the **Mercury Bay Museum** (☎07-866 0730; www.mercurybay museum.co.nz; 11a The Esplanade; adult/child $7.50/50¢;

67

DETOUR:
FAR NORTH COROMANDEL

Start: ❹ Colville

The rugged northernmost tip of the Coromandel Peninsula is well worth the effort required to reach it. The best time to visit is summer (December to February), when the gravel roads are dry and the pohutukawa trees are in their crimson glory. Three kilometres north of Colville at **Whangaahei**, the sealed road turns to gravel and splits to straddle each side of the peninsula. Following the west coast, ancient pohutukawa spread overhead as you pass turquoise waters and stony beaches. The small DOC-run **Fantail Bay campsite** (☏07-866 6685; www.doc.govt.nz; Port Jackson Rd; adult/child $10/5), 23km north of Colville, has running water and a couple of long-drop toilets under the shade of puriri trees. Another 7km brings you to the **Port Jackson campsite** (☏07-866 6932; www.doc.govt.nz; Port Jackson Rd; adult/child $10/5), a larger DOC site right on the beach. There's a spectacular **lookout** about 4km further on, where a metal dish identifies the various islands on the horizon. **Great Barrier Island** is only 20km away, looking every part the extension of the Coromandel Peninsula that it once was. The road stops at **Fletcher Bay** – a magical land's end. Although it's only 37km from Colville, allow an hour for the drive.

Note there is no road linking Fletcher Bay with the east coast of the peninsula, so you need to return to Whangaahei 3km north of Colville, before branching left to return to Coromandel Town via a spectacular east coast road taking in **Waikawau Bay** and **Kennedy Bay**. Sections of this road are unsealed gravel.

For the entire journey north from Colville to Fletcher Bay, back south to Whangaahei, and then around the east coast back to Coromandel Town, allow around four to five hours of driving time. For the Coromandel Town north to Colville section, add around 30 minutes.

⊙10am-4pm) commemorates his visit and that of British maritime explorer Captain James Cook in 1769. Whitianga is a fast-growing town and has some of the peninsula's best restaurants. For a relaxing break from driving, book a spa session at the **Lost Spring** (☏07-866 0456; www.thelostspring.co.nz; 121a Cook Dr; per 90min/day $38/68; ⊙10.30am-6pm Sun-Fri, to 8pm Sat), a thermal complex comprising a series of hot pools in a lush jungle-like setting complete with an erupting volcano.

✕ ⫘ p72

The Drive » Depart south on SH25, skirting Whitianga Harbour to the east. Stay on SH25 to Whenuakite (26km), and turn left into Hot Water Beach Rd. After 5km, veer left onto Link Rd for 3km, and turn right onto Hahei Beach Rd to Hahei (2km).

- - - - - - - - - - - - -

`TRIP HIGHLIGHT`

❼ Hahei

A sleepy holiday town that explodes with visitors across summer – especially during school holidays – Hahei is located close to **Cathedral Cove**. The cove's gigantic **stone arch** and natural **waterfall shower** is best enjoyed early or late in the day to avoid the tourist buses and the worst of the hordes. From the car park, a kilometre north of Hahei, it's a rolling walk of 30 to 40 minutes to the cove. On the way there's rocky **Gemstone Bay**, which has a snorkelling trail where you could see big snapper, crayfish and stingrays, and sandy **Stingray Bay**. The **Cathedral Cove Water Taxi** (☏027 919 0563; www.

cathedralcovewatertaxi.co.nz; return/one-way adult $25/15, child $15/10; ☺every 30min) runs frequent waterborne transport from Hahei Beach to the cove, a good idea to avoid the often busy car park. During the height of summer, a shuttle bus also runs from Hahei to the beginning of the track to the cove.

✗ p73

The Drive » From Hahei, depart on Hahei Beach Rd (2km)

for Link Rd, turn left on Link Rd and continue for around 3km, then left onto Hot Water Beach Rd to Hot Water Beach (3km).

- - - - - - - - - - -

TRIP HIGHLIGHT

8 Hot Water Beach

Hot Water Beach is extraordinary. For two hours either side of low tide, you can access an area of sand in front of a rocky outcrop at the middle of the beach where hot water oozes up

from beneath the surface. Bring a spade, dig a hole and you've got a personal spa pool. Spades ($5) can be hired from the **Hot Water Beach Store** (☎07-866 3006; Pye Pl; ☺9am-5pm), and local tourist information centres list tide schedules so you know when to rock up with scores of other fans of natural jacuzzis. Note the car park outside the Hot Water Beach Store is pay and display,

EXPLORING THE TE WHANGANUI-A-HEI MARINE RESERVE

Departing from either Whitianga Harbour or from Hahei, local operators provide exciting and scenic access to the beautiful 840 hectares of the Te Whanganui-A-Hei Marine Reserve and around the surrounding coastline of Mercury Bay. The reserve was gazetted in 1992 and is centred on Cathedral Cove (Whanganui-A-Hei in Māori).

Hahei Explorer (☎07-866 3910; www.haheiexplorer.co.nz; adult/child $85/50) Hour-long jetboat rides touring the coast.

Cathedral Cove Sea Kayaking (☎07-866 3877; www.seakayaktours.co.nz; 88 Hahei Beach Rd; half-/full day $105/170; ☺8.45am & 1.30pm) Guided kayaking trips around the rock arches, caves and islands in the Cathedral Cove and Mercury Bay area. The Remote Coast Tour heads the other way when conditions permit, visiting caves, blowholes and a long tunnel.

Banana Boat (☎07-866 5617; www.facebook.com/bananaboatwhitianga; rides $10-35; ☺26 Dec-31 Jan) Monkey around in Mercury Bay on the bright-yellow motorised Banana Boat – or split to Cathedral Cove.

Glass Bottom Boat (☎07-867 1962; www.glassbottomboatwhitianga.co.nz; adult/child $95/50) Two-hour bottom-gazing tours exploring the Te Whanganui-A-Hei Marine Reserve.

Cave Cruzer (☎07-866 0611; www.cavecruzer.co.nz; adult/child 1hr $50/30, 2hr $75/40) Tours on a rigid-hull inflatable.

Ocean Leopard (☎0800 843 8687; www.oceanleopardtours.co.nz; adult/child $80/45; ☺10.30pm, 1.30pm & 4pm) Two-hour trips around coastal scenery, naturally including Cathedral Cove. The boat has a handy canopy for sun protection, and a one-hour 'Whirlwind Tour' is also on offer.

Whitianga Adventures (☎0800 806 060; www.whitianga-adventures.co.nz; adult/child $75/45) A two-hour Sea Cave Adventure in an inflatable.

Windborne (☎027 475 2411; www.windborne.co.nz; day sail $95; ☺Dec-Apr) Day sails in a 19m, 1928 schooner.

COROMANDEL CRAFT BEER

Yes, the Kiwi craft beer revolution has washed up on the pristine waters of Mercury Bay, and two excellent breweries are located near Hahei and Hot Water Beach. Good cafes and restaurants around the Coromandel Peninsula also stock beers from the Pour House and Hot Water Brewing Co.

Home base for the Coromandel Brewing Company, **Pour House** (www.coromandelbrewingcompany.co.nz; 7 Grange Rd; ☺11am-11pm) in Hahei regularly features around five of their beers in a modern ambience. Platters of meat, cheese and local seafood combine with decent pizzas in the beer garden. Our favourite brew is the Code Red Irish Ale.

Located at the Sea Breeze Holiday Park in Whenuakite, **Hot Water Brewing Co** (✆07-866 3830; www.hotwaterbrewingco.com; Sea Breeze Holiday Park, 1043 SH25, Whenuakite; ☺11am-late) is a modern craft brewery with lots of outdoor seating. Standout brews include the hoppy Kauri Falls Pale Ale and the robust Walkers Porter. Platters and pizzas make it easy to order another beer, and the lamb burger is deservedly famous around these parts. Ask if the superb Barley Wine is available.

and it's enforced quite rigorously. Alternatively, park at the larger (free) car park before you get to the beach proper, and walk along the beach for a few hundred metres. Be aware that Hot Water Beach has dangerous rips, especially in front of the main thermal area. It's actually one of NZ's most dangerous beaches in terms of drowning numbers, but this is potentially skewed by the huge number of tourists flocking here. Regardless, swimming is definitely not safe if lifeguards aren't on patrol, and when they are on duty always swim between the flags.

✗ ☕ p73

The Drive ›› From Hot Water Beach, return by Hot Water Beach Rd to SH25 at Whenuakite, and continue south to Whangamata, 59km from Hot Water Beach. En route at Tairua, a steep 15-minute walk to the summit of Paaku offers great harbour views across to Pauanui. At Opoutere, the Wharekawa Wildlife Refuge is a breeding ground for the endangered NZ dotterel.

9 Whangamata

Outside of summer, 'Whanga' is a genteel seaside town (population 3560), but over Christ-

mas, New Year and other key holiday periods, it can be a much more energetic spot, and the population swells to around 40,000 with holiday-makers from Auckland and Hamilton. It's an excellent surf beach, and a popular destination for kayaking and paddle boarding is **Whenuakura (Donut) Island**, around 1km from the beach. There's also good snorkelling at **Hauturu (Clarke) Island**. Note that in an effort to boost the islands' status as wildlife sanctuaries, landing on them is not permitted. Boating around the islands is allowed however. The experienced team at **SurfSup** (✆021 217 1201; www.surfsupwhangamata.com; 101b Winifred Ave; hire half-/full-day surfboard $30/50, kayak from $40/60, 1/2hr paddle board $20/30) offer paddle-boarding and surfing lessons, and also run daily kayaking and paddle-boarding tours to Whenuakura from December to March.

✗ p73

The Drive ›› From Whangamata, SH25 continues its meandering route south to Waihi (30km).

TRIP HIGHLIGHT

10 Waihi

Gold and silver have been dragged out of Waihi's Martha Mine (NZ's richest) since 1878, and Seddon St, the town's main street, has interesting sculptures and information panels about Waihi's golden legacy. The superb **Gold Discovery Centre** (☏07-863 9015; www.golddiscoverycentre.co.nz; 126 Seddon St, Waihi; adult/child $25/12; ☻9am-5pm, to 4pm in winter) tells the area's gold-mining past, present and future through interactive displays, focusing on the personal and poignant to tell interesting stories. Holograms and short movies both feature, drawing visitors in and informing them through entertainment. Atmospherically lit at night, the skeleton of a derelict **Cornish Pumphouse** (1904) is the town's main landmark. From here the **Pit Rim Walkway** has fascinating views into the 250m-deep **Martha Mine**. To get down into the spectacular mine, join a 1½-hour excursion with **Waihi Gold Mine Tours** (☏07-863 9015; www.gold-discoverycentre.co.nz/tours; 126 Seddon St, Gold Discovery Centre, Waihi; adult/child $34/17; ☻10am & 12.30pm daily, additional tours in summer) departing from the Gold Discovery Centre.

The Drive ❯❯ Take SH2 south out of Waihi and turn left into Waihi Beach Rd after 3km.

- - - - - - - - - - - -

⑪ Waihi Beach

Separated from Waihi township by 11km of

HAURAKI RAIL TRAIL

From Waihi township, an excellent day excursion is to combine a train ride, on the heritage **Goldfields Railway** (☏07-863 8251; www.waihirail.co.nz; 30 Wrigley St, Waihi; adult/child return $18/10, bikes $2 extra per route; ☻departs Waihi 10am, 11.45am & 1.45pm Sat, Sun & public holidays), with a few hours' cycling part of the popular **Hauraki Rail Trail** through the scenic **Karangahake Gorge**. Bikes can be rented at the railway's terminus in the gorge, the **Waikino Station Cafe** (☏07-863 8640; www.waikinostationcafe.co.nz; SH2; mains $10-18; ☻9.30am-3pm), or at **Waihi Bicycle Hire** (☏07-863 8418; www.waihibicyclehire.co.nz; 25 Seddon St, Waihi; bike hire half-/full day from $30/40; ☻8am-5pm) in town and then carried on the train. This part of the Hauraki Rail Trail is spectacular as it winds on a gentle gradient through a beautiful river valley. Book ahead for lunch at **Bistro at the Falls Retreat** (☏07-863 8770; www.fallsretreat.co.nz; 25 Waitawheta Rd; pizzas $20-24, mains $25-28; ☻10am-10pm), located in a cosy wooden cottage in the the heart of a sun-dappled forest. Gourmet pizzas and rustic meat dishes emerge from the wood-fired oven on a regular basis, and there's a great little playground for children.

See www.haurakirailtrail.co.nz for detailed information, including trail maps and recommendations for other day rides on this popular cycle route linking Thames to the towns of Paeroa, Te Aroha and Waihi.

---

prime Waikato farmland, this low sandy surf beach stretches 9km to **Bowentown** on the northern limits of Tauranga Harbour. As well as being a prime summertime destination for the good people of Hamilton, Waihi Beach is also a growing foodie hot spot with a number of fine little cafes; even the pub has had a makeover and attracts locals and weekenders alike.

If you want to stretch your legs on more than the flat miles of golden beach, a good walk from the northern end of the beach leads to Orokawa Beach, 45 minutes away around the coastal headlands. In summer when the beachside pohutukawa was flowering there is no finer Coromandel sight than scarlet trees, white sand and turquoise water.

✗ ⌸ p73

Eating & Sleeping

AUCKLAND & THE NORTH **3** COROMANDEL PENINSULA

Coromandel Town ③

✕ Coromandel Mussel Kitchen
Seafood **$$**

(☎07-866 7245; www.musselkitchen.co.nz; cnr SH25 & 309 Rd; mains $18-21; ☺9am-3.30pm, plus dinner late Dec-Feb) This cool cafe-bar sits among fields 3km south of town. Mussels are served with Thai- and Mediterranean-tinged sauces or grilled on the half-shell. In summer the garden bar is perfect for a mussel-fritter stack and a frosty craft beer from MK Brewing Co, the on-site microbrewery. Smoked and chilli mussels and bottles of the beers are all available for takeaway.

⬛ Hush Boutique Accommodation
Studio **$$**

(☎07-866 7771; www.hushaccommodation. co.nz; 425 Driving Creek Rd; campervans $45, cabins & studios $145-175) Rustic but stylish studios are scattered throughout native bush at this easygoing spot. Lots of honey-coloured natural wood creates a warm ambience, and the shared Hush al fresco area with kitchen facilities and a barbecue is a top spot to catch up with fellow travellers. Hush Petite ($145) is a very cosy stand-alone one-bedroom cottage that was originally a potter's cottage.

Colville ④

✕ Hereford 'n' a Pickle
Cafe **$**

(☎021 136 8952; www.facebook.com/ hereford.n.a.pickle; Colville Town; pies $4-6; ☺9am-4pm; ☎) Good coffee, fresh fruit ice cream, and pies made from meat from local Hereford cattle are the standouts at this rustic self-described 'farm shop' that also boasts free wi-fi and sunny outdoor seating. Sausages and smoked meats are available to takeaway, along with loads of other local produce including fresh juices, jams and pickles.

Kuaotunu ⑤

✕ Luke's Kitchen & Cafe
Cafe, Pizza **$$**

(☎07 866 4420; www.lukeskitchen.co.nz; 20 Blackjack Rd, Kuaotunu; mains & pizza $15-28; ☺cafe & gallery 8.30am-3.30pm, restaurant & bar 11am-10pm, shorter hours in winter) In Kuaotunu village, Luke's Kitchen has a rustic surf shack ambience, cold brews (including craft bars from around NZ) and excellent wood-fired pizza. Occasional live music, local seafood and creamy fruit smoothies make Luke's an essential stop. Adjacent is Luke's new daytime cafe and gallery with very good coffee, home-baked goodies and eclectic local art for sale.

⬛ Kuaotunu Bay Lodge
B&B **$$$**

(☎07-866 4396; www.kuaotunubay.co.nz; SH25; s/d $270/295; ☎) An elegant B&B set among manicured gardens, offering a small set of spacious sea-gazing rooms.

Whitianga ⑥

✕ Salt Restaurant & Bar
Modern NZ, Seafood **$$$**

(☎07-866 5818; www.salt-whitianga.co.nz; 2 Blacksmith Lane; shared plates $12-30, mains $28-38; ☺11.30am-late) Views of the Whitianga marina – including the sleepy ferry crossing to Ferry Landing – provide the backdrop for relaxed but stylish dining at this restaurant attached to Whitianga Hotel. In summer the place to be is out on the deck, enjoying local wines with pan-seared fish with Cloudy Bay clams or Coromandel oysters from the raw bar.

⬛ Within the Bays
B&B **$$$**

(☎07-866 2848; www.withinthebays. co.nz; 49 Tarapatiki Dr; r $275-325; @ ☎) It's the combination of charming hosts and incredible views that make this B&B – set on a hill overlooking Mercury Bay – really worth considering. It's extremely well set up for guests with restricted mobility – there's even a wheelchair-accessible bush track on the property. Find it 5km from Whitianga town.

Hahei ➐

✖ The Church   Mediterranean $$

(☎07-866 3797; www.thechurchhahei.co.nz;
87 Hahei Beach Rd; shared plates $10-28;
🕑5.30pm-late Mon-Sat, shorter hours outside
summer) This ultra-charming wooden church
is Hahei's swankiest eatery with excellent
Spanish- and North African–inspired dishes
made to be shared, as well as a stellar, if pricey,
selection of Kiwi craft beers. Try the lamb tagine
with yoghurt and couscous or the Moroccan-
style steamed mussels. Booking ahead is
recommended as the dining room is cosy and
compact.

Hot Water Beach ➑

✖ Hot Waves   Cafe $$

(☎07-866 3887; 8 Pye Pl; mains $12-26;
🕑8.30am-4pm Mon-Thu & Sun, to 8.30pm Fri
& Sat) In summer everyone wants a garden
table at this excellent cafe. For a lazy brunch,
try the eggs Benedict with smoked salmon or
a breakfast burrito. It also rents out spades for
the beach ($5). Ask about occasional Friday-
night music sessions.

🛏 Hot Water Beach Top 10 Holiday
Park   Holiday Park $

(☎07-866 3116; www.hotwaterbeachholiday
park.com; 790 Hot Water Beach Rd; campsites
from $23, dm $30, units $90-180; @🐾)
Bordered by tall bamboo and gum trees, this is a
very well-run holiday park with everything from
grassy campsites through to a spacious and
spotless backpackers lodge and stylish villas
with arched ceilings crafted from NZ timber.

Whangamata ➒

✖ Argo Restaurant   Modern NZ $$

(☎07-865 7157; www.argorestaurant.co.nz;
328 Ocean Rd; mains $28-33; 🕑5.30-9.30pm
Thu-Sun & 9am-2.30pm Sat & Sun, daily from late
Dec-early Feb; 🐾) Whangamata's most stylish
restaurant offers a concise menu of innovative
bistro classics including garlic-infused linguine
with Coromandel mussels, and fish with a black-
rice risotto and a curry coconut sauce. The
starter of pork-belly croquettes go really well
with a hoppy IPA, and the airy deck is perfect for
a few lazy afternoon drinks.

Waihi Beach ⓫

✖ Flatwhite   Cafe $$

(☎07-863 1346; www.flatwhitecafe.co.nz; 21
Shaw Rd, Waihi Beach; mains brunch $14-20,
dinner $20-35; 🕑8am-late; 🐾) Funky, licensed
and right by Waihi Beach, Flatwhite has a lively
brunch menu, decent pizzas and flash burgers.
A recent makeover has added huge decks with
brilliant ocean views. Our favourite from the
new dinner menu is the blackened salmon with a
chargrilled-corn-and-saffron salsa.

🛏 Waihi Beach Lodge   B&B $$$

(☎07-863 5818; www.waihibeachlodge.
co.nz; 170 Seaforth Ave, Waihi Beach; d $295)
A short stroll from the beach, this boutique
accommodation features colourful, spacious
and modern rooms as well as a studio
apartment with its own kitchenette. Legendary
breakfasts are often served on a sunny deck.
Ask the friendly owners Greg and Ali how
they're going with their homemade honey
and limoncello, and hopefully look forward to
sampling both.

Waiheke Island Emerald waters lap sandy beaches

Waiheke Island Escape

4

An hour from the city, Auckland's favourite Hauraki Gulf island combines vineyard restaurants, active adventure and a thriving art scene, with beaches and coves definitely worth discovering.

TRIP HIGHLIGHTS

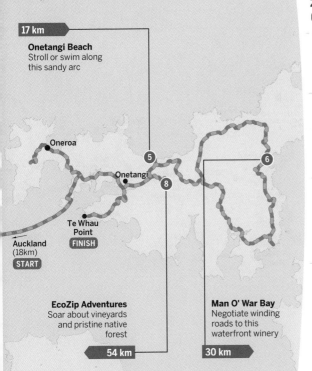

17 km

Onetangi Beach
Stroll or swim along this sandy arc

Oneroa

5

Onetangi

8

6

Te Whau Point
FINISH

Auckland (18km)
START

EcoZip Adventures
Soar about vineyards and pristine native forest

54 km

Man O' War Bay
Negotiate winding roads to this waterfront winery

30 km

2 DAYS
62KM / 38 MILES

GREAT FOR...

BEST TIME TO GO
February to April but try and avoid busy weekends and public holidays

ESSENTIAL PHOTO
Being launched onto the zipline at EcoZip Adventures

BEST FOR FOODIES
A leisurely lunch at a top vineyard restaurant

Waiheke
Island Escape

Tantalisingly close to Auckland and blessed
with its own warm, dry microclimate, blissful
Waiheke Island has long been a favourite
escape for both city dwellers and travellers. On
the island's landward side, emerald waters lap
at rocky bays, while its ocean flank has some
of the region's best sandy beaches. Vineyards
evoking a South Pacific spin on Tuscany or the
south of France are other sybaritic diversions.

❶ Auckland

One of the world's most
beautiful harbour cities,
Auckland is the gateway
to the islands of the
Hauraki Gulf – see its
highlights on our three-
hour walking tour (p82).
Regular ferries leave
from downtown Auck-
land and other locations
around the city to islands
promising wine, art,
walking and adventure.

The Drive ›› From Auckland,
Sealink (www.sealink.co.nz)
runs car ferries (adult/child/
car return $36.50/20/168)
to Kennedy Point on Waiheke

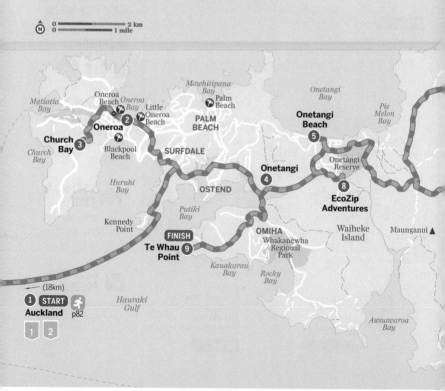

Island. Most leave from Half Moon Bay in east Auckland (45 to 60 minutes), but some depart from Wynyard Wharf in the city (60 to 80 minutes). From Kennedy Point to Oneroa, Waiheke's main town, is 3km.

② Oneroa

Waiheke's main settlement comprises a relaxed main street dotted with cafes, restaurants, gift shops and local stores. **Oneroa Beach** and the pretty cove of **Little Oneroa** nearby are both good for swimming. In town, attractions are conveniently centred on

the **Waiheke Island Art-works** (2 Korora Rd, Oneroa; 🛜) complex, and include the **Waiheke Community Art Gallery** (📞09-372 9907; www.waihekeartgallery.org. nz; ⏱10am-4pm) – featuring local artists and an excellent gift shop – and **Whittaker's Musical Museum** (📞09-372 5573; www.musicalmuseum. org; suggested donation $5; ⏱1-4pm, live shows 1.30pm Sat) with afternoon concerts played on heritage instruments. Drop in at the **Waiheke Wine Centre** (📞09-372 6139; www.waihekewinecentre.com; 153 Oceanview Rd, Oneroa; ⏱9.30am-7.30pm Mon-Thu, to 8pm Fri & Sat, from 11am Sun) featuring wine from all of Waiheke's 30-plus vineyards.

🍴 🛏 p81

The Drive ⟩⟩ Leave Oneroa on Oceanview Rd – up the hill – and after 500m turn left into Church Bay Rd. Look for the small brown sign indicating 'Wineries'. Continue on Church Bay Rd for 2.5km to Mudbrick.

③ Church Bay

With spectacular views back to central Auckland – including the imposing profile of the **Sky Tower** – the two vineyards above pretty Church Bay are deservedly very popular. Auckland and the gulf are at their glistening best when viewed from the picturesque veranda at **Mudbrick** (📞09-372 9050; www.mudbrick.co.nz; 126 Church Bay Rd; mains $46-49; ⏱11.30am-3.30pm & 6-10.30pm). The pretty formal gardens make it popular with weddings, which periodically take over the restaurant (be sure to book ahead). The winery also offers tastings (from $10, 10am to 4pm). One kilometre back down the hill towards Oneroa, **Cable Bay** (📞09-372 5889; www.cablebay. co.nz; 12 Nick Johnstone Dr; mains $42-44; ⏱noon-3pm Tue-Sun, 6pm-late Tue-Sat; 🛜) features contemporary architecture and more stunning vistas. There are two good restaurants and wine tasting ($10 for five wines, 11am to 5pm

LINK YOUR TRIP

1 Northland & the Bay of Islands

More great beaches and discovering NZ's shared Māori & European heritage.

2 East & West Coast Explorer

More food- and wine-related fun amid Aucklanders' favourite day trips.

Cactus Bay

Man O' War Bay ⑥

Te Haahi-Goodwin Reserve

Omaru Bay

Connells Bay ⑦

daily) takes place in a stylish tasting room.

p81

The Drive » Return to Oceanview Rd via Church Bay Rd and continue for 2.7km before turning right into Surfdale Rd. Continue on this road for 5.5km until you see a sign for 'Wild on Waiheke' on your left.

4 Onetangi

Three Waiheke attractions are handily adjacent amid Onetangi's rural ambience. **Wild on Waiheke** (☎09-372 3434; www.wildonwaiheke.co.nz; 82 Onetangi Rd; tastings per beer or wine $2-3; ⏰11am-4pm Thu-Sun, daily in summer; 🚻) combines a winery and a microbrewery with archery, laser clay shooting, pétanque and a giant chess board. A secondary route leads to nearby **Stonyridge** (☎09-372 8822; www.stonyridge. com; 80 Onetangi Rd; tastings per wine $4-18; ⏰11.30am-5pm; 🛜). Waiheke's most famous vineyard is home to world-beating reds, an atmospheric cafe, and tours ($10 including tastings of two wines, 30 minutes, 11.30am Saturday and Sunday). Combine a bottle with one of Stonyridge's deli platters and retreat to a garden cabana. Another nearby unsealed road meanders to the **Shed at Te Motu** (☎09-372 6884; www.temotu. co.nz/the-shed; 76 Onetangi Rd; shared plates small $12-18, large $22-36; ⏰noon-3pm daily, 6pm-late Fri & Sat Nov-Apr, reduced hours in winter). Te Motu is most famous for stellar Bordeaux-style red wines, and sophisticated shared plates imbued with global culinary influences are served under umbrellas in the restaurant's rustic courtyard.

p81

The Drive » Continue east along Onetangi Rod for 2.5km to Onetangi Beach.

TRIP HIGHLIGHT

5 Onetangi Beach

Waiheke's best beach is a 1.9m sandy arc bookended by forested headlands. The humble baches (simple holiday homes) of earlier decades have now largely been replaced by million-dollar homes with ocean views, but the beach is still accessible to all. It's a wonderful spot for a leisurely stroll, and the gently rolling breakers coming in from the Hauraki Gulf are often perfect for bodysurfing. At the beach's eastern end, **Charlie Farley's** (☎09-372 4106; www.charlie farleys.co.nz; 21 The Strand, Onetangi; ⏰8.30am-late) is the locals' favourite, and the pohutukawa-tree-shaded deck is a top spot for a New Zealand craft beer or a leisurely lunch or dinner.

The Drive » Return to Onetangi Rd and turn left after 300m into Waiheke Rd. Continue for 4.5km before turning left into Man O' War Bay Rd. Travel for 9km on an unsealed road with superb ocean views to Man O' War Bay. This road is narrow and winding in parts so take extra care.

TRIP HIGHLIGHT

6 Man O' War Bay

Yes, the drive to Man O' War Bay on unsealed roads can be bumpy, but it is definitely one of Waiheke's most beautiful

BLAINE HARRINGTON III / ALAMY STOCK PHOTO ©

Church Bay Gardens at Mudbrick Vineyard

spots. The beach is great for swimming, a slender wooden wharf stretches into the water, and there are great views of nearby **Pakatoa** and **Rotoroa Islands**. An essential island experience is to settle in with a tasting platter at the beachfront tasting room of the **Man O' War vineyard** (📞09-372 9678; www.manowarvineyards. co.nz; 725 Man O' War Bay

Rd; 🕐11am-6pm Dec-Feb, to 4.30pm Mar-Nov). The Valhalla chardonnay is an outstanding wine, and the rosé is highly recommended with tapas including charcuterie, cheeses and plump Waiheke olives. Beer fans can cool down with Man O' War's very own 'Great Harry' lager.

The Drive » Leave Man O' War Bay on the unsealed road

in front of the beach. Look for the heritage church that is used for summer weddings. Continue over the beach's southern headland for 6km before turning left down to Connells Bay.

❼ Connells Bay

Reached by a road in the island's remote southeastern corner, this private sculpture park in beautiful **Connells**

LOCAL KNOWLEDGE: TIME FOR AN ICE CREAM...

Before school, after school, and on weekdays and weekends, Waiheke locals crowd the funky shipping-container garden at **Island Gelato** (☎021 536 860; www.islandgelato.co.nz; 1 Oceanview Rd, Oneroa; ice cream from $5; ⏰7.30am-5pm Sun-Thu, to 8pm Fri & Sat) for delicious ice cream, coffee and bagels. Seasonal ice-cream flavours shine, including our favourite, the zingy kaffir-lime-and-coconut sorbet. You'll find all this irresistible goodness at the bottom end of Oneroa village.

Bay (☎09-372 8957; www.connellsbay.co.nz; 142 Cowes Bay Rd; adult/child $30/15; ⏰by appointment Nov-Mar) features a stellar roster of NZ artists. Around 30 different works punctuate the coastal terrain. Admission is by way of a two-hour guided tour, so visitors need to book ahead. Note the park is only open from late October to mid-April.

The Drive » Continue for 1.5km south on Cowes Bay Rd to the intersection with Orapiu Rd. Turn right into Orapiu Rd – this section is sealed again – and continue for 14km via Waiheke Rd to Onetangi Rd. Turn left on Onetangi Rd before turning left into Trig Hill Rd for 2km. Look for the sign to EcoZip Adventures.

TRIP HIGHLIGHT

8 EcoZip Adventures

Soar on a zipline above vineyards and native forest on Waiheke Island's most exciting experience. Three separate 200m-long stretches add up to a thrilling ride at **EcoZip Adventures** (☎09-372 5646; www.ecozipadventures.co.nz; 150 Trig Hill Rd; adult/child/family $119/79/$317; ⏰9am-5pm), but it's definitely a soft adventure suitable for most travellers. Look out to the skyline of Auckland's CBD as you're whizzing through the island air. Following the zipline, there is a pleasant 1.4km walk through the pristine forest. A few hundred metres further along Trig Hill Rd, **Peacock Sky**

(☎09-950 4386; www.peacocksky.co.nz; 152 Trig Hill Rd; ⏰noon-5pm) combines a rustic vineyard ambience with wine tasting (from $3), and main dishes ($25-32) and shared platters ($40) combining local produce and international flavours.

The Drive » Return via Trig Hill Rd to Onetangi Rd and continue left for 2.2km. Turn left into O'Brien Rd and then right onto Te Whau Dr for 4km out to the end of the Te Whau peninsula.

9 Te Whau Point

Perched on the end of the peninsula, the restaurant at **Te Whau** (☎09-372 7191; www.tewhau.com; 218 Te Whau Dr; mains $40-42; ⏰11am-5pm daily & 6.30-11pm Thu-Sat Dec & Jan, 11am-5pm Wed-Mon & 6.30-11pm Sat Feb-Easter, 11am-4.30pm Fri-Sun & 6.30-11pm Sat Easter-Nov) has exceptional views, food and service, and one of NZ's finest wine lists. The attached tasting room offers samples of its own impressive Bordeaux blends (11am to 5pm, four tastes for $12). En route stop at **Azurro Groves** (☎09-372 2700; www.azzurogroves.com; 152 Te Whau Dr; ⏰11.30am-3.30pm, reduced hours Jun-Aug) to taste (and purchase) some of Waiheke's finest olive oils.

Eating & Sleeping

Auckland ❶

See p50 and p60 for places to eat and stay in Auckland.

Oneroa ❷

✕ Dragonfired   Pizza $

(☑021 922 289; www.dragonfired.co.nz; Little Oneroa Beach, Oneroa; mains $10-18; ⊙10am-8pm daily Dec-Feb, 11am-7pm Fri-Sun Mar-Nov; ☑) Specialising in 'artisan woodfired food', this caravan by the beach serves the three Ps: pizza, polenta plates and pocket bread. It's easily Waiheke's best place for cheap eats. It has another location by the shop in **Palm Beach** (☑0272 372 372; www.dragonfired.co.nz; Matapana Reserve, Palm Beach; ⊙10am-8pm daily Dec-Feb, 11am-7pm Fri-Sun Mar-Nov).

✕ Wai Kitchen   Cafe $$

(☑09-372 7505; www.waikitchen.co.nz; 1/149 Oceanview Rd, Oneroa; mains $17-26; ⊙8.30am-3.30pm, extended hours in summer; ☑) Why? Well firstly there's the lively menu that abounds with Mediterranean and Asian flavours. Then there's the charming service and the breezy ambience of this glassed-in wedge, facing the *wai* (water).

⮕ Fossil Bay Lodge   Cabin $

(☑09-372 8371; www.fossilbay.net; 58 Korora Rd, Oneroa; s $60, d $85-90, tents $100-120, apt $130; ☑) Three cutesy cabins open onto a courtyard facing the main building, which houses the communal toilets, kitchen and living area, and a compact self-contained upstairs apartment. Best of all are the four 'glamping' tents, each with a proper bed and its own toilet.

Apart from the occasional squawking duck – or toddler from the adjacent Steiner kindergarten – it's a peaceful place.

⮕ Oyster Inn   Boutique Hotel $$$

(☑09-372 2222; www.theoysterinn.co.nz; 124 Oceanview Rd, Oneroa; r $395-450) With a breezy and cool ambience inspired by classic American Cape Cod style, The Oyster Inn has just three rooms in the heart of the Oneroa shops. There are no views to speak of and the rooms are small for the price, but you can expect ferry pickups, stellar bathroom products and personalised service.

Church Bay ❸

⮕ Cable Bay Views   Apartment $$$

(☑09-372 2901; www.cablebayviews.co.nz; 103 Church Bay Rd; r $300; ☑) These three modern, self-contained studio apartments have stellar vineyard views and are handy to a couple of Waiheke's best vineyard restaurants. Check the website for good midweek and off-peak discounts.

Onetangi ❹

✕ Casita Miro   Spanish $$

(☑09-372 7854; www.casitamiro.co.nz; 3 Brown St, Onetangi; tapas $12-20, ración $26; ⊙noon-3pm Thu-Mon, 6-10pm Fri & Sat) A wrought-iron and glass pavilion backed with a Gaudi-esque mosaic garden is the stage for a very entertaining troupe of servers who will guide you through the menu of delectable tapas and *raciónes* (larger dishes), designed to be shared. In summer the sides open up, but otherwise, at busy times, it can get noisy.

STRETCH YOUR LEGS
AUCKLAND

Start/Finish: Sky Tower

Distance: 5km

Duration: Three hours

Ascend the soaring Sky Tower for stunning views of Auckland's impetuous sprawl across two harbours, before discovering iconic New Zealand art, the city's proud maritime history, and emerging areas for great eating, drinking and shopping.

Take this walk on Trips

Sky Tower

At 328m, Auckland's Sky Tower (p106) is the southern hemisphere's tallest structure, and a lift reaches the observation decks in 40 stomach-lurching seconds. There's underground parking here, and adjacent **Federal St** is packed with excellent restaurants.

The Walk ≫ Walk along Federal St and turn left down Wellesley St to the Civic Theatre.

Civic Theatre

The **Civic Theatre** (☎09-309 2677; www.civictheatre.co.nz; cnr Queen & Wellesley Sts), built in 1929, is one of only seven 'atmospheric theatres' remaining in the world, and a fine survivor from cinema's Golden Age. The auditorium features lavish Moorish decoration, and the stunning foyer is an Indian confection with elephants and monkeys hanging from every fixture.

The Walk ≫ Cross Queen St and walk up Wellesley St before turning left into Kitchener St for the Auckland Art Gallery.

Auckland Art Gallery

Combining a modern glass-and-wood atrium with an 1887 French-chateau frame, the **Auckland Art Gallery** (☎09-379 1349; www.aucklandartgallery.com; cnr Kitchener & Wellesley Sts; ⊙10am-5pm) features the best of NZ art, along with important works by Picasso, Cézanne, Gauguin and Matisse. Highlights include the intimate, 19th-century portraits of tattooed Māori subjects by Charles Goldie, and the dramatic text-scrawled canvasses of Colin McCahon. Free tours at 11.30am and 1.30pm.

The Walk ≫ Turn right along Lorne St, which becomes High St and continues via Commerce St across Customs St to the Britomart Precinct.

Britomart Precinct

The Britomart Precinct is a compact enclave of historic buildings that has been transformed into one of the city's best eating, drinking and shopping precincts. Most of Auckland's top fashion designers have recently decamped

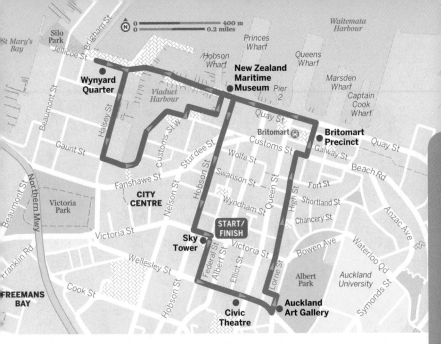

to the Britomart area from further uptown in High St.

The Walk » From the Britomart Precinct, walk along Quay St past Auckland's historic Ferry Building to the New Zealand Maritime Museum.

New Zealand Maritime Museum

This museum traces NZ's seafaring history from Māori voyaging canoes to America's Cup yachting. Re-creations include a 19th-century steerage-class cabin and a 1950s Kiwi bach (holiday home). The exhibit 'Blue Water Black Magic' is a tribute to Sir Peter Blake, the renowned and respected NZ yachtsman who was murdered in 2001 on an environmental monitoring trip in the Amazon.

The Walk » Continue past super yachts to the Wynyard Quarter. Te Wero Bridge is raised when boats need to access the inner harbour.

Wynyard Quarter

Wynyard Quarter opened in advance of 2011's Rugby World Cup, and with its public plazas, waterfront eateries and children's playground, it is a popular place for Aucklanders to gather. At the **Silo Park** area, down the western end, free outdoor Friday-night **movies** and weekend **markets** are summertime institutions. Most of Wynyard's better restaurants are one block back from the water on **Jellicoe St**.

The Walk » Leave the Wynyard Quarter on Halsey St and turn left onto Gaunt St to follow a pedestrian walkway around the marina to Viaduct Harbour (1.4km).

Viaduct Harbour

Once a busy commercial port, Viaduct Harbour was given a major makeover for the 1999/2000 and 2003 America's Cup yachting events. It's now a fancy dining precinct, and guaranteed to have at least a slight buzz any night of the week. Historical plaques, public sculpture and a line-up of millionaires' yachts make it a diverting place for a stroll.

The Walk » Follow Hobson St uphill for 700m to the Sky Tower.

Rotorua & the Central North Island Trips

CENTRED ON THE MASSIVE EXPANSE OF LAKE TAUPO, these journeys course through some of the North Island's most dramatic and powerful landscapes.

The three volcanic peaks of Tongariro National Park provide a mighty backdrop for superb hiking and mountain biking, and from Taupo north to Rotorua the land is alive with the powerful geothermal forces. Rotorua is also a hot spot of traditional Māori culture, with the city's famed *hangi* feasts and concerts.

To the northwest, the Waitomo Caves offer relaxed exploration or more exciting adventures to challenge Rotorua's compelling menu of extreme activities, and funky Raglan is the quintessential Kiwi surf town.

Lake Taupo Rock carvings at Mine Bay (Trip 6)

Redwoods Whakarewarewa Forest Walking one of the forest tracks

5 **Taranaki Wanderer 3 days**
A superb art gallery, great beaches and NZ's most photogenic mountain. (p88)

6 **Tongariro National Park Loop 3–4 days**
Alpine vistas and active adventures on two legs or two wheels. (p96)

7 **Thermal Discoverer 5–6 days**
Steaming volcanic thrills, Māori culture and the wonders of Tolkien. (p104)

8 **Waves & Caves to Whanganui 5 days**
World-renowned surf beaches segue to underground beauty and subterranean adventure. (p120)

☑ **DON'T MISS**

Len Lye Centre
New Plymouth's newest gallery combines stunning design with the kinetic art of world-renowned artist Len Lye. Get arty on Trip **5**

Whangamomona Hotel
At the heart of a self-proclaimed 'republic', get your passport stamped at this classic Kiwi pub that's a great watering hole on Trip **5**

Māori Rock Carvings
Take a boat trip or kayak to these towering works etched into the cliffs above Lake Taupo's Mine Bay. Paddle away on Trip **6**

'Smash Palace'
This quirky car-graveyard at sleepy Horopito was featured in a classic Kiwi movie in 1981. Now it's a worthy stop on Trip **6**

Rotorua Canopy Tours
Bridges, zip lines and platforms all combine within a native forest canopy. Time to fly high on Trip **7**

Oakura Beach *One of many black-sand beaches along Surf Highway*

Taranaki Wanderer

5

Explore the fascinating art of Len Lye in New Plymouth before charting a route around Mt Taranaki's perfect volcanic cone and exploring a historic and remote highway.

TRIP HIGHLIGHTS

43 km

Cape Egmont Lighthouse
Combine ocean views and graceful Mt Taranaki

0 km

New Plymouth
Explore the fascinating kinetic art of Len Lye

FINISH
Taumarunui

START
1

4

7

Stratford

Hawera

Dawson Falls
Base for walks around Egmont National Park

162 km

3 DAYS
345KM /
214 MILES

GREAT FOR...

BEST TIME TO GO

From November to March, Taranaki's gardens are at their most colourful

ESSENTIAL PHOTO

Mt Taranaki from the Cape Egmont Lighthouse

BEST FOR MUSIC FANS

New Plymouth's WOMAD world music festival in March

5 | Taranaki Wanderer

Taranaki is an interesting region often overlooked by travellers. Cradled by the coast, the city of New Plymouth combines urban smarts – courtesy of a stellar duo of art galleries – with a laid-back, beachy vibe. Mt Taranaki, surely New Zealand's best-looking volcano, anchors an area with a proud history of dairy farming, while sleepy roads meander down to rugged surf beaches from the famed Surf Highway (SH45).

TRIP HIGHLIGHT

❶ New Plymouth

Welcome to one of NZ's most interesting provincial cities. New Plymouth has a bubbling arts scene, excellent cafes and restaurants, and attractive parks and gardens. Opened in late 2015, the spectacular **Len Lye Centre** (☎06-759 6060; www.lenlyefoundation. com; 42 Queen St; ◷10am-6pm Mon, Wed & Fri-Sun, to 9pm Thu; 👪) is a thrilling architectural showcase of kinetic sculptures by NZ

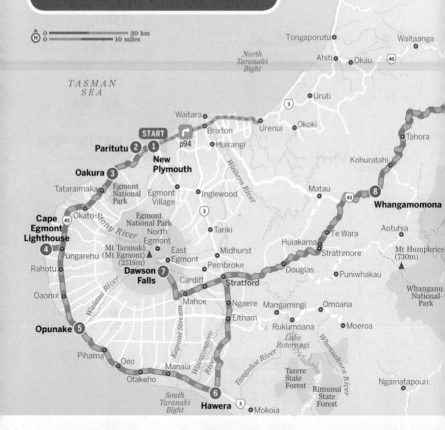

artist Len Lye (1901–80), and the adjacent **Govett-Brewster Art Gallery** ([📞]06-759 6060; www.govettbrewster.com; 42 Queen St; [🕐]10am-6pm Mon, Wed & Fri-Sun, to 9pm Thu) – arguably the country's best regional art gallery – presents more contemporary, experimental and provocative works. **Pukekura Park** ([📞]06-759 6060; www.pukekura.org.nz; Liardet St; [🕐]daylight hours) is the pick of the city's green spaces with 49 relaxing hectares of gardens, playgrounds, trails, streams and waterfalls.

[🍴][🛏] p95

The Drive » From central New Plymouth, drive southwest on St Aubyn St which merges into Breakwater Rd. Turn left into Ngamotu St and then right into Centennial Drive for Paritutu Centennial Park (around 5km from central New Plymouth).

- - - - - - - - - - - - - -

② Paritutu

Just south west of New Plymouth is Paritutu, a steep-sided, craggy hill (154m) whose name translates as 'Rising Precipice'. 'Precipice' is right – it's a seriously knee-trembling, 20-minute scramble to the top, the upper reaches over bare rock with a chain to grip on to. If you can ignore your inner screams of common sense and make it to the top, from the summit you can see for miles around: out to the **Sugar Loaf Islands**, down across the town and out to **Mt Taranaki** beyond.

The Drive » Continue south on Centennial Dr with superb ocean views on your right-hand

side. After 2.5km, Centennial Dr merges left into Beach Rd. At the end of Beach Rd, turn right onto SH45, known as the Surf Highway, and continue south towards Hawera. Stop at Oakura, 12km from Paritutu.

- - - - - - - - - - - - - -

③ Oakura

Negotiating the **Surf Highway** – named after the 105km route taken by surfers looking for the best waves – the first stop is Oakura. Wear footwear on the beach in summer as the black sand can get scorching hot. Highlights of Oakura's sleepy village vibe are good cafes, interesting **craft galleries** and the **world's biggest surfboard**. Around 7km south of Oakura turn right down Timaru Rd for 4km to the skeletal remains of the **SS Gairloch**, a vessel that foundered on the nearby Timaru Reef in 1903. From the shipwreck there are excellent views inland to the graceful profile of Mt Taranaki.

[🍴][🛏] p95

Nihoniho

Ohura

8

FINISH
Taumarunui **9** **4**

6

Tokirima   Te Maire

Ohura River

Kirikau

Maraekowhai

Whakahoro

Kaitieke

Retaruke

Mangapurua
(663m)

Manganuioteao River

Tohunga
Junction

Raetihi

Mangaetoroa

Pipiriki

6

Whanganui River

Jerusalem

[§] LINK YOUR TRIP

6 Tongariro National Park Loop

More mountains are showcased a short 42km drive south from Taumarunui at National Park Village.

8 Waves & Caves to Whanganui

Taumarunui is also a stop on this island-spanning route including the spectacular Waitomo Caves.

The Drive ›› Return to SH45 on Timaru Rd and turn right to continue 23km south to Cape Rd at Pungarehu. Turn right on Cape Rd towards the coast and the Cape Egmont Lighthouse. Total distance is 32km.

TRIP HIGHLIGHT

④ Cape Egmont Lighthouse

Located on a gentle rise with superb coastal views, this photogenic, cast-iron lighthouse was prefabricated in London then moved here from Mana Island near Wellington in 1881. The Dutch explorer Abel Tasman sighted this cape in 1642 and called it 'Nieuw Zeeland'. You can't get inside the lighthouse, but it retains a gracious heritage ambience. The best photo opportunity is from near the beach, looking back towards the lighthouse with Mt Taranaki in the background. En route to the lighthouse is Taranaki's distinctive rolling landscape of lahar mounds caused by an explosive volcanic past.

The Drive ›› Return to SH45 along Cape Rd and turn right to continue south to Opunake, 25km from the lighthouse.

⑤ Opunake

A summer town and the surfing epicentre of the Taranaki region, Opunake has a sheltered family beach and plenty of challenging waves fur-ther out. In town along SH45, many of the heritage buildings are dotted with colourful murals depicting the region's history. In front of the library is a **bronze statue** of legendary NZ middle-distance runner Peter Snell, born in Opunake in 1938, who won gold medals at the 1960 Rome and 1964 Tokyo Olympics.

✖ p95

The Drive ›› Continue south on SH45 to Hawera, a distance of 44km. Around 29km south from Opunake, the highway runs through sleepy Manaia, once designed on a grand scale to be one of NZ's main centres.

⑥ Hawera

The largest town in south Taranaki, Hawera is mainly an agricultural service centre for the surrounding region; the

Cape Egmont Lighthouse

dairy industry is very important here. Highlights include **KD's Elvis Presley Museum** (☏06-278 7624; www.elvismuseum.co.nz; 51 Argyle St; admission by donation; ⊙by appointment) – phone ahead to make an appointment – and the **Tawhiti Museum** (☏06-278 6837; www.tawhitimuseum.co.nz; 401 Ohangai Rd; adult/child $15/5; ⊙10am-4pm Fri-Sun, daily Jan, Sun only Jun-Aug) which showcases the traders, whalers and dairy farmers who developed the region. The Tawhiti Museum is near the corner of Tawhiti Rd, 4km north of town. Before you leave SH45 to travel inland to the north, ascend the **Hawera Water Tower** (☏06-278 8599; www.southtaranaki.com; 55 High St; adult/child/family $2.50/1/6; ⊙10am-2pm) for coastal and rural views – and hopefully also the glorious profile of Mt Taranaki if the region's often-capricious clouds are playing fair.

The Drive » From Hawera drive north to Stratford on SH3. Look forward to more stunning vistas of Mt Taranaki on the left. Depart Stratford west on Celia St and Opunake Rd, and turn right into Manaia Rd to drive

93

DETOUR: MIKE'S BREWERY, URENUI

Start: ❶ New Plymouth

Established in 1989, one of NZ's first craft breweries is still one the country's best purveyors of flavour-packed combinations of hops, malt and yeast. **Mike's** (☎06-752 3676; www.mikesbeer.co.nz; 487 Mokau Rd, Urenui; tastings/tours $15/25; ☺10am-6pm) is 35km north of New Plymouth on SH3, just past the summertime hot spot of Urenui Beach. Look forward to brewery tours (book ahead), takeaway bottles of draught beer, and leisurely tastings of a wide range of brews, some crafted with organic ingredients. Standout beers include the Taranaki India Pale Ale, THC (a zingy Hefeweizen wheat beer), and a smooth-as-silk barrel-aged whisky Porter.

north to Dawson Falls on the slopes of Mt Taranaki, 54km from Hawera.

TRIP HIGHLIGHT

❼ Dawson Falls

Located within Egmont National Park – the name of the mountain was changed back to Mt Taranaki from Mt Egmont in 1985 – Dawson Falls is an excellent base for walking. Shorter options include the **Wilkies Pools Loop** (1¼ hours return) or the **Kapuni Loop Track** (one-hour loop) which runs to the impressive 18m Dawson Falls themselves. You can also see the falls from the visitor centre via a 10-minute walk to a **viewpoint**. More challenging is the hike to **Fanthams Peak** (five hours return) which is snowed-in during winter. Definitely get

advice and source maps at the **Dawson Falls Visitor Centre** (☎06-443 0248; www.doc.govt.nz; Manaia Rd, Dawson Falls; ☺9am-4pm Thu-Sun, daily school holidays) before heading off.

The Drive ›› Return 23km back to Stratford and rejoin SH3. After around 1km heading north on SH3, turn right into SH43 towards Taumarunui. The tiny forest hamlet of Whangamomona is reached after 62km. Your last option for petrol on this road is Stratford, so fill up before you leave town.

❽ Whangamomona

Running 155km from Stratford northeast to Taumarunui, SH43 – also known as the **Forgotten Highway** – winds through hilly bush country, passing Māori *pa* (fortified villages) and abandoned coal mines en route. Excellent

lookout spots include the Whangamomona Saddle, 6km before Whangamomona. This quirky village declared itself an independent republic in 1989 after disagreements with local councils. The town celebrates **Republic Day** in January every odd-numbered year. Get your passport stamped at the grand old Whangamomona Hotel as you're waiting for one of their big country meals. There's also simple accommodation with shared bathrooms and a separate self-contained cottage.

The Drive ›› From Whangamomona it is another 87km on winding and narrow roads to Taumarunui. Around 12km is unsealed gravel, so drive carefully to minimise the risk of a tyre puncture.

❾ Taumarunui

On the edge of Taranaki and actually in the King Country region, Taumarunui is a good base for jetboating with **Taumarunui Jet Tours** (☎0800 853 886; www.taumarunuijettours.co.nz; 30/60min tours from $60/100) on the nearby Whanganui River, or mountain biking the 85km Timber Trail with **Epic Cycle Adventures** (☎022 023 7958; www.thetimbertrail.com; bike & shuttle $100).

✕ p95

Eating & Sleeping

New Plymouth ❶

✖ Federal Store　　　　　　Cafe $$
(☏06-757 8147; www.thefederalstore.com; 440
Devon St E; mains $10-20; ⊙7am-5pm Mon-Fri,
8am-5pm Sat, 9am-5pm Sun; 🖊 🖼) Super-
popular and crammed with retro furniture,
Federal conjures up a 1950s corner-store vibe.
Switched-on staff in dinky head scarves take
your coffee requests as you queue to order food
at the counter, keeping you buoyant until your
hot cakes, New Yorker sandwich or pulled-pork
bun arrive. Terrific cakes, tarts and pre-made
counter food (love the vegie frittata).

🛏 King & Queen Hotel
Suites　　　　　　Boutique Hotel $$$
(☏06-757 2999; www.kingandqueen.co.nz;
cnr King & Queen Sts; ste from $205; @🛜) A
relatively new kid on the NP accommodation
block, this regal hotel occupies the corner of
King and Queen Sts (get it?). Run by unerringly
professional staff, it's an interesting 17-room
affair over two levels. Each suite features
antique Moroccan and Euro furnishings, plush
carpets, lustrous black tiles, hip art, retro
leather couches and *real* flowers. Cafe/bean
roastery onsite.

Oakura ❸

✖ Kin & Co　　　　　　Cafe $
(☏06-752 7270; www.facebook.com/KinandCo;
1151 South Rd, SH45; snacks & mains $5-14;
⊙7am-6pm Tue-Fri, 9am-3pm Sat & Sun) A
cool combination of cafe and deli, Kin & Co
is the perfect stop before discovering the
Surf Highway south from Oakura. Colourful
macarons and fluffy brioches combine with
perfect coffee, and kombucha and gluten-free

options appeal to healthy-eating travellers.
Grab a sunny spot on the bean bags, or stock
up for on-the-road picnics with local artisan
produce.

🛏 Ahu Ahu Beach
Villas　　　　　　Boutique Hotel $$$
(☏06-752 7370; www.ahu.co.nz; 321 Lower Ahu
Ahu Rd; d/q from $295/650; 🛜) Pricey, but
pretty amazing. Set on a knoll overlooking the
big wide ocean, these luxury, architect-designed
villas are superbly eccentric, with huge recycled
timbers, bottles cast into walls, lichen-covered
French tile roofs and polished-concrete floors
with inlaid paua. A lodge addition sleeps four.
Rock stars stay here!

Opunake ❺

✖ Sugar Juice Café　　　　　　Cafe $$
(☏06-761 7062; 42 Tasman St; snacks $4-10,
mains $11-35; ⊙9am-4pm Sun-Wed, 9am-late
Thu-Sat, closed Mon Jun-Aug; 🖊) Happy, hippie
and wholesome, Sugar Juice Café has some
of the best food on SH45. It's brimming with
delicious, homemade, filling things (try the
crayfish-and-prawn ravioli or cranberry lamb
shanks). Terrific coffee, salads, wraps, tarts,
cakes and big brekkies – don't pass it by.

Taumarunui ❾

✖ Anna's Cafe　　　　　　Cafe $$
(☏07-896 7442; 75 Hakiaha St; mains $13-20;
⊙7am-4pm Mon-Fri, to 10pm Sat & Sun)
Anna's country kitchen style is brightened up
by big-format photos of food, and luckily the
menu fulfils this culinary promise. Wine, beer
and Taumarunui's coffee is all available along
with well-prepared versions of cafe classics like
hotcakes with mixed berries.

Tongariro National Park Outdoor
adventures amid dramatic volcanic scenery

Tongariro National Park Loop

6

The three volcanic peaks of Ruapehu, Ngauruhoe and Tongariro form the spectacular alpine hub of this exciting ramble combining expansive scenery, active adventure and family fun.

TRIP HIGHLIGHTS

0 km

Taupo
Visit spectacular Māori Rock Carvings on Lake Taupo

1 START

Lake Taupo

Turangi FINISH

131 km

National Park Village
Departure point for the Tongariro Alpine Crossing

5

Ohakune
Take on the Old Coach Road mountain bike trail

6

Waiouru

167 km

**3–4 DAYS
257KM / 160 MILES**

GREAT FOR...

BEST TIME TO GO
October to April for prime mountain-biking weather

ESSENTIAL PHOTO
Biking the 284m Hapuawhenua Viaduct on the Old Coach Road

BEST FOR FAMILIES
Rafting on the Tongariro River near Turangi

6

Tongariro National Park Loop

Tracing a circle around the North Island's biggest national park, this journey presents many energising opportunities to get active amid some of New Zealand's most inspiring scenery. But if mountain biking, rafting or hiking aren't on your agenda, trout fishing and boat trips around Lake Taupo offer more relaxing ways to be immersed in the spectacular scenery of the diverse Ruapehu region.

TRIP HIGHLIGHT

❶ Taupo

One of the North Island's most popular resort towns, Taupo is deservedly busy with holidaying Kiwi families across summer (December to February). Located a short walk from Lake Taupo, the **Taupo Museum** (☏07-376 0414; www.taupodc.govt.nz; Story Pl; adult/child $5/free; ☺10am-4.30pm) features an excellent Māori gallery and quirky displays, including a 1960s caravan

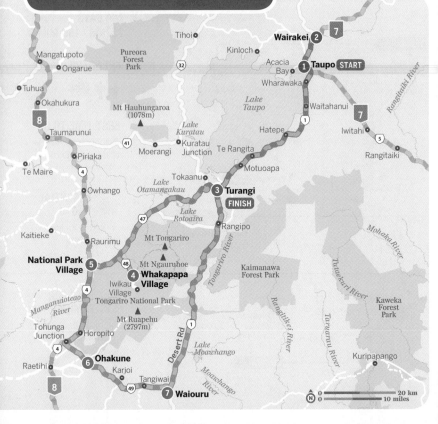

set up as if the occupants have just popped down to the lake. The centre-piece of the museum is an elaborately carved Māori meeting house, Te Aroha o Rongoheikume. To see the lake more closely, boat operators run regular trips taking in spectacular 10m-high **Māori Rock Carvings** that have been etched into the cliffs of Mine Bay. They depict Ngatoro-i-rangi, the visionary Māori navi-gator who guided the Tu-wharetoa and Te Arawa tribes to the Taupo area a thousand years ago.

✕ ⌂ p103

The Drive » Head out of Taupo north on the Thermal Explorer Hwy – with the glorious lake behind you – and turn right to meander along Huka Falls Rd before linking with Karetoto Rd to Wairakei, 7km from Taupo.

LINK YOUR TRIP

7 **Thermal Discoverer**

This journey through the North Island's geologically active centre also includes Taupo.

8 **Waves & Caves to Whanganui**

National Park Village is a stop on this island-spanning adventure.

---

② Wairakei

Scattered around Ka-retoto Rd in Wairakei are several interesting diversions. The **Volcanic Activity Centre** (☎07-374 8375; www.volcanoes.co.nz; Karetoto Rd; adult/child $12/7; ☺9am-5pm Mon-Fri, 10am-4pm Sat & Sun) explains all about the region's geothermal and volcanic activity, including a live seismograph keeping a watch on what's current-ly going on underground. A favourite exhibit with children is the **Earthquake Simulator**, a little booth complete with teeth-chattering shudders and jarring wobbles. Further down the hill, the **Huka Prawn Park** (www.hukaprawnpark. co.nz; Karetoto Rd; adult/child $28/16; ☺9am-4pm) – a geothermally heated freshwater prawn farm – offers prawn 'fishing', Killer Prawn Golf and a restaurant serving up... yep, you guessed it. Near-by, **Hukafalls Jet** (☎0800 485 253, 07-374 8572; www. hukafallsjet.com; 200 Karetoto Rd; adult/child $115/69) runs 30-minute thrill rides to the spray-filled foot of the **Huka Falls**.

The Drive » Return down the hill to Taupo and continue south along the lake's edge before rejoining SH1 just after pretty Five Mile Bay and reaching Turangi after 60km. Look forward to a winding road and stunning lake views.

---

③ Turangi

Once a service town for the nearby hydroelectric power station, sleepy Turangi's claim to fame nowadays is as the 'Trout Fishing Capital of the World'. Contact **Greig's Sporting World** (☎07-386 6911; www.greigsports.co.nz; 59 Town Centre; ☺7.30am-5pm Mon-Sat) for fishing gear and licences, or to book a local fishing guide. Around 4km south of Turangi, the **Tongariro National Trout Centre** (☎07-386 8085; www. troutcentre.com; SH1; adult/child $12/free; ☺10am-4pm Dec-Apr, 10am-3pm May-Nov) has educational displays and freshwater aquari-ums. A gentle stroll leads to the hatchery, an underwater viewing chamber, and a riverside picnic area. Turangi also offers superb white-water rafting. The team at **Rafting NZ** (☎07-386 0352, 0800 865 226; www.rafting-newzealand.com; 41 Ngawaka Pl) run a four-hour, Grade III trip on the Tongariro River with an optional waterfall jump (adult/child $129/119), and a family-fun trip over more relaxed rapids (Grade II, adult/child $90/70, three hours).

✕ ⌂ p103

The Drive » Leave Turangi on SH41 before turning left into SH47 – Te Ponanga Saddle Rd – and skirting the northern edge of Tongariro National Park. Turn left into SH48 for the final push to the village, 48km from Turangi. In fine weather, there are views of the park's three volcanic peaks, Mts Ruapehu, Tongariro and Ngauruhoe.

④ Whakapapa Village

Located within the bounds of Tongariro National Park on the lower slopes of Mt Ruapehu, Whakapapa Village (pronounced 'fa-ka-pa-pa'; altitude: 1140m) is the gateway to the park and home of the park's **visitor centre** (☏07-892 3729; www.doc.govt.nz; Whakapapa Village; ⊙8am-5pm). During winter, the village is packed with skiers and snowboarders heading up to the slopes, but in summer hiking is the main attraction. Most gentle is the **Whakapapa Nature Walk**, a 15-minute loop track beginning 250m above the visitor centre and passing through beech forest and scrubby alpine gardens. The **Taranaki Falls Track** is a two-hour, 6km loop track from the village to the eponymous falls, which plunge 20m over an old lava flow into a boulder-fringed pool. The visitor centre sell the *Walks In and Around Tongariro National Park* brochure ($3) detailing 30 walks and tramps in the park. Whakapapa's most elegant building is the **Chateau Tongariro** (☏0800 242 832, 07-892 3809; www.chateau.co.nz;

Whakapapa Village; d from $245; @🛜🍴), one of NZ's most historic hotels.

The Drive » It's just 16km through scrubby alpine tussock back to SH47 and then west to National Park Village.

TRIP HIGHLIGHT

⑤ National Park Village

This compact sprawl of a town lies at the junction of SH4 and SH47 at 825m above sea level. In ski season the township is packed, but in summer it's sleepier and a handy base for activities in and around the park. The most popular spring and summer activity is tackling the Tongariro Alpine Crossing, renowned as one of the best one-day walks in the world. Embark on this relatively challenging hike independently – regular shuttles run to trail heads – or join a guided walk with **Adrift Guided Outdoor Adventures** or **Adventure Outdoors** (p128). National Park Village is also a great hub for mountain biking on the nearby Fishers Track, 42 Traverse, Old Coach Road and Bridge to Nowhere trails. Contact **Kiwi Mountain Bikes** (p128) for bike rental and transport.

The Drive » From National Park Village to Ohakune (36km) on SH4 and SH49, verdant farmland gradually takes over from more sparse alpine

JENNY & TONY ENDERBY / GETTY IMAGES ©

Whakapapa Village Whakapapa ski field

MOUNTAIN BIKING THE OLD COACH ROAD

The **Ohakune Old Coach Road** (www.ohakunecoachroad.co.nz) is a fantastic adventure for moderately fit cyclists, with local operators in National Park Village and Ohakune making it easy with gear hire and transport.

The dual use (walking and cycling) track follows the original 15km coach track from Ohakune to Horopito which was used from 1886 until 1909, when SH49 opened. Largely forgotten and overgrown, the Old Coach Road was resurrected by locals and restored to glory.

One of NZ's most enjoyable half-day (three to four hours) rides, the gently graded route passes unique engineering features including the historic **Hapuawhenua Viaduct**. It also negotiates ancient forests of giant rimu and totara that survived the Taupo blast of AD 180 as they were in the lea of Mt Ruapehu.

The best start point is **Horopito** as this provides more downhill action overall. A few pushes uphill are required on the way to Ohakune, but sweeping downhill runs on historic cobblestones make it all worthwhile.

vegetation. Stop at Horopito to see the quirky car-graveyard known as 'Smash Palace'.

TRIP HIGHLIGHT

6 Ohakune

Packed with ski bunnies in winter, Ohakune also offers many warmer-weather outdoor adventures, including the superb half-day Old Coach Road mountain bike trail. Contacts to help you get active include **Mountain Bike Station** (06-385 8797; www.mountainbikestation.co.nz; 60 Thames St) – ask about the 17km Turoa Downhill Madness ride down the

Mt Ruapehu ski field access road – and **Canoe Safaris** (06-385 9237, 0800 272 3353; www.canoe-safaris.co.nz; 6 Tay St) for one- to five-day guided trips on the Whanganui or Rangitikei Rivers. Walking opportunities around Ohakune include the **Mangawhero River Walkway**, a leafy amble taking around 25 minutes, and the **Waitonga Falls Walk** (1½ hours return, 4km), which heads to Tongariro's highest waterfall (39m) and includes magnificent views of Mt Ruapehu.

✖ 🛏 p103

The Drive » Stellar views of Mt Ruapehu and bucolic dairy farms feature on the 27km drive east on SH49 from Ohakune to Waiouru.

7 Waiouru

At the junction of SH1 and SH49, Waiouru (altitude 792m) is primarily an army base and a refuelling stop for the 56km-long Desert Rd leading north to Turangi. Housed in a large, concrete bunker at the south end of the township, the **National Army Museum** (06-387 6911; www.armymuseum.co.nz; adult/child $15/5; 9am-4.30pm) preserves the history of the NZ army and its various campaigns from colonial times to the present. Moving stories are told through displays of arms, uniforms, medals and memorabilia. Until mid-2018, the museum will be hosting a series of special exhibitions marking the centenary of WWI. Heading north on the **Desert Road**, the sparse landscape is the result of two million years of volcanic activity, especially during the massive Taupo eruption around two millennia ago that coated the land with thick deposits of pumice and destroyed all vegetation.

The Drive » Back on SH1, it's 63km north through the moon-like landscape of the Desert Rd back to Turangi, near Lake Taupo's southern end.

Eating & Sleeping

Taupo ❶

✗ The Bistro   Modern NZ $$

(☏07-377 3111; www.thebistro.co.nz; 17 Tamamutu St; mains $24-36; ⏰5pm-late) Popular with locals – bookings are recommended – the Bistro focuses on doing the basics very, very well. That means harnessing local seasonal produce for dishes such as confit duck with truffle potatoes or crab-and-pork-belly tortellini, and channelling an intimate but unpretentious ambience. A small but perfectly formed beer and wine list makes it a very reliable choice.

🛏 Waitahanui Lodge   Motel $$

(☏07-378 7183, 0800 104 321; www.waitahanuilodge.co.nz; 116 SH1, Waitahanui; d $119-179; 🛜) Ten kilometres south of Taupo, this enclave of genuine retro bach-style units is ideally positioned for swimming, fishing and superb sunsets. Pick of the bunch are the two absolute-lakefront units, but all have lake access, sociable communal areas plus free use of rowboats and kayaks. The units are all self-contained with kitchenettes, or you can fire up the shared barbecue.

For more places to eat and stay in Taupo see p119.

Turangi ❸

✗ Lakeland House   International $$

(☏07-386 6442; www.braxmere.co.nz; 88 Waihi Rd, Tokaanu; mains lunch $16-25, dinner $38-40; ⏰10am-3pm & 6pm-late) Destination dining at the southern end of Lake Taupo, with generous pastas, salads and chowder dominating the daytime menu. Craft beer from Tuatara Brewing is on tap, and come evening diners can salivate over duck breast with a star-anise-and-honey glaze rounded off with a slice of New York baked cheesecake. Eight kilometres from Turangi, just off SH41.

🛏 Braxmere   Motel $$

(☏07-386 6449; www.braxmere.co.nz; 88 Waihi Rd, Tokaanu; apt from $180) Braxmere is a collection of stylish self-contained apartments arrayed on a grassy lawn with absolute lakefront views. The spacious one-bedroom units all have decks and private courtyards, the decor is chic and modern, and also on-site is the excellent Lakeland House restaurant. Turangi is around 8km away.

Ohakune ❼

✗ Eat   Cafe $

(☏027 443 1426; 49 Clyde St; snacks & mains $9-14; ⏰9am-4pm) Bagels, innovative salads, and tasty American and Tex Mex–influenced dishes combine with the best coffee in town at this modern spot on Ohakune's main drag. There's a strong focus on organic ingredients and sustainable practices, and dishes such as the breakfast burrito or the chicken tacos with carrot-and-cumin slaw really hit the spot after a busy day's adventuring.

🛏 Ruapehu Country Lodge   B&B $$$

(☏06-385 9594; www.ruapehucountrylodge.co.nz; 630 Raetihi–Ohakune Rd; d $287; 🛜) Around 4km south of Ohakune on the road to Raetihi, Ruapehu Country Lodge perfectly combines elegance and classy decor with a friendly welcome from Heather and Peter, the well-travelled and thoroughly unpretentious hosts. Framed by expansive gardens and situated on 2 hectares, the lodge is separated from the local golf course by a meandering river.

Auckland *Adrenaline-packed sports and sedate waterfront wanders*

Classic Trip

Thermal Discoverer

7

Crossing the rugged volcanic heart of the North Island, this expansive journey also includes Māori culture, and plenty of opportunities to get active in the Kiwi outdoors.

TRIP HIGHLIGHTS

START
Auckland

192 km

Matamata
Middle Earth comes to life at Hobbiton

Hamilton

3

4 5

262 km

Rotorua
Māori culture, cuisine and active adventures aplenty

264 km

Redwood Whakarewarewa Forest
Walking and mountain biking amid soaring trees

10

Taupo

Orakei Korako
Geysers, silica terraces and a stunning natural cavern

403 km

Napier
FINISH

5–6 DAYS
591KM / 367 MILES

GREAT FOR...

BEST TIME TO GO
February to April for warm and settled weather

ESSENTIAL PHOTO
Channelling your inner Bilbo or Frodo at Hobbiton

BEST FOR OUTDOORS
Zipping through the Redwoods Whakarewarewa Forest on two wheels

105

Classic Trip

7 Thermal Discoverer

Sitting in the caldera of a volcano that began erupting about 300,000 years ago, Lake Taupo is at the centre of this diverse and spectacular region. Northeast to Rotorua, the idiosyncratic landscape is punctuated by steaming, bubbling geothermal attractions, and destinations to the north and south include the fascinating make-believe world of Hobbiton and the art-deco architectural heritage of Napier, itself a reaction to a devastating earthquake in 1931.

1 Auckland

Start as you mean to go on – further south Rotorua and Taupo both have extreme activities on tap – by experiencing a more adventurous side of NZ's biggest city. With **Auckland Bridge Climb & Bungy** (☏09-360 7748; www.bungy.co.nz; 105 Curran St, Westhaven; adult/child climb $125/85, bungy $160/130, both $230), there's the option of negotiating the arches of this city landmark before taking a bungy leap of faith towards the waters of the **Waitemata Harbour**. The Sky Tower (p82), at 328m, is another Auckland icon, and riding the elevator to the observation decks is trumped by the spine-tingling thrills of the **SkyWalk** (☏0800 759 925; www.skywalk.co.nz; Sky Tower, cnr Federal & Victoria Sts; adult/child $145/115; ⏱10am-4.30pm) or the **SkyJump** (☏0800 759 586; www.skyjump.co.nz; Sky Tower, cnr Federal & Victoria Sts; adult/child $225/175; ⏱10am-5.15pm). Alternatively, take a more sedate wander through the city

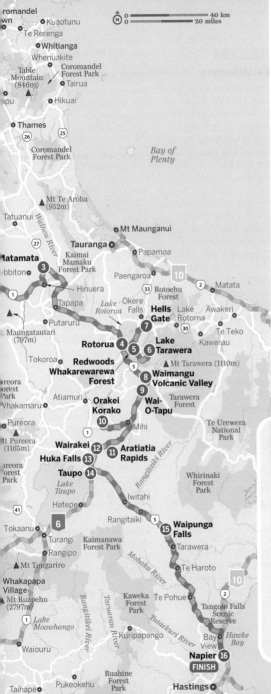

on our walking tour showcasing Auckland's interesting waterfront (p82).

✕ p118

The Drive » Depart Auckland on the Southern Motorway (SH1) and continue south for 125km to Hamilton. At times the road skirts the wide Waikato River.

2 Hamilton

One of NZ's most bustling provincial cities, Hamilton combines excellent cafes and restaurants for an on-the-road breakfast or lunch with a compact riverside arts and culture precinct. The interesting **Waikato Museum** (www.waikatomuseum.co.nz; 1 Grantham St; admission by donation; ◷10am-4.30pm) has five main areas: an art gallery; interactive science galleries; Tainui

§ **LINK YOUR TRIP**

6 Tongariro National Park Loop

From Taupo, explore the outdoor adventures of North Island's biggest national park.

10 Pacific Coast Explorer

Napier is an interesting stop on this exploration of New Zealand's Pacific coastal fringes.

Classic Trip

galleries housing Māori treasures, including the magnificently carved *waka taua* (war canoe), Te Winikawaka; a WWI exhibition entitled 'For Us They Fell'; and a Waikato River exhibition. Adjacent to the museum, **ArtsPost** (www.waikato museum.co.nz/artspost; 120 Victoria St; ⏰10am-4.30pm) is a contemporary gallery and gift shop housed in a grand, former post office. It focuses on the best of local art: paintings, glass, prints, textiles and photography.

✗ p118

The Drive » Depart Hamilton south on Anglesea St and Cobham Dr, which becomes SH1. After 44km turn left into SH29, then left into SH27 after 14km, continuing a further 10km to Matamata. If you're joining a tour at the Hobbiton site, turn left into Buckland Rd 10km

after the intersection of SH1 and SH29.

TRIP HIGHLIGHT

❸ Matamata

Matamata was a pleasant country town you usually drove through until Peter Jackson's film trilogy *Lord of the Rings* put it on the map. During filming, 300 locals got work as extras, and following the subsequent filming of *The Hobbit*, the town has ardently embraced its Middle Earth credentials. There's a spooky statue of **Gollum** in the main street, and the **Matamata i-SITE** (☎07-888 7260; www.matamatanz.co.nz; 45 Broadway; ⏰9am-5pm) has been transformed into a wonderful Hobbit gatehouse. Tours to **Hobbiton** (☎0508 446 224 866, 07-888 1505; www. hobbitontours.com; 501 Buckland Rd, Hinuera; adult/child tours $79/39.50, dinner tours $190/100; ⏰tours 10am-4.30pm) – including a very entertaining bus ride –

leave from the i-SITE, and it's also possible to travel there with your own transport. Booking ahead is strongly recommended. The Evening Dinner Tours on Sunday and Wednesday include a banquet dinner.

✗ p118

The Drive » Leave Matamata on its main street and continue via SH28 and SH24 reaching Tapapa after 24km. Turn left into SH5 and continue for 43km through forest and farmland to Rotorua, 67km from Matamata.

TRIP HIGHLIGHT

❹ Rotorua

Home to spurting geysers, steaming hot springs and exploding mud pools, Rotorua is NZ's most dynamic thermal area. The Māori revered this place, naming one of the most spectacular springs Wai-O-Tapu (Sacred Waters). Today 35% of Rotorua's population is Māori, and the best places to experience their culture and the fascinating geothermal terrain are **Te Puia** (☎0800 837 842, 07-348 9047; www.tepuia.com; Hemo Rd; adult/child tours $49.50/23, daytime tour & performance combos $58/29, evening tour, performance & hangi combos $140/70; ⏰8am-6pm Oct-Apr, to 5pm May-Sep) and **Whakarewarewa Village** (☎07-349 3463; www.whakarewarewa. com; 17 Tyron St; tour & cultural performance adult/child

LOCAL KNOWLEDGE: TAUPIRI'S SACRED SLOPES

About 26km north of Hamilton on SH1 is Taupiri (287m), the sacred mountain of the Tainui people. You'll recognise it by the cemetery on its slopes and the honking of passing car horns – locals saying hi to their loved ones as they pass by. In August 2006 thousands gathered here as the much-loved Māori queen, Dame Te Atairangikaahu, was transported upriver by *waka* (canoe) to her final resting place, an unmarked grave on the summit.

$35/15; ⏱8.30am-5pm, tours hourly 9am-4pm & cultural performances 11.15am & 2pm). The Tudor-style **Rotorua Museum** (☏07-350 1814; www.rotoruamuseum.co.nz; Queens Dr, Government Gardens; adult/child $20/8; ⏱9am-5pm Mar-Nov, to 6pm Dec-Feb, tours hourly 10am-4pm, plus 5pm Dec-Feb) tells the story of the area's heritage as an elegant spa retreat.

Entertainment celebrating Māori culture is big business in Rotorua and, although it is commercialised, it's a great opportunity to learn about the indigenous culture of NZ. The two big activities are concerts and *hangi* feasts, often packaged together in an evening's entertainment featuring the famous *hongi* (Māori greeting; the pressing of foreheads and noses, and sharing of life breath) and *haka* and *poi* dances. **Tamaki Maori Village** (☏0508 826 254, 07-349 2999; www.tamakimaorivillage.co.nz; booking office 1220 Hinemaru St; adult/family $115/310, child $25-65; ⏱tours depart 5pm, 6.15pm & 7.30pm Nov-Apr, 6.15pm May-Oct) and family-run **Mitai Maori Village** (☏07-343 9132; www.mitai.co.nz; 196 Fairy Springs Rd; adult/family $116/315, child $23-58; ⏱6.30pm) are established favourites. **Te Puia** (p108) and **Whakarewarewa Village** (p108) also put on shows, and many of the big hotels offer mainstream Māori concerts and hangi.

🍴 🛏 p118

The Drive » Leave Rotorua on Hinemaru St, turn left onto SH30, then right into Tarawera Rd for the Redwoods Whakarewarewa Forest, 4km from town.

- - - - - - - - - - -

TRIP HIGHLIGHT

⑤ Redwoods Whakarewarewa Forest

This magical forest park was originally home to over 170 tree species, planted from 1899 to see which could be grown successfully for timber. Mighty Californian redwoods give the park its grandeur today. Walking tracks range from a half-hour wander through the **Redwood**

WORLD-CLASS MOUNTAIN BIKING

On the edge of Rotorua is the Redwoods Whakarewarewa Forest, home to some of the best mountain bike trails in the country. There are close to 100km of tracks to keep bikers of all skill levels happy for days on end. Note that not all tracks in the forest are open to bikers, so adhere to the signposts. Pick up a trail map at the forest visitor centre.

Another essential destination for mountain bikers is the new **Skyline MTB Gravity Park** (☏07-347 0027; www.skyline.co.nz/rotorua; Fairy Springs Rd; 1/15 gondola rides with bike $28/55; ⏱9am-5pm) where access up Mt Ngongotaha is provided by a gondola.

Mountain Bike Rotorua (☏0800 682 768; www.mtbrotorua.co.nz; Waipa State Mill Rd; mountain bikes per 2hr/day from $35/45, guided half-/full-day rides from $130/275; ⏱9am-5pm) hires out bikes and runs guided half- and full-day rides at the Waipa Mill car park entrance to the Redwoods Whakarewarewa Forest, the starting point for the bike trails. You can also stop by their new central Rotorua **adventure hub** (☏07-348 4290; www.mtbrotorua.co.nz; 1128 Hinemoa St; ⏱9am-5pm) for rentals, mountain biking information, and a cool little cafe, and they can also fit you out with a bike at the Skyline MTB Gravity Park.

For more information, the **Rotorua i-SITE** (☏0800 768 678, 07-348 5179; www.rotoruanz.com; 1167 Fenton St; ⏱7.30am-6pm) has a special display area dedicated to the city's world class mountain biking scene. Online, see www.riderotorua.com.

Classic Trip

WHY THIS IS A CLASSIC TRIP
BRETT ATKINSON, WRITER

Born in Rotorua, experiencing this region's volcanic energy feels like a warm and familiar embrace when I return to my home town. Around the central North Island a roll call of geothermal attractions unfolds, each more improbably impressive than the previous one. Māori culture underpins the natural spectacle, and mountain biking and hiking fast-track immersion into the outdoors.

Top: Champagne Pool, Wai-O-Tapu Thermal Wonderland
Left: Redwoods Whakarewarewa Forest
Right: Māori woman and man greet with a traditional *hongi*

Grove to a whole-day route to the **Blue and Green Lakes**. Most walks start from the **Redwoods i-SITE** (☎07-350 0110; www.redwoods.co.nz; Long Mile Rd, off Tarawera Rd; ⏰8.30am-5.30pm Mon-Fri, 10am-5pm Sat & Sun Oct-Mar, closes 1hr earlier Apr-Sep).

A recent addition is the spectacular **Redwoods Treewalk** (☎07-350 0110; www.treewalk.co.nz; Redwoods Whakarewarewa Forest; adult/child $25/15; ⏰8.30am-6pm), a suspended walkway combining 21 wooden bridges between century-old trees. Aside from walking, the forest park is great for picnics, and is acclaimed for its accessible mountain biking.

🍴 p119

The Drive » Continue along Tarawera Rd for 22km to Lake Tarawera, passing the beautiful Blue and Green Lakes en route.

- - - - - - - - - - - - - -

6 Lake Tarawera

Pretty Lake Tarawera offers swimming, fishing, and walks, and **Lake Tarawera Water Taxi & Eco Tours** (☎07-362 8080; www.ecotoursrotorua.co.nz; 1375 Tarawera Rd; adult/child $65/35; ⏰departs at 2pm) runs boat trips around the lake. Around 4km before the lake is the **Buried Village** (☎07-362 8287; www.buriedvillage.co.nz; 1180 Tarawera Rd; adult/child/family $32.50/10/65; ⏰9am-5pm Nov-Mar, to 4.30pm Apr-Oct) of Te Wairoa, interred by the 1886 eruption of Mt

Tarawera. Te Wairoa was the staging post for travellers coming to see the famed Pink and White Terraces, spectacular silica travertines that were destroyed by the same eruption. Today a museum houses objects dug from the ruins, and guides in period costume escort groups through the excavated sites. There's also a walk to the 30m **Te Wairoa Falls** and a cafe. Tarawera means 'Burnt Spear', named by a Māori

hunter who left his bird spears in a hut, and on returning the following season found both the spears and the hut had been incinerated.

The Drive » Return to SH30 and turn right, skirting Lake Rotorua and the airport on SH30 to Tikitere (30km in total).

❼ Hells Gate

Known as Tikitere to Māori, **Hells Gate** (☎07-345 3151; www.hellsgate.co.nz; SH30, Tikitere; admission adult/child/family $35/17.50/85, mud bath & spa $75/35/185; ⊕8.30am-8.30pm) is an impressive geothermal reserve 16km northeast of Rotorua

on the Whakatane road (SH30). The reserve covers 10 hectares, with a 2.5km walking track to the various attractions, including a hot thermal waterfall. You can see a master woodcarver at work, and learn about flax weaving and other Māori traditions. Long regarded by Māori as a place of healing, Tikitere also houses the **Wai Ora Spa** where you can get muddy with a variety of treatments.

The Drive » Return to Rotorua on SH30 along the edge of Lake Rotorua, with Mokoia Island on the right. Just after the geothermal steam of Whakarewarewa and Te Puia, continue onto SH5 then turn

THE LEGEND OF HINEMOA & TUTANEKAI

Hinemoa was a young woman of a *hapu* (subtribe) that lived on the western shore of Lake Rotorua, while Tutanekai was a young man of a Mokoia Island *hapu*. The pair met and fell in love during a regular tribal meeting. While both were of high birth, Tutanekai was illegitimate, so marriage between the two was forbidden.

Home on Mokoia, the lovesick Tutanekai played his flute for his love, the wind carrying the melody across the water. Hinemoa heard his declaration, but her people took to tying up the canoes at night to ensure she wouldn't go to him.

Finally, Tutanekai's music proved impossible to resist. Hinemoa undressed and swam the long distance from the shore to the island. When she arrived on Mokoia, Hinemoa found herself in a quandary. Having shed her clothing in order to swim, she could hardly walk into the island's settlement naked. She hopped into a hot pool to think about her next move.

Eventually a man came to fetch water from a cold spring beside the hot pool. In a deep man's voice, Hinemoa called out, 'Who is it?' The man replied that he was Tutanekai's slave on a water run. Hinemoa grabbed the slave's calabash and smashed it to pieces. More slaves came, but she smashed their calabashes too, until finally Tutanekai came to the pool and demanded that the interloper identify himself. Astonished when it turned out to be Hinemoa, he secreted her in his hut.

Next morning, after a suspiciously long lie-in, a slave reported that someone was in Tutanekai's bed. The two lovers were rumbled, and when Hinemoa's superhuman efforts to reach Tutanekai had been revealed, their union was celebrated.

Descendants of Hinemoa and Tutanekai still live around Rotorua today.

left into Waimangu Rd for 6km through sparse scrub to Waimangu Volcanic Valley, a total distance of 38km from Hells Gate.

⑧ Waimangu Volcanic Valley

The downhill stroll through the **Waimangu Volcanic Valley** (☎07-366 6137; www.waimangu.co.nz; 587 Waimangu Rd; adult/child walking tours $37/12, boat cruises $42.50/12; ⏰8.30am-5pm, to 6pm Jan, last admission 3pm, 4pm Jan), created during the eruption of Mt Tarawera in 1886, passes spectacular thermal and volcanic features, including **Inferno Crater Lake**, where overflowing water can reach 80°C, and **Frying Pan Lake**, the largest hot spring in the world. The walk continues down to **Lake Rotomahana** (Warm Lake), where options include a return shuttle or a 45-minute lake boat trip past steaming cliffs and the former site of the Pink and White Terraces. Waimangu (Black Water) refers to the dark, muddy colour of much of the water here.

The Drive » From Waimangu Volcanic Valley continue on Okaro Rd past compact Lake Okaro and turn left back onto SH5. After 1km turn left into Waiotapu Loop Rd and on to Wai-O-Tapu, 10km from Waimangu Volcanic Valley.

---

⑨ Wai-O-Tapu Thermal Wonderland

'Sacred Waters' or **Wai-O-Tapu** (☎07-366 6333; www.waiotapu.co.nz; 201 Waiotapu Loop Rd, off SH5; adult/child/family $32.50/11/80; ⏰8.30am-5pm, last admission 3.45pm) has several interesting geothermal features packed into a small area, including the boiling, multihued **Champagne Pool**, a bubbling mud pool, stunning mineral terraces and **Lady Knox Geyser**, which spouts off (with a little prompting from an organic soap) punctually at 10.15am and gushes up to 20m for about an hour (be here by 9.45am to see it). Wai-O-Tapu is 27km south of Rotorua along SH5 (towards Taupo), and a further 2km from the marked turn-off down Waiotapu Loop Rd.

The Drive » Return on the loop road to SH5 and continue left en route to Taupo. Rural endeavours – including a few very expansive sheep farms – characterise the landscape, and just after the tiny hamlet of Mihi, turn right into Tutukau Rd, then follow Orakei Korako Rd for 14km to Orakei Korako, 39km from Wai-O-Tapu.

TRIP HIGHLIGHT

⑩ Orakei Korako

Slightly off the beaten track, **Orakei Korako** (☎07-378 3131; www.orakeikorako.co.nz; 494 Orakei Korako Rd; adult/child $36/15; ⏰8am-4.30pm) gets fewer visitors than other thermal areas. Yet, since the destruction of the Pink and White Terraces, it is arguably NZ's best thermal area, even though two-thirds of the original site now lies beneath a dammed section of the Waikato River. A walking track follows stairs and boardwalks around the colourful silica terraces for which the park is famous, and passes geysers and **Ruatapu Cave**, an impressive natural cavern with a jade-green pool. Allow 1½ hours. Entry includes a boat ride across the lake from the visitor centre and cafe. Back at Mihi, the **Mihi Cafe** (☎07-333 8909; www.facebook.com/mihicafe; 4089 SH5, Reporoa; mains $10-22; ⏰8am-3pm Mon-Thu, 8am-3pm & 6-8pm Fri, 9am-3pm Sat & Sun) is an excellent Kiwiana-themed eatery.

The Drive » Depart Orakei Korako and turn right into Tutukau Rd. Continue left onto SH1 then take a left into SH5 followed by a right into Aratiatia Rd, 32km from Orakei Korako.

---

⑪ Aratiatia Rapids

Two kilometres off SH5, this was a spectacular part of the Waikato River until the government constructed a hydroelectric dam across the water way, shutting off the flow. The spectacle hasn't disappeared completely, with the floodgates opening from October to March at 10am, noon,

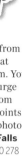

2pm and 4pm, and from April to September at 10am, noon and 2pm. You can see the water surge through the dam from two good vantage points. For an even better photo opportunity, **Huka Falls River Cruise** (📞0800 278 336; www.hukafallscruise. co.nz; Aratiatia Dam; adult/ child $37/15; ⏰10.30am, 12.30pm & 2.30pm year-round, plus 4.30pm Dec-Feb) offers a relaxed jaunt (80 minutes) departing from the nearby Aratiatia Dam to Huka Falls.

The Drive » Return to SH5 and continue over busy SH1 to Wairakei Terraces & Thermal Health Spa, 5km from Aratiatia Rapids.

⑫ Wairakei

Wairakei is the site of NZ's only geothermal electricity generation enterprise. The landscape features huge pipes and other infrastructure, and shape-shifting clouds of steam often drift across the highway. At **Wairakei Terraces & Thermal Health Spa** (📞07-378 0913; www.wairakeiterraces. co.nz; Wairakei Rd; thermal walk adult/child $18/9; pools $25, massage from $85; ⏰8.30am-8.30pm Fri-Wed, to 7pm Thu), mineral-laden waters from the geothermal steamfield cascade

over silica terraces into pools (open to those 14 years and older) nestled in native gardens. Take a therapeutic soak and a self-guided tour on the **Terraces Walkway** featuring a re-created Māori village, carvings depicting the history of NZ, Māori and local *iwi* (tribe) Ngāti Tuwahretoa, and artificially made geysers and silica terraces echoing – on a smaller scale – the famous Pink and White Terraces that were destroyed by the Tarawera eruption in 1886. The night-time **Māori Cultural Experience** – which includes a traditional challenge, welcome, concert, tour and *hangi* meal – gives an insight into Māori life in the geothermal areas (adult/child $104/52).

The Drive » Turn right from Wairakei Terraces & Thermal Health Spa back onto SH5, before turning left into Huka Falls Rd after 2km and following this road down past a lookout to the falls car park.

⑬ Huka Falls

Clearly signposted and with a car park and kiosk, these **falls** (Huka Falls Rd) mark where NZ's longest river, the Waikato, is slammed into a narrow chasm, making a dramatic 10m drop into a surging pool. From the footbridge you can see the full force of this torrent that the Māori called Hukanui

(Great Body of Spray). Take one of the short walks around the area to really get a handle on the spectacular river scenery surrounding the falls. On sunny days the water is crystal clear, making for stunning photographs of the raging and roiling cascade.

The Drive » Continue on Huka Falls Rd with the Waikato River on your left. After around

Matamata Hobbiton film set

3km this route rejoins the main road for a final 2km downhill push featuring excellent lake views to Taupo.

- - - - - - - - - - -

⑭ Taupo

With a postcard-perfect setting on the north-eastern shores of the lake, Taupo is one of the North Island's premier resort towns. There are lots of adrenaline-pumping activities on offer, but for those with no appetite for white knuckles, there's plenty of enjoyment to be had simply meandering by the lake and enjoying the scenery. The **Great Lake Walkway** is a pleasant path following the Taupo lakefront south from the Taupo Boat Harbour to Five Mile Bay (10km). It's flat and offers easy walking or cycling along public-access beaches. To rent a bike, see **Top Gear Cycles** (☏07-377 0552; www.topgearcycles. co.nz; Suncourt Plaza, 19 Tamamutu St; rental full day $35; ◷8.30am-5pm Mon-Fri, 9am-2pm Sat) in central Taupo. For views across the lake to the mountains of Tongariro National Park, grab an outdoor table at the **Lakehouse**

Classic Trip

(☎07-377 1545; www.lake-housetaupo.co.nz; 10 Roberts St; ◷7.30am-midnight) on the waterfront and order a Hairy Hop IPA from Taupo-based Lakeman Brewing.

✕ 🛏 p119

The Drive ≫ Departing Taupo south along the lakefront, Lake Tce passes pretty Two Mile Bay before heading away from the lake on SH5, the Taupo–Napier road. Passing through rugged semi-alpine scenery and sprawling commercial forests, it's 54km from Taupo to the Waipunga Falls.

⑮ Waipunga Falls

Falling up to 40m, the Waipunga Falls are on the left travelling from Taupo to Napier, around 50km from the intersection of Lake Tce and SH5. Native scrub frames the falls, and the spidery surges of three parallel cascades are best

GETTING ACTIVE

Amid the forests, rivers and lakes of the spectacular central North Island, there are many exciting, fun, and sometimes downright quirky opportunities to get active and energised.

Around Rotorua

River Rats (☎07-345 6543, 0800 333 900; www.riverrats.co.nz) Kayaking, river rafting and exciting white-water sledging.

Rotorua Rafting (☎0800 772 384; www.rotorua-rafting.co.nz; per person $85; ◷Oct-May) Grade V rafting action – including the 7m-high Tutea waterfalls – on the Kaituna River.

Ogo (☎0800 646 768, 07-343 7676; www.ogo.co.nz; 525 Ngongotaha Rd; rides from $45; ◷9am-5pm, to 6.30pm Dec-Feb) Your chance to roll down a hillside in a giant, inflatable sphere. No, we're not making this up.

Rotorua Canopy Tours (☎07-343 1001, 0800 226 679; www.canopytours.co.nz; 173 Old Taupo Rd; 3hr tours per adult/child/family $139/95/419; ◷8am-8pm Oct-Apr, to 6pm May-Sep) Explore a 1.2km web of bridges, flying foxes, ziplines and platforms, 22m high in a lush native forest canopy

Around Taupo

Rapids Jet (☎0800 727 437, 07-374 8066; www.rapidsjet.com; Nga Awa Purua Rd; adult/child $105/60; ◷9am-5pm summer, 10am-4pm winter) This sensational 35-minute jetboat ride shoots along the lower part of the Aratiatia Rapids.

Taupo Bungy (☎0800 888 408, 07-377 1135; www.taupobungy.co.nz; 202 Spa Rd; solo/tandem jump $169/338; ◷9am-5pm, extended hours summer) High above the Waikato River, this picturesque bungy site is the North Island's most popular. There is also the Cliffhanger Giant Swing.

Taupo Kayaking Adventures (☎0274 801 231, 07-376 8981; www.tka.co.nz; Acacia Bay) Runs guided kayaking trips from its base in Acacia Bay to the Māori rock carvings.

Skydive Taupo (☎0800 586 766, 07-378 4662; www.skydivetaupo.co.nz; Anzac Memorial Dr; 12,000ft/15,000ft jump from $249/339) High above the lake, Taupo is one of NZ's most scenic locations for skydiving.

CYCLING HAWKE'S BAY

Buoyed by the fun of mountain biking around Rotorua, here's your chance to explore the Hawke's Bay region around Napier – this time more gently combining a few refreshing and re-energising stops at some of the area's best vineyards.

Bike About Tours (📞06-845 4836, 027 232 4355; www.bikeabouttours.co.nz; tours half-/full day from $35/45) Offers a range of self-guided tours around Napier including several winery options, with tours extending as far as Cape Kidnappers, Hastings and Havelock North.

Coastal Wine Cycles (📞06-875 0302; www.winecycles.co.nz; tours per day $40) Self-guided tours of the wineries out towards Cape Kidnappers on comfy bikes with guaranteed 'no wedgie' seats!

Fishbike (📞06-833 6979, 0800 131 600; www.fishbike.nz; 22 Marine Pde, Pacific Surf Club; bike hire per half-/full day $30/40, tandems per hour $30; 🕑9am-5pm) Napier itself is very cycle-friendly, particularly along Marine Pde where you'll find this outfit renting comfortable bikes – including tandems for those willing to risk divorce.

On Yer Bike Winery Tours (📞06-650 4627; www.onyerbikehb.co.nz; full day with/without lunch $60/50) Offering fully geared-up tours around the bay, with wineries the top priority. Kids' bikes are available, too.

Tākaro Trails (📞06-835 9030; www.takarotrails.co.nz; day rides from $40) Self-guided tours around Hawke's Bay including winery routes and mountain bike adventures at Pan Pac Eskdale MTB Park.

seen from the adjacent car park that's just a short drive from the main road. Located on a relatively benign and flat plateau, the energy and spectacle of the falls are actually quite surprising, and to the left of the main cascade visitors can usually sneak a peak of the smaller, but equally spectacular **Waiarua Falls**.

The Drive » SH5 continues its winding and hilly way through spectacular country en route to Napier. Note that conditions on this road can often be misty and raining. The final stages of the 88km journey from Waipunga Falls to Napier meander through vineyards and orchards around Eskdale, before joining SH2 and running down the Pacific Coast to Napier.

- - - - - - - - - -

🔞 Napier

With a relaxed ambience and a sparkling collection of art-deco buildings – much of the city was rebuilt in the architectural fashion of the day following a devastating 1931 earthquake – Napier is an elegant and ordered Pacific city that contrasts with the rough and tumble of the geothermal activity from earlier in this trip. The vineyards around nearby Eskdale and Taradale showcase some of the country's oldest and most-established wineries, and the restaurants, bars and cafes of the re-energised Ahuriri waterfront area, 2km northwest of town, are essential diversions after the long drive south. Napier's cultural heart is **MTG Hawke's Bay** (Museum Theatre Gallery; 📞06-835 7781; www.mtghawkesbay.com; 1 Tennyson St; adult/child $10/free; 🕑10am-5pm), a gleaming-white museum-theatre-gallery space by the water. Look forward to live performances, film screenings, and regularly changing gallery and museum displays together with touring and local exhibitions.

✕ 🛏 p119

Classic Trip

Eating & Sleeping

Auckland ❶

For places to eat and stay in Auckland see p50 and p60

Hamilton ❷

✗ Chim Choo Ree   Modern NZ $$$

(☏07-839 4329; www.chimchooree.co.nz; 14 Bridge St; mains $36-37; ⊘11.30am-2pm & 5pm-late Mon-Sat) In an airy heritage building beside the river, Chim Choo Ree focuses on small plates like Thai fish-and-papaya salad, gin-cured salmon and confit pork belly, plus larger, equally inventive mains using duck, lamb, venison and snapper. Local foodies wash it all down with a great wine list and flavourful NZ craft beers.

✗ Hazel Hayes   Cafe $$

(☏07-839 1953; www.hazelhayes.co.nz; 587 Victoria St; mains $10-23; ⊘7am-4pm Mon-Fri, 8am-2pm Sat) This mash-up of country-kitchen decor showcases inventive cafe fare. Free-range and organic options punctuate the short, focused menu, and both the service and coffee are very good. Try the homemade hash browns with salmon and a rich hollandaise sauce and you'll definitely be set for the day.

For more places to eat and stay in Hamilton see p130.

Matamata ❸

✗ Workman's Cafe Bar   Cafe $$

(☏07-888 5498; 52 Broadway; mains $12-30; ⊘7.30am-late) Truly eccentric (old transistor radios dangling from the ceiling; a wall-full of art-deco mirrors; Johnny Cash on the stereo), this funky eatery has built itself a reputation that extends beyond Matamata. It's also a decent bar later at night.

Rotorua ❹

✗ Abracadabra Cafe Bar   Middle Eastern $$

(☏07-348 3883; www.abracadabracafe. com; 1363 Amohia St; mains $15-30, tapas $10-15; ⊘10.30am-11pm Tue-Sat, to 3pm Sun) Channelling Spain, Mexico and Morocco, Abracadabra is a magical cave of spicy delights, from beef-and-apricot tagine to king-prawn fajitas and Tijuana pork chilli. There's a great beer terrace out the back – perfect for combining a few local craft brews and shared tapas. We can highly recommend the breakfast burrito and a revitalising bottle of kombucha for the morning after.

✗ Gold Star Bakery   Bakery $

(☏07-349 1959; 89 Old Taupo Rd; pies $4-5; ⊘6am-3pm Mon-Sat) As you head into Rotorua from the north, it's essential that you stop at this award-winning bakery with a stellar reputation for turning out some of NZ's best pies. Great-value savoury treats to devour include chicken and mushroom, or the classic steak 'n' cheese. Good luck choosing from the huge selection.

🛏 Mokoia Downs Estate B&B   B&B $$$

(☏07-332 2930; www.mokoiadowns.com; 64 Mokoia Rd; s/d $200/250; 🛜🐾) The B&B accommodation here is very comfortable, but the real appeal is the warm welcome from the English-Irish owners Mick and Teresa, plus the other attractions at this great semirural retreat. Say hi to the sheep, donkeys and miniature horses, kick back in the private cinema and library, or sample Mick's liqueurs made from local organic fruit in his microdistillery.

Redwoods Whakarewarewa Forest ⑤

✗ Mistress of Cakes   Bakery $

(☏07-345 6521; www.mistressofcakes.co.nz; Shop 2, 26 Lynmore Ave; snacks $4-8; ◷8.30am-5.30pm Tue-Fri, 9am-3pm Sat & Sun) Fab muffins, slices, biscuits, scones and quiches, too, all homemade with local ingredients. Mistress of Cakes is now in a new location handily close to the Redwoods Whakarewarewa Forest. A coffee and a stonking sausage roll could be just the thing when you've been walking or mountain biking. Pop in also to see what takeaway ready-made meals are available.

Taupo ⑭

✗ Spoon & Paddle   Cafe $$

(☏07-378 9664; www.facebook.com/spoonandpaddle; 101 Heu Heu St; mains $12-19; ◷8am-4pm) Filling a spacious and airy 1950s house with colourful decor, Spoon & Paddle is more evidence that you'll find great cafes pretty well anywhere in NZ. Excellent coffee partners with a concise beer and wine list, and the energetic and youthful owners focus on delivering dishes like tasty lamb-shoulder tortillas, and just maybe the country's best eggs Benedict.

✗ Storehouse   Cafe $$

(☏07-378 8820; www.facebook.com/storehousenz; 14 Runanga St; shared plates $7-14; ◷7am-4pm Mon-Wed, 7am-10pm Thu-Fri, 8am-10pm Sat, 8am-3.30pm Sun) Hands-down Taupo's coolest eatery, Storehouse does tasty double duty as a cool daytime cafe serving a hipsters' holy trinity of bagels, sliders and coffee, before morphing into a night-time bar with craft beer on tap, cocktails, wine, and shared plates including tacos, empanadas, and garlic-and-chilli prawns. Leave room for dessert of the salted caramel and macadamia ice-cream sundae. On Friday nights there's often live music. Check Facebook for details.

⌖ Lake   Motel $$

(☏07-378 4222; www.thelakeonline.co.nz; 63 Mere Rd; d $155-185; @ ⧈) A reminder that 1960s and '70s design wasn't all Austin Powers–style groovaliciousness, this boutique motel is crammed with furniture from the era's signature designers. The four one-bedroom units have kitchenettes and dining and living areas, and everyone has use of the pleasant garden at the back. Some of the units are enlivened with stunning paintings of well-known musos by the owners' son.

For more places to eat and stay in Taupo see p103.

Napier ⑯

✗ Café Ujazi   Cafe $$

(☏06-835 1490; www.facebook.com/ujazicafe; 28 Tennyson St; mains $10-22; ◷8am-5pm; ⌖) The most bohemian of Napier's cafes, Ujazi folds back its windows and lets the alternative vibes spill out onto the pavement. It's a long-established, consistent performer offering blackboard meals and hearty counter food (vegetarian and vegan dishes are a speciality). Try the classic *rewana* special – a big breakfast on traditional Māori bread. Oooh – homemade limeade!

⌖ Pebble Beach Motor Inn   Motel $$

(☏06-835 7496, 0800 723 224; www.pebblebeach.co.nz; 445 Marine Pde; r $145-295; ⧈) Unlike the majority of NZ motels, this one is owner-operated (they own the building, rather than lease it from a higher power) – so maintenance and service top the list of staff priorities. There are 25 immaculate rooms over three levels, all with kitchens, spas, balconies and ocean views. Full to capacity most nights.

For more places to eat and stay in Napier see p157.

Waitomo Caves *Thrilling underground adventures and twinkly glowworms*

Waves & Caves to Whanganui

8

Wild west coast black-sand beaches and the subterranean thrills and spectacle of the Waitomo Caves combine with one of the planet's finest one day hikes.

156 km

Raglan
A laidback and arty surf town with great eating

219 km

Hamilton
Experience the city's beautiful gardens beside the Waikato River

Auckland
START

2 4

7 Te Kuiti

295 km

Waitomo Caves
Seek subterranean relaxation or underground thrill-seeking

National Park Village

Raetihi

Whanganui
This riverside city has a historic and cultural vibe

FINISH 10 **560 km**

**5 DAYS
560KM /
343 MILES**

GREAT FOR...

BEST TIME TO GO
November to April for the Tongariro Alpine Crossing

ESSENTIAL PHOTO
Emerging back into the daylight after a Waitomo Caves adventure

BEST FOR OUTDOORS
Paddle boarding on Lake Otamangakau in Tongariro National Park

Waves & Caves to Whanganui

8

On this journey traversing the western side of the North Island, the urban attractions of Auckland and Hamilton give way to a rugged surf-fringed coastline, viewing New Zealand's national bird at Otorohanga, and experiencing the flickering glowworms at Waitomo. Further south there's spectacle and adventure amid the Tongariro and Whanganui National Parks, before reaching the historic and arty riverside city of Whanganui.

---

1 Auckland

Before heading south, explore the historical side of NZ's biggest and most cosmopolitan city. In the **Auckland Museum** (☎09-309 0443; www.auckland museum.com; Auckland Domain, Parnell; adult/child $25/10; ◷10am-5pm), the displays of Pacific Island and Māori artefacts on the ground floor are essential viewing. Highlights include a 25m war canoe and a carved meeting house (remove your shoes before entering). Dominating the **Auckland Domain**, the museum is housed in an imposing neoclassical temple (1929), capped with an impressive copper-and-glass dome (2007). The grand building is a prominent part of the Auckland skyline, especially when viewed from the harbour. Admission packages can be purchased incorporating a highlights tour and a Māori cultural performance ($45 to $55). Or take a stroll along the harbour on our walking tour (p82).

The Drive ›› Leave Auckland on the Southern Motorway and continue south on SH1 to Ngaruawahia. Turn right on SH39 to Whatawhata before turning right on SH23 and continuing to Raglan. Look out for the 28 wind turbines of the Te Uku Wind Farm on the hills above Raglan, 161km from Auckland.

TRIP HIGHLIGHT

2 Raglan

Laid-back Raglan may well be NZ's perfect surfing town. It's small enough to have escaped mass development, but big enough to have great eateries and a couple of pubs that attract big-name bands in summer. Along with famous surf spots to the south, the harbour just begs to be explored. **Raglan Water sports** (☎07-825 0507; www.raglanwatersports. co.nz; 5a Bankart St; group/ private paddle-boarding lessons per person $45/65) offer paddle-boarding, kayaking and kiteboarding tours. There's also an excellent arts scene – check out **Jet Collective** (☎07-825 8566; www. jetcollective.co.nz; 19a Bow St; ◷10am-4pm Wed-Mon) for local crafts and **Toi Hauāuru Studio** (☎021 174 4629, 07-825 0244; www. toihauauru.com; 4338 Main Rd; ◷10am-5pm Wed-Sun) for contemporary Māori design – and at the Raglan Wharf, **Soul Shoes** (☎07-825 8765; www.soulshoes. co.nz; Wallis St, Raglan Wharf; ◷9.30am-5pm) and **Tony Sly Pottery** (☎0800 825 037; www.tonyslypottery.com; 90 Wallis St, Raglan Wharf; ◷9am-5pm) both offer unique styles hand-made in Raglan.

✕ ⊨ p130

The Drive ›› Leave Raglan on Wainui Rd and after 4km turn

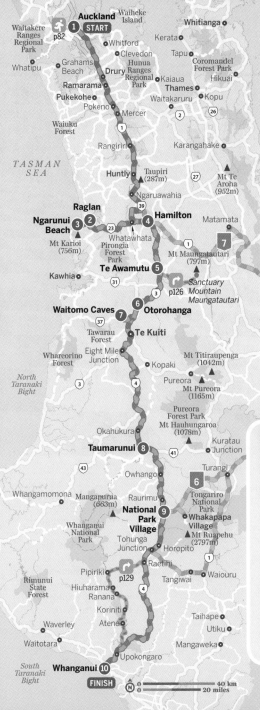

right into Ngarunui Rd down to
the carpark above the beach.

❸ Ngarunui Beach

Welcome to the wild
west of NZ's North
Island, a rugged series
of black-sand surf
beaches stretching all
the way down the coast
to Taranaki. Ngarunui's
broad expanse is packed
during summer – it is the
area's best ocean beach
for swimming – and is
protected by lifeguards
from October to April.
Around 2.5km south of
Ngarunui Beach, **Manu
Bay** is a legendary surf
spot said to have the
longest left-hand break
in the world. The elon-
gated uniform waves are
created by the angle at
which the Tasman Sea
swell meets the coastline.
The Manu Bay car park
is a great spot to watch
local surfers taking on

🔗 LINK YOUR TRIP

6 Tongariro National Park Loop

Around National Park
Village, explore the North
Island's biggest national
park in detail.

7 Thermal Discoverer

Combine Hobbiton and
Rotorua's geothermal
activity on this trip which
also incorporates Hamilton.

the waves. Accessed by Calvert Rd, **Whale Bay** is another world-renowned surf spot around 1km west of Manu Bay.

The Drive » Return from Whale Bay to Raglan (8km), leave Raglan on SH23 and continue a further 46km to Hamilton.

TRIP HIGHLIGHT

❹ Hamilton

Hamilton is the Waikato region's biggest city, and university students contribute a dynamism to the more conservative vibe of the surrounding agricultural hinterland. Vibrant restaurants, cafes and bars punctuate Hood and Victoria Sts, and southeast of the city centre, the glorious **Hamilton Gardens** (☏07-838 6782; www.hamiltongardens.co.nz; Cobham Dr; guided tour adult/child $15/8; ⏰enclosed gardens 7.30am-5pm, info centre 9am-5pm, guided tours 11am Sep-Apr) **incorporate** Italian Renaissance, Chinese, Japanese, English, American and Indian gardens complete with colonnades, pagodas, and even a mini Taj Mahal. It's a wonderful area to have a picnic or stretch your legs. Look for the impressive Nga Uri O Hinetuparimaunga (Earth Blanket) Māori sculpture at the main gates. Hamilton Gardens is also the departure point for scenic 1½-hour cruises on the **Waikato**

KIM HOWELL / SHUTTERSTOCK ©

River Explorer (☏0800 139 756; www.waikatoexplorer.co.nz; Hamilton Gardens Jetty; adult/child $29/15; ⏰Wed-Sun, daily 26 Dec-6 Feb).

✕ 🛏p130

The Drive » Depart central Hamilton south via Anglesea St and Cobham Dr, and turn right after 2km into SH3. Continue on SH3 south to Te Awamutu, 30km from Hamilton.

❺ Te Awamutu

Deep into dairy-farming country, Te Awamutu (which means 'The River Cut Short'; the Waikato beyond this point was unsuitable for large canoes), is a pleasant rural service centre. With a blossom tree–lined main street and good cafes, TA (aka Rose Town) is an ap-

Hamilton Greenhouse in Hamilton Gardens

pealing stop. The town's **Rose Garden** (cnr Gorst Ave & Arawata St; ⏰24hr) has around 2500 colourful bushes, and from November to May there's always a blooming good display. The **Te Awamutu Museum** (☎07-872 0085; www.tamuseum.org.nz; 135 Roche St; admission by donation; ⏰10am-4pm Mon-Fri, to 2pm Sat) showcases a superb collection of Māori

taonga (treasures) – the highlight is the revered **Te Uenuku** (The Rainbow), an ancient Māori carving estimated to be up to 600 years old. The museum also features an interesting display on the Waikato War between Māori and British colonial forces in the 1860s.

🍴 p130

The Drive ›› From Te Awamutu to Otorohanga on SH3, it's a pleasant 30km journey through bucolic farmland dotted with black-and-white Friesian cows. Yes, it does look like a *Far Side* cartoon waiting to happen.

- - - - - - - - - - - -

❻ Otorohanga

Before heading underground at the nearby Waitomo Caves, visit the **Otorohanga Kiwi House**

DETOUR:
SANCTUARY MOUNTAIN MAUNGATAUTARI

Start: ❺ Te Awamutu

Can a landlocked volcano become an island paradise? Inspired by the success of pest eradication and native species reintroduction in the Hauraki Gulf, a community trust has erected 47km of pest-proof fencing around the triple peaks of Maungatautari (797m) to create the impressive **Sanctuary Mountain Maungatautari** (www.sanctuarymountain.co.nz; adult/child $18/8). This atoll of rainforest dominates the skyline between Te Awamutu and Karapiro and is now home to its first kiwi chicks in 100 years. There is also a 'tuatarium', where NZ's iconic reptile the tuatara can be seen.

The main entrance is at the visitor centre at the sanctuary's southern side, 30km east of Te Awamutu and reached by SH3 and Arapuni Rd. There is a handy map on the Sanctuary's website. **Guided tours** (adult/child $35/15) leaving from the visitor centre from Tuesday to Sunday include an afternoon wetlands tour, and morning and afternoon departures exploring the bird and insect life of the sanctuary's Southern Enclosure. Online or phone bookings for guided tours must be made at least 24 hours in advance.

Out in the Styx (☑07-872 4505; www.styx.co.nz; 2117 Arapuni Rd, Pukeatua; dm/s/d $95/155/260) is a lodge near the southern end of the Maungatautari that offers guided night walks. The three stylishly furnished themed rooms (Polynesian, African or Māori) are especially nice, plus there are bunk rooms and a spa for soothing weary legs. Prices include a four-course dinner and breakfast. They also provide a drop-off service (per person $10, minimum $40) if you wish to walk across the mountain from south to north (around six hours).

& Native Bird Park (☑07-873 7391; www.kiwihouse.org.nz; 20 Alex Telfer Dr; adult/child $24/8; ☺9am-5pm, kiwi feedings 10am,1.30pm & 3.30pm daily) to see NZ's national bird, the kiwi, scurrying around a nocturnal enclosure searching for food with its long beak. This is one of the only places where you can see a great spotted kiwi, the biggest of the three kiwi species. The bird park is at the northern end of town arriving from Te Awamutu. In Otorohanga's main street, the **Ed Hillary Walkway** – named after the NZ mountaineer who was one of the first two people to conquer Mt Everest in 1953 – shows cherished icons of Kiwiana including sheep, jandals, the All Blacks and NZ's beloved pavlova dessert.

The Drive » Depart Otorohanga south on SH3 for 8km and turn right at the large roundabout into Waitomo Caves Rd (SH37). From the intersection it is around 7.5km to the centre of Waitomo Caves village.

TRIP HIGHLIGHT

❼ Waitomo Caves

The labyrinth of limestone caves, caverns and underground rivers under the Waitomo region is one of the North Island's top attractions, and experiencing the subterranean wonders can either be gentle and reflective, or crammed with action and adventure. The name Waitomo comes from *wai* (water) and *tomo* (hole or shaft): dotted across this region are numerous shafts dropping into underground cave systems and streams. Bookings to visit the big-three Waitomo Caves – Glowworm, Ruakuri and Aranui – can be made online or at the **Waitomo Caves Visitor Centre** (☑0800 456 922; www. waitomo.com; Waitomo Caves Rd; ◷9am-5pm). For cave tours, try to avoid the large tour groups, most of which arrive between 10.30am and 2.30pm. Other Waitomo operators provide more thrilling ways to experience the underworld including abseiling, climbing and negotiating underground

rivers on inflatable inner tubes.

✗ 🛏 p131

The Drive » Return to the intersection of SH37 and SH3. Turn right and head south on SH3 to Te Mapara, then turn right into SH4 to Taumarunui, 100km from Waitomo Caves.

- - - - - - - - - - - -

❽ Taumarunui

Once a bustling stop on the main trunk railway line from Auckland to Wellington, Taumarunui is now a sleepy combination of provincial service town and base for exciting outdoor adventures. Go jetboating with Taumarunui Jet Tours (p94) on the nearby Whanganui River, or

tackle the 85km Timber Trail on a mountain bike with **Epic Cycle Adventures** (p94). Also based in Taumarunui, **Forgotten World Adventures** (☑0800 7245 2278; www. forgottenworldadventures. co.nz; 1 Hakiaha St; 1/2 days from $210/495; ◷booking office 9am-2pm) runs trips on converted golf carts along an abandoned railway line to the tiny hamlet of Whangamomona in the Taranaki region. The most spectacular trip takes in 20 tunnels. Overnight stays in the heritage Whangamomona Hotel (☑06-762 5823; www. whangamomonahotel.co.nz; r per person incl breakfast $75) are also available.

SECRET LIFE OF A GLOWWORM

Glowworms are the larvae of the fungus gnat. The larva glowworm has luminescent organs that produce a soft, greenish light. Living in a sort of hammock suspended from an overhang, it weaves sticky threads that trail down and catch unwary insects attracted by its light. When an insect flies towards the light it gets stuck in the threads – the glowworm just has to reel it in for a feed.

The larval stage lasts from six to nine months, depending on how much food the glowworm gets. When it has grown to about the size of a matchstick, it goes into a pupa stage, much like a cocoon. The adult fungus gnat emerges about two weeks later.

The adult insect doesn't live very long because it doesn't have a mouth. It emerges, mates, lays eggs and dies, all within about two or three days. The sticky eggs, laid in groups of 40 or 50, hatch in about three weeks to become larval glowworms.

Glowworms thrive in moist, dark caves but they can survive anywhere if they have the requisites of moisture, an overhang to suspend from and insects to eat. Waitomo is famous for its glowworms but you can see them in many other places around NZ, both in caves and outdoors.

When you come upon glowworms, don't touch their hammocks or hanging threads, try not to make loud noises and don't shine a light right on them. All of these things will cause them to dim their lights. It takes them a few hours to become bright again, during which time the grub will go hungry. The glowworms that shine most brightly are the hungriest.

The Drive >> From Taumarunui, continue south on SH4 for 43km to National Park Village. The vegetation becomes alpine scrub and Tongariro's mountains rise above the near horizon.

- - - - - - - - - - - -

9 National Park Village

On the western edges of Mt Ruapehu in Tongariro National Park, this settlement is packed with skiers and snowboarders during winter, and is growing in popularity with visitors across warmer months as the base for undertaking the Tongariro Alpine Crossing. Combining thrilling scenery, steaming hot springs, crazy rock formations and quirky moonscapes, this moderately challenging hike is regarded as one of the world's best one-day adventures, and can be tackled independently (if you're properly equipped) or with local operators including **Adrift Guided Outdoor Adventures** (www.adriftnz. co.nz) or **Adventure Outdoors** (0800 386 925; www.adventureoutdoors. co.nz). Other outdoor activities include mountain biking with **Kiwi Mountain Bikes** (0800 562 4537; www.kiwimountainbikes. com) and stand-up paddle boarding on nearby Lake Otamangakau with **My Kiwi Adventure** (021 784 202, 0800 784 202; www.mykiwiadventure. co.nz; 15 Findlay St; paddle boarding $50, mountain biking $45-95).

✗ ☐ p131

The Drive >> Continue south on SH4 via Raetihi (35km) before travelling a further 87km to Whanganui. The final 15km skirting the Whanganui River is particularly scenic.

GOING UNDERGROUND

Waitomo excels with a range of exciting, challenging and unique ways to explore the area's subterranean wonders. Note that most operators offer a discount for prebooking online, and during summer this strategy is also recommended to avoid disappointment.

Legendary Black Water Rafting Company (0800 782 5874; www.waitomo.com/ black-water-rafting; 585 Waitomo Caves Rd; Black Labyrinth tour 9am, 10.30am, noon, 1.30pm & 3pm, Black Abyss tour 9am & 2pm, Black Odyssey tour 10am & 3pm) Don a wetsuit and float down an underground river in an inner tube. Other options incorporate a flying fox and negotiating high wires.

CaveWorld (0800 228 338, 07-878 6577; www.caveworld.co.nz; cnr Waitomo Caves Rd & Hotel Access Rd) Black-water rafting on inner tubes through glowworm-filled Te Anaroa. The Footwhistle Glowworm Cave Tour incorporates a forest stop for a mug of restorative *kawakawa* bush tea.

Kiwi Cave Rafting (07-873 9149, 0800 228 372; www.blackwaterraftingwaitomo.co.nz; 95 Waitomo Caves Rd) An adventurous combination of abseiling, tubing, caving and rock climbing.

Waitomo Adventures (0800 924 866, 07-878 7788; www.waitomo.co.nz; 654 Waitomo Caves Rd) A variety of intrepid excursions incorporating rock climbing, abseiling, swimming, caving and a subterranean flying fox.

Spellbound (07-878 7622, 0800 773 552; www.glowworm.co.nz; 10 Waitomo Caves Rd; adult/child $75/26; 3hr tours 10am, 11am, 2pm & 3pm) Small-group tours access the heavily glowworm-dappled Mangawhitiakau cave system in a raft. Still an exciting experience, and you get to stay dry.

DETOUR:
WHANGANUI RIVER ROAD

Start: ❾ National Park Village

The direct route on SH4 south from National Park Village to Whanganui is definitely no slouch visually, but this alternative route following the Whanganui River to the coast is a real stunner. It's a winding route on narrow but sealed roads that is around one hour longer than the 70 minutes it takes on SH4.

Instead of continuing on SH4 south of Raetihi, turn west to travel 27km to tiny Pipiriki, a sleepy river town that was once a humming holiday hot spot serviced by river steamers and paddle boats.

Heading south on the Whanganui River Rd, the graceful spire of **St Joseph's Church** (📞06-342 8190; www.compassion.org.nz; Whanganui River Rd; ⏰9am-5pm) stands tall on a spur of land above a deep river bend near Hiuharama (aka Jerusalem), around 15km south of Pipiriki. A French Catholic mission led by Suzanne Aubert established the Daughters of Our Lady of Compassion here in 1892, and esteemed NZ poet James K Baxter (1926–72) founded a commune here in the late 1960s. He is also buried in Hiuharama.

Moutoa Island, the site of an historic 1864 battle, is just downriver, followed by the remote Māori villages of Ranana, Koriniti and Atene as you continue south. There are several Māori meeting houses, but ask a local out of courtesy before you go looking around. Just south of Ranana, the **Kawana Flour Mill** (📞04-472 4341; www.nzhistory. net.nz/media/photo/kawana-flourmill; Whanganui River Rd; ⏰dawn-dusk) is testament to when the river was a trade route, and at Atene, about 22km north of the junction with SH4, the **Atene Viewpoint Walk** is a one-hour ascent offering great views of the Whanganui National Park. The Whanganui River Rd rejoins SH4 just north of Upokongaro and continues 15km south to Whanganui.

TRIP HIGHLIGHT

❿ Whanganui

This historic town lies on the banks of the wide Whanganui River. Despite the occasional flood – much of the city centre was underwater in June 2015 – the town centre has been rejuvenated, the local arts community is thriving and old port buildings are being turned into glass-art studios. At the **Chronicle Glass Studio** (📞06-347 1921; www.chronicleglass.co.nz; 2 Rutland St; ⏰9am-5pm Mon-Fri, 10am-3pm Sat & Sun, closed Sun & Mon Jun-Sep) visitors can watch glass-blowers in action, check out the gallery, or take a one-hour 'Make a Paperweight' lesson ($100). Across City Bridge from downtown Whanganui, the **Durie Hill Elevator** (📞06-345 8525; www.wanganui.govt.nz; Anzac Pde; adult/child one-way $2/1; ⏰8am-6pm Mon-Fri, 10am-5pm Sat & Sun) was built with grand visions for the city's residential future. A tunnel burrows 213m into the hillside, from where a 1919 elevator rattles 65.8m to the top. At the summit you can climb the 176 steps of the War Memorial Tower and scan the horizon for Mt Taranaki and Mt Ruapehu.

✕ ▭ p131

129

Eating & Sleeping

Auckland ❶

For places to eat and stay in Auckland see p50 and p60.

Raglan ❷

✕ Shack
International $$

(www.theshackraglan.com; 19 Bow St; tapas $6-14, mains $12-21; ⊙8am-5pm Sun-Thu, until late Fri & Sat; 🛜🍴) Brunch classics – try the chickpea-and-corn fritters – and interesting shared-plate mains like tempura squid and star anise-chicken feature at the best cafe in town. A longboard strapped to the wall, wobbly old floorboards, up-tempo tunes and international staff serving Kiwi wines and craft beers complete the picture.

✕ Raglan Fish
Fish & Chips $

(☎07-825 7544; www.facebook.com/raglanfishshop; 92 Wallis St, Raglan Wharf; fish & chips $7-10; ⊙9am-7pm) Super-fresh fish and chips and funky decor at this locals' favourite, right on Raglan's recently restored wharf about a kilometre north of town. Fresh oysters, mussels and seafood salads are also available.

🛏 Bow St Studios
Apartment $$

(☎07-825 0551; www.bowstreet.co.nz; 1 Bow St; studios $170-195, cottages $170-235; 🛜) With a waterfront location right in town, Bow St has self-contained studios and a historic cottage. The cool and chic decor is stylish and relaxing. The property is surrounded by a subtropical garden and shaded by well-established pohutukawa trees.

Hamilton ❹

✕ Duck Island Ice Cream
Ice Cream $

(☎07-856 5948; 300 Grey St; ice cream from $4; ⊙11am-6pm Tue-Thu & Sun, to 8pm Fri & Sat) A dazzling array of ever-changing flavours – how does crab-apple crumble or coconut and kaffir lime sound – make Duck Island quite probably NZ's best ice-cream parlour. The sunny corner location is infused with a hip retro vibe, and the refreshing house-made sodas and ice-cream floats are other worthy reasons to cross the river to Hamilton East.

✕ Gothenburg
Tapas $$

(☎07-834 3562; www.gothenburg.co.nz; ANZ Centre, 21 Grantham St; shared plates $7-24; ⊙9am-11pm Mon-Fri, 11.30am-late Sat) Relocated to a scenic river-side spot with high ceilings and a summer-friendly deck, Gothenburg has morphed from a bar into our favourite Hamilton restaurant. The menu of shared plates effortlessly spans the globe – try the pork-and-kimchi dumplings or the beef-and-chorizo meatballs – and the beer list features rotating taps from local Waikato craft brewers.

🛏 City Centre B&B
B&B $$

(☎07-838 1671; www.citycentrebnb.co.nz; 3 Anglesea St; r $90-125; @🛜🐾) At the quiet river-side end of a central city street (five minutes' walk to the action on Victoria and Hood Sts), this sparkling self-contained apartment opens onto a swimming pool. There's also a bedroom available in a wing of the main house. Self-catering breakfast is provided.

For more places to eat and stay in Hamilton see p118.

Te Awamutu ❺

✕ Walton St Coffee
Cafe $

(☎022 070 6411; www.facebook.com/waltonstreetcollective; 3 Walton St; snacks & meals $6-12; ⊙6.30am-3pm Tue-Fri, to 1pm Sat) In a rustic building with exposed beams and retro furniture, this combo of cafe, gallery and performance space is Te Awamutu's top spot for a coffee. The menu has a strong focus on organic and gluten-free options. Try the Buddha Bowl, a changing concoction of fresh seasonal vegies and the grain of the day, topped with a cashew-and-herb dressing.

Waitomo Caves ❼

✕ Huhu
Modern NZ $$

(📞07-878 6674; www.huhucafe.co.nz; 10 Waitomo Caves Rd; small plates $8-15, mains $19-34; ⏱noon-late; 📶) Huhu has views from the terrace and sublime contemporary NZ food. Sip a Kiwi wine or craft beer – including brews from the local King Country Brewing Co – or graze through a seasonal tapas-style menu of delights like slow-cooked lamb, teriyaki salmon and organic rib-eye steak. Downstairs is a small King Country Brewing beer bar that's open mainly in summer.

🛏 Abseil Inn
B&B $$

(📞07-878 7815; www.abseilinn.co.nz; 709 Waitomo Caves Rd; d from $150; 📶) A *veeery* steep driveway takes you to this delightful B&B with four themed rooms, great breakfasts and witty hosts. The biggest room has a double bath and valley views.

National Park Village ❾

✕ Station Cafe
Cafe $$

(📞07-892 2881; www.stationcafe.co.nz; cnr Findlay St & Station Rd; mains lunch $15-20, dinner $28-34; ⏱9am-4pm Mon-Tue, to 9pm Wed-Sun) Count your blessings ye who find this little railway station along the line, a lovely old dear, restored with care and now serving eggy brunches, sandwiches, coffee and yummy cakes, plus an impressive à la carte evening menu. Try the grilled pork tenderloin with a creamy blue cheese sauce. Three-course Sunday night roasts ($40) are world famous around these parts.

🛏 Parkview Apartments
Apartment $$$

(📞0800 727 588; www.parkviewnationalpark. com; 24 Waimarino–Tokaanu Rd; d $280; 📶) Stylish and thoroughly modern accommodation comes to National Park Village at these recently built apartments. Both two-bedroom apartments sleep up to four people, and expansive picture windows make it easy to take in the beautiful alpine scenery outside. Indoor distractions such as big-screen TVs, gas fireplaces and contemporary kitchens could well delay your eventual enjoyment of the surrounding area.

Whanganui ❿

✕ Mischief on Guyton
Cafe $

(📞06-347 1227; 96 Guyton St; mains $10-25; ⏱7.30am-3pm Mon-Fri) 'I believe in reality every now and then' says the little sign in the window. How mischevous. Step inside for cafe classics (eggs Benedict, savoury mince) and globally inspired lunch mains (Thai green prawn curry, Moroccan beef sirloin, chicken-and-bean tortillas). Excellent counter cakes and salads; little courtyard out back. Good stuff!

🛏 151 on London
Motel $$

(📞06-345 8668, 0800 151 566; www.151onlondon.co.nz; 151 London St; d $115-160, apt $200-280; 📶) This six-year-old, snappy-looking spaceship of a motel wins plenty of fans with its architectural angles, quality carpets and linen, natty lime/silver/ black colour scheme and big TVs. At the top of the price tree are some excellent upstairs/ downstairs apartment-style units sleeping six: about as ritzy as Whanganui accommodation gets. There is a cafe across the car park.

Wellington & the East Coast Trips

ARRAYED AROUND A COMPACT HARBOUR Wellington, combines urban art and culture with a cosmopolitan eating and drinking scene and is a good base for journeys in the lower North Island.

There's stellar birdwatching on Kapiti Island, superb vineyards around Martinborough and the coastline is punctuated by remote beaches and lighthouses.

Continuing up the east coast, Napier, Hastings and Gisborne are all thriving regional cities caressed by the sun and celebrating local food scenes and more excellent wine. New Zealand's Pacific coast extends past the islands of Whakaari and Moutuhora to the sunny beaches and popular coastal hub of Tauranga and Mt Maunganui in the Bay of Plenty region.

Mt Maunganui Mt Maunganui and Tauranga Harbour (Trip 10)

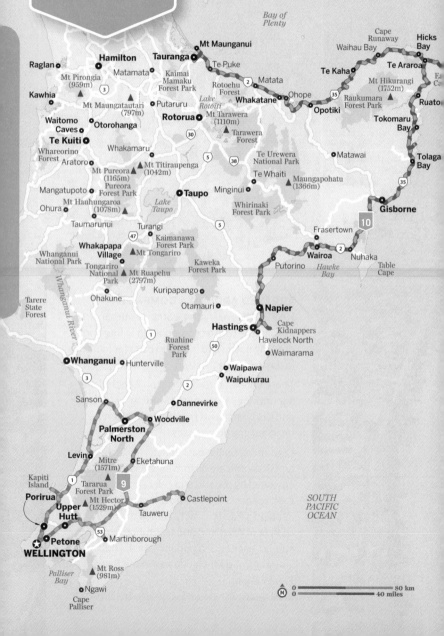

Wellington & the East Coast Trips

Cape Kidnappers Gannet colony

9 North Island Southern Loop 3–4 days
Urban culture combines with a bird sanctuary and damn fine wine. (p136)

Classic Trip
10 Pacific Coast Explorer 5–7 days
Everything from beaches and islands to sunny vineyards and art-deco architecture. (p144)

☑ **DON'T MISS**

Wellington Craft Beer
Find out why the capital's hoppy and diverse beer scene is one of the most exciting on the planet. Drink up on Trip 9

Weta Cave
Make the pilgrimage to this combination of museum and studio that's been behind some of history's biggest movies. It's lights down on Trip 9

Lake Ferry Hotel
Have a leisurely pub lunch before continuing to the end-of-the-road location of the Cape Palliser Lighthouse. Time to get remote on Trip 9

Cape Kidnappers
Catch a lift in a 4WD or on a tractor-pulled trailer to this isolated coastal gannet colony on Trip 10

Te Mata Peak
On fine days, this 399m peak can offer views all the way to Tongariro National Park. Gaze away on Trip 10

Castlepoint *A truly awesome, end-of-the-world place*

North Island Southern Loop

9

From the compact and cosmopolitan capital city of Wellington, embark on a diverse journey combining brilliant bird life, remote lighthouses, world-beating wine and NZ's national sport.

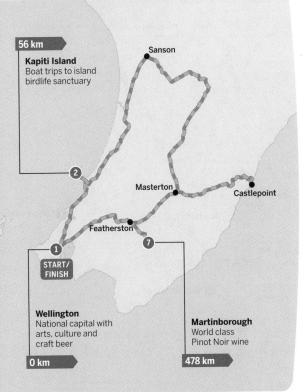

56 km

Kapiti Island
Boat trips to island birdlife sanctuary

Sanson

2

Masterton

Castlepoint

Featherston

7

1

START/
FINISH

Wellington
National capital with arts, culture and craft beer

0 km

Martinborough
World class Pinot Noir wine

478 km

**3–4 DAYS
559KM /
347 MILES**

GREAT FOR...

BEST TIME TO GO
Expect more blue skies from November to April

ESSENTIAL PHOTO
A wild and windswept selfie at the Castlepoint Lighthouse

BEST FOR WINE BUFFS
Tasting the world-renowned pinot noir of Martinborough

9 North Island Southern Loop

This rambling sojourn covers the agricultural and wine-making heartland north of Wellington. The island sanctuary of Kapiti offers excellent walking and birdlife, and the regional city of Palmerston North showcases just why the sport of rugby is so important to NZ. In nearby Masterton there's the opportunity to see wildlife unique to NZ – including the beloved kiwi – and east coast diversions include remote, windswept lighthouses.

TRIP HIGHLIGHT

1 Wellington

Wellington is famous for being NZ's constitutional and cultural capital. Downtown, the compact CBD vibrates with museums, theatres, galleries and boutiques, and tasty diversions include great cafes and restaurants, plus an excellent craft beer scene. See www.craftbeercapital.com for the hoppy local lowdown, or try our walking tour (p158). With a spectacular harbour-

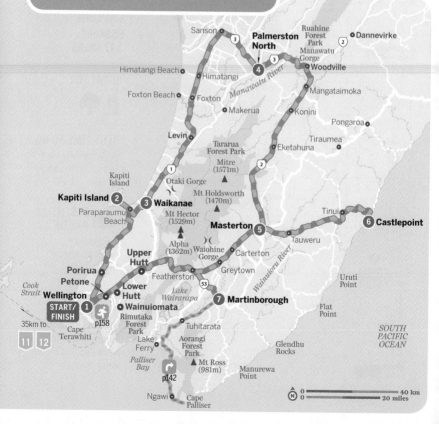

side location, Te Papa (p158) is NZ's national museum, and crammed with interactive, fun and informative displays telling the nation's story. For exhibition highlights, the one-hour 'Introducing Te Papa' tour (adult/child $15/7) runs at 10.15am, noon and 2pm daily. Film buffs will dig the **Weta Cave** (☎04-909 4100; www.wetanz.com; cnr Camperdown Rd & Weka St, Miramar; admission & tour adult/child $25/12, with return transport $65/40; ◉9am-5.30pm), a mind-blowing mini-museum of the Academy Award–winning special-effects company that brought *The Lord of the Rings*, *King Kong* and *The Hobbit* to life. It's 9km from town in Miramar.

✕ ⊨ p143

LINK YOUR TRIP

11 **Kaikoura Coast**
Catch the ferry to Picton and continue down the east coast to Christchurch for more wineries and the odd whale sighting along the way.

12 **Sunshine & Wine**
The inter-island ferry port of Picton is the starting point for this luscious loop around the top of the South Island.

The Drive » Head north to Paraparaumu Beach (53km) on SH1 with west coast views of Kapiti Island on the near horizon.

TRIP HIGHLIGHT

❷ Kapiti Island

Paraparaumu Beach is the departure point to Kapiti Island, a 10km by 2km sanctuary that has been a protected reserve since 1897, and is home to bird species now rare or extinct on the mainland. The island is open to day walkers, limited each day to 100 at Rangatira, where you can hike up to the 521m high point, Tuteremoana; and to 60 visitors at the northern end, which has gentle walks to viewpoints and around a lagoon.

To visit the island, it's essential to book in advance with one of three licensed operators. Reconfirm arrangements on the morning of departure, as sailings are weather dependent. Contact **Kapiti Marine Charter** (☎027 655 4739, 0800 433 779; www.kapitimarinecharter.co.nz; adult/child from $75/40), **Kapiti Tours** (☎04-237 7965, 0800 527 484; www.kapititours.co.nz; adult/child $75/40, with guided tour $95/50) and **Kapiti Island Nature Tours** (☎06-362 6606, 021 126 7525; www.kapitiislandnature-tours.co.nz; transport per person $75, day tours $165) to book the short 15-minute

hop from Paraparaumu Beach.

The Drive » From Paraparaumu Beach to Waikanae is around 12km along busy SH1.

---

❸ Waikanae

Around 60km north of Wellington, Waikanae is a seaside suburban enclave, good for some salt-tinged R&R and natural-realm experiences. The **Nga Manu Nature Reserve** (☎04-293 4131; www.ngamanu.co.nz; 281 Ngarara Rd, Waikanae; adult/child/family $18/8/38; ◉10am-5pm; 🅿) is a 15-hectare bird sanctuary dotted with picnic areas, bush walks, aviaries and a nocturnal house with kiwis, owls and tuataras. The eels are fed at 2pm daily; guided bird-feeding tours run at 11am daily (adult/child $25/12 including admission). To get here, turn seawards from SH1 onto Te Moana Rd then right down Ngarara Rd and follow the signs.

The Drive » From Waikanae, follow SH1 north through dairy-farming country to Sanson. The west coast beaches of Foxton (14km return) and Himatangi (16km return) are broad and shallow. At Sanson, turn east on SH3 to Palmerston North, 117km from Waikanae.

---

❹ Palmerston North

On the banks of the Manawatu River, Palmerston North lies at the

heart of the agriculturally prosperous Manawatu region. Massey University, NZ's largest, informs the town's cultural and social structures. As a result 'Palmy' has an open-minded, rurally bookish vibe. Find out all about NZ's national game at the **New Zealand Rugby Museum** (📞06-358 6947; www.rugbymuseum. co.nz; Te Manawa Complex, 326 Main St; adult/child/family $12.50/5/30; ⏰10am-5pm), an amazing space overflowing with rugby paraphernalia and history. NZ won back-to-back Rugby World Cups in 2011 and 2015, so quiz the friendly staff about the All Blacks' prospects for 2019. Adjacent **Te Manawa** (📞06-355 5000; www.temanawa.co.nz; 326 Main St; ⏰10am-5pm; 👶) merges a museum and art gallery into one experience, with vast collections joining the dots between art, science and history. The city's heart and soul is **the Square,** (⏰24hr; 📞) with 17 spacious acres featuring a clock tower, Māori carvings and modern art.

✕ p143

The Drive ›› Leave Palmerston North northeast on SH3 and follow the spectacular Manawatu Gorge before linking with SH2 at Woodville and continuing south to Masterton (107km from Palmerston North) through fields dotted with sheep.

⑤ Masterton

The hub of the agriculturally rich Wairarapa region, Masterton's main claim to immortality is the 50-year-old sheep-shearing competition, the international **Golden Shears** (www.goldenshears. co.nz; ⏰Mar), held annually in the first week of March. In keeping with the ovine theme, the **Wool Shed** (📞06-378 8008; www.thewoolshednz. com; 12 Dixon St, Masterton; adult/child/family $8/2/15; ⏰10am-4pm) is a great little museum dedicated to NZ's sheep-shearing and wool-production industries. It's a good spot to pick up a home-knitted hat. About 30km north of Masterton, the 1000-hectare **Pukaha Mt**

Nga Manu Nature Reserve Pukeko (Purple swamphen)

Bruce National Wildlife Centre (☎06-375 8004; www.pukaha.org.nz; 85379 SH2, Masterton; adult/child/family $20/6/50, guided walks incl admission adult/child $45/22.50; ⏰9am-4.30pm) is one of NZ's most successful wildlife and captive breeding centres. The scenic 1½-hour loop walk gives a good overview, and on display are kiwi and tuatura, NZ's unique reptile.

The Drive » From Masterton east to Castlepoint is 68km through farming country. Allow around one hour for the one way journey, but it's definitely worth it.

- - - - - - - - - -

❻ Castlepoint

On a rugged coastline east of Masterton, Castlepoint is a truly awesome, end-of-the-world place, with a reef, the lofty 162m-high Castle Rock, some safe swimming and walking tracks. There's an easy (but sometimes ludicrously windy) 30-minute return walk across the reef to the lighthouse, where 70-plus shell species are fossilised in the cliffs. A one-hour return walk runs to a huge limestone

DETOUR: CAPE PALLISER

Start: ❼ Martinborough

From Martinborough, the road wends through picturesque farmland before hitting the coast along Cape Palliser Road. Impossibly scenic, this route hugs the coast between wild ocean and black-sand beaches on one side and sheer cliffs on the other. The shadows of the South Island are sometimes visible on a clear day.

Further south, the wind-worn fishing village of Ngawi is where rusty beach-bound bulldozers are used to drag fishing boats ashore. Next stop is a malodorous seal colony, the North Island's largest breeding area for these fellers. In your quest for a photo, don't get between the territorial seals and their escape route to the sea.

Just beyond stands the **Cape Palliser Lighthouse**, where 250-steps climb to its base for excellent views. It's a great place to linger if there isn't a southern gale.

On the way there or back, take a short detour to the crusty waterside settlement of Lake Ferry, overlooking Lake Onoke. There's the characterful old **Lake Ferry Hotel** (📞06-307 7831; www.lakeferryhotel.co.nz; 2 Lake Ferry Rd, Lake Ferry; mains $14-30; ⏱noon-3pm & 6-9pm) here, plus ranks of grey, shingled dunes at the river mouth. This is a classic coastal corner of NZ where nothing ever happens but there's plenty to see. From Martinborough to the lighthouse is 67km, but allow around one and a quarter hours driving time to get there.

cave (take a torch), or take the 1½-hour return track from Deliverance Cove to Castle Rock. Keep well away from the lower reef when there are heavy seas.

The Drive » Returning 68km to Masterton from Castlepoint, it's a further 53km journey on SH2 and SH53 to Martinborough via Carterton and Featherston. Around 24km south of Masterton, Greytown's heritage centre includes boutique accommodation, good eateries and three high-street pubs.

❼ Martinborough

A photogenic town with a leafy town square and charming heritage architecture, Martinborough is surrounded by rolling pasture and well-ordered grapevines. It is famed for its wine – especially the pinot noir. An excellent spot to buy local wine and taste a few is **Martinborough Wine Merchants** (📞06-306 9040; www.martinboroughwinemerchants.co.nz; 6 Kitchener St; ⏱9.30am-5.30pm Sun-Thu, to 6pm Fri & Sat). They also rent out bikes (per half/full day $25/35) for cellar-door adventures or you can join a tour with **Green Jersey Cycle Tours** (📞021 074 6640; www.greenjersey.co.nz; 3-4hr guided tours incl lunch $120, bike hire per half/full day $30/40; 🚲). The Wairarapa Visitor Guide (available from local i-SITEs) has plenty

of info on the region's vineyards, and www.winefrommartinborough.com details leading wineries including **Ata Rangi,** (📞06-306 9570; www.atarangi.co.nz; 14 Puruatanga Rd; ⏱noon-4pm) **Margrain** (📞06-306 9292; www.margrainvineyard.co.nz; cnr Ponatahi & Huangarua Rds; ⏱11am-5pm Sat & Sun, daily Jan) and **Palliser Wines** (📞06-306 9019; www.palliser.co.nz; Kitchener St; ⏱11am-4pm).

🍴 p143

The Drive » Return to Featherston northwest on SH53 and pick up SH2 to travel across the hilly Rimutaka Ranges back to Wellington (81km from Martinborough) through the Hutt Valley.

Eating & Sleeping

Wellington ❶

🍴 Nikau Cafe   Cafe $$

(📞04-801 4168; www.nikaucafe.co.nz; City
Gallery, Civic Sq; mains $15-27; ⊗7am-4pm
Mon-Fri, 8am-4pm Sat; 🚼) An airy affair at
the sophisticated end of Wellington's cafe
spectrum, Nikau consistently dishes up simple
but sublime stuff (pan-fried halloumi, sage
eggs, legendary kedgeree). Refreshing aperitifs,
divine sweets and a sunny courtyard complete
the package. The organic, seasonal menu
changes daily. Good one!

🍴 Ortega Fish Shack   Seafood $$$

(📞04-382 9559; www.ortega.co.nz; 16
Majoribanks St; mains $34-39; ⊗5.30pm-
late Tue-Sat) Mounted trout, salty portraits,
marine-blue walls and Egyptian floor tiles cast
a Mediterranean spell over Ortega – a magical
spot for a seafood dinner. Fish comes many
ways (roasted with laksa sauce; with mango
chutney and raita), while desserts continue the
Med vibes with Catalan orange crêpes and one
of Welly's best cheeseboards. Excellent stuff.

🛏 City Cottages   Rental Houses $$

(📞021 073 9232; www.citybedandbreakfast.
co.nz; 5 & 7 Tonks Gr; d/q $185/219; 🅿🛜)
These two tiny 1880 cottages squat amid a
precinct of historic Cuba St buildings. Clever
conversion has transformed them into all-
mod-con, self-contained one-bedroom pads,
comfortable for two but sleeping up to four
(thanks to a sofa bed). Hip, convenient and
totally Cuba. It's not the quietest location in the
city, but it's the coolest.

Palmerston North ❹

🍴 Café Cuba   Cafe $$

(📞06-356 5750; www.cafecuba.co.nz; cnr
George & Cuba Sts; mains brunch $10-26, dinner
$25-32; ⊗7am-late Mon-Sat; 🚼🍴) Need a
sugar shot? Proceed to day-turns-to-night Café
Cuba – the cakes here are for professional
chocoholics only. Supreme coffees and cafe
fare (risottos, salads, curries, corn fritters) also
draw the crowds. The halloumi-and-eggplant
stack is bodacious. Kid-friendly, too.

Martinborough ❼

🍴 Tirohana Estate   Modern NZ $$

(📞06-306 9933; www.tirohanaestate.com; 42
Puruatanga Rd; lunch mains $12-22, 3-course
dinners $59; ⊗11.30am-3pm & 6pm-late
Mon-Sat, 6pm-late Sun) Enjoy a casual lunch
over a glass or two on the terrace at this
pretty vineyard, then come back for dinner in
the elegant dining room (quite the occasion).
Food (salmon fishcakes, lamb shanks, bread-
and-butter pudding) is amply proportioned,
proficiently prepared and impeccably served.
Dinner bookings essential.

🛏 Aylstone
Retreat   Boutique Hotel $$$

(📞06-306 9505; www.aylstone.co.nz; 19
Huangarua Rd; d incl breakfast $230-260; 🛜)
Set among the vines on the edge of the village,
this elegant retreat is a winning spot for the
romantically inclined. Six en suite rooms exude
flowery French-provincial charm and share
a posh reading room. The whole shebang is
surrounded by micro-mansion gardens sporting
lawns, box hedges and chichi furniture.

Pacific Coast Explorer

10

Beaches, vineyards, modern coastal cities and authentic Māori culture are all featured in this trip, along with lots of gazing out to the wild blue of the Pacific Ocean.

TRIP HIGHLIGHTS

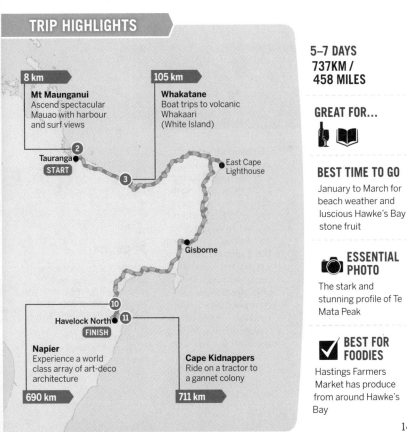

8 km

Mt Maunganui
Ascend spectacular Mauao with harbour and surf views

105 km

Whakatane
Boat trips to volcanic Whakaari (White Island)

Tauranga
START

East Cape Lighthouse

Gisborne

Havelock North
FINISH

Napier
Experience a world class array of art-deco architecture

690 km

Cape Kidnappers
Ride on a tractor to a gannet colony

711 km

**5–7 DAYS
737KM /
458 MILES**

GREAT FOR...

BEST TIME TO GO

January to March for beach weather and luscious Hawke's Bay stone fruit

ESSENTIAL PHOTO

The stark and stunning profile of Te Mata Peak

BEST FOR FOODIES

Hastings Farmers Market has produce from around Hawke's Bay

Classic Trip

10 Pacific Coast Explorer

Describing a languid arc around New Zealand's Pacific Ocean coastline, this epic journey combines sandy beaches, spectacular scenery and day excursions to rugged and idiosyncratic islands. Māori culture is thriving in Whakatane, Opotiki and around the remote East Cape, and the bountiful food scenes of Hastings and Gisborne are complemented by sun-kissed vineyards. In Napier, a classy art-deco architectural legacy echoes a stylish past.

❶ Tauranga

Tauranga (pronounced 'toe-rung-ah') has been booming since the 1990s, and remains one of NZ's fastest-growing cities. Restaurants and bars line the waterfront, fancy hotels rise high, and the city with an easygoing maritime vibe offers both cultural and natural attractions. The **Tauranga Art Gallery** (☏07-578 7933; www.artgallery.org.nz; cnr Wharf & Willow Sts; ◷10am-4.30pm) presents historic and contemporary art, and houses a permanent collection along with local and visiting exhibitions. Touring the ground-floor and mezzanine galleries will take around an hour. For a diverse day on the ocean, **Bay Explorer** (☏021 605 968; www.bayexplorer.co.nz; adult/child $115/65) offer a popular cruise incorporating wildlife spotting – potentially including whales, dolphins and birdlife – with the opportunity to go paddle boarding, kayaking and snorkelling around nearby Motiti Island.

✕ ⊨ p156

The Drive » Depart Tauranga northeast across Tauranga Harbour on SH2. Once across the harbour, turn left onto Totara St and drive through Tauranga's port area before merging left onto Maunganui Rd. From Tauranga to Mt Maunganui is 8km.

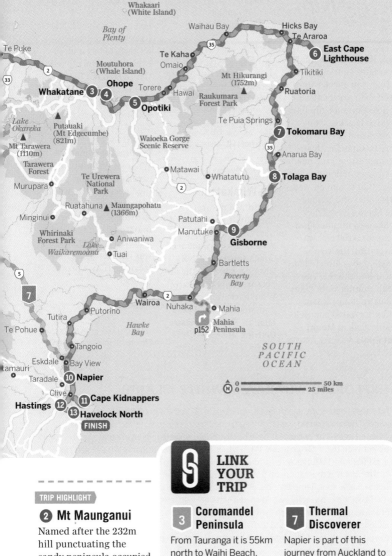

0 ——————— 50 km
0 ——————— 25 miles

TRIP HIGHLIGHT

2 Mt Maunganui

Named after the 232m hill punctuating the sandy peninsula occupied by the township, Mt Maunganui is often just called 'the Mount', or Mauao, which translates as 'caught by the light of

LINK YOUR TRIP

3 Coromandel Peninsula

From Tauranga it is 55km north to Waihi Beach.

7 Thermal Discoverer

Napier is part of this journey from Auckland to Hawke's Bay through the North Island's volcanic landscapes.

Classic Trip

day'. It's considered part of greater Tauranga, but is really an enclave unto itself with great cafes and restaurants, hip bars and fab beaches. Sunseekers and surfers flock here in summer. Meandering through the magical groves of pohutukawa trees that bloom between November and January, the Mauao Base Track (3.5km, 45 minutes) is a pleasant stroll circumnavigating the area's most famous forest-clad natural highlight. The steep summit walk takes about an hour return, and afterwards a muscle-easing soak at **Mount Hot Pools** (www.tcal.co.nz;

9 Adams Ave; adult/child/family $11/8/31; ⊘6am-10pm Mon-Sat, 8am-10pm Sun) is an essential reward.

🍴 p156

The Drive ❯❯ Depart Mt Maunganui along Maunganui Rd onto SH2. After 13km, the Tauranga Eastern Link toll road begins, but stay on SH2 to take the more scenic route via Te Puke and on to Whakatane, 97km from Mt Maunganui.

- - - - - - - - - - - -

TRIP HIGHLIGHT

③ Whakatane

Cradling a natural harbour at the mouth of the Whakatane River, Whakatane (pronounced 'fokka-tar-nay') is NZ's sunniest city, and the departure point for nearby Whakaari (White Island) and Moutuhora (Whale Island). The **Whakatane District Museum** (📞07-306 0509; www.whakatane

museum.org.nz; Esplanade Mall, Kakahoroa Dr; admission by donation; ⊘9am-5pm Mon-Fri, 10am-2pm Sat & Sun) has excellent displays on early Māori and European settlement, and the **Te Manuka Tutahi Marae** (📞07-308 4271; www.mataatua.com; 105 Muriwai Dr; 90min cultural tours adult/child $49/15; ⊘9am-4pm Dec-Feb, reduced hours Mar-Nov) features the Mataatua Wharenui, a beautifully carved 1875 Māori meeting house. In 1879 it was dismantled and shipped to Sydney, before spending 71 years in the Otago Museum from 1925. It was only returned to the local Ngāti Awa people in 1996.

🛏 p156

The Drive ❯❯ Depart Whakatane south on McAllister St, turn left into Gorge Rd and

EXPLORING WHAKAARI (WHITE ISLAND)

NZ's most active volcano (it last erupted in 2013) lies 49km off the Whakatane coast. The small island was originally formed by three separate volcanic cones of different ages. The two oldest have been eroded, while the younger cone has risen up between them. Geologically, Whakaari is related to Moutuhora (Whale Island) and Putauaki (Mt Edgecumbe), as all lie along the Taupo Volcanic Zone.

The island is dramatic, with hot water hissing and steaming from vents over most of the crater floor. Temperatures of 600°C to 800°C have been recorded.

The island is privately owned so you can only visit it with a licensed tour operator. Fixed-wing air operators run flyover tours, while boat and helicopter tours usually include a walking tour around the island, including a visit to the ruins of the sulphur-mining factory. Most tours depart Whakatane; scenic flights are also possible ex-Tauranga and Rotorua.

Operators include **White Island Tours** (📞0800 733 529, 07-308 9588; www.whiteisland.co.nz; 15 The Strand, Whakatane; 6hr tours adult/child $199/130; ⊘departures 7am-12.30pm), **Frontier Helicopters** (📞0800 804 354; www.whiteislandvolcano.co.nz; Whakatane Airport; flights per person from $650) and **White Island Flights** (📞0800 944 834; www.whiteislandflights.co.nz; Whakatane Airport; flights per person $249).

then right into Ohope Rd. Look forward to stunning coastal views on the 7km journey over the hill to Ohope.

-----

④ Ohope

Ohope has great beaches, perfect for lazing or surfing, and is backed by sleepy Ohiwa Harbour. Based on the shores of Ohiwa Harbour, **KG Kayaks** (☏07-315 4005, 027 272 4073; www.kgkayaks. co.nz; 93 Kuatere Wharf Rd, Kuatere; tours $85-155, 2hr hire s/d $45/70) offers guided tours and kayak hire. Popular guided options include around Ohiwa Harbour, four-hour boat trips to Moutuhora (Whale Island), and a coastal adventure between Whakatane and Ohope. Owned by friendly Ohope locals, **Moanarua Tours** (☏07-312 5924; www.moanarua.co.nz; 2 Hoterini St; 3hr boat tours per person $80, bike/kayak rental from $10/15) offers boat trips with a Māori cultural and historical focus, plus sunset tours and fishing trips. There's also bike and kayak hire to explore Ohope's glorious beach, an arcing stretch of sand often rated NZ's finest.

The Drive » Leave Ohope Beach on Wainui Rd and skirt Ohiwa Harbour for 17km before turning left to rejoin SH2 to Opotiki, a further 20km with rural and coastal views.

DAY TRIP TO MOUTUHORA

Nine kilometres off Whakatane is Moutuhora (Whale Island) – so called because of its leviathan shape. This island is another of the volcanoes along the Taupo Volcanic Zone but is much less active, although there are hot springs along its shore. The summit is 353m high and the island has several historic sites, including an ancient *pa* (fortified village) site.

Whale Island was originally home to a Māori settlement. In 1829 Māori massacred sailors from the trading vessel *Haweis* while it was anchored at Sulphur Bay. In 1867 the island passed into European ownership and remains privately owned, although since 1965 it has been a DOC-protected wildlife refuge for seabirds and shorebirds. NZ fur seals are also frequently spotted.

Operators departing from Whakatane include **White Island Tours** (☏0800 733 529; www.moutuhora. co.nz; 15 The Strand East, Whakatane; adult/child $90/60; ⏱10am-1.30pm), **Diveworks Dolphin & Seal Encounters** (☏07-308 2001, 0800 354 7737; www. whaleislandtours.com; 96 The Strand; dolphin & seal swimming adult/child $160/130, diving incl gear from $215) and **KG Kayaks** (p149).

-----

⑤ Opotiki

The Opotiki area was settled from at least 1150, some 200 years before the larger 14th-century Māori migration. Māori traditions are well preserved here, with the work of master carvers lining the main street and the occasional facial *moko* (tattoo) passing by. The town is a gateway to the East Coast, and top beaches nearby include Ohiwa and Waiotahi. The **Opotiki Museum** (☏07-315 5193; www.opotikimuseum. org.nz; 123 Church St; adult/child/family incl Shalfoon & Francis Museum $10/5/25; ⏱10am-4pm Mon-Fri, to 2pm Sat) has interesting heritage displays including Māori *taonga* (treasures), militaria and historic shopfronts. Part of the **Motu Trails** (☏04-472 0030; www.motutrails.co.nz), the nearby Dunes Trail is a 19km one-day mountain biking diversion. See www.motucycletrails. com for shuttles and bicycle hire.

✕ p156

The Drive » Leaving Opotiki on SH35, after 42km this mainly coastal road crosses the broad and pebble-strewn Motu River, before continuing via the fishing town of Te Kaha and Hicks Bay to Te Araroa and the East Cape

Classic Trip

WHY THIS IS A CLASSIC TRIP
BRETT ATKINSON, WRITER

For sheer diversity, this exploration of New Zealand's Pacific fringes is hard to beat. Tauranga and nearby Mt Maunganui combine as a vibrant city, while traditional Māori values underpin more remote areas further east. The islands of Whakaari and Moutuhora are essential day trips, and Gisborne, Napier and Hastings all offer summertime beaches and some of the country's most established and respected vineyards.

Top: Tauranga beach
Left: Market at Hastings
Right: Mt Maunganui

Fresh
Crisp
Apple
Fill The
B...

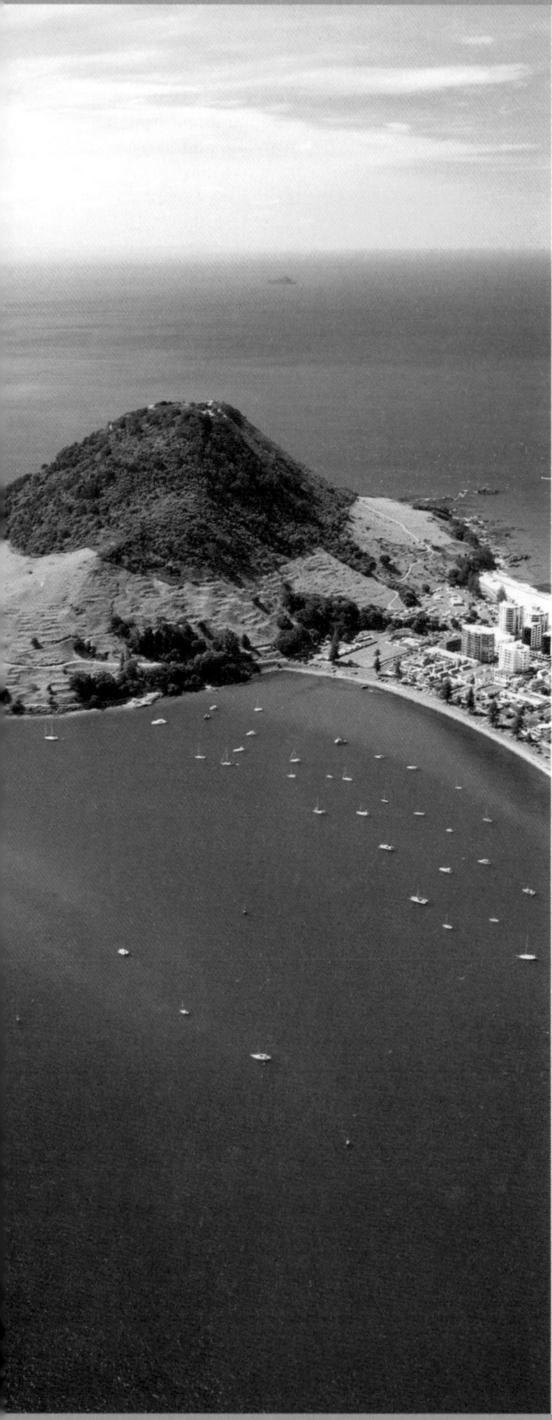

DAVID WALL PHOTO / GETTY IMAGES ©

Lighthouse. Allow two and a half hours for the winding 179km journey from Opotiki.

❻ East Cape Lighthouse

Around 10km east of Hicks Bay is Te Araroa, a lone-dog village with a few shops, a petrol station, and a beautifully carved *marae* (Māori meeting house). The geology changes here from igneous outcrops to sandstone cliffs, all blanketed by dense native bush. More than 350 years old, 20m high and 40m wide, Te-Waha-O-Rerekohu is allegedly NZ's largest pohutukawa tree, and it dominates the Te Araroa schoolyard. From Te Araroa, drive out to see the East Cape Lighthouse, the easterly tip of mainland NZ. It's 21km (30 minutes) east of town along a winding, mainly unsealed road, with a 25-minute climb (750 steps!) to the lighthouse.

The Drive » Returning from the lighthouse to SH35, travel through rough-hewn farmland to Tokomaru Bay (79km), stopping to see the fascinating Māori-style interior at St Mary's Church in Tikitiki (24km from Te Araroa). Dominating the inland horizon is Mt Hikurangi (1752m), the first spot on Earth to see the sun each day.

❼ Tokomaru Bay

With a broad beach framed by sweeping cliffs, sleepy Tokomaru

Bay is one of SH35's most scenic spots. The town has weathered hard times since the freezing works closed in the 1950s, but it still sports several attractions including good surfing for beginners, swimming, and a great pub. Heading south from Tokomaru Bay is a bucolic 22km stretch of highway to the turn-off to Anaura Bay, 6km away. It's a definite 'wow' moment when the bay springs into view far below. Captain James Cook arrived here in 1769 and commented on the 'profound peace' in which the local Māori people

were living and their 'truly astonishing' cultivations.The **Anaura Bay Walkway** (www.doc.govt. nz; off Anaura Bay Rd, Anaura Bay) is a two-hour, 3.5km ramble through steep bush and grassland, starting at the northern end of the bay.

The Drive ›› Back on SH35 from Anaura Bay, it's a further 14km south to Tolaga Bay – population around 800 – and the largest community along the East Cape.

8 Tolaga Bay

The longest in the southern hemisphere at 660m, Tolaga Bay's historic wharf was built in 1929 and was commercially functional until 1968. Now it is caught somewhere between rusty decay, and dedicated,

but costly, preservation. Nearby is **Cooks Cove Walkway**, an easy 5.8km, 2½-hour loop through farmland and native bush to a cove where the erstwhile captain landed. At the northern end of the beach, the **Tatarahake Cliffs Lookout** is reached by a sharp 10-minute walk. Just off the main street, the **Tolaga Bay Cashmere Company** (06-862 6746; www.cashmere.co.nz; 31 Solander St, Tolaga Bay; ⏰10am-4pm Mon-Fri) inhabits the art-deco former council building. Watch the knitters knit, then perhaps purchase one of their delicate works: call to check they're open. Around 40km south of Tolaga Bay, the **Te Tapuwae o Rongokako Marine Reserve** is a 2450-hectare haven for fur seals, dolphins and whales. **Dive Tatapouri** (06-868 5153; www.dive tatapouri.com; 532 SH35, Tatapouri) offers dive trips, reef tours and snorkelling.

The Drive ›› From Tolaga Bay, SH35 meanders 55km south to Gisborne.

9 Gisborne

Squeezed between surf beaches and a sea of chardonnay, Gisborne proudly claims to be the first city on Earth to see the sun. It's a good place to hit the beach, and there's safe swimming

DETOUR: MAHIA PENINSULA

Start: 9 Gisborne

Between Gisborne and Napier, the Mahia Peninsula's eroded hills, sandy beaches and vivid blue sea make it a mini-ringer for the Coromandel Peninsula, but without the tourist numbers and with the bonus of dramatic Dover-ish cliffs. It's an enduring holiday spot for East Coasters, who come largely for boaty, beachy stuff. A day or two can be spent exploring the scenic reserve and the bird-filled **Maungawhio Lagoon**, or hanging out at the beach for a spectacular sunset. Mahia has several small settlements offering between them a few guesthouses, a holiday park, a bar-bistro and a couple of stores. From Gisborne, drive south on SH2 to Nuhaka (66km), and then turn left (east) for 17km to Mahia Beach.

THE BEST OF NZ'S PACIFIC COAST WINERIES

Napier & Hastings

The Hawke's Bay and East Coast regions are home to some of New Zealand's finest wineries.

The area around Napier, Hastings and Havelock North was once famous for its orchards. Today grapes have top billing, and Hawke's Bay is NZ's second-largest wine-producing region (behind Marlborough). Expect excellent Bordeaux-style reds, syrah and chardonnay. Pick up the *Hawke's Bay Winery Guide* map at the **Hastings i-SITE** (📞06-873 0080; www.visithastings.co.nz; Westermans Bldg, cnr Russell St & Heretaunga St E; ⏰9am-5pm Mon-Fri, to 3pm Sat, 10am-2pm Sun) or **Napier i-SITE** (📞06-834 1911; www.napiernz.co.nz; 100 Marine Pde; ⏰9am-5pm, extended hours Dec-Feb; 📶), or download at www.winehawkesbay.co.nz.

Black Barn Vineyards (📞06-877 7985; www.blackbarn.com; Black Barn Rd, Havelock North; ⏰9am-5pm Mon-Fri, 10am-5pm Sat & Sun) This hip winery near Havelock North has a bistro, art gallery, and a popular summer Saturday farmers' market.

Mission Estate (📞06-845 9354; www.missionestate.co.nz; 198 Church Rd, Taradale; ⏰9am-5pm Mon-Sat, 10am-4.30pm Sun) NZ's oldest winery (established 1851) has a tree-lined driveway leading to a restaurant and cellar door inside a restored Catholic seminary. Call to book a guided tour.

Waipaoa River Valley

With hot summers and fertile loam soils, the Waipaoa River valley to the northwest of Gisborne is another renowned grape-growing area. The region is traditionally famous for its chardonnay, and is increasingly noted for gewürztraminer and pinot gris. See www.gisbornewine.co.nz for a cellar-door map. Opening hours scale back out of peak season.

Matawhero (📞06-867 6140; www.matawhero.co.nz; Riverpoint Rd, Matawhero; ⏰noon-4pm Sat & Sun) Home of a particularly buttery chardonnay. Enjoy a picnic in bucolic splendour, accompanied by a flight of fine wines.

Millton (📞06-862 8680; www.millton.co.nz; 119 Papatu Rd, Manutuke; ⏰10am-5pm Mon-Sun, reduced winter hours) Sustainable, organic and biodynamic wines. Another fine option for a picnic surrounded by sturdy-trunked vines.

between the flags at **Waikanae** and **Midway Beach**. Focusing on East Coast Māori and colonial history, the **Tairawhiti Museum** (www.tairawhiti museum.org.nz; Kelvin Rise, Stout St; adult/child $5/ free, Mon free; ⏰10am-4pm Mon-Sat, 1.30-4pm Sun) is Gisborne's arts hub with rotating exhibits and excellent historic photographic displays.

The **Gisborne Botanic Gardens** (📞06-867 2049; www.gdc.govt.nz/botanical-gardens; Aberdeen Rd; ⏰24hr; 🚻) beside the Taruheru River is a beaut spot for a picnic. Wiggle through the NZ native Bushland Walkway that thrives in Gisborne's often balmy climate. Also doing well is the local produce sold at Saturday morning's **Gisborne Farmers**

Market (📞027 251 8608; www.gisbornefarmersmarket.co.nz; cnr Stout & Fitzherbert Sts; ⏰9.30am-12.30pm Sat). Stock up on fresh fruit, macadamia nuts, honey, herbs, cheese and Gisborne oranges... all of it locally grown or produced.

🍴 p156

The Drive » From Gisborne south, SH2 combines rural

Classic Trip

vistas and occasional views of the sea to run 214km to Napier. At Wairoa, 98km south of Gisborne, the Eastend Cafe is an essential refreshment stop.

TRIP HIGHLIGHT

⑩ Napier

Today's Napier – a sunny city with the air of an affluent English seaside resort – is the silver lining of the dark cloud that was the city's deadly 1931 earthquake. Rebuilt in the popular architectural styles of the time, Napier retains a unique concentration of art-deco buildings. Offering one-hour guided walks and two-hour guided tours, the centrally-located **Deco Centre** (☎06-835 0022; www.artdeconapier.com; 7 Tennyson St; ⊙9am-5pm; 🚻) is the best place to start, and architectural highlights of the city include the **Daily Telegraph Building** (☎06-834 1911; www.heritage.org.nz/the-list/details/1129; 49 Tennyson St; ⊙9am-5pm Mon-Fri) and the **National Tobacco Company Building** (☎06-834 1911; www.heritage.org.nz/the-list/details/1170; cnr Bridge & Ossian Sts, Ahuriri; ⊙lobby 9am-5pm Mon-Fri). More heritage style lingers along Marine Pde, an elegant seaside avenue lined with huge Norfolk Island pines.

🍴 🛏 p157

The Drive ⟫ Depart Napier along Marine Pde (SH2), and just after Clive (10km), turn left into Mill Rd for 6km before turning left into East Rd. Turn right into Clifton Rd and continue another 450m to the Clifton waterfront, 21km from Napier.

TRIP HIGHLIGHT

⑪ Cape Kidnappers

From mid-September to late April, Cape Kidnappers erupts with squawking gannets. These big ocean birds usually nest on remote islands but here they settle for the mainland, completely unfazed by human spectators. The birds nest as soon as they arrive, and eggs take about six weeks to hatch with the chicks arriving in early November. The colony is best viewed between early November and late February when the gannets are here in the greatest numbers. Take a guided tour with **Gannet Safaris** (☎06-875 0888; www.gannet-safaris.co.nz; 396 Clifton Rd, Te Awanga; adult/child $75/35; 🚻), through farmland in a 4WD, or with **Gannet Beach Adventures** (☎06-875 0898, 0800 426 638; www.gannets.com; 475 Clifton Rd, Clifton; adult/child/family $44/24/106; 🚻) on a tractor-pulled trailer along the beach. Prebooking is essential.

The Drive ⟫ Return to SH2 at Clive (11km), and turn left

to Hastings, 21km from Cape Kidnappers.

⑫ Hastings

Like Napier, Hastings was devastated by the 1931 earthquake and also boasts some fine art-deco and Spanish Mission buildings built in the aftermath. Main-street highlights include the **Westerman's Building** (cnr Russell St & Heretaunga St E), arguably the Bay's best example of the Spanish Mission style. The Hastings i-SITE (p153) stocks the *Art Deco Hastings* brochure ($1) detailing walking tours. The compact but interesting **Hastings City Art Gallery** (HCAG; ☎06-871 5095; www.hastingscityartgallery.co.nz; 201 Eastbourne St E; ⊙10am-4.30pm) presents contemporary NZ (including Māori) and international art in a bright, purpose-built space, and Sunday morning's **Hastings Farmers Market** (☎027 697 3737; www.hawkes bayfarmersmarket.co.nz; Showgrounds, Kenilworth Rd; ⊙8.30am-12.30pm Sun) is one of the country's best.

🍴 🛏 p157

The Drive ⟫ From central Hastings, Heretaunga St runs southeast to lead into Havelock St, and then on to Havelock North after 5km.

⑬ Havelock North

Positioned at the centre of the Hawke's Bay fruit

Napier Art-deco National Tobacco Company Building

bowl, busy Hastings is the commercial hub of the region, but a few kilometres of orchards still separate it from the rural village ambience of Havelock North. Excellent cafes and restaurants dot this prosperous burg, and 16km to the south lies the dramatic 399m profile of **Te Mata Peak** (📞06-873 0080; www.tematapark.co.nz; off Te Mata Rd, Havelock North) and the 99-hectare Te Mata Trust Park. The summit road passes sheep trails, rickety fences and vertigo-inducing stone escarpments, all cowled in a bleak, lunar-meets–Scottish Highlands atmosphere. On a clear day, views stretch to the Mahia Peninsula and distant Mt Ruapehu. The park's 30km of trails offer walks ranging from 30 minutes to two hours: pick up the *Te Mata Park's Top 5 Walking Tracks* brochure from local i-SITEs.

🍴 p157

Classic Trip

Eating & Sleeping

Tauranga ①

✕ Macau   Asian $$

(☎07-578 8717; www.dinemacau.co.nz; 59
The Strand; shared plates $14-31; ⊙11am-late
Mon-Fri, 10am-late Sat) Zingy Asian flavours take
centre stage at this recent addition to the strip
along the Strand. Plates – small and large – are
all designed to be shared. Menu highlights
include crispy Sichuan-spiced eggplant, and the
moreish steamed buns with roasted pork belly.
Stylish decor, Asian-inspired cocktails and a
good craft beer list make this one of Tauranga's
best.

⊨ Tauranga on the
Waterfront   Motel $$

(☎07-578 7079; www.thetauranga.co.nz; 1
Second Ave; r/ste from $165/215; 🛜) A short
stroll from central Tauranga, this well-
established motel has recently renovated
studios with compact private courtyards,
and brilliant harbour suites with huge picture
windows and outstanding views. Sunlight
streams in to brighten the chic and stylish
decor, modern bathrooms are equipped with
premium toiletries, and compact self-contained
kitchenettes come with Nespresso machines for
the first coffee of the day.

Mt Maunganui ②

✕ Post Bank   Modern NZ $$$

(☎07-575 4782; www.postbank.co.nz; 82
Maunganui Rd; mains $24-34; ⊙noon-2.30pm
Tue-Fri, 5pm-late nightly) Bookcases crammed
with an eclectic range of tomes give Post Bank
the ambience of a gentlemen's club, but there's
nothing stuffy about the food on offer. Asian
and Mediterranean influences combine in a
menu playfully divided up into 'Chapter 1, 2 and
3'. Highlights have included the Vietnamese
beef-and-prawn salad, and a great Thai chicken

curry. The smoothly professional team behind
the bar concoct classy cocktails worthy of a
1920s speakeasy.

Whakatane ③

⊨ One88 on Commerce   Motel $$

(☎07-307 0915; www.one88commerce.co.nz;
188 Commerce St; d/ste from $160/200) This
new motel features spacious rooms and extra-
large super-king suites. Most options feature
spa baths and private courtyards; together with
classy kitchen appliances and huge flat-screen
TVs, it all adds up to the best rooms in town.
One88 is in a quiet location a 10-minute walk
from central Whakatane. Welcome to one of the
best new hotels in NZ.

Opotiki ⑤

✕ Two Fish   Cafe $

(☎07-315 5448; 102 Church St; snacks $5-10,
mains $7-21; ⊙8am-3pm Mon-Fri, to 2pm Sat)
Decent eating options are thin on the ground
in Opotiki, but this cafe serves up robust
homemade burgers, chowder, toasties, steak
sandwiches, fab muffins and salads, plus a
jumbo selection in the cabinet. Two Fish has
happy staff, Cuban tunes and a retro-groovy
interior and courtyard. And super coffee!
Sorted.

Gisborne ⑨

✕ USSCO Bar & Bistro   Modern NZ $$$

(☎06-868 3246; www.ussco.co.nz; 16 Childers
Rd; mains $38-45; ⊙4.30pm-late) Housed
in the restored Union Steam Ship Company
building (USSCO – get it?), this place is all class.
Silky kitchen skills shine in a highly seasonal
menu featuring the likes of soy-glazed pork
belly with caramelised yams, parsnip puree and

toasted nut salad. Devilishly good desserts, plus plenty of local wines and NZ craft beers. Generous portions and multicourse deals.

🛏 Ahi Kaa Motel   Motel $$

(📞06-867 7107; www.ahikaa.co.nz; 61 Salisbury Rd; d $110-180; @ 🛜) An uptown motel offering in a quiet backstreet, a short sandy-footed stroll across the road from Waikanae Beach. Fancy linen, tasteful bathrooms, double glazing, outdoor showers, recycled timbers, solar power and recycling savvy – nice one!

Napier 🔟

✖ Mister D   Modern NZ $$

(📞06-835 5022; www.misterd.co.nz; 47 Tennyson St; mains $25-33; ⊙7.30am-4pm Sun-Wed, to late Thu-Sat) This long, floorboarded room with its green-tiled bar is the pride of the Napier foodie scene. Hip and slick but not unaffordable, with quick-fire service delivering the likes of pulled pork with white polenta or roast-duck risotto. Novelty of the Year award: doughnuts served with syringes full of chocolate, jam or custard (DIY injecting). Bookings essential.

🛏 Sea Breeze B&B   B&B $$

(📞06-835 8067; www.seabreezebnb.co.nz; 281 Marine Pde; r incl breakfast $100-135; 🛜) Inside this Victorian seafront earthquake survivor (1906) are three richly coloured themed rooms (Chinese, Indian and Turkish), decorated with a cornucopia of artefacts. It's all tastefully done, avoiding the risk of being over the top. The price and location are right. Self-serve continental breakfast and free wi-fi included.

For more places to eat and stay in Napier see p119.

Hastings 🔢

✖ Opera Kitchen   Cafe $$

(📞06-870 6020; www.operakitchen.co.nz; 312 Eastbourne St E, Hastings; mains $9-26; ⊙7.30am-4pm Mon-Fri, 9am-3pm Sat & Sun; 🗷) Set your rudder right with whisky porridge with cream and giant oats at this mod, stylish cafe abutting the Hawke's Bay Opera House (has the earthquake-proofing construction finished?). For a more practical start to the day, the farmer's breakfast is also a winner. Heavenly pastries, great coffee and snappy staff.

🛏 Millar Road   Villa $$$

(📞06-875 1977; www.millarroad.co.nz; 83 Millar Rd, Hastings; villas/house from $400/650; 🛜🏊) Set in the Tuki Tuki Hills with vineyard and bay views, Millar Road is architecturally heaven-sent. Two plush villas (each sleep four) and a super-stylish house (sleeps eight) are filled with NZ-made furniture and local artworks. Explore the 20-hectare grounds or look cool by the pool.

Havelock North 🔢

✖ Deliciosa   Tapas $$

(📞06-877 6031; www.deliciosa.co.nz; 21 Napier Rd, Havelock North; tapas $10-22; ⊙4pm-late Mon & Tue, 11am-late Wed-Sat) Great things come in small packages at this rosy little tapas bar. The kitchen delivers sassy, locally sourced edibles such as pork belly with pomegranate jus, and salt-and-pepper squid with orange and parsley. The wine list roams from Spain to Italy and back. Terrific beer list and breezy front terrace, too.

Start/Finish Te Papa

Distance 5km

Duration Three hours

Harbour views, hip urban style and expansive public spaces feature on this diverse stroll through New Zealand's capital city. Look forward to exploring museums and galleries to fast-track your understanding of the country's history, art and culture.

Take this walk on Trip

9

Te Papa

New Zealands's national museum is interactive, fun and full of surprises: 'Te Papa Tongarewa' loosely translates as 'treasure box'. Riches include Māori artefacts and the museum's own colourful *marae* (meeting ground); natural history exhibitions; Pacific and NZ history galleries; and the **National Art Collection**. Museum tours (adult/child $15/7) run at 10.15am, noon and 2pm daily, and there's a 'Māori Highlights' tour daily at 2pm ($20/10).

The Walk >> Leave your car in Te Papa's underground car park and stroll along Wellington's waterfront crossing to Frank Kitts Park and the Wellington Museum. Art en route includes the Four Plinths project and the Albatross Fountain.

Wellington Museum

Occupying an 1892 Bond Store, the **Wellington Museum** (✆04-472 8904; www.museumswellington.org.nz; Bond Store, Queens Wharf; ⊙10am-5pm;) presents the city's social and maritime history. Highlights include a moving documentary on the *Wahine*, the inter-island ferry that sank in the harbour in 1968 with the loss of 51 lives. Māori legends are dramatically told using tiny holographic actors and special effects.

The Walk >> From the museum, walk through Post Office Sq and then up Grey St to Lambton Quay. Make a short hop right to Cable Car Lane.

Wellington Cable Car

This little red **cable car** (✆04-472 2199; www.wellingtoncablecar.co.nz; Cable Car Lane, rear 280 Lambton Quay; adult/child one way $4/2, return $7.50/3.50; ⊙departs every 10min, 7am-10pm Mon-Fri, 8.30am-10pm Sat, 9am-9pm Sun;) has been trundling up the steep slope from Lambton Quay to Kelburn since 1902. At the top are the Wellington Botanic Gardens, the **Carter Observator**y and the small-but-evocative **Cable Car Museum** (✆04-475 3578; www.museumswellington.org.nz; Upland St, Kelburn; ⊙9.30am-5pm). Look forward to Wellington harbour views.

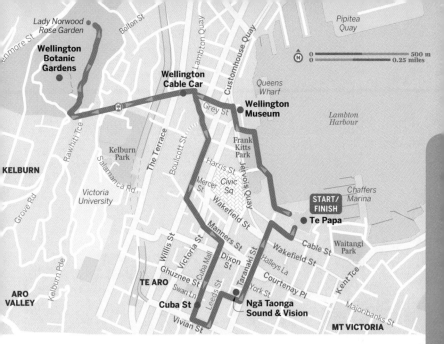

The Walk >> From the cable car terminus it's around 900m through the Wellington Botanic Gardens downhill to the treehouse visitor centre.

Wellington Botanic Gardens

These hilly, 25-hectare botanic **gardens** (☏04-499 4444; www.wellington.govt.nz; 101 Glenmore St, Thorndon; ⏱daylight hours) boast original native forest, the beautiful Lady Norwood Rose Garden, 25,000 spring tulips, and international plant collections. Fountains, sculptures, a duck pond, a cafe and city skyline views make it a very pleasant place to stroll.

The Walk >> Having explored the gardens, walk back uphill to catch the cable car down to the CBD, and continue via Lambton Quay, Willis St and Manners Mall to the quirky Bucket Fountain.

Cuba Street

Cuba Mall's retail strip is enlivened by the kooky and colourful tilt-and-pour mechanism of the **Bucket Fountain**. Try not to get splashed before exploring Cuba St's more bohemian southern end. Essential shopping includes **Slow Boat Records** (☏04-385 1330; www. slowboatrecords.co.nz; 183 Cuba St; ⏱9.30am-5.30pm Mon-Thu, to 7.30pm Fri, 10am-5pm Sat & Sun), and **Ombra** (☏04-385 3229; www. ombra.co.nz; 199 Cuba St; snacks $5-14, mains $12-19; ⏱10am-late Mon-Fri, 8am-late Sat & Sun; ☏) is a hip refreshment stop.

The Walk >> From the corner of Cuba and Vivian Sts, walk via Marion St and Ghuznee St to Ngā Taonga Sound & Vision.

Ngā Taonga Sound & Vision

Dive into NZ culture at this wonderful **visual archive** (☏04-384 7647; www. ngataonga.org.nz; cnr Taranaki & Ghuznee Sts; screenings from $8; ⏱library noon-5pm Tue-Fri) with more than 30,000 moving images including feature films, documentaries, short films, home movies, TV shows and advertisements. There are regular screenings in the cinema (check the website), a viewing library (free) where you can watch films, and a groovy on-site cafe.

The Walk >> Continue down Taranaki St and turn right into Cable St and Te Papa.

Marlborough & Nelson Trips

WELCOME TO WARM AND SUNNY MARLBOROUGH AND NELSON, the first port of call for travellers crossing the Cook Strait from windy Wellington to the 'Mainland'.

These top-of-the-South neighbours have much in common beyond an amenable climate: both boast renowned coastal holiday spots, plus more mountain ranges than you can poke a Leki-stick at. Both produce delicious food and drink, from game and seafood to summer fruits, hops for craft beer and grapes for world-class wines. Combined, Marlborough and Nelson make for splendid road-trip country with an emphasis on sunshine and good times.

Marlborough Vineyard near Blenheim (Trips 11, 12 & 14)
DOUG PEARSON / GETTY IMAGES ©

Marlborough & Nelson Trips

Cape Farewell
Whariariki Beach
Puponga
Farewell Spit
Pakawau
Collingwood
Onekaka
Pohara
Totaranui
Takaka
Abel Tasman National Park
Devil River Peak (1775m)
13
Marahau
Mt Domett (1646m)
Upper Takaka
Kaiteriteri
Riwaka
Motueka

TASMAN SEA

Marlborough Sounds

Kohaihai
Kahurangi National Park
Mt Arthur (1795m)
Mapua
60
Nelson
Havelock
12
Waikawa
Picton
Oparara
Karamea
Brightwater
Richmond

Little Wanganui
Mt Kendall (1762m)
Tapawera
Wakefield
Pelorus River
Renwick
Blenheim

Karamea Bight
67
Mt Owen (1875m)
6
Mt Richmond Forest Park
Wairau River

Granity
Hector
Kawatiri
Seddon
Westport
Lyell
14
Lake Rotoroa
63
Grassmere
Cape Campbe
Charleston
Inangahua
Murchison
St Arnaud
Ward
Mt Uriah (1525m)
69
Mt Travers (2338m)
Lake Rotoiti
Severn (2027m)
Molesworth Station
Tapuae-o-Uenuku (2885m)
Paparoa National Park
Reefton
Victoria Forest Park
65
Nelson Lakes National Park
Homestead
Kekerengu
Ikamatua
Mt Una (2300m)
St Bernard (2256m)
Clarence River
Mt Haast (1587m)
Faerie Queen (2237m)
Dillon Cone (2173m)
Manakau (2610m)
Clarence
Stillwater
Springs Junction
Mt Fyffe (1602m)
Moana
Mt Ajax (1832m)
Lake Sumner Forest Park
Hanmer Forest Park
Mt Lyford
Kaikoura
Lake Brunner (Moana)
Hanmer Springs
70
Goose Bay
Jacksons
Lake Sumner
Mt Longfellow (1898m)
7
Waiau
Oaro
Arthur's Pass National Park
Culverden
1
Otira
Hurunui River
Parnassus
Arthur's Pass
Hurunui
Cheviot
Mt Murchison (2408m)
7
Bealey
Cass
11
73
Waipara
SOUTH PACIFIC OCEAN
Lake Coleridge
Oxford
Amberley
Springfield
Woodend
Sheffield
Kaiapoi
Pegasus Bay
Windwhistle
Belfast
Mt Hutt
Darfield
Christchurch
Methven
Rolleston
Lyttelton
Dunsandel
Diamond Harbour

0   50 km
0   25 miles

Kaikoura Māori carving

 DON'T MISS

Kaikoura Peninsula Walkway
Spot seals and sea birds against a staggering mountain and ocean backdrop on Trip **11**

Great Taste Trail
Hop on a bike for easy, scenic riding around the Nelson region's beaches, cafes, wineries and galleries on Trips **12** **13**

Kerr Bay Jetty
Snap the classic lake pic and watch wriggly eels, then take a flying leap into the drink on Trips **12** **14**

Te Waikoropup Springs
Admire the the clearest freshwater spring in the world (reputedly) on Trip **13**

Omaka Aviation Heritage Centre
View the collection of Great War and WWII aircraft in displays created by Peter Jackson and Weta Workshop on Trip **12**

Gore Bay Cathedral Cliffs are sculpted
by wind and rain

Kaikoura Coast

11

The inter-island ferry port of Picton and New Zealand's southern capital, Christchurch, are linked by a scenic highway wending through pretty countryside and along the wild Pacific Coast.

TRIP HIGHLIGHTS

0 km

Picton
Pretty waterside town and hub for Marlborough Sounds' adventures

1 START

Blenheim ●

157 km

3

Kaikoura
Marine-mammal encounters ahoy with a stunning mountain backdrop

Cheviot ●
● Gore Bay

5

299 km

Pegasus Bay Winery
Fantastic food, wine and setting

FINISH ● Christchurch

3–4 DAYS
352KM / 219 MILES

GREAT FOR...

BEST TIME TO GO

The scenery, wine and wildlife are great all year round

ESSENTIAL PHOTO

Queen Charlotte Sound snapped from the Snout Track

BEST FOR WILDLIFE

Kaikoura's ocean teems with dolphins, whales, seals and seabirds

165

11 Kaikoura Coast

This stretch of State Hwy 1 is a relatively quick and convenient route between the South Island's two major traveller gateways, Picton and Christchurch, but it also boasts several of the South Island's major highlights. The beautiful Marlborough Sounds, Blenheim's world-class wineries and Kaikoura's marine tours can hardly be missed, but hidden, low-key and up-and-coming attractions also abound.

TRIP HIGHLIGHT

❶ Picton

The inter-island ferry port town of Picton doubles as the departure point for adventures throughout the labyrinthine **Marlborough Sounds** (p176). Often overlooked, however, are Picton's many enjoyable adventures for landlubbers, including some great walks.

For an elevated perspective that makes the sounds seem very much like the drowned valleys they are, follow the **Snout Track** (three hours return) along the headland flanking the harbour's east side. If the short, sharp climb to the ridge line isn't quite what you had in mind, indulge in Picton's simplest and most popular activity, namely lolling about in the pretty foreshore park for a picnic, ice cream or fish and chips, and watch the comings and goings on both land and sea.

✕ ⨝ p171

The Drive » Following SH1, it's only 28km to Blenheim through the Tuamarina river valley and Para Wetlands, then into the broad plains of the Wairau Valley.

❷ Blenheim

Approaching the town of Blenheim you'll be left in no doubt that you've

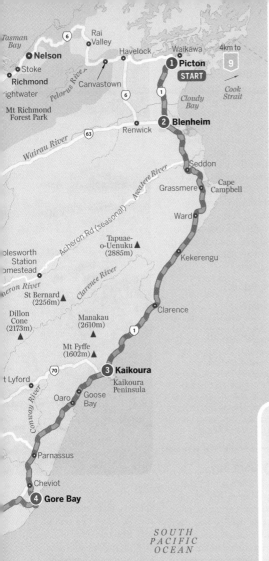

entered wine country, and fortunately it's easy to dip a toe into Marlborough's wine barrels without straying too far from the highway.

Just 3km off SH1, north of Blenheim, **Saint Clair** (www.saintclair. co.nz; 13 Selmes Rd, Rapaura; ⊘9am-5pm) is a long-standing, family owned operation crafting some of NZ's most interesting and well-regarded wines, including the Pioneer Block range showcasing Marlborough's varied terroir. The adjacent cafe is an atmospheric spot for the obligatory vineyard lunch.

The good news for wine-lovers is that the bulk of Marlborough's 35 or so cellar doors are scattered through the valley within a 15-minute

LINK YOUR TRIP

9 North Island Southern Loop

Across the Cook Strait, enjoy a trip taking in the nation's compact and cosmopolitan capital, brilliant bird life, remote lighthouses and world-beating wine.

21 Southern Alps Circuit

Christchurch is a common departure point for a grand tour of the mountainous south.

drive. The **Vines Village**
(www.thevinesvillage.co.nz; 193
Rapaura Rd; ⊙10am-5pm) is
a good place to obtain a
winery map and advice,
along with a bike if you'd
rather wobble around on
two wheels.

✕ ⛶ p171

The Drive ≫ From Blenheim,
SH1 cuts inland through
Marlborough's second-largest
grape-growing region, the
Awatere Valley. Beyond the
Clarence River, 88km from
Blenheim, the peaks of the
Seaward Kaikoura Range start
to fill the picture, as does the
spectacular coastline the
road follows for much of the
remaining 41km to Kaikoura.

- - - - - - - - - - - - - -

TRIP HIGHLIGHT

❸ Kaikoura

Kaikoura is a pretty
coastal town with a
dramatic, snowy-peak
backdrop. Its hand-
some peninsula is the
place where – according
to Māori legend – the
demigod Māui placed his
feet when he fished the
North Island up from the
depths.

Most people come
here for marine tours,
particularly whale-
watching, but the town
also sports a particularly
good walk. Starting from
town, the three-to-four
hour **Peninsula Walkway**
is a mighty fine way to
soak up the scenery, and
offers the chance to see
seals, shearwaters and
other seabirds while
learning about the area

via a series of insightful
information panels.

The walkway begins
by following the town
quay out to the penin-
sula's end, Point Kean,
where seals laze around
seemingly oblivious to
the attention of hordes
of human gawpers.
From there the pathway
climbs gently to the top
of limestone cliffs from
where there are vast
views in every direction.
On reaching South Bay,
the trail heads across the
isthmus back towards
the town.

✕ ⛶ p171

The Drive ≫ SH1 hugs the
coast, occasionally burrowing
through odd tunnels in the
rock, before climbing over the
Hundalee Hills and heading
down onto the bucolic
Canterbury Plains. A 'Tourist
Drive' signpost in the centre of
Cheviot township directs you
left down McQueen Rd to reach
Gore Bay, 77km and a little over
an hour from Kaikoura.

- - - - - - - - - - - - - -

❹ Gore Bay

This is old-school NZ:
aged beach-side baches
(holiday cottages), some
dating back to 1865, and
a long beach good for
swimming and surfing.
Gore Bay's permanent
population of around a
dozen people balloons in
the summer, mainly with
Kiwi campers, but any
time of the year you'll
still have plenty of sand
to yourself.

Towards the northern
end of the beach is a

short track leading along
the Jed River to a small,
hilltop cemetery, con-
taining just a handful of
tombstones. It has lovely
views of the wetland and
beach, and is a peaceful
spot to enjoy the last of
the day's sun.

Gore Bay is also
known for its **Cathe-
dral Cliffs**, which can
be reached by car or a
brutally steep 10-minute

MICAH WRIGHT / DESIGN PICS / GETTY IMAGES ©

Kaikoura Kekeno (New Zealand fur seal)

walk at the southern end of the village. Sculpted by wind and rain – in the evocatively named process known as badlands erosion – the clay gully walls resemble a cathedral's organ pipes, also known as hoodoos.

The Drive » Head south out of Gore Bay to complete the Gore Bay Tourist Drive, up and over the coastal hills to meet the braided Hurunui River, and soon hitting SH1 where you head south to Waipara. Total distance to Waipara is 59km.

TRIP HIGHLIGHT

5 Waipara Valley

Conveniently stretched along SH1 near the Hanmer Springs turn-off, this resolutely rural area makes for a mouth-watering pit stop en route to Christchurch. The valley's warm dry summers and cool autumn nights have proved a winning formula for growing grapes. While it accounts for less than 3% of NZ's wine production, it's responsible for some of the country's finest cool-climate

WHALE WORLD

Few places in the world are home to such a panoply of easily spottable marine wildlife. Whales, dolphins, NZ fur seals, penguins, shearwaters, petrels and several species of albatross all live in the area or swing by.

Marine animals converge here due to ocean-current and continental-shelf conditions: the seabed gradually slopes away from the land before plunging to more than 800m where the southerly current hits the continental shelf. This creates an upwelling of tasty nutrients from the ocean floor into the feeding zone.

Top-of-the-food-chain sperm whales congregate here all year round, but depending on the time of year you may also spy humpbacks, southern rights and even behemoth blue whales, the heaviest animals ever to have graced this earth.

With knowledgeable guides and fascinating 'world of whales' on-board animation, the town's biggest operator, **Whale Watch Kaikoura** (✆ 0800 655 121, 03-319 6767; www.whalewatch.co.nz; Railway Station; 3½hr tours adult/child $150/60), heads out on boat trips (with admirable frequency) to introduce you to some of the big fellas. It'll refund 80% of your fare if no whales are sighted (success rate: 95%), but if this trip is a must for you, allow a few days' flexibility in case the weather turns bad.

wines including riesling and pinot noir.

It's fitting that Waipara Valley's premier winery, **Pegasus Bay** (✆ 03-314 6869; www.pegasusbay.com; Stockgrove Rd; ☉ tastings 10am-5pm), should also have the loveliest setting and one of Canterbury's best restaurants. The beautiful gardens and sun-drenched lawn encourage a very long linger over contemporary cuisine and luscious wines; try the Canterbury lamb matched with Prima Donna pinot noir.

To fully indulge in the valley's bounty, pick up a copy of the *Waipara Valley Map* (www.waiparavalleynz.com). Otherwise, you'll spot several of the main players from the highway.

The Drive » Breaking out onto the Canterbury Plains south of Waipara, it's a flat and reasonably featureless 59km drive from Waipara to central Christchurch.

- - - - - - - - - - - -

⑥ Christchurch

Christchurch is a city in transition, rebuilding from the 2010 and 2011 earthquakes that left 186 people dead and all but hollowed out the heart of the CBD.

While many historic buildings were destroyed, you can see architectural survivors on the walking tour (p286), including Canterbury Museum. Its Māori galleries contain beautiful *pounamu* (greenstone) carvings, while Christchurch St is an atmospheric walk through the colonial past. The must-see is Fred & Myrtle's gloriously kitsch Paua Shell House, Kiwiana at its best.

The museum is also strong on natural history, but to see some of NZ's native animals in the flesh (or more likely feather), visit Willowbank Wildlife Reserve (p223). As well as a rare opportunity to view kiwi, NZ's national bird, the reserve has a recreated Māori village where Ko Tane (p223) cultural performances are held in the evenings.

✗ ⌂ p171

Eating & Sleeping

Picton ❶

✖ Picton Village Bakkerij Bakery $
(cnr Auckland & Dublin Sts; bakery items $2-8; ⏰6am-4pm Mon-Fri, to 3.30pm Sat; ✈) Dutch owners bake trays of European goodies here, including interesting breads, filled rolls, cakes and custardy, tarty treats. An excellent stop before or after the ferry, or to stock a packed lunch.

🛏 Picton Top 10 Holiday Park Holiday Park $
(☎0800 277 444, 03-573 7212; www. pictontop10.co.nz; 70 Waikawa Rd; sites from $36, units $75-185; @🛜🛝) About 500m from town, this compact, well-kept park has plenty of lawn and picnic benches, plus crowd-pleasing facilities including a playground, barbecue area and swimming pool.

For more places to eat and stay in Picton see pages 183 and 201.

Blenheim ❷

✖ Burleigh Deli $
(☎03-579 2531; 72 New Renwick Rd; pies $6; ⏰7.30am-3pm Mon-Fri, 9am-1pm Sat) The humble pie rises to stratospheric heights at this fabulous deli; try the sweet pork-belly or savoury steak and blue cheese, or perhaps both. Fresh-filled baguettes, local sausage, French cheeses and great coffee also make tempting appearances. Avoid the lunchtime rush.

🛏 171 on High Motel $$
(☎0800 587 856, 03-579 5098; www.171onhighmotel.co.nz; 171 High St; d $145-185; 🛜) A welcoming option close to town, these tasteful, splash-o-colour studios and apartments are bright and breezy in the daytime, warm and shimmery in the evening. Expect a wide complement of facilities and 'extra mile' service.

For more places to stay in Blenheim see p183.

Kaikoura ❸

✖ Kaikoura Seafood BBQ Seafood $
(Fyffe Quay; items from $5; ⏰10.30am-6pm) Conveniently located on the way to the Point Kean seal colony, this long-standing roadside barbecue is a great spot to sample local seafood, including crayfish (half/full from $25/50) and scallops, at an affordable price.

🛏 Kaikoura Cottage Motels Motel $$
(☎0800 526 882, 03-319 5599; www. kaikouracottagemotels.co.nz; cnr Old Beach & Mill Rds; d $140-160; 🛜) This enclave of eight modern tourist flats looks mighty fine, surrounded by attractive native plantings. Oriented for mountain views, spick-n-span self-contained units sleep four between an open plan studio-style living room and one private bedroom. Lovely hosts seal the deal.

For more places to eat and stay in Kaikoura see p227.

Christchurch ❻

✖ Supreme Supreme Cafe $
(☎03-365 0445; www.supremesupreme.co.nz; 10 Welles St; breakfast $7-18, lunch $10-20; ⏰7am-4pm Mon-Fri, 8am-4pm Sat & Sun; ✈) With so much to love, where to start? Perhaps with a kimchi Bloody Mary, a chocolate-fish milkshake, or maybe just an exceptional espresso alongside ancient-grain muesli or pulled corn-beef hash. One of New Zealand's best coffee roasters presents a right-now cafe of splendid style, form and function.

🛏 Merivale Manor Motel $$
(☎03-355 7731; www.merivalemanor.co.nz; 122 Papanui Rd; d $165-229; P 🛜) A gracious 19th-century Victorian mansion is the hub of this elegant motel, with units both in the main house and in the more typically motel-style blocks lining the drive. Accommodation ranges from studios to two-bedroom apartments, and there's a complimentary continental breakfast.

For more places to eat and stay in Christchurch see pages 227, 235, 245, 260 and 284.

Blenheim It's easy to visit Marlborough's vineyards without straying too far from the highway

Sunshine & Wine

12

This tour around the sunny top of the South Island serves up a seductive blend of wineries, alfresco dining and gentle leisure activities.

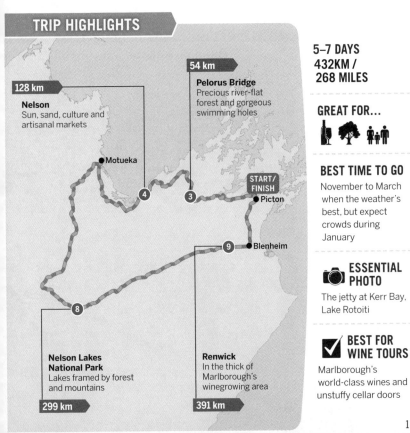

54 km

Pelorus Bridge
Precious river-flat forest and gorgeous swimming holes

128 km

Nelson
Sun, sand, culture and artisanal markets

● Motueka

④

③

START/FINISH
● Picton

⑨ ● Blenheim

⑧

Nelson Lakes National Park
Lakes framed by forest and mountains

299 km

Renwick
In the thick of Marlborough's winegrowing area

391 km

5–7 DAYS
432KM /
268 MILES

GREAT FOR...

BEST TIME TO GO

November to March when the weather's best, but expect crowds during January

ESSENTIAL PHOTO

The jetty at Kerr Bay, Lake Rotoiti

BEST FOR WINE TOURS

Marlborough's world-class wines and unstuffy cellar doors

Classic Trip

12 Sunshine & Wine

Blenheim and Nelson vie annually for the crown of New Zealand's sunniest centre, so odds are on for blue skies on this trip around the top of the South. A high concentration of attractions and short driving times allow you to maximise enjoyment of outdoor adventures in hot spots such as Queen Charlotte Sound and Nelson Lakes National Park, as well as meander in a leisurely fashion around wineries and restaurants.

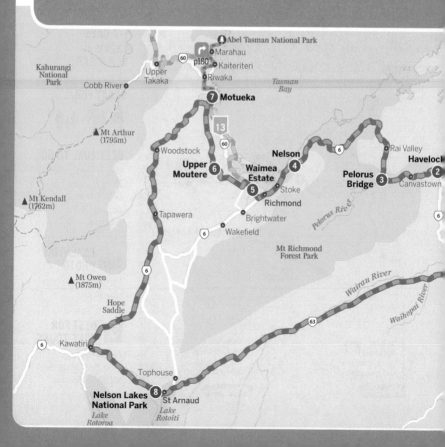

1 Picton

Spread around two pretty bays secreted deep within Queen Charlotte Sound, Picton is much more than just the inter-island ferry port and departure point for trips throughout the Marlborough Sounds.

The town and its environs can be surveyed from the popular **Snout Track** (three hours return), sidling along the Victoria Domain headland flanking the harbour's east side. A side track makes for a shorter walk to **Bob's Bay** (one hour return), a good spot for a swim.

One of Picton's lesser-known but worthy attractions is **Tirohanga Track**, a two-hour leg-stretching loop around a hill just behind the town. Taking you much higher than the Snout Track, it affords dress-circle views of the town and the endless ridges of the Sounds beyond.

✗ ⌂ p183

The Drive » Follow signs for Queen Charlotte Dr, which winds around bay after bay for 34km through to Havelock, providing a panoramic Marlborough Sounds' snapshot.

2 Havelock

The western bookend of the Queen Charlotte Dr, the little town of Havelock is the hopping-off point for forays into Kenepuru and Pelorus Sounds.

It is also the self-proclaimed 'Greenshell Mussel Capital of the World'. You can familiarise yourself with this ubiquitous bivalve on the three-hour **Greenshell Mussel Cruise** (☎03-577 9997, 0800 990 800; www.marlboroughtourcompany.co.nz; Havelock Marina; adult/child $125/45; ⊙departs 1.30pm), which provides a broad introduction to the Marlborough Sounds and, crucially, a sampling of steamed mussels and sauvignon blanc so you can tick the region's ultimate wine and food match off your list.

Another attraction that might float your boat can be found inside the **Havelock i-SITE** (☎03-577 8080; www.pelorusnz.co.nz; 61 Main Rd, Havelock; ⊙9am-5pm summer only). This local information centre shares its home with the **Eyes On Nature** museum, a menagerie of frighteningly lifelike replica birds, fish and other critters. Colourful, fun and certainly surprising, it'll be a hit with nature lovers of all ages.

The Drive » Follow SH6 west along the Pelorus River past the old gold-mining settlement of Canvastown and on to Pelorus Bridge, 20km away.

N 0 —— 20 km
0 —— 10 miles

Waikawa
1 Picton
START/FINISH
1

Cloudy Bay

9 10 Blenheim
Renwick

11

Awatere River
Seddon

Grassmere
Cape Campbell
1
Ward

LINK YOUR TRIP

11 Kaikoura Coast
From Picton you can head down the east coast to Christchurch taking in more wineries and the odd whale along the way.

13 Tasman & Golden Bays
Nelson is the starting point for this trip around two of NZ's sunniest bays.

Classic Trip

TRIP HIGHLIGHT

❸ Pelorus Bridge

A peaky pocket of deep, green forest tucked between paddocks of bog-standard pasture, the **Pelorus Bridge Scenic Reserve** (www.doc.govt. nz) contains one of the last stands of river-flat forest in Marlborough. It survived only because a town planned in 1865 didn't get off the ground by 1912, by which time loggers' obliteration of surrounding forest made this little remnant look precious.

Explore the reserve's many tracks, admire the historic bridge, take a dip in the crystal-clear Pelorus River (alluring enough to star in Peter Jackson's *The Hobbit*), and then partake in some home baking at the cafe.

If you're travelling in a campervan or with a tent, consider overnighting here in DOC's small but perfectly formed **Pelorus Bridge Campground** (☎03-571 6019; www.doc.govt.nz; Pelorus Bridge, SH6; powered/unpowered sites per person $15/7.50), with its snazzy facilities building, lush lawns and riverside setting. Come sundown keep an eye out for long-tailed bats, known to Māori as pekapeka – the reserve is home to one of the last remaining populations in Marlborough.

The Drive » The 74km drive to Nelson along SH6 winds over the scenic Whangamoa hills. If you have a spare day, turn right 9km from Pelorus Bridge and head out to French Pass (or even D'Urville Island) for some big-picture framing of the outer Marlborough Sounds.

TRIP HIGHLIGHT

❹ Nelson

Dishing up a winning combination of sandy beaches, parks and forest reserves, sophisticated art and culinary scenes, and lashings of sunshine, Nelson deserves its laurels as one of NZ's most liveable cities and a fulfilling holiday destination for visitors.

Nelson has an inordinate number of galleries, most of which are listed in the *Art & Crafts Nelson City brochure* (with walking-trail map) widely available around town. A particularly vibrant side of the city's creative scene is on show at the **World of WearableArt Museum** (WOW; ☎03-547 4573; www.wowcars.

MARLBOROUGH SOUNDS

The Marlborough Sounds are a scenic labyrinth of peaks, bays, beaches and watery reaches, formed when the sea flooded deep river valleys after the last ice age. They are very convoluted, accounting for almost one fifth of NZ's total coastline.

Exploring the Sounds is invariably quicker by boat, with driving times up to three times longer. Accordingly, an armada of vessels offers scheduled and on-demand boat services, with the bulk operating out of Picton for the Queen Charlotte Sound, and some from Havelock for Kenepuru and Pelorus Sounds.

Indulgence combined with gentle recreation is a Queen Charlotte Sound speciality, with lunch cruises de rigueur. A fine choice is schmick **Bay of Many Coves Resort** (☎0800 579 9771, 03-579 9771; www.bayofmanycoves.co.nz; Bay of Many Coves; 1-/2-/3-bedroom apt $710/930/1100; 🛜🍴). Nestled into a secluded bay, it offers a dreamy one-stop-shop of bushwalks, kayaking, swimming and a day spa, all on top of experiencing some of the region's best cuisine. You could do the whole shebang on a day trip, but luxurious all-mod-cons apartments overlooking the water make an overnighter pretty irresistible.

FOOD, GLORIOUS FOOD

Nelson's belt almost bursts with the weight of its restaurants and cafes, plumped up with fresh regional produce. Fortunately, visitors can readily source some for themselves from roadside stalls and regular markets.

The must-do on Saturday morning is a noodle through **Nelson Market** (☎03-546 6454; www.nelsonmarket.co.nz; Montgomery Sq; ⏰8am-1pm Sat). 'Bustling' ain't the half of it, so tightly packed is this weekly affair with fresh fruit and vegies, food stalls, artisan cheese and pickles, not to mention an array of art, craft and homespun fashions. Pork-lovers should snuffle straight for Doris' caravan serving up the tastiest bratwurst outside the Mutterland.

The much smaller mid-week **Farmers Market** (☎022 010 2776; www.nelsonfarmersmarket.org.nz; Morrison Sq, cnr Morrison & Hardy Sts; ⏰11pm-4pm Wed) is an abundant alternative spruiking seasonal produce from asparagus to zucchini with bread, chocolate and other commendable edibles filling the gaps.

For a healthy blend of drinking, eating and exercise – with a super-sized helping of scenery on the side – hire a bike to ride the **Tasman's Great Taste Trail** (www.heartofbiking.org.nz). Mainly off-road and accessible from various points around Nelson and Motueka, this cycle route can easily be sliced and diced into an assortment of adventures.

co.nz; 1 Cadillac Way; adult/child $24/10; ⏰10am-5pm), where you can ogle around 70 past entries of NZ's most inspiring fashion pageant. You name it, they've made a garment out of it: wood, metal, shells, cable ties, dried leaves, even ping-pong balls. Revel in sensory overload as you wander around the museum's galleries including a glow-in-the-dark room, and buxom 'Bizarre Bras' exhibition.

🍴 🛏 p183

The Drive » Take the scenic route out of town via waterfront SH6, through Tahunanui and Stoke, and alongside Waimea Inlet through to Richmond. Turn right on to SH60 to reach Waimea Estate, 16km from the centre of Nelson.

❺ Waimea Estate

Less of a global superstar than Marlborough, its behemoth, sauvignon-swirling neighbour, Nelson's wine region is quietly going about its business producing a variety of excellent drops including Old World-challenging pinot noir, chardonnay and riesling. **Waimea Estate** (☎03-544 6385; www.waimeaestates.co.nz; 59 Appleby Hwy, Richmond; ⏰10am-5pm Mon-Wed, to 9pm Thu-Sun) is a firm favourite for fine examples of these varietals as well as more adventurous drops like Trev's Red, a plummy co-fermentation of three grape varieties, and the delightfully bright and quaffable Albariño – a rare bird on these shores.

Pop in for one of the region's friendliest and most interesting wine tastings before retiring to the stylish conservatory or vine-view garden for a relaxed lunch of homemade pasta or local salmon.

The Drive » Continue along SH60 for 5km before turning left onto the inland Moutere Hwy. Traversing gently rolling countryside dotted with farms, orchards and lifestyle blocks, it's a scenic and fruitful drive, particularly in high summer when roadside stalls may be heaving with produce. Upper Moutere is 14km from the SH60 turn-off.

❻ Upper Moutere

Upper Moutere was first settled by German immigrants and originally

Classic Trip

WHY THIS IS A CLASSIC TRIP
SARAH BENNETT, WRITER

This small but perfectly formed loop serves up so much that is good about NZ, starting – most importantly – with scenery from snowy mountains to sandy beaches and all sorts of other lovely landscapes in between. Add in blue skies, beach time, fine wine and juicy fruit, and you're getting pretty close to my holiday nirvana. But I would say that – I grew up here.

Top: Neudorf Vineyards, Upper Moutere, Nelson
Left: Greenshell mussels, Kenepuru Sound
Right: Abel Tasman National Park

named Sarau. Today it's a sleepy hamlet with a pretty church and a couple of shops, including the **Old Post Office** (☎03-543 2780; www.theoldpostoffice.co.nz; 1381 Moutere Hwy, Upper Moutere; ☺9am-4pm Mon-Fri, 10am-4pm Sat & Sun), an endearing blend of micro-deli and cafe (stocking scrumptious local jam), with a gallery and gift shop on the side.

With jam in your bag, you're ready for a pint at the local pub. Reputedly NZ's oldest, complete with questionably retro interior, the **Moutere Inn** (☎03-543 2759; www.moutereinn.co.nz; 1406 Moutere Hwy, Upper Moutere) is a welcoming establishment serving honest meals and predominantly local craft beer. Sit in the sunshine with a beer-tasting platter, or settle down on the sofa on folk-flavoured music nights.

Four kilometres from Upper Moutere, just off the highway to Motueka, bijou **Neudorf Vineyards** (☎03-543 2643; www.neudorf.co.nz; 138 Neudorf Rd, Upper Moutere; ☺11am-5pm daily Oct-Apr, Mon-Fri only May, Jun & Sep, closed Jul & Aug) is one of the Nelson region's most celebrated wineries. Signature tipples include pinot noir and some of NZ's finest chardonnay, available to taste in the agriculturally chic cellar door.

Classic Trip

The Drive » From Upper Moutere, continue north on the Moutere Hwy to its end 18km away at Motueka. In the distance, northwest of the town, you'll see the beech-forest-clad Mt Arthur in Kahurangi National Park.

7 Motueka

Motueka (pronounced 'mott-oo-ecka' and meaning 'Island of Weka') is a bustling agricultural town that doubles as an ace visitor destination due to its ample accommodation, decent cafes and shops, and marginally salty setting along the shore of Tasman Bay.

The town's buzzy aerodrome gives rise to several hair-raising activities, including skydiving in one of NZ's most scenic drop-zones.

Skydive Abel Tasman (☏ 03-528 4091, 0800 422 899; www.skydive.co.nz; Motueka Aerodrome, 60 College St; jumps 13,000ft/16,500ft $299/399) will spiral you up to 16,500ft and throw you out of a perfectly good plane strapped to a professional adrenaline junkie, at which point – if you can keep your eyes open – you can see Abel Tasman, Nelson Lakes and Kahurangi national parks, and as far away as the North Island.

Fancy the thrill without the spill? Skydive's front lawn is a lovely spot to spectate while soaking up some sun.

✕ ⨼ p183

The Drive » Motueka Valley Hwy is clearly signposted from the high street, heading down College St towards the aerodrome. Follow the highway 54km inland until its final juncture at SH6, turn right, and drive 39km to Kawatiri. Head left on SH63 following the Buller River to St Arnaud, 25km away. In all, this scenic drive into the mountains should take around 90 minutes.

TRIP HIGHLIGHT

8 Nelson Lakes National Park

Located at the northern end of the Southern Alps,

DETOUR: ABEL TASMAN NATIONAL PARK

Start: 7 Motueka

Blanketing the coast and hill country between Tasman and Golden Bays, NZ's smallest national park is famed for its picture-perfect arcs of golden sand lapped by seas of shimmering blue. Slightly less likely to make the postcard rack are its myriad other natural features such as limpid lagoons, sculpted granite cliffs and gorges, and spectacular karst caves concealed in its rugged interior.

Hiking the **Abel Tasman Coast Track** is by far the most popular activity in the park, as is evident by the hordes that troop along it in high season. It's hardly a seething mass of humanity, however, with disadvantages limited largely to chock-a-block hut and campsite bookings, and the occasional risk of a photobomb.

Limit your exposure on a day trip. Boat cruises galore are offered from Kaiteriteri, the built-up holiday resort 16km from Motueka. If you're up for paddle power, however – arguably the best way to experience the park – bypass Kaiteriteri and head instead for Marahau, a mere 3km further away, where **Kahu Kayaks** (☏ 0800 300 101, 03-527 8300; www.kahukayaks.co.nz; 11 Marahau Valley Rd) can launch you on your way to glorious Anchorage beach from where you can walk south along the Coast Track back to base.

MARLBOROUGH'S VINOUS COLOSSUS

Marlborough is NZ's vinous colossus, producing around three-quarters of the country's wine. At last count, there were 229 sq km of vines planted throughout the Wairau and Awatere valleys – that's approximately 26,500 rugby pitches! Sunny days and cool nights create the perfect conditions for cool-climate grapes: world-famous sauvignon blanc, top-notch pinot noir, and notable chardonnay, riesling, gewürztraminer, pinot gris and bubbly.

Drifting between tasting rooms and dining among the vines is a quintessential South Island experience. Around 35 of Marlborough's 168 wineries have cellar doors, most open from around 10.30am till 4.30pm in summer (reduced hours in winter).

Contrary to rumours propagated by supermarket sauvignon blanc, Marlborough's terroir is extremely varied. To sniff out the interesting stuff hone in on smaller and independent wineries, rather than the big boys you recognise.

Picks of the bunch include **Framingham** (www.framingham.co.nz; 19 Conders Bend Rd, Renwick; ⊙10.30am-4.30pm), **Te Whare Ra** (www.twrwines.co.nz; 56 Anglesea St, Renwick; ⊙11am-4.30pm Mon-Fri, 12pm-4pm Sat & Sun Nov-Mar) and **Huia** (www.huiavineyards.com; 22 Boyces Rd, Blenheim; ⊙10am–5pm Oct-May),. Two top-notch winery lunch options are **Rock Ferry** (☏03-579 6431; www.rockferry.co.nz; 80 Hammerichs Rd, Blenheim; mains $23-27; ⊙11.30am-3pm) and **Wairau River** (www.wairauriverwines.com; 11 Rapaura Rd; ⊙10am-5pm).

With ample parking and bike hire, the boutique **Vines Village** (p168) shopping centre, 5km north of Renwick, is a good place to get your bearings and collect the Marlborough Wine Trail map (www.wine-marlborough.co.nz). If you'd rather not drive, a host of wine-tour companies await to roll you around the traps, including long-standing **Highlight Wine Tours** (☏03-577 9046, 027 434 6451; www.highlightwinetours.co.nz).

Nelson Lakes National Park is a glacier-carved landscape of rugged greywacke mountains, ancient beech forest, and two stunning lakes – Rotoiti and Rotoroa ('small lake' and 'long lake' respectively in Māori). St Arnaud, the tiny national park village, lies alongside the shore of Rotoiti.

The park's visitor hub is the National Park Visitor Centre (☏03-521 1806; www.doc.govt.nz; View Rd; ⊙8am-4.30pm, to 5pm in summer), well worth a visit for its informative displays on the park's ecology and history. It will also pay to call in to check the forecast and track conditions if you're venturing out onto the park's trails.

Changeable weather and tough terrain certainly make for some serious wilderness-hiking country, but numerous day walks offer more achievable options. Easy nature trails head off hither and zither from Lake Rotoiti's **Kerr Bay**, offering a chance to smell sweet beech trees and eyeball the bird life. Reasonably fit walkers, however, should aim higher; a good pick is the five-hour **Mt Robert Circuit Track**, which circumnavigates the mountain, with an optional side trip along Robert Ridge offering staggering views into the heart of the national park.

🛏 p183

The Drive » The 92km drive down the Wairau Valley to Renwick is pretty as a picture, complete with shingle peaks, a braided river, and golden paddocks that eventually give way to the endless rows of grapevines dominating the lower plains.

Classic Trip

TRIP HIGHLIGHT

❾ Renwick

Not so long ago an unremarkable dot, the little town of Renwick now occupies an enviable position at the centre of Marlborough's growing wine industry. An island in a sea of vines, with more than 20 cellar doors in its ambit – along with an increasing amount of accommodation and traveller services – it's a pleasant and convenient base for exploring NZ's premier wine country.

To cut straight to the wine chase, hire a bike from **Bike2Wine** (☎03-572 8458, 0800 653 262; www. bike2wine.co.nz; 9 Wilson St, Renwick; standard/tandem per day $30/60, pick ups from $10), whose friendly staff will happily advise on the best two-wheeled tour for your schedule, fitness and inclinations.

**The Drive ›› ** Drive east on SH6 for 13km to Blenheim, passing Marlborough Airport after around 4km. If you can't see vines, vines, vines all the way after that, you're lost, very lost.

---

❿ Blenheim

Servicing the viticultural endeavours that carpet most of the Wairau Plains between the Wither Hills and Richmond Ranges, Blenheim is a bustling town with a fairly farmy, workaday feel. In recent years, however, town beautification projects and wine industry spin-offs (such as decent places to eat and pubs you can take your children to) are inching Blenheim closer to a fully fledged tourist town.

Threatening to blow the wine out of the water is the brilliant **Omaka Aviation Heritage Centre** (☎03-579 1305; www.omaka. org.nz; 79 Aerodrome Rd; adult/child $30/12, family from $45; ⊙9am-5pm Dec-Mar, 10am-4pm Apr-Nov). It houses a collection of original and replica Great War and WWII aircraft, brought to life in a series of lifelike dioramas (created by associates of *Lord of the Rings* director, Peter Jackson, who also owns the centre's Great War collection), depicting dramatic wartime scenes such as the demise of the Red Baron. Budding aces can take to the skies on vintage biplane flights.

🛏 p183

**The Drive ›› ** Head north on SH1 for 28km to return to Picton. After leaving the wide Wairau Plains, the views narrow as you head up the Tuamarina Valley and past the Para Wetlands towards the Marlborough Sounds.

Eating & Sleeping

Picton ①

✕ Le Café
Cafe **$$**

(www.lecafepicton.co.nz; London Quay; lunch $14-25, dinner $24-30; ⊙7.30am-10.30pm; 🍴) A spot perennially popular for its quayside location, dependable food and Havana coffee. The likes of salami sandwiches and sweets are in the cabinet, while a good antipasto platter, generous pasta dishes, local mussels, and lamb and fish dishes feature à la carte. The laid-back atmosphere, craft beer and occasional live gigs make this a good evening hang-out.

▭ Bay Vista Waterfront Motel
Motel **$$**

(📞03-573 6733; www.bayvistapicton.co.nz; 303 Waikawa Rd, Waikawa; d $130-185; 🛜) This smart motel enjoys an enviable position on Waikawa foreshore, with views down Queen Charlotte Sound. All units have their own patio and share a big, lush lawn. Located 4km from Picton (courtesy transfer available).

For more places to eat and stay in Picton see pages 171 and 201.

Nelson ④

✕ DeVille
Cafe **$$**

(📞03-545 6911; www.devillecafe.co.nz; 22 New St; meals $12-21; ⊙8am-4pm Mon-Sat, 8.30am-2.30pm Sun; 🍴) Most of DeVille's tables lie in its sweet walled courtyard, a hidden boho oasis in the inner city and the perfect place for a meal or morning tea. The food's good and local – from fresh baking to a chorizo-burrito brunch, Caesar salad and proper burgers, washed down with regional wines and beers. Open late for live music Fridays in summer.

▭ Palazzo Motor Lodge
Motel **$$**

(📞03-545 8171, 0800 472 5293; www.palazzomotorlodge.co.nz; 159 Rutherford St; studios $130-249, apt $230-390; 🛜) This modern, Italian-tinged motor lodge offers stylish studios and one- and two-room apartments featuring enviable kitchens with decent cooking equipment, classy glassware and a dishwasher.

Its comfort and convenient location easily atone for the odd bit of dubious art.

For more places to eat and stay in Nelson see p193.

Motueka ⑦

✕ Toad Hall
Cafe **$$**

(📞03-528 6456; www.toadhallmotueka.co.nz; 502 High St; breakfast $10-20, lunch $10-23; ⊙8am-6pm, to 9pm summer) This fantastic cafe serves smashing breakfasts, such as smoked salmon rösti, and wholesome yet decadent lunches including pork-belly burgers. The outdoor space is home to live music and pizza on Friday and Saturday nights in summer. Inside is a fine selection of smoothies, juices, baked goods, pies and selected groceries.

▭ Equestrian Lodge Motel
Motel **$$**

(📞0800 668 782, 03-528 9369; www.equestrianlodge.co.nz; Avalon Ct; d $125-158, q $175-215; 🛜🏊) No horses, no lodge, but no matter. This excellent motel is close to town (off Tudor St) and features expansive lawns, rose gardens, and a heated pool and spa alongside a series of continually refreshed units. Cheerful owners will hook you up with local activities.

For more places to stay in Motueka see p193.

Nelson Lakes National Park ⑧

For places to stay in Nelson Lakes National Park see p201.

Blenheim ⑩

▭ St Leonards
Cottage **$$**

(📞03-577 8328; www.stleonards.co.nz; 18 St Leonards Rd; d incl breakfast $125-320; 🛜🏊) Tucked into the 4.5-acre grounds of an 1886 homestead, these five stylish and rustic cottages offer privacy and a reason to stay put. Each is unique in its layout and perspective on the gardens and vines. Our pick is the capacious and cosy Woolshed, exuding agricultural chic.

For more places to eat and stay in Blenheim see p171.

Farewell Spit Colossal, crescent-shaped dunes with panoramic views

Tasman & Golden Bays

13

Follow the coast around the top of the South Island for some of New Zealand's finest beaches and the low-key, land's end feel of Golden Bay.

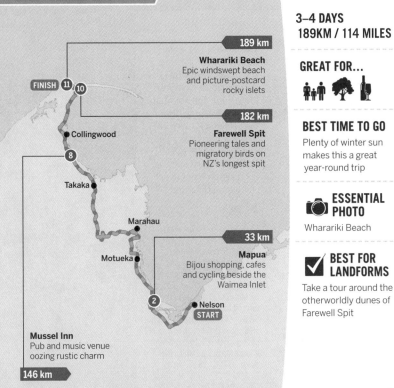

189 km

Wharariki Beach
Epic windswept beach and picture-postcard rocky islets

182 km

Farewell Spit
Pioneering tales and migratory birds on NZ's longest spit

● Collingwood

8

Takaka ●

Marahau ●

33 km

Mapua
Bijou shopping, cafes and cycling beside the Waimea Inlet

Motueka ●

2

● Nelson
START

FINISH **11** **10**

Mussel Inn
Pub and music venue oozing rustic charm

146 km

3–4 DAYS
189KM / 114 MILES

GREAT FOR...

BEST TIME TO GO

Plenty of winter sun makes this a great year-round trip

ESSENTIAL PHOTO

Wharariki Beach

☑ BEST FOR LANDFORMS

Take a tour around the otherworldly dunes of Farewell Spit

13 Tasman & Golden Bays

This trip skirts two big bays at the top of the South Island. Centred on artsy Nelson city, Tasman Bay is sprinkled with relaxed coastal settlements and swathed in seaside fun. It's a winding drive over Takaka Hill to Golden Bay, a smaller and quieter region blending rural charm with enviable beaches. Abel Tasman National Park and Farewell Spit round out this trip in wild style.

TASMAN SEA

FINISH
Farewell Spit
Wharariki Beach 11
10
Puponga
Pakawau

9 **Collingwood**
Aorere
Tukurua
8 **Onekaka**
Bainham
60

Te Waikoropupū Springs 7
Takaka 6

Devil River Peak (1775m)
60

Kahurangi National Park
Cobb River
Upper Takaka

Mt Arthur (1795m)
Woodstock
12
Tapawera

❶ Nelson

Vying every year for the title of NZ's sunniest centre, Nelson's a great place for outdoor adventure. With three national parks and numerous other scenic reserves within easy reach, it boasts land-based adventure galore, but its situation along sandy Tasman Bay makes the seaside the first port of call for playtime.

Number one in the popularity stakes is Tahunanui Beach, less than 10 minutes' drive from the centre of Nelson. It's a big one alright, with the bonus of pretty dunes and a large, grassy reserve alongside.

The beach's vast, sandy shallows make for safe swimming, while offshore conditions favour kitesurfing and stand-up paddle boarding. **Kite Surf Nelson** (☏0800 548 363; www.kitesurfnelson.co.nz) and **Moana SUP** (☏027 656 0268; www.moananzsup. co.nz) are on hand to get you out on the water.

✕ ⊨ p193

The Drive ⟩⟩ From Nelson (or Tahunanui), head southwest along SH6 through Stoke, and alongside Waimea Inlet through to Richmond, before turning onto SH60 signposted for Motueka. Continue past the turn-off for Rabbit Island, 22km from Nelson, and then turn right off SH60 after 9km on to Mapua Dr (signposted Ruby Bay Scenic Route); Mapua is 2km further along.

TRIP HIGHLIGHT

② Mapua

Mapua wharf, near the mouth of the picturesque Waimea River, is home to arty shops and eateries. The quintessential experience is to order fish and chips from the **Smokehouse** (www.smokehouse.co.nz; Mapua Wharf, Mapua; fish and chips $8-12; ⊘11am-8pm), then eat them by the water under the watchful gaze of greedy seagulls. A cold lager from **Golden Bear Brewing Company** (www.goldenbearbrewing.com; Mapua Wharf, Mapua; meals $10-16) is a refreshing way to wash them down.

Mapua is also a popular setting-off point for cycling adventures on the **Great Taste Trail** (p192). Hire a bike from **Wheelie**

LINK YOUR TRIP

11 Kaikoura Coast

From Picton, 107km east of Nelson, you can head down the east coast visiting more wineries and spotting the odd whale along the way.

12 Sunshine & Wine

Nelson and Motueka both feature on this indulgent loop which also takes in Marlborough's wineries and Picton.

187

Fantastic (☎03-543 2245; www.wheeliefantastic.co.nz; Mapua Wharf, Mapua; self-guided tours from $95, bike hire per day from $30) then board the little ferry across the inlet to Rabbit Island/Moturoa, where there are various forest trails and an idyllic swimming beach.

The Drive » Continue along the Ruby Coast Scenic Route for around 10km before rejoining SH60 around a small settlement named Tasman. From here the highway runs beside the pretty Moutere Inlet; after 9km you'll reach the centre of Motueka.

❸ Motueka

Although it's not obvious from the town centre, Motueka is just a stone's throw from the coast. To get the lay of the land, head along the estuary walkway, either on foot or by hiring a bike from the **Bike Shed** (☎03-929 8607; www.motuekabikeshed.co.nz; 145b High St; half-/full-day hire from $25/40).

What it lacks in sandy beaches it more than makes up for with seabirds, saltwater baths and even a shipwreck. To find everything, just follow your nose or pick up a town map from the **i-SITE** (☎03-528 6543; www.motuekaisite.co.nz; 20 Wallace St; ⏰8.30am-5pm Mon-Fri, 9am-4pm Sat & Sun), where you can also get the *Motueka Art Walk* pamphlet pinpointing sculptures, murals and occasional peculiarities around town.

As the last major town before Abel Tasman National Park and Golden Bay, Motueka is also a good place to stock up on supplies.

🛏 p193

The Drive » Head north on SH60. At Riwaka, 4km north of Motueka, keep an eye out for Hop Federation Brewery and various fruit stalls for another chance to sample local goodies. Continue for 3km before turning right to drive the winding 6km over to Kaiteriteri.

❹ Kaiteriteri

This seaside hamlet is a holiday resort popular with both locals and overseas tourists who flock here during summer for its golden-sand beach, pretty lagoon playground and proximity to Abel Tasman National Park.

It could be argued that Kaiteriteri has jumped the shark with an ugly camping ground complex now dominating the waterfront, but by lolling about on your beach towel – facing outwards – you should have little trouble conjuring up a chilled-out, seaside vibe.

Lined up in the aforementioned camping ground complex are a bunch of tour operators itching to get you out into **Abel Tasman National Park**, just

around the corner. Long-standing **Wilsons** (☎03-528 2027, 0800 223 582; www.abeltasman.co.nz; 409 High St, Motueka) runs an excellent cruise/walk combo starting with a scenic boat trip to pretty Medlands Beach, followed by a four-hour walk through lush coastal forest and across a lofty swing bridge. The walk finishes at Anchorage, one of the park's

Collingwood Mussel Inn

finest beaches, where you can enjoy a spot of swimming before being collected for the cruise back to Kaiteriteri.

The Drive » From the beach, head up and over the hill along meandering Kaiteriteri–Sandy Bay Rd for 6km then turn right onto Sandy Bay–Marahau Rd. After tracing the shore of the pretty Otuwhero Inlet for 2km you'll arrive at Marahau.

5 Marahau

Less developed than Kaiteriteri, Marahau is the main walking and kayaking gateway for Abel Tasman National Park (p180) and a laid-back place to while away a day or two. Three respectable dining options and two horse trekking outfits should fill up any

downtime, as will Marahau's rather lovely beach.

Revealed at low tide, the sand flats and knee-deep pools conceal a delicious local delicacy – cockles *(tuangi)*. If such seafood tickles your fancy and you don't mind sand under your finger-nails (and quite possibly in your pants), you can readily gather a dinner's worth in the shallows a couple of hours either side of low tide. Be sure to collect only what you need, heeding daily limits posted beside the beach. Cockles marinières or cockles casino – what's it to be?

✖ 🛏 p193

The Drive ›› The steep, winding drive over Takaka Hill will take around an hour. From Marahau it's 9km along Riwaka–Sandy Bay Rd to the junction with SH60, where you turn right and climb over Takaka Hill, reaching the summit after 10km, with panoramic views of Kahurangi National Park and Golden Bay. From here, Takaka is 33km away.

❻ Takaka

Boasting a high concentration of conscious consumers and alternative lifestylers, Takaka is Golden Bay's 'big' centre and a lovable little town to boot. You'll find most things you need here, and a few you don't, but we all have an unworn pair of yoga pants in our wardrobe, don't we?

It's certainly easy to get sucked into a spot of recreational shopping along Takaka's parade of interesting, independent businesses with a colourful, crafty bent. If you've a hankering for an old-school hardware store or a pottery shop stocking free-range eggs, you may just have found retail nirvana.

Takaka's great for a chow-down, too, with kale and quinoa not *quite* the only game in town by the time you've factored in pizza from the **Dangerous Kitchen** (📞03-525 8686; 46a Commercial St; meals $13-28; ⊙9am-8pm Mon-Sat; 🍴), wicked espresso from **Paul's Coffee Cart** (Takaka Library car park; ⊙8am-1pm Mon-Sat), and a burger (and perhaps a beer) at groovy **Roots Bar** (www.rootsbar.co.nz; 1 Commercial St; ⊙2pm-late; 🛜).

The Drive ›› Four kilometres north of Takaka, follow the signpost right for Te

KARST IN STONE

Golden Bay may look pretty bushy but closer inspection reveals a remarkable karst landscape formed by millions of years of erosion and weathering, which dissolved the marble rock. Its smooth beauty is revealed on the one-hour drive over **Takaka Hill**, a precipitous, serpentine route punctuated by spectacular lookout points and a smattering of other interesting stops.

Around 4km shy of the Takaka Hill summit are the **Ngarua Caves** (SH60; adult/child $17/7; ⊙45min tours hourly 10am-4pm Sep-May, open Sat & Sun only Jun-Aug), a rock-solid attraction where you can see myriad subterranean delights including hundreds of stalactites and stalagmites, and skeletal displays of moa, NZ's extinct giant bird. Access is restricted to tours – you can't go solo spelunking.

Reached at the end of an 11km gravel road, signposted just before Takaka Hill summit, is **Canaan Downs Scenic Reserve** (www.doc.govt.nz). This area stars in both *The Lord of the Rings* and *The Hobbit* movies, but **Harwoods Hole** is the most famous feature here. It's one of the largest *tomo* (caves) in the country at 357m deep and 70m wide, with a 176m vertical drop. You can peer into the cave entrance via a 30-minute walk from the car park; the cave is off-limits to all but the most experienced cavers.

Further along SH60 is the car park for **Takaka Hill Walkway**, a three-hour loop through crazy rock gardens, native forest and farmland. Further along the road **Harwood Lookout** affords tantalising views of Kahurangi National Park's peaks, and down the Takaka River Valley to Takaka and Golden Bay. For more walks on the sunny side of the hill, see DOC's brochure *Walks in Golden Bay*.

Waikoropupū Springs, another 3km further on.

7 Te Waikoropup Springs

Commonly known as **Pupū Springs** (www.doc.govt.nz), this hidden gem is the largest freshwater spring in the southern hemisphere, and reputedly the clearest in the world except for that beneath Antarctica's frozen Weddell Sea – measurements indicate a visibility of over 60m! The colourful little lake is refreshed with around 14,000L of water per second surging from underground vents. A 30-minute forest loop takes in the waters, which are *tapu* (sacred) and therefore off-limits for a plunge.

The Drive » From the Pupū Springs turn-off on SH60, it's another 11km, predominantly rural drive to the Mussel Inn at Onekaka, albeit with glimpses of ocean seaward and bush-clad hills inland.

TRIP HIGHLIGHT
8 Mussel Inn

One of the country's most beloved brewery-taverns can be found sitting largely alone amid farmland, halfway between Takaka and Collingwood. The **Mussel Inn** (☎03-525 9241; www.musselinn.co.nz; 1259 SH60, Onekaka; all-day snacks $5-17, dinner $13-30; ⊙11am-late, closed Jul-Aug) is rustic

NZ at its most genuine, complete with creaking timbers, a rambling beer garden with a brazier, and hearty, homemade food. Try the signature 'Captain Cooker', a brown beer brewed naturally with manuka.

If you can, coincide your visit with one of its immensely entertaining, regular live-music or open-poetry nights. The Mussel Inn is a firm favourite with touring musos, so don't be surprised if you see one of NZ's best or up-and-coming acts playing here. Also be prepared for the possibility of dancing on tables and other sundry merry-making.

🛏 p193

The Drive » Should you exercise self control at the Mussel Inn, drive north on SH60, passing the turn-off for Tukurua after 3km. Around halfway to Collingwood (12km) you will pass the pretty Parapara Inlet, while grand mountains vistas open up to the southwest as you look up the Aorere River valley.

9 Collingwood

Far-flung Collingwood (population 240) is the last town in Golden Bay and exudes a real end-of-the-line vibe. It's also the bay's oldest town, and boomed so big during the late 1850s' gold rushes that a few folk suggested it become the nation's capital.

Such stories are retold in the town's twin historical repositories, on the main street. **Collingwood Museum** (Tasman St, Collingwood; admission by donation; ⊙9am-6pm) fills a tiny, unstaffed corridor with an idiosyncratic collection of saddlery, Māori artefacts, moa bones, shells and old typewriters, while the adjacent **Aorere Centre** has an on-rotation slide show featuring the works of the wonderful pioneer photographer, Fred Tyree.

No visit to Collingwood would be complete without poking your nose into **Rosy Glow** (54 Beach Rd, Collingwood; chocolates $3-10; ⊙10am-5pm Sat-Thu). Chocoholics will go nuts for handmade confections produced with love, and displayed like jewels in glass cabinets.

🛏 p193

The Drive » From Collingwood, SH60 follows the coast north for most of the 24km to Puponga Farm visitor centre at the base of Farewell Spit. On the way, you'll pass the pretty village of Pakawau, sited handsomely on a long and oft-deserted beach.

TRIP HIGHLIGHT
10 Farewell Spit

Bleak, exposed and positively sci-fi, Farewell Spit is a wetland of international importance and a renowned bird sanctuary – the summer home of thousands of

THE GREAT TASTE TRAIL

In a stroke of genius inspired by great weather and easy topography, the Tasman region has developed one of New Zealand's most popular cycle trails. Why is it so popular? Because no other is so frequently punctuated by stops for food, wine, craft beer and art, as it passes through a range of landscapes from bucolic countryside to estuary boardwalk.

The **Great Taste Trail** (www.heartofbiking.org.nz) stretches 174km from Nelson to Kaiteriteri, with plans afoot to propel it further inland. While it can be ridden in full over a few days, staying in accommodation en route, it lends itself even better to day trips tailored to suit various interests and levels of ability.

Nelson, Mapua and Motueka are all good places to set off from, with numerous bike tour companies offering freedom hire, maps and advice. Highlights include wine touring around the Waimea area, Rabbit Island's easy forest trails, and the particularly scenic section from Motueka to Kaiteriteri traversing a fun mountain-bike park along the way.

migratory waders, notably the godwit (which flies all the way from the Arctic tundra), Caspian tern and Australasian gannet. Walkers can explore the first 4km of the spit via a network of tracks (see DOC's *Farewell Spit & Puponga Farm Park* brochure; www.doc.govt.nz).

Beyond that, point access is limited to trips with the brilliant **Farewell Spit Eco Tours** (📞0800 808 257, 03-524 8257; www.farewellspit.com; 6 Tasman St, Collingwood; tours $125-165), scheduled according to the tide. Operating for more than 70 years and led by passionate local guides, this company runs memorable tours ranging from two to 6½ hours. Depart-

ing from Collingwood, tours take in the spit, the lighthouse, and up to 20 species of bird. The spit's 35km beach features colossal, crescent-shaped dunes, from where panoramic views extend across Golden Bay and a vast low-tide salt marsh. Expect ripping yarns aplenty.

The Drive » From Puponga Farm, it's 7km along the unsealed Whariki Rd to the Whariki Beach car park.

- - - - - - - - - - - -

🕚 Whariki Beach

The 20-minute walk across undulating farmland is a welcome build-up to the grand reveal of one of NZ's most windswept and interest-

ing beaches. Desolate Whariki Beach is quite the introduction to the wild West Coast, with mighty dune formations, looming rock islets just offshore and a seal colony at its eastern end (keep an eye out for seals in the stream on the walk here). As inviting as a swim may seem, just forget it. There are strong undertows here, and what the sea wants, the sea shall have...

For a different perspective, befitting of the area's frontier feel, saddle up with **Cape Farewell Horse Treks** (📞03-524 8031; www.horsetreksnz.com; McGowan St, Puponga; treks from $80) for its three-hour trip taking in the beach and farmland.

Eating & Sleeping

Nelson ❶

✖ Urban Oyster   Modern NZ $$

(☎03-546 7861; www.urbaneatery.co.nz; 278
Hardy St; dishes $13-27; ⏰4pm-late Mon,
11am-late Tue-Sat) Slurp oysters from the shell,
or revitalise with sashimi and ceviche, then sate
your cravings with street-food dishes such as
Korean fried chicken, or popcorn prawn tacos
and a side of devilish poutine chips. Black
butchery tiles, edgy artwork and fine drinks
bolster this metropolitan experience.

🛏 Te Maunga House   B&B $$

(☎03-548 8605; www.
nelsoncityaccommodation.co.nz; 15 Dorothy
Annie Way; s $90, d $125-145; 🛜) Aptly named
('the mountain'), this grand old family home
has exceptional views and a well-travelled host.
Two doubles and a twin have a homely feel with
comfy beds and their own bathrooms. Your
hearty breakfast can be walked off up and down
that hill, a 10-minute climb with an extra five
minutes to town. Closed May to October.

For more places to eat and stay in Nelson see
p183.

Motueka ❸

🛏 Eden's Edge Lodge   Hostel $

(☎03-528 4242; www.edensedge.co.nz; 137
Lodder Lane, Riwaka; sites from $18, dm $31,
d/tr with bathroom $99/86; 🛜) Surrounded
by farmland, 4km from the bustle of Motueka,
this purpose-built lodge comes pretty close to
backpacker heaven. Well-designed facilities
include a gleaming kitchen and inviting
communal areas including a grassy garden.
There's bike hire for tackling the Great Taste
Trail, but it's also within walking distance of
beer, ice cream and coffee.

For more places to eat and stay in Motueka see
p183.

Marahau ❺

✖ Fat Tui   Burgers $

(cnr Marahau-Sandy Bay & Marahau Valley Rds;
burgers $13-18; ⏰noon-8pm daily summer,
Wed-Sun winter) Everyone's heard about this
place, based in a caravan that ain't rollin'
anywhere fast. Thank goodness. Superlative
burgers, such as the Cowpat (beef), the Ewe
Beaut (lamb) and Roots, Shoots & Leaves
(vege). Fish and chips, and coffee, too.

🛏 Abel Tasman Marahau
Lodge   Motel $$

(☎03-527 8250; www.abeltasmanlodge.
co.nz; 295 Sandy Bay-Marahau Rd; d $145-
175, q $200-260; @🛜) There are 15 studios
and self-contained units with groovy styling
and cathedral ceilings, opening out on to
landscaped gardens. There's also a fully
equipped communal kitchen, plus spa and
sauna. Cuckoos, tui and bellbirds squawk and
warble in the bushy surrounds.

Tukurua

🛏 Adrift   Cottage $$$

(☎03-525 8353; www.adrift.co.nz; 53 Tukurua
Rd, Tukurua; d $250-540; 🛜) Adrift on a
heavenly bed of beachside bliss is what you'll
be in one of these five cottages dotted within
beautifully landscaped grounds, right on the
beach. Tuck into your breakfast hamper, then
self-cater in the fully equipped kitchen, dine on
the sunny deck, or soak in the spa bath.

Collingwood ❾

🛏 Innlet Backpackers &
Cottages   Hostel $

(☎03-524 8040, 027 970 8397; www.theinnlet.
co.nz; 839 Collingwood-Puponga Rd, Pakawau;
dm/d $34/80, cabins from $90; ⏰closed
Jun-Aug; 🛜) This charmer is 10km from
Collingwood on the way to Farewell Spit. The
main house has elegant backpacker rooms,
and there are self-contained options including
a cottage sleeping six; campers can enquire
about sites.

193

Going West: from Picton to Westport

14

Head for the South Island's West Coast via two distinct valleys – the wide, sun-drenched Wairau and the serpentine Buller Gorge.

TRIP HIGHLIGHTS

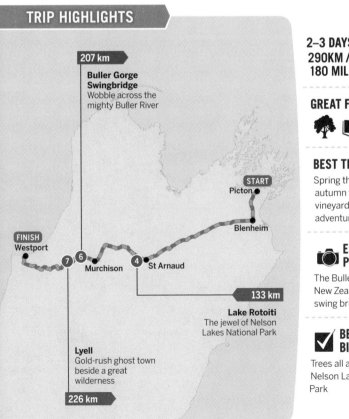

207 km

Buller Gorge Swingbridge
Wobble across the mighty Buller River

START
Picton

Blenheim

FINISH
Westport

7 6

Murchison

4 St Arnaud

133 km

Lake Rotoiti
The jewel of Nelson Lakes National Park

Lyell
Gold-rush ghost town beside a great wilderness

226 km

2–3 DAYS
290KM /
180 MILES

GREAT FOR...

BEST TIME TO GO

Spring through autumn for leafy vineyards and alpine adventures

ESSENTIAL PHOTO

The Buller Gorge from New Zealand's longest swing bridge

BEST FOR BIRD LIFE

Trees all a-twitter in Nelson Lakes National Park

Going West: from Picton to Westport

This coast-to-coaster is a journey of contrasts. The dry Wairau Valley – its lower plains lined with grapevines and the upper valley blanketed in golden meadows – looks like a different planet compared to the lush, forested mountain country surrounding the Buller Gorge. Between the two, Nelson Lakes National Park is reason enough to travel this route, but wineries and pioneer history should clinch the deal.

① Picton

Sitting prettily at the head of Queen Charlotte Sound, the ferry port of Picton was first settled by Māori who collected *kaimoana* (seafood) in the area. Once Captain James Cook found the place, whalers and sealers soon followed.

Dial back to such salty old stories at the **Edwin Fox Maritime Museum** (www.edwinfoxsociety.co.nz; Dunbar Wharf; adult/child $15/5; ◷9am-5pm), home to purportedly the world's ninth-oldest

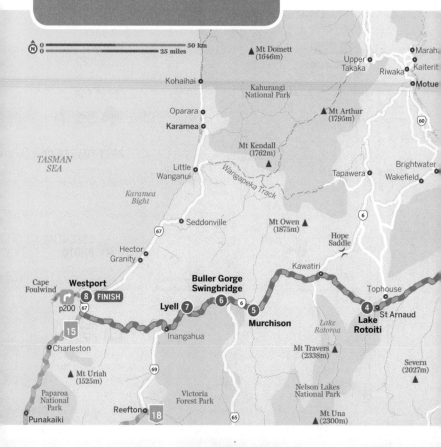

surviving wooden ship. Built near Calcutta and launched in 1853, the *Edwin Fox* carried troops to the Crimean War, convicts to Australia and immigrants to New Zealand. Here she is displayed in dry dock alongside the museum, which houses related maritime exhibits.

✕ 🛏 p201

The Drive » Following SH1, it's a quick 28km zip to Blenheim through the Tuamarina Valley and Para Wetlands, into the broad Wairau Valley.

➋ Blenheim

Workaday Blenheim is majorly preoccupied servicing the 170-odd wineries that carpet most of the Wairau Plains between the Wither Hills and Richmond Ranges.

In a town as flat as a pancake, 11-sq-km **Wither Hills Farm Park** provides rare views. Around 60km of walking and mountain-biking trails survey the Wairau Valley and Cloudy Bay. Signposts on Redwood St and Taylor Pass Rd lead to two of several entrances, where there are toilets and ample parking. A rewarding 6km loop starts at Redwood St and follows Sutherland Stream up to Covenant Loop Track, which takes in the summit of Mt Vernon (422m).

The Drive » Drive west on SH6 for 13km to reach Renwick, passing Marlborough Airport sandwiched between endless rows of vines.

➌ Renwick

This small town occupies an enviable position at the centre of Marlborough's wine-touring area, surrounded by more than 20 cellar doors. A satisfying way to explore it is on two wheels; hire a bike from Bike2Wine (p182) and follow the roadside paths and back roads among the vines. Pick up a copy of the *Marlborough Wine Trail* map

LINK YOUR TRIP

15 The West Coast Road

Westport is the starting gate for the classic journey down the wild West Coast.

18 Two Passes

From Westport, head south for 102km to Greymouth for the scenic circuit over Arthur's and Lewis passes.

Tasman Bay

Marlborough Sounds

Rai Valley ●

● **Nelson** ⑥ Havelock

● Stoke

Richmond

Waikawa ●

● Picton
START

Mt Richmond Forest Park

Peloru's River

⑥

①

Wairau River

Cloudy Bay

➌ ⑥ ➋ **Blenheim**
Renwick

㊿

Seddon ●

Awatere River

Grassmere ● Cape Campbell

Ward ●

Tapuae-o-Uenuku (2885m) ▲

Molesworth-Acheron Rd (seasonal)

Clarence River

Kekerengu ●

Molesworth Station Homestead ●

St Bernard ▲ (2256m)

197

(www.wine-marlborough. co.nz) to avoid getting lost.

If you're short on time, the Vines Village (p168), 5km north of Renwick, is a good one-stop shop, with Whitehaven's cellar door, boutique shopping and a decent cafe all within its ambit.

✗ ⊨ p201

The Drive » SH63 follows the Wairau Valley 92km up to St Arnaud (for Lake Rotoiti) through scenic wine country and sheepy upper reaches. Drive time is around 1¼ hours.

TRIP HIGHLIGHT

④ Lake Rotoiti

Nelson Lakes National Park, as the name suggests, is dominated by bodies of water, in particular its two main lakes – Rotoiti and Rotoroa. It's also a mountainous and forested haven for bird life and hikers. Near Rotoiti's northern shore, the small village of **St Arnaud** is home to the helpful DOC Visitor Centre (p181), a smattering of locals, and warm hospitality at the long-standing lodge.

The park has plenty of hardcore country, but you don't have to go far to survey its splendours. From Kerr Bay, just 500m from the village, take the easy **Bellbird** and **Honeydew Walks** through lakeside beech forest. You'll likely hear the sweet song of tui and

bellbirds and enjoy the attentions of inquisitive fantails and tomtits – the fruits of local conservationists' labours.

While at Kerr Bay, snap a photograph from the jetty – the classic Nelson Lakes shot. Below it, slithering eels will soon scarper should you brave a leap into the drink. The sandflies, however, won't be so kind.

✗ ⊨ p201

The Drive » Follow SH63 down the bushy upper Buller River valley to Kawatiri, 25km from St Arnaud. Turn left onto SH6 and follow it 45km to Murchison, situated on the Four Rivers Plain.

⑤ Murchison

Murchison is a mecca for trout anglers and whitewater addicts who converge on the area's many waterways, including the Buller, which runs alongside the town.

It's a small and quiet place, frequented by passing travellers since the 19th century. Its landmark moment of recent times was the 1929 earthquake (magnitude 7.8), which rocked the town and triggered landslides that left Murchison stranded for several months. This and other local tales are recounted in the old-fashioned **Murchison Museum** (60 Fairfax St; admission by donation; ⊙10am-4pm). The butchery a few doors

down sells properly cured bacon and local honey.

⊨ p201

The Drive » SH6 heads west through farmland before the valley walls close in. At the SH65 junction, around 11km along, continue right on SH6; Buller Gorge Swingbridge is another 4km on.

Westport Cape Foulwind

TRIP HIGHLIGHT

6 Buller Gorge Swingbridge

Here's an opportunity to put some splash and dash into your drive, starting with a wobble across the **Buller Gorge Swingbridge** (☎0800 285 537; www.bullergorge.co.nz; SH6; bridge crossing adult/ child $10/5; ⏱8am-7pm Dec-Apr, 9am-5.30pm May-Nov), NZ's longest at 110m. On the other side are short walkways around **White Creek Faultline**, epicentre of the 1929 earthquake. There's also the jetty for **Buller Canyon Jet** (☎03-523 9883; www.buller-canyonjet.co.nz; SH6; adult/ child $105/60; ⏱Sep-Apr), one of NZ's most scenic and best-value jetboat trips – 40 minutes of zipping and spinning along the beautiful river. The ultimate return trip across the river is via the flying fox, either seated (adult/child $30/15) or 'Supaman' style ($60). Whoo-hoo!

The Drive >> SH6 continues down the bushy Upper Buller Gorge for 19km to the Lyell historic reserve.

DETOUR: CAPE FOULWIND

Start: 8 Westport

Accessed from SH67A, 14km from Westport, you'll find Omau and the start of the **Cape Foulwind Walkway** (www.doc.govt.nz), a wonderful 1½-hour-return amble traversing coastal hills between Omau and Tauranga Bay. Towards the southern end is the seal colony where – depending on the season – up to 200 kekeno (NZ fur seals) loll about on the rocks. Tauranga Bay (4km by road from the Omau car park) is popular with surfers who dodge its rocky edges.

Dutch explorer Abel Tasman was the first European to sight the cape, in 1642, naming it Clyppygen Hoek (Rocky Point). However, it was re-christened by James Cook in 1770, who clearly found it less than pleasing. If you visit on a bad day, the name change will make perfect sense.

TRIP HIGHLIGHT

7 Lyell

The once-bustling gold-rush town of Lyell has long gone, but the historic reserve in its place is a popular camping and rest stop. A short walk through beech forest takes you to overgrown **Lyell Cemetery** – a magical place of rest.

Lyell is also the start of one of NZ's gnarliest new backcountry trails, the 85km **Old Ghost Road** (www.oldghostroad.org.nz), which follows a miners' track that was started in the 1870s but never completed as the gold rush petered out. It takes three to five days to walk or cycle its full length, but an easy, two-hour return walk still provides plenty of interest, including rusty relics of the remote gold-mining settlements Gibbstown and Zalatown.

The Drive » Head west on SH6, which crosses the Buller via an impressive old iron bridge after 3km. Ignore the Reefton turn-off (SH69), and soak up the splendid scenery of the Lower Buller Gorge. At the SH67 junction, 57km from Lyell, turn right towards Westport, 7km away.

8 Westport

Westport is the gateway to Karamea and the rest of the northern coast's less-visited, totally underrated reaches. The town itself is lined with low-rise heritage buildings. There's also an atmospheric old wharf ripe for redevelopment, and **Coaltown Museum** (www.coaltown.co.nz; 123 Palmerston St; ⊙9am-5pm Mon-Fri, 10am-4pm Sat & Sun; adult/child $10/2), a modern affair that should stoke your interest for a couple of hours.

North Beach is a great place for a stroll; start at the Buller River mouth and walk to the end of the massive breakwater. If there's a big swell, keep an eye out for local fishing boats trying to cross the treacherous bar, battling menacing, rolling waves. Walk north along the driftwood-strewn beach to peaceful **Orowaiti Lagoon**. Bird life here includes herons, ducks and dotterel, joined in spring and summer by one of the great distance aviators, the bar-tailed godwit.

✕ ⊨ p218

Eating & Sleeping

Picton ❶

✖ Café Cortado
Cafe $$

(www.cortado.co.nz; cnr High St & London Quay; mains $16-34; ⏰8am-late) A pleasant corner cafe and bar with sneaky views of the harbour through the foreshore's pohutukawa and palms. This consistent performer turns out fish dishes, homemade cheeseburgers and decent pizza.

🛏 Harbour View Motel
Motel $$

(📞03-573 6259, 0800 101 133; www.harbourviewpicton.co.nz; 30 Waikawa Rd; d $145-185; 🛜) Its elevated position means this motel commands good views of Picton's mast-filled harbour from its smart, self-contained studios with timber decks.

For more places to eat and sleep in Picton see pages 171 and 183.

Blenheim ❷

For places to eat and sleep in Blenheim see pages 171 and 183.

Renwick ❸

✖ Arbour
Modern NZ $$$

(📞03-572 7989; www.arbour.co.nz; 36 Godfrey Rd, Renwick; mains $31-38; ⏰3pm-late Tue-Sat year-round, 6pm-late Mon Jan-Mar; 🖍) Located in the thick of Renwick wine country, this elegant restaurant offers 'a taste of Marlborough' by focusing on local produce fashioned into contemporary yet crowd-pleasing dishes. Settle in for a three-, four- or multiple-course à la carte offering ($73/85/98), or an end-of-the-day nibble and glass or two from the mesmerising wine list.

🛏 Olde Mill House
B&B $$

(📞03-572 8458; www.oldemillhouse.co.nz; 9 Wilson St, Renwick; d $160; 🛜) On an elevated section in otherwise flat Renwick, this charming old house is a treat. Dyed-in-the-wool local hosts run a welcoming B&B, with stately decor, and home-grown fruit and homemade goodies for breakfast. Free bikes, an outdoor spa and

gardens make this a tip-top choice in the heart of the wine country.

St Arnaud (Lake Rotoiti) ❹

🛏 Alpine Lodge
Lodge $$

(📞03-521 1869; www.alpinelodge.co.nz; Main Rd, St Arnaud; d $155-210; @🛜) Family owned and a consistent performer, this large lodge complex offers a range of accommodation, the pick of which are the split-level doubles with mezzanine bedroom and spa. If nothing else, go for the inviting in-house restaurant – a snug affair sporting an open fire, mountain views, good food (meals $10 to $32; takeaway pizza $20) and local beer.

Murchison ❺

🛏 Kiwi Park Motels & Holiday Park
Motel $

(📞0800 228 080, 03-523 9248; www.kiwipark.co.nz; 170 Fairfax St; sites unpowered/powered from $20/25, cabins $65-85, motels $140-225; @🛜) This leafy park on the edge of town has plenty of accommodation options, from a campervan and tent area graced with mature trees, through to basic cabins, and roomy motel units nestled among the blooms. Cheery hosts and a menagerie of friendly farm animals make this one happy family.

Westport ❽

🛏 Carters Beach Top 10 Holiday Park
Holiday Park, Motel $

(📞03-789 8002, 050 893 7876; www.top10westport.co.nz; 57 Marine Pde, Carters Beach; sites from $38, units $70-205; @🛜) Right on Carters Beach and conveniently located 4km from Westport and 12km to Tauranga Bay, this tidy complex has pleasant sites as well as comfortable cabins and motel units. It's a good option for tourers seeking a peaceful stop-off, and perhaps even a swim.

For more places to eat and stay in Westport see p218.

Canterbury & the West Coast Trips

SOME OF NEW ZEALAND'S FINEST ROAD TRIPS ARE FOUND IN THESE CONTRASTING REGIONS, lying astride the Southern Alps.

Most start in Christchurch, the country's second-largest city, still recovering from devastating earthquakes but inspiring with its attitude and spirit. South Island highlights lie in all directions, from bay-lined Banks Peninsula to wineries, hot springs, and tussocky high-country across the plains. NZ's highest peak, Aoraki/Mt Cook, stands sentinel in the south. Alpine passes lead to the wilderness West Coast. Its long, often winding highway is loaded with end-of-the-road vibe, even around hotspots such as Punakaiki and the glaciers, Franz Josef and Fox.

Aoraki/Mt Cook National Park Mt Cook reflected in Hooker Lake (Trips 19, 20 & 21)
MATTEO COLOMBO / GETTY IMAGES ©

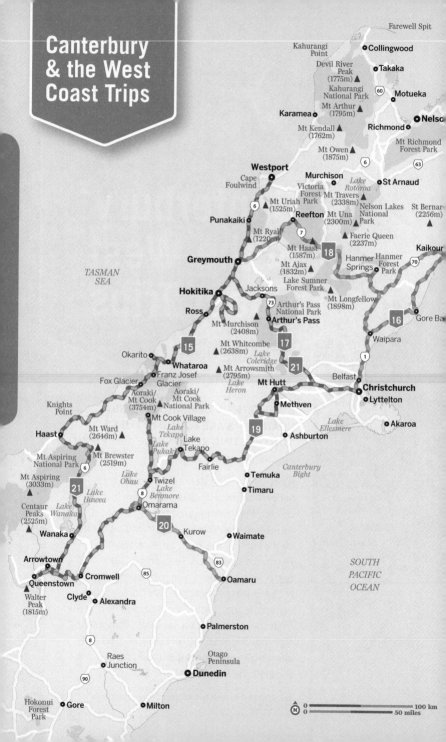

Canterbury & the West Coast Trips

Farewell Spit

Kahurangi Point

Collingwood

Devil River Peak
(1775m) ▲

Takaka

Kahurangi
National Park

60

Motueka

Mt Arthur
(1795m) ▲

Karamea

Mt Kendall
(1762m)

Richmond

Nels○

Mt Richmond
Forest Park

Mt Owen
(1875m) ▲

6

63

Westport

Cape
Foulwind

6

Murchison

Victoria
Forest
Park

Lake
Rotoroa

St Arnaud

Mt Travers
(2338m) ▲

St Bernar
(2256m) ▲

Mt Uriah
(1525m) ▲

Reefton

Nelson Lakes
National
Park

Punakaiki

7

Mt Una
(2300m) ▲

Mt Ryall
(1220m) ▲

▲ Faerie Queen
(2237m)

18

Greymouth

Mt Haast
(1587m) ▲

Hanmer
Springs

Hanmer
Forest
Park

Kaikour

70

Mt Ajax
(1832m) ▲

Hokitika

Jacksons

Lake Sumner
Forest Park

*TASMAN
SEA*

Ross

73

Arthur's Pass
National Park

Mt Longfellow
(1898m) ▲

16

Gore Ba

Waipara

15

Mt Murchison
(2408m) ▲

Arthur's Pass

17

Mt Whitcombe
(2638m) ▲

*Lake
Coleridge*

21

Belfast

1

Okarito

Whataroa

Franz Josef
Glacier

Mt Arrowsmith
(2795m) ▲

*Lake
Heron*

Mt Hutt

Christchurch

Lyttelton

Fox Glacier

Aoraki/
Mt Cook
(3754m) ▲

Aoraki/
Mt Cook
National Park

Methven

19

Akaroa

Knights
Point

Mt Cook Village

*Lake
Tekapo*

*Lake
Ellesmere*

Haast

Mt Ward
(2646m) ▲

*Lake
Pukaki*

Lake
Tekapo

Ashburton

*Canterbury
Bight*

Mt Aspiring
National Park

Mt Brewster
(2519m) ▲

6

*Lake
Ohau*

Fairlie

Temuka

Mt Aspiring
(3033m) ▲

21

*Lake
Hawea*

Twizel

*Lake
Benmore*

Timaru

Centaur
Peaks
(2525m) ▲

*Lake
Wanaka*

8

Omarama

20

Kurow

Waimate

Wanaka

Arrowtown

Cromwell

85

83

Oamaru

*SOUTH
PACIFIC
OCEAN*

Queenstown

Clyde

Alexandra

Walter
Peak
(1815m) ▲

Palmerston

8

Raes
Junction

*Otago
Peninsula*

90

Dunedin

Hokonui
Forest
Park

Gore

Milton

N

0 ————— 100 km
0 ————— 50 miles

Oparara Basin Moria Gate Arch

Classic Trip
15 **The West Coast Road 6–8 days**
A spectacle of epic wilderness, flinty history and big, blue ocean. (p206)

16 **Alpine Pacific Triangle 3–4 days**
Encounter Kaikoura's marine-life and relax in Hanmer's hot springs. (p220)

17 **Coast to Coast 2–3 days**
Survey the distinct landscapes either side of the mighty Southern Alps. (p228)

18 **Two Passes 4–5 days**
Wilderness scenery, hot springs and historic sites along Arthur's and Lewis Passes. (p236)

Classic Trip
19 **Inland Scenic Route 4–6 days**
Survey NZ's highest mountain, golden highlands, surreal blue lakes and bucolic countryside. (p246)

20 **Alps to Ocean 3–4 days**
Big skies and ever-changing, colourful landscapes from mountain high to valley low. (p262)

Classic Trip
21 **Southern Alps Circuit 12–14 days**
A seriously grand tour taking in sublime scenery and stacks of sights. (p270)

 DON'T MISS

Oparara Basin
Discover a hidden wonderland where ancient forest conceals limestone arches on Trip 15

Lake Kaniere
Go jump in the lake then dry off and warm up again on a rainforest walk on Trips 15 21

Ship Creek
Combine rainforest wilderness class 101 with sublime beach scenery on Trips 15 21

Lake Ohau
Venture into a remote, glacier-carved valley filled with wild waters and surrounded by rocky ranges on Trip 20

Akaroa Summit Rd
Get a bird's-eye view winding around the crater rim of an ancient volcano on Trip 26

Classic Trip

The West Coast Road

15

Running the length of New Zealand's longest and least populated region, the West Coast road reveals spectacular natural landscapes and flinty pioneer history alongside eyefuls of big, blue ocean.

TRIP HIGHLIGHTS

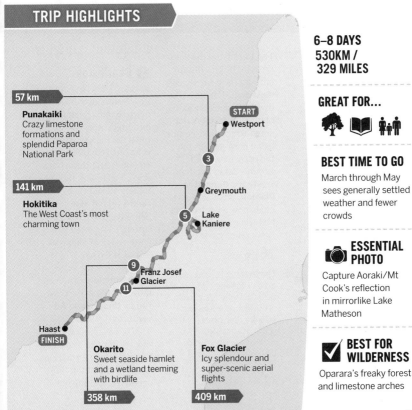

57 km

Punakaiki
Crazy limestone formations and splendid Paparoa National Park

141 km

Hokitika
The West Coast's most charming town

START
● Westport

● Greymouth

● Lake Kaniere

9 ● Franz Josef Glacier

11

Haast ●
FINISH

Okarito
Sweet seaside hamlet and a wetland teeming with birdlife
358 km

Fox Glacier
Icy splendour and super-scenic aerial flights
409 km

6–8 DAYS
530KM /
329 MILES

GREAT FOR...

BEST TIME TO GO

March through May sees generally settled weather and fewer crowds

📷 ESSENTIAL PHOTO

Capture Aoraki/Mt Cook's reflection in mirrorlike Lake Matheson

✓ BEST FOR WILDERNESS

Oparara's freaky forest and limestone arches

15 The West Coast Road

A serious contender for NZ's most scenic road trip, the end-to-end journey along the West Coast offers deep immersion in the rich wilderness that covers 90% of the region. Nature is interrupted by a series of rustic old gold- and coal-mining towns, dotting the highway and nestling into nooks in the mountain ranges. Along the way, the wild Tasman Sea beats an ever-present rhythm.

❶ Westport

Flinty Westport typifies the towns of the West Coast, its fortunes waxing and waning on the output of its mines. The coal that has kept it stoked up for much of its existence is on the way out, but it leaves behind a legacy of low-rise heritage buildings, an old wharf precinct ripe for rejuvenation, and myriad industrial curios both in town and beyond. Lovers of gritty history will dig Westport.

A good introduction to the area's life and times is the Coaltown Museum (p200), a thoroughly modern affair with well-composed yarns and evocative photographs.

The Denniston displays are a highlight, illuminating one of the Coast's most beguiling ghost towns, famous for its fantastically steep 'incline', down which hurtled fully laden coal wagons and the occasional coffin. Around 25km north of Westport, **Denniston Plateau** (www.doc.govt. nz) is now a captivating historic reserve with rusty relics galore.

❌ 🛏 p218

The Drive » Heading south along SH6, swing into Mitchell's Gully Gold Mine, 22km south of Westport, to meet a gold pioneer's descendants and the odd trapdoor spider, before continuing another 5km to the unassuming village of Charleston.

❷ Charleston

It's hard to believe that Charleston, now little more than a clutch of buildings, was a boom town during the 1860s gold rush, complete with 80 hotels and three breweries. The town's thirsty miners staked their claims inland along the Nile River, which wends through a forested valley on the edge of Paparoa National Park.

Nowadays the valley is the setting for trips deep into the Nile River Caves, run by **Underworld Adventures** (☎03-788 8168, 0800 116 686; www.caverafting.com; SH6, Charleston). The limestone formations set the imagination into overdrive, making out

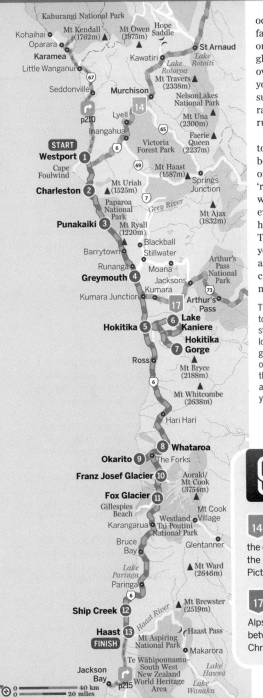

odd creatures, strange faces, angel wings and organ pipes. A galaxy of glow-worms twinkles overhead as you make your way towards the subterranean river, then raft towards the exit on a rubber tyre.

The cave rafting tour ($175, four hours) begins with a fun ride on the narrow gauge 'rainforest railway' – it's worth a trip in itself, even if you don't fancy heading underground. The caving crew will give you the full low-down at their adventure-base-cum-cafe on Charleston's main road.

The Drive » The 30km to Punakaiki is packed with staggering panoramas of lowland pakihi scrub and lush green forest alongside a series of bays dramatically sculpted by the ocean's relentless fury. Drive as slowly as the traffic behind you will allow.

LINK YOUR TRIP

14 **Going West**
Westport bookends the cross-island journey to the inter-island ferry port of Picton.

17 **Coast to Coast**
Cross the Southern Alps through Arthur's Pass between Greymouth to Christchurch.

- - - - - - - - - -
TRIP HIGHLIGHT

❸ Punakaiki

A small settlement beside the rugged **Paparoa National Park** (www.doc.govt.nz), Punakaiki has a claim to fame in **Dolomite Point**, where a layering-weathering process called stylobedding has carved the limestone into what looks like piles of pancakes (hence its nickname **Pancake Rocks**).

The thoughtfully landscaped walkway that meanders around the point affords various views of the rocks as well as epic ocean lookouts, but the X-factor relies entirely on time and tide. If possible, visit at high tide on a big sea, when the waves surge into caverns and boom menacingly through blowholes. Even better, aim for a high tide at sunset, when the pancakes turn mellow yellow and the fluttering flax flickers with light.

🛏 p218

The Drive ›› Part of the aptly named Great Coast Rd, the 45km stretch between Punakaiki and Greymouth is flanked by white-capped waves and rocky bays on one side and the steep, bushy ranges of Paparoa National Park on the other.

- - - - - - - - - -

❹ Greymouth

Welcome to the West Coast's 'Big Smoke', crouched at the mouth of the imaginatively named

---

DETOUR: OPARARA BASIN

Start: ❶ Westport

Heading north of Westport, the 111km stretch of highway to the end of the line at Kohaihai is much less travelled than the southerly route. But skip it and you miss a stack of spectacular sights including one of the West Coast's true gems, **Oparara Basin**. To quote a local: 'If this were anywhere else, there'd be hordes streaming in.' Too true.

Lying within Kahurangi National Park, this is a natural spectacle of the highest order – a remote valley concealing limestone arches and strange caves within a dense forest of massive, moss-laden trees that tower over Dr Seuss–esque undergrowth in every imaginable hue of green.

The valley's signature sight is the 200m-long, 37m-high **Oparara Arch**, spanning the picturesque Oparara River – home to the endangered, super-cute blue duck (whio) – reached on an easy, 45-minute walk. The smaller but no less stunning **Moria Gate Arch** (43m long, 19m high) is reached via a divine forest loop walk (1½ hours).

Just a 10-minute walk from the second car park are the Crazy Paving and Box Canyon Caves. Take your torch to enter a world of weird subterranean forms and rare, leggy spiders. Spiders, caves, darkness…sound like fun?

Beyond this point are the superb **Honeycomb Hill Caves and Arch**, accessible only on guided tours (three-/five-/eight-hour tours $95/150/240) run by the **Karamea Information & Resource Centre** (☏03-782 6652; www.karameainfo.co.nz; Market Cross; ◷9am-5pm Mon-Fri, 10am-1pm Sat & Sun, shorter hours May-Dec).

From Karamea, the Coast's northernmost settlement, it's 10km to the Oparara turn-off at McCallum's Mill Rd, and another 14km into the basin itself.

Grey River and known to Māori as Mawhera.

This is a town with hidden charms, some so well hidden that you may question their very existence. But by the time you've checked out the unpretentious town centre, wandered along the Floodwall Walk, and followed the river to its mouth at the wild break-water where waves come crashing in, you might *just* find yourself bitten by the Greymouth bug.

The town is actually home to one of the Coast's biggest tourist attractions, **Shantytown** (www.shantytown.co.nz; Rutherglen Rd, Paroa; adult/child/family $33/16/78; ⏰8.30am-5pm), a recreated pioneer village assembled from an array of original gold rush buildings. It offers a pretty good history lesson on the Coast's early settlement, enhanced with sweeteners such as gold-panning, steam-train rides, holographic movies and period-costume photo shoots in the old saloon. The squeamish may wish to skip the iron lung and other gory hospital exhibits.

✗ 🛏 p218

The Drive » The 39km drive to Hokitika hugs the coastline most of the way, passing the turn-off to Arthur's Pass around the halfway point, at Kumara Junction. Keep trucking south on SH6.

TRIP HIGHLIGHT

⑤ Hokitika

The setting for numerous NZ novels – including 2013 Man Booker award-winner *The Luminaries* by Eleanor Catton – Hokitika is yet another West Coast town founded on gold. Today it is the stronghold of indigenous *pounamu* (greenstone). Master carvers jostle for position alongside jewellers, glass-blowers and various craftspeople, making Hokitika a mecca for art lovers.

The town also boasts some admirable historic buildings, including the 1908 Carnegie Building housing **Hokitika Museum** (www.hokitika museum.co.nz; 17 Hamilton St; adult/child $6/3; 10am-5pm Nov-Mar, 10am-2pm Apr-Oct). An exemplary provincial repository – and easily the best on the Coast – it has intelligently curated and wide-ranging displays covering such topics as Māori and their use of *pounamu*, the gold-rush era, and the region's natural and social history.

Five minutes' walk from the town centre is **Sunset Point**. A spectacular vantage point at any time of day, this is – as the name suggests – the primo place to watch the light fade. Surfers, seagulls, drifting sands and fish and chips: *this* is NZ.

✗ 🛏 p218

The Drive » From central Hokitika, drive inland on Stafford St, then follow signs to Lake Kaniere Scenic Reserve, 20km away.

⑥ Lake Kaniere

At the foot of Mt Tuhua, and surrounded by classic West Coast rainforest, **Lake Kaniere** (www.doc.govt.nz) is a tranquil place even in high season. The reserve's hub is grassy **Hans Bay** where there are campsites, toilets and a jetty to jump off should you wish to avoid the tortuous tiptoe in. There are also numerous bush walks including a half-hour return amble to Canoe Cove and the two-minute zip to Dorothy Falls.

The Drive » Continue clockwise around the lake and then head back towards the coast on a gravel road to the small settlement of Kokatahi. From there zigzag on rural back roads signposted for the Hokitika Gorge. Total driving distance is 37km.

⑦ Hokitika Gorge

Through this ravishing granite ravine flow unbelievably turquoise waters, tinted by glacial 'flour'. The surreal scene can be photographed from various angles via a short forest walkway, complete with swing bridge, and a toe may be tentatively dipped in the drink.

Classic Trip

WHY THIS IS A CLASSIC TRIP
LEE SLATER, WRITER

With conservation land covering around 90% of the West Coast and just 1% of NZ's population living here, it can feel like you've got the whole place to yourself, especially if you deviate from SH6 to discover its hidden surprises. The weather keeps you on your toes and makes every visit unique. Will it rain? Probably. Will Aoraki/Mt Cook reveal itself? Maybe...

Top: Pancake Rocks, Punakaiki
Left: A walk through the rainforest, Ship Creek
Right: Coastline near Greymouth

The Drive » Return to Hokitika via Kaniere–Kowhitirangi Rd, then head south on SH6 where you'll encounter the historic Mananui Tramline, which is definitely worth a wander. The rest of the drive to Whataroa (136km in total) passes a mixture of pasture and forest with teasing glimpses of the snow-capped Southern Alps.

- - - - - - - - - -

⑧ Whataroa

A dot of a town strung out along SH6, Whataroa is the departure point for tours to the **Kotuku Sanctuary**, NZ's only nesting site for the kotuku (white heron), which roosts between November and February.

The only way to visit the nesting site is with **White Heron Sanctuary Tours** (☎0800 523 456, 03-753 4120; www.whiteherontours.co.nz; SH6, Whataroa; adult/child $120/55; ⏱4 tours daily late Aug-Mar) on an enjoyable 2½-hour tour involving a gentle jetboat ride and a short boardwalk to a viewing hide. Observing scores of birds perched in the bushes is a magical experience whether you're a seasoned twitcher or just a general nature lover.

The Drive » Following the highway south for 14km, you'll reach the turn-off to The Forks, which branches west for 10km to Okarito. If it's raining down here in glacier country (and it often is), don't be surprised if the clouds open up as you reach the coast – just one reason we love Okarito.

Classic Trip

TRIP HIGHLIGHT

9 Okarito

The sweet, seaside hamlet of Okarito sits alongside **Okarito Lagoon**, the largest unmodified wetland in NZ and a superb place for spotting birds including rare kiwi and the majestic kotuku.

There are numerous walks to enjoy, from the easy Wetland Walk (20 minutes) to the three-hour Three Mile Pack Track, which includes an invigorating (but tide-dependent) amble along Okarito's wild beach (a superb sunset spot, with the possibility of a beach bonfire).

If you're even remotely into kayaking, a paddle on the lagoon is a must-do. **Okarito Nature Tours** (☎03-753 4014, 0800 652 748; www.okarito.co.nz; kayaking half-/full day $65/75; 📶) will kit you up and recommend a suitable adventure – most commonly a noodle across the lagoon's open waters and up into luxuriant rainforest channels where all sorts of feathered creatures hang out.

A more passive but equally memorable excursion is a bird-spotting boat trip with **Okarito Boat Tours** (☎03-753 4223; www.okaritoboattours.co.nz), the most fruitful of which is the 'early bird'. The later-morning, two-hour 'ecotour' offers a broader insight into this remarkable natural area.

🛏 p219

The Drive » Return to SH6. The 18km stretch of highway south to Franz Josef Glacier winds past pretty Lake Mapourika, where you can stop for an obligatory jetty photo, or even a quick dip, if a sandfly bite on the bum doesn't bother you.

10 Franz Josef Glacier

Franz Josef and its twin glacier, Fox, are the biggest drawcards of **Westland Tai Poutini National Park**. How close you get to either of them will depend on your budget.

In both cases, the cheapest option is also the easiest – an independent walk up the glacier valley to various viewpoints. From the

GLACIERS – THE COLD, HARD FACTS

Franz Josef and Fox Glaciers are peculiar – in no other place at this latitude do glaciers come so close to the ocean. Buzzing above them on an aerial sightseeing tour or walking on the ice, you'll be greeted not just by a snowy, mountainous spectacle, but also by panoramic views of the Tasman Sea and the lush rainforest that cloaks the alpine foothills and lowlands to the west.

The glaciers' existence is largely due to the West Coast's weather systems. A surfeit of snow falls in the glaciers' broad accumulation zones, fuses into clear ice at around 20m deep and begins creeping down the steep valleys.

During the last ice age (15,000 to 20,000 years ago), the twin glaciers reached the sea. In the ensuing thaw they may have crawled back even further than their current positions, but in the 14th century a mini ice age caused them to advance to their greatest modern-era extent around 1750. Terminal moraines from this time are still visible.

Climate change, however, has brought a consistent retreat over recent years, drastically reducing opportunities for viewing these glaciers on foot. Both glacier terminal faces are roped off to prevent people from being caught in icefalls and river surges, and the only way to get close to or on to the ice safely is with a guided tour.

DETOUR: JACKSON BAY ROAD

Start: 13 Haast

In fine weather, this is an intensely scenic journey between the Southern Alps and the wild coast, passing farms settled by some of the hardiest souls the South ever saw. Cemeteries and other heritage sites betray the settlers' wrangles on both land and sea.

Wilderness, however, has always reigned supreme here, as is evident in the vast World Heritage Area that blankets the inland ranges. It's largely impenetrable to all but hardy hunters and super-keen hiking types, but a unique perspective is offered by **Waiatoto River Safaris** (☎03-750 0780, 0800 538 723; www.riversafaris.co.nz; 1975 Haast-Jackson Bay Rd, Hannahs Clearing; adult/child $199/139; ☺trips 10am, 1pm & 4pm). One of NZ's best backcountry jetboat tours, the two-hour trip takes passengers upriver deep into pristine forest, then all the way back down to the salt-misted river mouth. Magical.

Without stops, it's less than an hour to drive the entire 51km from Haast to the fishing village of Jackson Bay, the only natural harbour on the West Coast. With good timing you'll arrive when the **Cray Pot** (fish and chips $17-29; ☺12-4pm, hours may vary) is open. This place is just as much about the dining room (a caravan) and location (looking out over the bay) as it is about the honest seafood, including fish and chips, crayfish, chowder and whitebait.

Walk off your fries on the **Wharekai–Te Kou Walk** (40 minutes return) to Ocean Beach, pounded by waves and lined with interesting rock pools. DOC's *Walks and Activities in the Haast Area* pamphlet details this and other jaunts along Jackson Bay Rd.

---

small but bustling Franz Josef village, it's 5km to the trail car park. From here you can take a 10-minute stroll to **Sentinel Rock**, or **Ka Roimata o Hine Hukatere Track** (1½ hours return), which leads you up the glacier valley to the best view of the terminal face.

If this faraway view doesn't cut the mustard, consider an aerial sightseeing trip with one of the swarm of operators lined up on the village's main road. Alternatively, take a hike on the ice with **Franz Josef Glacier**

Guides (☎0800 484 337, 03-752 0763; www.franzjosef-glacier.com; 63 Cron St). The two-to-three hour tours require a helicopter hop on and off the ice; the easier 'Heli Hike' ($435) combines a 10-minute flight with around two hours on the ice in the glacier's upper reaches.

✗ ⮕ p219

The Drive » The serpentine 23km drive between Franz Josef Glacier and Fox Glacier townships could well be NZ's most scenic half-hour drive. As you near Fox, the valley reveal is the icing on the cake.

TRIP HIGHLIGHT

11 Fox Glacier

Compared to Franz Josef, Fox Glacier village is relatively small and sedate, with a more farmy feel and open aspect. It's glacier viewing options are remarkably similar, namely a scenic flight (with operators lined up in the same fashion along the main road), and a choice of independent or guided walks up into the Fox valley. On-the-ice glacier hikes offered by **Fox Glacier Guiding**

NIRAD J / SHUTTERSTOCK ©

NIRAD J / SHUTTERSTOCK ©

Classic Trip

(www.foxguides.co.nz; ☎03-751 0825, ☎0800 111 600) also require a helicopter trip.

There are, however, another couple of notable natural wonders in Fox Glacier's ambit. From the village it's just 6km down Cook Flat Rd to forest-fringed **Lake Matheson** (www.doc.govt.nz), the famous 'mirror lake' in which the Southern Alps (including Aoraki/Mt Cook) are reflected, when conditions are ideal.

Another 15km further down Cook Flat Rd you will hit the Tasman coast at black-sand **Gillespies Beach** (www.doc.govt. nz). Interesting walks from here include a five-minute zip to the old miners' cemetery, and the 3½-hour return walk to Galway Beach, home to herds of seals.

✗ ☒ p219

The Drive 》 Allow 90-minutes to reach Ship Creek, 103km away along a scenic stretch of highway chopped through lowland forest and occasional pasture, with views inland to sheer-sided valleys, and intermittent but grand views seaward. This section of highway only opened in 1965, as commemorated at Knights Point lookout, 6km beyond Lake Moeraki. Stop there for awesome Tasman Sea views.

⑫ Ship Creek

Ship Creek, 14km north-east of Haast River, is a terrific place to stretch the legs. It boasts two great short walks with fascinating information panels: the Dune Lake Walk, all sand dunes and stunted forest, leading to a surprising view; and the unsurprisingly boggy Kahikatea Swamp Forest Walk, featuring sections of handsome boardwalk.

The Drive 》 This 18km stretch of the SH6 clings to the coast before cutting inland to cross the mighty Haast River on NZ's longest single-lane bridge. Just after it is Haast Junction, the turn-off for Jackson Bay; 3km further along is Haast township from where SH6 leads south to Central Otago via Haast Pass.

Fox Glacier On-the-ice glacier hiking

13 Haast

The Haast region bookends the West Coast road. It's a vast and rich wilderness of kahikatea and rata forests, wetlands, sand dunes, seal and penguin colonies, birdlife and sweeping beaches, all aiding its inclusion in **Te Wāhipounamu–South**

West New Zealand World Heritage Area. There's not a huge amount to see and do in Haast township itself, with the exception of dropping into the Department of Conservation **Visitor Centre** (☎03-750 0809; www.doc.govt.nz; cnr SH6 & Jackson Bay Rd; ◷9am-6pm Nov-Mar, to 4.30pm Apr-Oct)

and having a meal at one of the pubs.

Haast is, however, the gateway to one of NZ's best off-the-beaten-track drives – the dead-end road leading south to Jackson Bay.

 p219

Eating & Sleeping

Westport ❶

✕ PR's Cafe — Cafe $

(☎03-789 7779; 124 Palmerston St, Westport; meals $10-20; ☻7am-4.30pm Mon-Fri, 7am-3pm Sat & Sun; 🛜) Westport's sharpest cafe has a cabinet full of sandwiches and pastries, and a counter groaning under the weight of cakes (Dutch apple, banoffee pie) and cookies. An all-day menu delivers carefully composed meals such as salmon omelette with dill aioli, spanakopita, and fish and chips.

✕ Star Tavern — Pub Food $$

(☎03-789 6923; 6 Lighthouse Rd, Omau; meals $9-30; ☻4pm-late Mon-Fri, noon-late Sat & Sun) A motto of 'arrive as strangers, leave as friends' is backed up at this rural tavern handily positioned near Cape Foulwind. It dishes up generously proportioned grub in its old-fashioned dining room, a warm welcome, a pool table and a jukebox in its unprepossessing public bar, and relaxation in the garden. Proper hospitality, that's what this is.

🛏 Archer House — B&B $$

(☎0800 789 877, 03-789 8778; www.archerhouse.co.nz; 75 Queen St, Westport; d incl breakfast $190; @🛜) This beautiful 1890 heritage home sleeps up to eight in three rooms with private bathrooms, all sharing no fewer than three lounges, plus peaceful gardens. Lovely hosts, complimentary sherry and generous continental breakfast make this Westport's most refined accommodation option.

For more places to stay in Westport see p201.

Punakaiki ❸

🛏 Hydrangea Cottages — Cottage $$

(☎03-731 1839; www.pancake-rocks.co.nz; SH6; d $165-320; 🛜) On a hillside overlooking the Tasman, these six standalone and mostly self-contained cottages (largest sleeping up to six) are built from salvaged timber and stone. It's a classy but relaxed enclave, with splashes of colourful mosaic tile, some outdoor baths, and pretty cottage gardens. The owners also run Punakaiki Horse Treks.

Greymouth ❹

✕ DP1 Cafe — Cafe $

(104 Mawhera Quay; meals $7-23; ☻8am-5pm Mon-Fri, 9am-5pm Sat & Sun; 🛜) A stalwart of the Greymouth cafe scene, this hip joint serves great espresso, along with good-value grub. Groovy tunes, wi-fi, local art and quayside tables make this a welcoming spot to linger. Swing in for the $6 morning muffin and coffee special.

🛏 Ardwyn House — B&B $

(☎03-768 6107; ardwynhouse@hotmail.com; 48 Chapel St; s/d incl breakfast from $65/100; 🛜) This old-fashioned, homey B&B nestles amid steep gardens on a quiet dead-end street. Mary, the well-travelled host, cooks a splendid breakfast.

For more places to eat and stay in Greymouth see p235.

Hokitika ❺

✕ Dulcie's Takeaways — Fish & Chips $

(cnr Gibson Quay & Wharf St; fish & chips $6-12; ☻11am-9pm Tue-Sun) Net yourself some excellent fish and chips (try the turbot or blue cod), then scoff them down the road at Sunset Point for an extra sprinkle of sea salt.

🛏 Teichelmann's B&B — B&B $$$

(☎03-755 8232; www.teichelmanns.co.nz; 20 Hamilton St; d $235-260; 📶) Once home to surgeon, mountaineer and professional beard-cultivator Ebenezer Teichelmann, this old gem is now a charming B&B with amicable hosts. All rooms have an airy, restorative ambience along with their own bathrooms, including the more private Teichy's Cottage in the garden.

For more places to eat and stay in Hokitika see p284.

Okarito ⑨

🛏 Okarito Beach House — Lodge $

(☎03-753 4080; www.okaritobeachhouse.com; The Strand; d & tw $85-105; 📶) The Okarito Beach House has a variety of accommodation. The weathered, self-contained 'Hutel' ($120, sleeping two people) is worth every cent. The Summit Lodge has commanding views and the best dining-room table you've ever seen.

Franz Josef Glacier ⑩

🍴 Alice May — Modern NZ $$

(☎03-752 0740; www.alicemay.co.nz; cnr Cowan & Cron Sts; mains $20-32; ⏱4pm-late) A faux Tudor corner pub with pastoral chic, mellow vibe and family-friendly attitude, Alice May serves up meaty meals with $20 options, including a daily roast, pasta, and venison burger, with sirloin steak and fish at the upper end. Sticky toffee pudding also features, as does happy hour and mountain views from outdoor tables.

🛏 Glenfern Villas — Apartment $$$

(☎0800 453 633, 03-752 0054; www.glenfern. co.nz; SH6; d $217-239; 📶) A desirable 3km from the tourist hubbub, these delightful one- and two-bedroom villas sit amid groomed grounds with private decks surveying mountain scenery. Top-notch beds, full kitchens, bike hire and family-friendly facilities strongly suggest 'holiday', not 'stop-off'.

Fox Glacier ⑪

🍴 Matheson Cafe — Modern NZ $$

(☎03-751 0878; www.lakematheson.com; Lake Matheson Rd; breakfast & lunch $10-21, dinner $17-33; ⏱8am-late Nov-Mar, to 4pm Apr-Oct) Next to Lake Matheson, this cafe does everything right: sharp architecture that maximises inspiring mountain views, strong coffee, craft beers and upmarket fare from a smoked-salmon breakfast bagel, to slow-cooked lamb followed by berry crumble. Part of the complex is the ReflectioNZ Gallery next door, stocking quality, primarily NZ-made art and souvenirs.

🛏 Fox Glacier Top 10 Holiday Park — Holiday Park $

(☎0800 154 366, 03-751 0821; www.fghp.co.nz; Kerrs Rd; sites $42-45, cabins & units $73-255; @ 📶) This park has options to suit all budgets, from grassy and hard campervan sites, to lodge rooms and upscale motel units. Excellent amenities include a modern communal kitchen and dining room, playground and spa pool, but it's the mountain views that give it the X-factor.

For more places to eat and stay at Fox Glacier see p284.

Haast ⑬

🍴 Hard Antler — Pub Food $$

(☎03-750 0034; Marks Rd, Haast Village; dinner mains $20-30; ⏱11am-late, dinner 5-9pm) This display of deer antlers confirms that you're in manly territory, as does the general ambience of this bold but welcoming and well-run pub. Plain, meaty food on offer with bain-marie action on the side.

🛏 Collyer House — B&B $$

(☎03-750 0022; www.collyerhouse.co.nz; Cuttance Rd, Okuru; d $180-250; @ 📶) This gem of a B&B has thick bathrobes, quality linen, beach views and a sparkling host who cooks a terrific breakfast. This all adds up to make Collyer House a comfortable, upmarket choice. Follow the signs off SH6 for 12km down Jackson Bay Rd.

Christchurch Endless beaches along the Pacific Ocean coast

Alpine Pacific Triangle

16

Cruise up the Pacific Ocean coast to marine-life-capital Kaikoura before heading inland to spa town Hanmer Springs and back to resurgent Christchurch.

TRIP HIGHLIGHTS

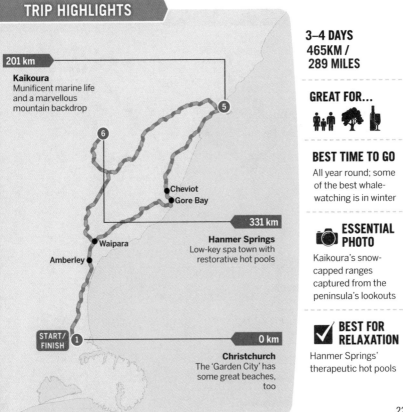

201 km

Kaikoura
Munificent marine life and a marvellous mountain backdrop

⑤

⑥

Cheviot
Gore Bay

331 km

Hanmer Springs
Low-key spa town with restorative hot pools

Waipara

Amberley

START/ FINISH ①

0 km

Christchurch
The 'Garden City' has some great beaches, too

**3–4 DAYS
465KM /
289 MILES**

GREAT FOR...

BEST TIME TO GO

All year round; some of the best whale-watching is in winter

ESSENTIAL PHOTO

Kaikoura's snow-capped ranges captured from the peninsula's lookouts

BEST FOR RELAXATION

Hanmer Springs' therapeutic hot pools

16 Alpine Pacific Triangle

Travellers making a beeline for Kaikoura may be interested to find they can turn A to B into a terrific triangle. The highway behind the Seaward Kaikoura Ranges adds not only a quiet sojourn through quintessential inland Canterbury countryside, but also the hot pools of Hanmer Springs, various outdoor pursuits and the spectacular Molesworth high-country farm.

TRIP HIGHLIGHT

❶ Christchurch

Christchurch boasts a host of urban attractions such as museums, galleries and restaurants, and it's a great place to stretch your legs on a walking tour (p286). Don't miss the **Botanic Gardens** (www.ccc.govt.nz; Rolleston Ave; ⏰7am-8.30pm Oct-Mar, to 6.30pm Apr-Sep), a peaceful oasis in the heart of the city occupying 30 blissful hectares of arboreal and floral splendour.

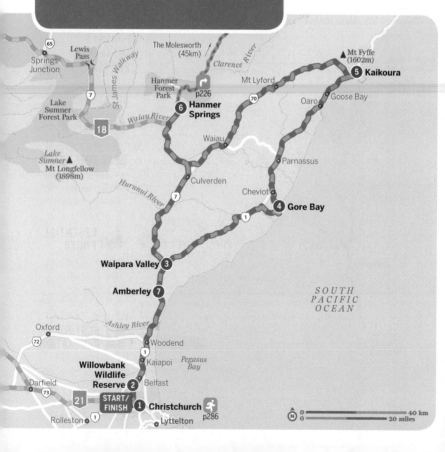

Beach bums, however, will also find satisfaction along the Pacific Ocean coast. The seaside superstar is **Sumner** – a perennially popular hotspot for its vibrant little village and holiday vibe. Closer to the city centre is **New Brighton**, with its distinctive pier reaching 300m out to sea. Our pick, however, is **Waimairi**, a little further north: a fine place for a swim or bodyboard between the flags.

✖ 🛏 p227

The Drive » Head north on Manchester St, then Cranford St until you meet Main North Rd. Keep driving north for 2km then turn left onto Styx Mill Rd, following the signs to Willowbank, a 12km journey in total, which should take 20 minutes out of peak times.

❺ LINK YOUR TRIP

18 Two Passes
Join this scenic circuit over Arthur's and Lewis Passes at Christchurch, Waipara or Hanmer Springs.

21 Southern Alps Circuit
Christchurch is also the start and end point of an epic loop around NZ's majestic alpine scenery.

❷ Willowbank Wildlife Reserve

This family-friendly **wildlife reserve** (☏03-359 6226; www.willowbank.co.nz; 60 Hussey Rd, Northwood; adult/child $28/11; ☯9.30am-7pm Oct-Apr, to 5pm May-Sep) focuses on native NZ critters, heritage farmyard animals and hands-on enclosures with wallabies, deer and lemurs. The Natural New Zealand experience combines some of the country's precious native birdlife with some of their introduced predators, but luckily not in the same enclosures. Among a fleet of birds are four varieties of kiwi, plus the speedy NZ falcon and the muscular takahe – the heaviest rail in the world.

The reserve also houses a re-created Māori village, the setting for the **Ko Tane** (www.kotane. co.nz; 60 Hussey Rd, Northwood; adult/child $135/68; ☯5.30pm) cultural experience that takes place in the evenings. After your *pōwhiri* (welcome), you'll learn about Māori traditions, see a rousing performance involving the famous *haka* (war dance), and enjoy a traditional *hangi* (earthen oven) feast.

The Drive » From Willowbank, follow signposts 750m to SH1, then follow it north 52km to Waipara through the flat Canterbury Plains and across

the braided Waimakariri and Ashley Rivers. The Hurunui hills appear before you around Amberley.

❸ Waipara Valley

Waipara Valley may be the pint-sized cousin of heavyweight Marlborough to the north, but it certainly punches above its weight when it comes to knockout wines with some of NZ's champion pinot noir, riesling and gewürztraminer produced here.

Waipara Springs (www. waiparasprings.co.nz; SH1; mains $24-28; ☯11am-5pm; 🍴), 3km northeast of the township, is one of the valley's oldest vineyards. Its riesling can be enjoyed in the charming garden cafe, which serves platters and hearty salads. A further 2km along the highway, **Black Estate** (☏03-314 6085; www.blackestate.co.nz; 614 Omihi Rd/SH1; ☯10am-5pm Wed-Sun, daily Dec-Jan), occupying an architecturally striking black barn overlooking the valley, presents excellent wines alongside cuisine championing local producers (mains $25 to $40). As well as common Waipara varieties, sniff out its interesting pinot-chardonnay rosé and seductive chenin blanc.

The valley's 16 or so other producers can be found on the *Waipara Valley Map* (www. waiparavalleynz.com).

The Drive » Drive northeast on SH1 through the Omihi and Greta Valleys. Around 12km on, turn right onto the Gore Bay Tourist Drive (Hurunui Mouth Rd) to head over the hills to the coast, 59km from Waipara.

④ Gore Bay

Gore Bay is a great place to get out of the car and among the waves, with the southern end sandy and good for swimming, when conditions are conducive. One of Canterbury's better surfing breaks lends the little holiday village a touch of *Point Break* vibe.

A pathway at the northern end of the settlement leads up to an old cemetery with lovely views of the wetland and beach; it's a serene spot come late afternoon. The Bay, however, is probably best known for its peculiar gully with walls sculpted by the elements to resemble church organ pipes. **Cathedral Cliffs** are located at the top of a bun-tightening 10-minute climb at the southern end of 'town'.

The Drive » Head northwest along Gore Bay Rd 8km to reach SH1 at Cheviot. Follow the rural highway north, then over the Hundalee Hills to reach the coast at Oaro, 46km from Cheviot. SH1 hugs the craggy coast for the remaining 23km to Kaikoura, passing through the odd tunnel blasted into the rock.

TRIP HIGHLIGHT

⑤ Kaikoura

According to Māori lore, Kaikoura Peninsula (Taumanu o te Waka o Māui) is where the demi-god Māui placed his feet when he fished up the North Island. Kaikoura's people have maintained strong links with the sea – firstly Māori who prized the area for its *kaimoana* (seafood), and latterly European settlers who hunted the southern right and sperm whale that frequented the coast.

Free from such savagery, Kaikoura's resident and visiting whale populations are now targeted by tourists' viewfinders on world-famous whale-watching tours (p170). An abundance of other marine tours runs the gamut from albatross-spotting to swimming with seals.

Yes, you heard right. While seals can readily be seen lolling slothfully at various Kaikoura coastal colonies, NZ fur seals (kekeno) can also be observed performing their aquabatics on two-hour snorkelling trips with **Seal Swim Kaikoura.** (☎0800 732 579, 03-319 6182; www.sealswim-kaikoura.co.nz; 58 West End; tours $70-110, viewing adult/child $55/35; ☽Oct-May)

✕ ▭ p227

The Drive » Head back on SH1 for 5km, then take SH70 inland towards Waiau. Around 14km further on, turn right into Flintoft Mouse Point Rd, right again at the SH7 junction, then right again at SH7A. The 130km drive to Hanmer Springs should take two hours, tops.

TRIP HIGHLIGHT

⑥ Hanmer Springs

This pretty little mountain town is famous for its hot springs resort, **Hanmer Springs Thermal**

MATTHEW MICAH WRIGHT / GETTY IMAGES ©

Hanmer Springs Soaking in hot pools at Hanmer Springs Thermal Pools

Pools (www.hanmersprings. co.nz; 42 Amuri Ave; ☎03-315 0000; adult/child $22/11, locker $2), a large, pleasantly landscaped complex with pools aplenty, a day spa and a cafe. There is also the Superbowl that whirls you whooping down the plughole – do that 10 times.

More relaxation can be found by way of nature-based activities. The town's primary outdoor playground is Hanmer Forest Park, less than 10 minutes' walk from the centre. The signature hike is the 1½-hour round trip up to **Conical Hill Lookout**. Mountain biking is also popular, not only around the park but through the town's quiet streets and cruisy Dog Stream trails. Bike hire is readily available around town; the **i-SITE** (☎03-315 0020, 0800 442 663; www.visithanmersprings. co.nz; 40 Amuri Ave; ◷10am-5pm) stocks a *Forest Park Walks* booklet and a mountain biking map.

✕ ⊨ p227

The Drive » Head back along SH7A for 9km to rejoin SH7, and continue south through the Waiau River valley, staying on SH7 to the junction with

DETOUR: THE MOLESWORTH

Start: ❻ Hanmer Springs

Spread over 1807 sq km of high country between Hanmer Springs and Blenheim, Molesworth Station is NZ's biggest cattle farm, ranging across a landscape so special it is protected by the Department of Conservation. Cutting through the station is the spectacularly scenic **Acheron Rd**, starting 8km from Hanmer via Jacks Pass Rd. A return day trip is a highly memorable outing.

The Molesworth is a geology-lovers' dream, sporting more glacial features than you can lob a rock at. It's also ecologically significant, inhabited by dozens of threatened plant species competing with the beautiful but unwelcome briar rose. Amid many heritage farm buildings are two cob cottages, including the 1862 **Accommodation House** near the Hanmer end, which houses historic displays.

The Acheron Rd – via which it's possible to reach Blenheim, 207km (six hours) away – is usually only open from November to early April, weather permitting, with the gates open 7am to 7pm. Overnight camping is permitted in certain areas. For more information, see DOC's *Molesworth Station* brochure, available at the **Hanmer Springs i-SITE** (p225).

Guided tours are available from Hanmer Springs with **Molesworth Heritage Tours** (☎027 201 4536, 03-315 7401; www.molesworth.co.nz; tours $198-750; ☺Oct-May), and from the Blenheim end with **Molesworth Tours** (☎03-572 8025; www.molesworthtours.co.nz).

SH1; then drive south for 10km to Amberley. It's 87km from Hanmer Springs to Amberley and should take just over one hour.

- - - - - - - - - - - - - -

❼ Amberley

The Waipara Valley's 'other town', Amberley is home to a delightfully diminutive brewery, **Brew Moon** (☎03-314 8036; www.brewmoon.co.nz; 12 Markham St, Amberley; ☺3pm-late Wed-Fri, noon-late Sat & Sun). Bedecked with striking street art, its out-of-this-world creations include the nicely balanced Hophead IPA and the hard-hitting Wee Heavy Scottish Ale. Stop in to fill a rigger (flagon) to take away, or sup an ale with a platter or a pizza (food from 3pm).

✕ p227

The Drive ⟩⟩ Drive for 47km south along SH1, across stranded rivers and the Canterbury Plains, then through the outer suburbs before hitting Christchurch. Just after Leithfield, around 6km from Amberley, look for Pukeko Junction cafe if you're feeling peckish.

Eating & Sleeping

Christchurch ❶

✖ Saggio di Vino — European $$$

(📞03-379 4006; www.saggiodivino.co.nz; 179 Victoria St; mains $40-43; ⏰5pm-late) **Elegant** Italo-French restaurant that's up there with Christchurch's best. Expect delicious, modern takes on terrine, rack of lamb and *Café de Paris* steak, plus a well-laden cheese trolley to finish. The wine list makes long, interesting reading.

🛏 George — Hotel $$$

(📞03-379 4560; www.thegeorge.com; 50 Park Tce; r $356-379, ste $574-761; P @ 🛜) The George has 53 handsome rooms within a defiantly 1970s-looking building on the fringe of Hagley Park. Staff attend to every whim, and ritzy features include huge TVs, luxury toiletries, glossy magazines and two highly rated restaurants – Pescatore and 50 Bistro.

For more places to eat and stay in Christchurch see pages 171, 227, 235, 245, 260 and 284.

Kaikoura ❺

✖ Green Dolphin — Modern NZ $$$

(📞03-319 6666; www.greendolphinkaikoura. com; 12 Avoca St; mains $26-39; ⏰5pm-late) Kaikoura's consistent top-ender dishes up high-quality local produce including seafood, beef, lamb and venison, as well as seasonal flavours such as fresh tomato soup. There are lovely homemade pasta dishes, too. The hefty drinks list demands attention, featuring exciting aperitifs, craft beer, interesting wines and more. Booking ahead is advisable.

🛏 Nikau Lodge — B&B $$$

(📞03-319 6973; www.nikaulodge.com; 53 Deal St; d $190-290; @ 🛜) A waggly tailed welcome awaits at this beautiful B&B high on the hill with grand-scale vistas. Five en suite rooms are plush and comfy, with cafe-quality breakfasts accompanied by fresh local coffee. Good humour, home baking, free wi-fi, complimentary drinks, a hot tub and blooming gardens: you may want to move in.

For more places to eat and stay in Kaikoura see p171.

Hanmer Springs ❻

✖ Coriander's — Indian $$

(📞03-315 7616; www.corianders.co.nz; Chisholm Cres; mains $14-22; ⏰11.30am-2pm Mon-Fri, 5-10pm daily; 🖉) Spice up your life at this brightly painted North Indian restaurant complete with bhangra-beats soundtrack. It's a beef-free zone, but there are plenty of tasty lamb, chicken and seafood dishes to choose from, plus a fine vegetarian selection.

🛏 Woodbank Park Cottages — Cottage $$

(📞03-315 5075; www.woodbankcottages.co.nz; 381 Woodbank Rd; d $190-210) These two plush cottages in a woodland setting are a six-minute drive from Hanmer, but feel a million miles away. Decor is crisp and modern, bathrooms and kitchens are well appointed, and wooden decks come equipped with gas barbecues and rural views. Log burners, and complimentary fresh juices and cheese platters, seal the deal.

For more places to eat and stay in Hanmer Springs see p245.

Amberley ❼

✖ Little Vintage Espresso — Cafe $

(20 Markham St, Amberley; brunch $8-18; ⏰7.30am-4.30pm Mon-Sat) This little cracker of a cafe just off SH1 serves up the best coffee in town with food to match. High-quality, contemporary sandwiches, slices and cakes are gobbled up by locals and tourists alike.

Leithfield

✖ Pukeko Junction — Cafe, Deli $$

(📞03-314 8834; www.pukekojunction.co.nz; 458 Ashworths Rd/SH1, Leithfield; mains $15-21; ⏰9am-4.30pm; 🖉) A deservedly popular roadside pit stop, this cafe in Leithfield (south of Amberley) serves delicious baked goods including gourmet sausage rolls and lamb shank pies. As well as arts and crafts, the shop next door stocks an excellent selection of local wine.

Castle Hill/Kura Tawhiti Other-wordly rock formations in the alpine foothills

Coast to Coast

17

From the agricultural plains of Canterbury to virgin West Coast rainforest – with the awesome Southern Alps in between – this drive from coast to coast takes in landscapes of extremes.

FINISH
Greymouth

Kumara

154 km

Arthur's Pass National Park
Mountain, forest and river splendour

⑤

Cave Stream

③

101 km

Castle Hill/Kura Tawhiti
Eerie limestone formations in alpine foothills

Darfield

①
START

0 km

Christchurch
Dynamic, rejuvenating cityscapes

**2–3 DAYS
250KM / 155 MILES**

GREAT FOR...

BEST TIME TO GO
Any time for scenery; summer for alpine hikes

ESSENTIAL PHOTO
The outsize, oddball rocks of Kura Tawhiti

BEST FOR MOUNTAINS
Arthur's Pass, the pinnacle of this trip through the alps

229

17 Coast to Coast

Early Māori forged this path through the Southern Alps long before Arthur Dobson's 1864 'discovery' led to the building of a coach road. It remains the most popular route between the east and west coasts, not just for convenience and quality tarmac but also for scenery that never gets old. Epic vistas through successive valleys include the spectacular, braided Waimakariri River and the craggy peaks of Arthur's Pass National Park.

TRIP HIGHLIGHT

❶ Christchurch

The transitional state of the South Island's largest city offers endless fascination for the curious traveller. Amid precious architecture that survived the earthquakes are construction sites aplenty and shiny new buildings. In the gaps are pocket parks and street-art projects alongside pop-up cafes and bars, augmenting what is already an exciting and dynamic culinary

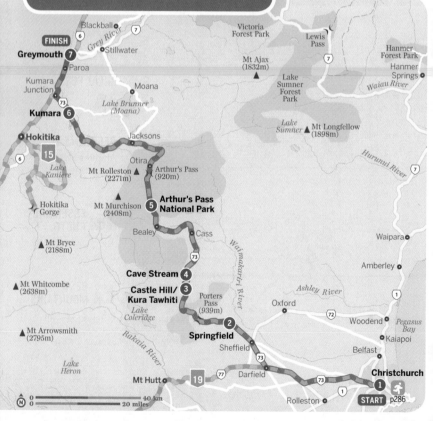

scene. Brace yourself for sensory overload.

To immerse yourself in this somewhat crazy scene – or to just watch from the sidelines – take a tour on the **Tram** (☑03-377 4790; www.tram.co.nz; adult/child $20/free; ☺9am-6pm Oct-Mar, 10am-5pm Apr-Sep). Beautifully restored trams and excellent driver commentary make this so much more than a handy loop around the CBD. The full 17-stop circuit takes just under an hour, but you can you can hop-on and hop-off all day taking in highlights such as Cathedral Sq and New Regent St.

🗴 🛏 p235

The Drive » Once out of the city on SH73, the Canterbury Plains open out before you

LINK YOUR TRIP

15 The West Coast Road

From Greymouth, head north or south along an epic wilderness coast, the east again via Haast, Lewis or SH6 through the Buller Gorge.

19 Inland Scenic Route

Linking Christchurch and Queenstown, this journey meanders through foothills and traverses the iconic Mackenzie Country.

backdropped by the snow-capped Southern Alps. It's 71km to Springfield, but pastry lovers should call in at the Famous Sheffield Pie Shop, 10km shy of Springfield.

② Springfield

The highly scenic Great Alpine Hwy (SH73) pierces the heart of the Selwyn district on its journey between Christchurch and the West Coast. Before it leaves the Canterbury Plains, it passes through the little settlement of Springfield (population 300), which is distinguished by a monument to notable local **Rewi Alley** (1897–1987) who became a great hero of the Chinese Communist Party. His life story is a tale indeed, retold well in a series of information panels.

The town's other major and more irreverent memorial is a giant pink-iced doughnut, originally erected to promote *The Simpsons Movie* but now a permanent feature. Is that an #InstaDonut I feel coming on?

The Drive » SH73 heads west from Springfield, over Porters Pass into the mountainous folds of the Torlesse and Big Ben Ranges with the Southern Alps looming ever larger. The crazy forms of Castle Hill/Kura Tawhiti appear around 30km from Springfield.

TRIP HIGHLIGHT

③ Castle Hill/Kura Tawhiti

Scattered across lush paddocks in a high tussock basin, these limestone formations are so odd they were named 'treasure from a distant land' (Kura Tawhiti) by early Māori. Exploring this supersized rock garden, it's easy to see why the weather-sculpted outcrops attract amateur and professional photographers alike.

You may come across charcoal drawings, secreted among the strange boulders by the Waitaha people some 500 years ago. Today, **Castle Hill/Kura Tawhiti** is still revered by the associated Ngāi Tahu *iwi* (tribe) and is considered *tapu* (sacred). While access on foot is unrestricted and there are rock-climbing guidelines in place, *tangata whenua* (people of the land) prefer that visitors don't clamber all over the delicate karst landforms.

The Drive » Heading north with the Craigieburn Range rising impressively to your left, it's a short but scenic 6km scoot along SH73 to Cave Stream Scenic Reserve.

④ Cave Stream

Near Broken River Bridge, around 3km northeast of Castle Hill

village, a car park signals access to **Cave Stream** (www.doc.govt.nz), so named for the 594m-long limestone grotto carved out by rain and melt waters over thousands of years. Walking through it is an achievable subterranean adventure, even for beginners, but only with a dependable torch, warm clothing and a mole-like disregard for claustrophobia.

It's safest and easiest to enter from the stream outlet and travel upstream. Don't attempt it during or after heavy rain, if the pool at the first corner is more than waist deep, or if the water is really cold. Heed all notices, take necessary precautions and revel in the spookiness. The cave's twists and turns, plus several small waterfalls, will take around an hour to conquer but the memories will last much, much longer.

Nonspelunkers can explore the reserve's sculpted limestone formations and river terraces above ground, on two short tracks to the cave entrance and exit.

The Drive » Around 25km north, SH73 traces the Waimakariri River westwards towards Arthur's Pass. The scree-scarred greywacke peaks, grassy flats and alluvial terraces presents a classic NZ panorama. After crossing the river, the highway squeezes through steep-sided Bealey Valley on the final leg of this 47km drive.

TRIP HIGHLIGHT

5 Arthur's Pass National Park

Straddling the Southern Alps and known to Māori as Ka Tiriti o te Moana (Steep Peak of Glistening White), this vast alpine wilderness became the South Island's first national park in 1929. It's a 1148 sq km ruggedly mountainous area, cut by deep valleys blanketed with pristine mountain beech in the east and temperate rainforest in the west.

The park's hub is **Arthur's Pass Village** (population 62), NZ's highest-altitude settlement at 900m. Plenty of well-marked walks start here, including the

SHAUN JEFFERS / SHUTTERSTOCK ©

Arthur's Pass National Park Kea (alpine parrots)

popular one-hour return amble to Devils Punchbowl falls, and the steep walk to Temple Basin (three hours return) with impressive views of Mt Rolleston (2271m). If the weather's good, the fit and sure-footed may consider tackling Avalanche Peak, the region's classic summit hike. Regardless of the forecast, always arrive prepared for rain.

Pick up or download a copy of DOC's *Discover Arthur's Pass* booklet for more information.

✖ ⊨ p235

The Drive ❯❯ Continue north over the pass proper (920m), pausing at the 10km mark for an obligatory snap of the Otira Viaduct and a possible encounter with the world's only alpine parrot, the kea. Wild mountain vistas soften as the highway winds for 61km to the western side of the Southern Alps where you'll reach Kumara.

⬤ Kumara

Kumara is a busy goldrush town that ground to a halt, leaving behind a thin posse of flinty citizens. In recent times its claims to fame have been as a welcome pit stop for cyclists on the 136km **West Coast Wilderness**

233

THE TRANZALPINE

Paralleling SH73 for much of its way between the Pacific Ocean and Tasman Sea, the **TranzAlpine** (☎0800 872 467, 03-341 2588; www.kiwirailscenic.co.nz; one way adult/child from $99/69) is one of the world's great train journeys. Leaving Christchurch daily at 8.15am, and returning from Greymouth at 1.45pm, the 4½-hour chug serves up a sequence of dramatic landscapes, from the flat, alluvial Canterbury Plains, to the beech-forested river valleys and narrow alpine gorges of the Southern Alps, through an 8.5km tunnel and past a lake fringed with cabbage trees. Popular as a return day trip from Christchurch, it can also be factored in as one-way passage on this Coast to Coast driving trip.

Trail (www.westcoast wildernesstrail.co.nz), and a slow-burning regentrification.

The town's recent upswing is most obvious at the show-stopping **Theatre Royal Hotel** (☎03-736 9277; www. theatreroyalhotel.co.nz; 81 Seddon St, SH73, Kumara; d $100-290; ☺10am-late; 🛜). With its classy restaurant and sumptuous accommodation styled with full historic honours, the fully restored beauty has kicked Kumara well and truly into the 21st century. Stop in to enjoy some of the best food on the West Coast, or for a drink and a yarn with the locals.

For a short walk, seek out **Londonderry Rock**, 1km east of Kumara.

Not only will you get to see the massive 'glacial erratic' boulder that proved problematic for local miners, there are also huge and curious boulder banks apparently assembled by aliens.

The Drive » Carry on along SH73, dead straight and flat for 7km to Kumara Junction. Then drive north on SH6, beside the Tasman Sea, to Greymouth, 18km away. At Paroa, 8km shy of Greymouth, is the turn-off for Shantytown, an outdoor museum that evocatively re-creates the West Coast's 19th-century gold-rush days.

- - - - - - - - - - - -

❼ Greymouth

The riverside town of Greymouth is a gritty, unpretentious place with its roots in coal and gold mining, and is of growing interest to the passing tourist traffic. 'Passing' is all too often the operative word – those who fail to linger and dig a little risk missing some interesting lessons in history, such as those at the **History House Museum** (www.greydc.govt. nz; 27 Gresson St; adult/child $6/2; ☺10am-4pm Mon-Fri). Predominantly pictorial and decidedly old fashioned, the museum nevertheless provides fulsome background on the region's trials and tribulations and is good place to pull up a chair on a rainy day (and the odds are on for that).

There's also loads of history at **Monteith's Brewing Co** (☎03-768 4149; www.monteiths.co.nz; cnr Turumaha & Herbert Sts; guided tour $22; ☺11am-8pm). Cynics might suggest it's merely brand HQ for mainstream product brewed mostly elsewhere, but the brewery's original home base still delivers heritage in spades through its guided tours, which include generous samples (25 minutes; four tours daily). Besides which, the flash tasting room-cum-bar is now Greymouth's most exciting watering hole.

🍴 🛏 p235

Eating & Sleeping

Christchurch ❶

✖ Addington Coffee Co-op   Cafe $

(📞03-943 1662; www.addingtoncoffee.org.nz; 297 Lincoln Rd; meals $8-21; ⏰7.30am-4pm Mon-Fri, 9am-4pm Sat & Sun; 🛜✖) You will find one of Christchurch's biggest and best cafes packed to the rafters most days. A compact shop selling fair-trade gifts jostles for attention with delicious cakes, gourmet pies and the legendary house breakfasts (until 2pm). An on-site launderette completes the deal for busy travellers.

✖ Twenty Seven Steps   Modern NZ $$$

(📞03-366 2727; www.twentysevensteps.co.nz; 16 New Regent St; mains $30-40; ⏰5pm-late Tue-Sat) Upstairs on the Edwardian New Regent St strip, the pared-back interior of this elegant restaurant puts the focus firmly on a menu showcasing local produce. Mainstays include modern renditions of lamb, beef, venison and seafood, but there's also outstanding risotto and desserts such as caramelised lemon tart.

🛏 Christchurch Top 10   Holiday Park $

(📞03-352 9176; www.christchurchtop10.co.nz; 39 Meadow St, Papanui; sites $35-52, units with/without bathroom from $94/76; 🅿@🛜✖) Family owned and operated for nearly 50 years, this large holiday park has a wide range of accommodation along with various campervan nooks and grassy tent sites. It has a raft of facilities and bike hire, too. Enthusiastic staff provide travel advice and bookings.

For more places to eat and sleep in Christchurch see pages 171, 227, 245, 260 and 284.

Sheffield

✖ Famous Sheffield Pie Shop   Bakery $

(www.sheffieldpieshop.co.nz; 51 Main West Rd, Sheffield; pies $5-6; ⏰7.30am-4pm) Heaven forbid you should blink and miss this roadside bakery, a stellar purveyor of meat pies produced here in more than 20 varieties. While you're at it, snaffle a bag of its exemplary afghan biscuits – such cornflakey, chocolatey goodness!

Arthurs Pass National Park ❺

✖ Wobbly Kea   Cafe $$

(www.wobblykea.co.nz; 108 Main Rd; breakfast $10-17, mains $24-26; ⏰9am-8pm) Don your big-eatin' pants for breakfast, lunch or dinner at the Wobbly Kea which offers a short menu of stodgy but tasty home-cooked meals such as meaty stew and curry. Pricey pizza ($33) is available to takeaway, as is fish and chips.

🛏 Arthur's Pass Village B&B   B&B $$

(📞021 394 776; www.arthurspass.org.nz; 72 School Tce; d $140-160; 🛜) This lovingly restored former railway cottage is now a cosy B&B, complete with two guest bedrooms (share bathroom), free-range bacon and eggs, and freshly baked bread for breakfast, and the company of interesting owners. Home-cooked dinners are also available ($35). Ask about the scorched floorboard.

For more places to stay in Arthurs Pass National Park see p245.

Greymouth ❼

✖ Recreation Hotel   Restaurant $$

(📞03-768 5154; www.rechotel.co.nz; 68 High St; mains $17-26; ⏰11am-late) A strong local following fronts up to 'the Rec' for its smart public bar serving good pub grub, such as a daily roast, burgers and local fish and chips amid pool tables and the TAB. Out the back, Buccleugh's dining room offers fancier fare such as venison backstrap and pork fillet wrapped in parma ham (mains $18 to $34).

🛏 Global Village   Hostel $

(📞03-768 7272; www.globalvillagebackpackers.co.nz; 42 Cowper St; sites per person $18, dm/d/tr $30/76/102; @🛜) A collage of African and Asian art is infused with a passionate travellers' vibe here. Free kayaks – the Lake Karoro wetlands reserve is just metres away – and mountain bikes are on tap, and relaxation comes with a spa, sauna, barbecue and fire pit.

For more places to eat and stay in Greymouth see p218.

Christchurch *Museums, galleries and the splendid Botanic Gardens and Hagley Park*

Two Passes

18

This trip loops through two distinctly different Southern Alps passes – Arthur's and Lewis – boasting national park and other fine wilderness scenery, as well as hot springs and historical sites.

TRIP HIGHLIGHTS

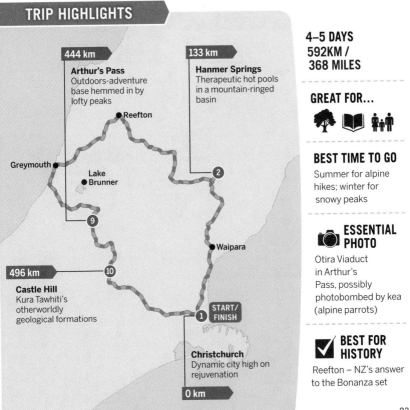

444 km

Arthur's Pass
Outdoors-adventure base hemmed in by lofty peaks

● Reefton

Greymouth ●

● Lake
Brunner

9

133 km

Hanmer Springs
Therapeutic hot pools in a mountain-ringed basin

2

● Waipara

496 km

Castle Hill
Kura Tawhiti's otherworldly geological formations

10

START/ FINISH
1

Christchurch
Dynamic city high on rejuvenation

0 km

4–5 DAYS
592KM / 368 MILES

GREAT FOR...

BEST TIME TO GO
Summer for alpine hikes; winter for snowy peaks

ESSENTIAL PHOTO
Otira Viaduct in Arthur's Pass, possibly photobombed by kea (alpine parrots)

BEST FOR HISTORY
Reefton – NZ's answer to the Bonanza set

18 Two Passes

These two Southern Alps passes provide a richly rewarding loop between the distinctly different east and west coasts. Debate rages about which is more beautiful – the lusher Lewis Pass or crag-tastic Arthur's. In and around them are lakes, braided rivers and a very odd rock garden, plus a series of small, interesting towns including the hot-pool resort of Hanmer Springs.

TRIP HIGHLIGHT

❶ Christchurch

Christchurch surely boasts more road cones and repurposed shipping containers per capita than anywhere else in the world, all waypoints in an epic rebuild across the CBD. But don't be put off by the rubble, dust, piledrivers and rumbling trucks, because there is as much to see as ever, if not more.

As you'd expect, there are notable buildings, old and new. There are mu-

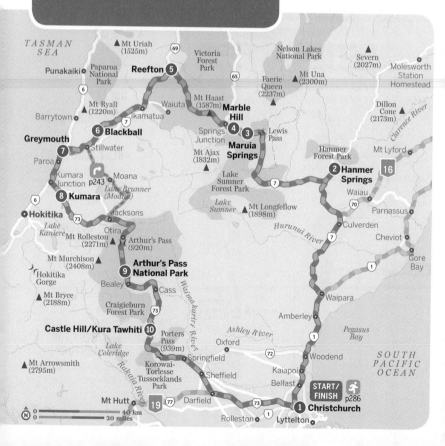

seums and galleries, too, along with the splendid **Botanic Gardens** (www.ccc.govt.nz; Rolleston Ave; ⏰7am-8.30pm Oct-Mar, to 6.30pm Apr-Sep) and adjacent **Hagley Park**. There's also exciting dining and nightlife. But this is also a city full of surprises – street art and sculpture, pocket parks and pop-up performance spaces, much of it transient, tongue-in-cheek and downright fun.

A walking tour is a great way to explore the city on foot (p286); taking to the streets with a local will deepen your experience. **Christchurch Bike & Walking Tours** (☎0800 733 257; www.chchbiketours.co.nz; 2 Cambridge Tce) offers an insightful two-hour trip taking in a stack of major sights.

LINK YOUR TRIP

16 Alpine Pacific Triangle

At Hanmer Springs you can hop on to this inland and coastal spin between Christchurch and Kaikoura.

19 Inland Scenic Route

Linking Christchurch and Queenstown, this journey meanders along alpine foothills and traverses the iconic Mackenzie Country.

✖ 🛏 p245

The Drive » Exit Christchurch on SH1, which stop-starts through a series of settlements on the Canterbury Plains. Just under an hour into the journey you'll reach the up-and-coming Waipara Valley wine region where you can stock up on a bottle before turning right, inland on SH7, towards Hanmer Springs via the pretty Weka Pass and Culverden. Total distance is 133km.

- - - - - - - - - - - -

TRIP HIGHLIGHT

❷ Hanmer Springs

This tree-lined town's *raison d'être* is the Hanmer Springs Thermal Pools (p225), a large complex forming the heart of the town. Unless you're made of sugar or other circumstances forbid it, a visit is all but obligatory.

There is, however, heaps more to Hanmer than just the pools. The mountain-ringed basin in which the town sits is the setting for all sorts of adventures, starting with the walking and mountain bike trails throughout Hanmer Forest Par, handily located on the edge of town.

Other hiking and biking opportunities abound, but if you're looking to up the adrenaline buzz, head to **Thrillseekers Adventures** (☎03-315 7046, 0800 661 538; www.thrillseekers.co.nz; 839 Hanmer Springs Rd; 🖥), where you can jetboat up and down the Waiau River or bungy jump off

---

its bridge. The river's gentle flows also host family-friendly rafting or inflatable kayak trips.

✖ 🛏 p245

The Drive » Follow SH7A back to SH7 and turn right, following the river-lined road deep into the virgin beech forest of Lewis Pass Scenic Reserve. As the road enters the Buller District, it gets tight and winding before topping out at the pass proper (864m) and dropping down to Maruia 6km away, just under an hour's drive (78km) from Hanmer Springs.

- - - - - - - - - - - -

❸ Maruia Springs

Right on the highway, perched on a riverbank surrounded by dense beech forest, **Maruia Springs** (☎03-523 8840; www.maruiasprings.co.nz; SH7; adult/child $22/12, guests free; ⏰pools 8am-7.30pm; 🖥) is a small Japanese-inspired hot spring resort. Much smaller and more relaxing than Hanmer – sandflies notwithstanding – it's an atmospheric spot for a therapeutic soak.

Maruia's waters, peppered with black mineral flakes known as 'hot spring flowers', are pumped into a series of outdoor rock pools and private pools. Spartan accommodation and simple cafe fare was on offer when we last visited, but the arrival of new owners signalled changes afoot. Regardless, if the hot waters flow, that's reason enough to go.

The Drive >> Continuing westwards from Maruia Springs, it's another 7km of forest-lined highway to Marble Hill, less than 10 minutes away.

- - - - - - - - - - - -

KHORISHUNOVA OLGA / SHUTTERSTOCK ©

➍ Marble Hill

Within **Lewis Pass Scenic Reserve** is **Marble Hill** (www.doc.govt.nz; SH7) home to one of NZ's most beautiful DOC camping grounds – a row of sites tucked into beech forest, overlooking a grassy meadow, encircled by forested mountains.

This special place represents a landmark victory for NZ's conservation movement. Back in the 1970s, this significant forest was saved from the chop by a 341,159-signature petition known as the 'Maruia Declaration', which played a part in the Department of Conservation's establishment in 1987.

A more concrete feature of the reserve is **Evison's Wall**. A highly unsuccessful geological experiment started in 1964, the 24m-long wall was built along the Alpine Fault to establish how the fault was in fact moving. Such measuring methods have clearly been superseded, so now it's just a straight-as-a-die wall in an out-of-the-way place.

For a spot of exercise, head out on the **Lake Daniells Track.** You don't have to go all the

Lake Brunner

way – it's four to six hours return – but even a short foray will reveal all sorts of native flora such as matagouri, mistletoe and sweet-smelling beech trees.

The Drive >> The highway soon encounters Springs Junction, with the right fork (SH65) leading north towards Nelson Lakes. The two passes journey, however, continues along a northwest track towards Reefton through the stunning mountainous forest of Victoria Forest Park. The drive will take around 40 minutes (49km).

⑤ Reefton

For generations, Reefton's claims to fame have been mining and the town's early adoption of the electricity grid and street lighting – hence the tag line, 'the city of light'. With crusty old buildings and a slight sniff of the Wild West, it's a fascinating town for a stroll. To find out who lived where and why, undertake the short **Heritage Walk** outlined in the *Historic Reefton* leaflet ($1), available from the **Reefton i-SITE** (📞03-732 8391; www.reefton.co.nz; 67 Broadway; ⏰9am-4.30pm Mon-Fri, 9.30am-2pm Sat, 9.30am-1pm Sun). Meanwhile, the free *Reefton* leaflet details short walks, including the **Bottled Lightning Powerhouse Walk** (40 minutes), which has its own mobile app. Reefton – the city of the internet!

The town's gritty history hub is **Blacks Point Museum** (📞03-732 8391; blksptmus@hotmail.co.nz; Franklyn St, Blacks Point, SH7; adult/child/family $5/3/15; ⏰9am-noon & 1-4pm Wed-Fri & Sun, 1-4pm Sat Oct-Apr, plus school holidays during winter). Housed in an old church 2km east of town, this museum is crammed with prospecting paraphernalia. Just up the driveway is the still-functional **Golden Fleece Battery**, used for crushing gold-flecked quartz. The Blacks Point walks also start from here.

✖ 🛏 p245

The Drive >> From Reefton, head southwest out of town on SH7. At the small farming settlement of Ikamatua (26km), turn right down Atarau Rd, signposted to Blackball, and follow it along the true right of the broad Grey River. Blackball is around an hour away in all (57km), just off Atarau Rd.

⑥ Blackball

Blackball was established in 1866 to service gold diggers, with coal mining kicking in between 1890 and 1964. A widely broadcast but not uncontested claim stakes it as the birthplace of the Labour Party, as a result of major strikes in 1908 and 1931.

Alongside you will find the hub of the town, **Formerly the Blackball Hilton** (📞03-732 4705, 0800 425 225; www.blackballhilton.co.nz; 26 Hart St; s/d incl breakfast $55/110; 🛜), where you can collect a copy of the helpful *Historic Blackball* map. This old dear has memorabilia galore, hot meals ($15 to $34), cold beer, heaps of afternoon sun and a host of rooms oozing yesteryear charm.

Competing with the Hilton in the fame stakes is **Blackball Salami Co** (📞03-732 4111; www.blackballsalami.co.nz; 11 Hilton St; ⏰8am-4pm Mon-Fri, 9am-2pm Sat), manufacturer of tasty salami, and sausages ranging from chorizo to black pudding.

Blackball's other claim to fame is as the southern end of the **Croesus Track**, a one- to two-day hike (or MTB ride) clambering over to Barrytown. In the next few years it will form part of the new Pike River Great Walk.

The Drive >> Back at the Blackball turn-off, head west towards Greymouth on the Taylorville–Blackball Rd, passing the historic Brunner Mine Site on the way to Cobden Bridge and Greymouth on the south side of the river. It's a short, 30-minute (24km) drive in all.

⑦ Greymouth

Known to Māori as Mawhera, Greymouth is the West Coast's utilitarian administrative hub, and the western terminus for the world-famous TranzAlpine scenic rail journey (p234).

Despite its monotone moniker there are some colourful sights to be seen in this workaday town, especially at the **Left Bank Art Gallery** (www.leftbankarts.org.nz; 1 Tainui St; admission by donation; ⏲11am-4.30pm Tue-Fri, 11am-2pm Sat). Deposited within a dashing 95-year old former bank are contemporary NZ jade carvings, prints, paintings, photographs and ceramics. The gallery also fosters and supports a wide society of West Coast artists, so don't forget to pop a gold coin or two into the *koha* (donation) box.

✕ p245

The Drive ≫ Head south on SH6 for 18km to Kumara Junction; from here, head inland on the Great Alpine Hwy (SH73) to Kumara, another 7km away.

- - - - - - - - - - - -

❽ Kumara

Kumara, a wee dot on the Great Alpine Hwy, is yet another West Coast gold town that ground to a screeching halt. However, it has been greatly re-energised in recent years, largely due to the development of the West Coast Wilderness Trail (p233), the 136km, multiday cycleway between Greymouth and Ross. Arguably the best day-ride section is between Kumara and Hokitika.

The town's star is Theatre Royal Hotel (p234), which has undergone a major and sympathetic restoration and now showcases some of the best food and accommodation on the West Coast.

Kumara's glittering history is entertainingly

CANTERBURY & THE WEST COAST **18** TWO PASSES

↱ **DETOUR:
LAKE BRUNNER**

Start: ❼ Greymouth

Lying inland from Greymouth, **Lake Brunner** (www.golakebrunner.co.nz) is the largest of the West Coast region's many lakes and a tranquil spot for tramping, bird spotting and various water sports including boating and fishing. The local boast is that the lake and Arnold River are 'where the trout die of old age', which implies that the local fish are particularly clever or the fisherfolk need to tighten their lines. Greymouth i-SITE can hook you up with a guide if you fancy an angle.

There are several short walks, as detailed in DOC's *Walks in the Lake Brunner/ Moana Area* pamphlet (www.doc.govt.nz). A couple of these start at Moana, the main lakeshore settlement, and feature ravishing rainforest complete with mighty miro and rimu trees. Moana's marina area is also great for a swim. Note the suspension bridge over the Arnold River, not that we'd ever advocate leaping off it (would we?).

Moana has a couple of places to eat, including a cafe opposite the train station where the **TranzAlpine** (p234) train pulls in, and a pub with a sunny deck overlooking the lake. There are also numerous accommodation options, the best of which is the atmospheric motel and holiday park, 2km inland on the Arnold Valley Rd.

There are two reasonably equidistant routes to Lake Brunner from the Two Passes trip. From Greymouth, head east on SH7 for 13km to Stillwater and follow Arnold Valley Rd for 22km to Moana. Alternatively, detour north to the lake from the Great Alpine Hwy at Jacksons, from where it's 32km to Moana.

🛏 p245

retold in the information panels opposite the hotel, while some of the town's boom-time relics can be viewed on short walks around town. Cut through regenerating native bush, Payn Track follows an old tram route. At the SH73 end of the track you'll find the historic baths, which in the town's heyday formed the largest swimming pool in NZ.

The Drive » SH73 winds east through the mountains of Arthur's Pass, 71km/one hour away. The actual pass is signposted (920m above sea level), after which you should stop for the obligatory snap of the Otira Viaduct and a possible encounter with the world's only alpine parrot, the kea.

TRIP HIGHLIGHT

⑨ Arthur's Pass National Park

The South Island's first national park, established in 1929, Arthur's Pass straddles the Southern Alps and thus befits its Māori name of Ka Tiriti o te Moana – 'Steep Peak of Glistening White'. The human heart

of the park is Arthur's Pass Village, home to a permanent population of around 60 and existing almost entirely as a base for visitors venturing out on various outdoor adventures.

While there are plenty of short walks from the village, the park's mountains and valleys are also a mecca for multiday hikers. The **Goat Pass Track**, starting at Greyneys Shelter, 5km south of the village, is a popular option for those new to pass-hopping and route finding. The two-day hike takes you over the 1070m pass, and along much of the easy-to-follow route that snakes beside the Mingha and Deception Rivers. The highlight is a night spent at Goat Pass Hut, above the bushline.

🏁 p245

The Drive » SH73 continues south and east through the Bealey and Waimakariri Valleys with their braided river beds, terraced meadows, and scree-scarred greywacke peaks. The Craigieburn Range rises impressively to your right as you approach Kura Tawhiti, 52km

(around 45 minutes' drive) from Arthur's Pass.

TRIP HIGHLIGHT

⑩ Castle Hill/ Kura Tawhiti

These otherworldly rocky outcrops, some up to 12m tall, were named Kura Tawhiti (treasure from a distant land) by Ngāi Tahu Māori. European settlers saw them in a different light, likening them to the crenellations or battlements of a castle, hence the area's two names.

Whichever way you look at them they're a beguiling sight, and a spectacular place to explore. The karst (eroded limestone) formations, with the craggy Craigieburn and Torlesse Ranges serving as dramatic backdrops, are highly Instagrammable from just about every angle.

The Drive » Follow SH73 east, leaving the mountainous folds of the Big Ben and Torlesse Ranges, over Porter's Pass down to the Canterbury Plains. It's 96km (90 minutes) to Christchurch.

Eating & Sleeping

Christchurch ❶

🍷 Pomeroy's Old Brewery Inn   Pub $$

(☎03-365 1523; www.pomspub.co.nz; 292 Kilmore St; ◷3-11pm Tue-Thu, noon-11pm Fri-Sun) For fans of great beer, there's no better place than Pomeroy's for supping a drop or two alongside comforting pub food. The newest addition, pretty **Little Pom's** cafe, serves super-fine fare (meals $14 to $22) until mid-afternoon.

🛏 Amber Kiwi Holiday Park   Holiday Park $

(☎03-348 3327, 0800 348 308; www.amberpark.co.nz; 308 Blenheim Rd, Riccarton; sites $42-50, units $82-200; 🛜) Blooming lovely gardens and close proximity to the city centre make this urban holiday park a great option for campervaners and tenters. Tidy cabins and more-spacious motel units are also available.

For more places to eat and stay in Christchurch see pages 171, 227, 235, 260 and 284.

Hanmer Springs ❷

🍴 Powerhouse Cafe   Cafe $$

(☎03-315 5252; www.powerhousecafe.co.nz; 8 Jacks Pass Rd; brunch $15-24; ◷7.30am-3pm; 🛜) Power up with a huge High Country breakfast, or a Highland Fling caramelised whisky-sodden porridge. Return for a burger, laksa or salmon salad for lunch, then finish with one of the lavishly iced friands.

🛏 Scenic Views   Motel $$

(☎03-315 7419, 0800 843 974; www.hanmerscenicviews.co.nz; 2 Amuri Ave; d $140-240; 🛜🐾) An attractive timber-and-stone complex with modern studios (one with an outdoor spa pool) and two- and three-bedroom apartments. Mountain views come standard, as do free wi-fi and plunger coffee.

For more places to eat and stay in Hanmer Springs see p227.

Reefton ❺

🍷 Wilson's Hotel   Pub $$

(☎03-732 8800; 32 Broadway; ◷noon-11pm Mon-Sat, 4-9pm Sun) A solid town pub pleasing all, from smokin' youth through to soup-slurping pensioners. Meat and three veg dominate the menu (mains $20 to $28), but it's all hearty and homemade. Occasional bands and DJs raise the excitement to somewhere under fever pitch.

🛏 Lantern Court Motels   Motel $$

(☎0800 526 837, 03-732 8574; www.lanterncourtmotel.co.nz; 63 Broadway; old units d $115-140, new units d $155-195; 🛜) This heritage hotel offers great value, with self-catering options for everyone from singles to family groups, while the well-assimilated motel block next door offers all mod cons.

Greymouth ❼

For places to eat and stay in Greymouth see pages 218 and 235.

Lake Brunner

🛏 Lake Brunner Country Motel   Motel, Campground $

(☎03-738 0144; www.lakebrunnermotel.co.nz; 2014 Arnold Valley Rd; sites from $34, cabins $62-72, cottages d $135-150; 🛜) This is a wonderful place for a night or two. Cabins, cottages and campervan sites are tucked into native plantings, while tenters can enjoy the lush grassy camping. field down the back.

Arthur's Pass National Park ❾

🛏 Arthur's Pass Alpine Motel   Motel $$

(☎03-318 9233; www.apam.co.nz; 52 Main Rd; d $125-150; 🛜) On the southern approach to the village, this cabin-style motel complex combines the homey charms of yesteryear with the beauty of double-glazing and the advice of active, enthusiastic hosts.

Lake Tekapo Be blown away by the brilliance of the stars

Classic Trip

Inland Scenic Route

19

New Zealand's highest mountain, golden tussock country and two of its bluest lakes are just some of the highlights on this trip through the middle of the South Island.

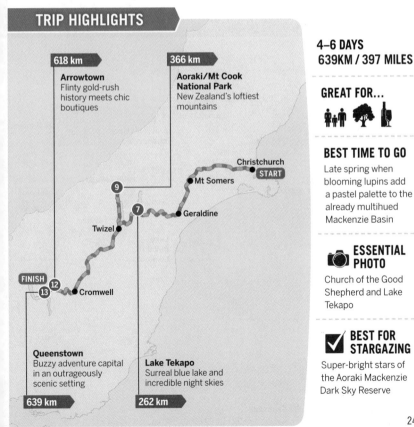

618 km

Arrowtown
Flinty gold-rush history meets chic boutiques

366 km

Aoraki/Mt Cook National Park
New Zealand's loftiest mountains

Christchurch
START

Mt Somers

9

7

Geraldine

Twizel

FINISH
13 12 Cromwell

Queenstown
Buzzy adventure capital in an outrageously scenic setting

639 km

Lake Tekapo
Surreal blue lake and incredible night skies

262 km

4–6 DAYS
639KM / 397 MILES

GREAT FOR...

BEST TIME TO GO
Late spring when blooming lupins add a pastel palette to the already multihued Mackenzie Basin

ESSENTIAL PHOTO
Church of the Good Shepherd and Lake Tekapo

BEST FOR STARGAZING
Super-bright stars of the Aoraki Mackenzie Dark Sky Reserve

247

Classic Trip

19 Inland Scenic Route

They don't called it 'inland' and 'scenic' for nothing, although 'spectacular' is a more fitting description. Yes, the most over-used superlative in the world of travel writing finds its nirvana here – on a road trip that sidles across the Canterbury Plains, around and over the Southern Alps' foothills, through the legendary Mackenzie Country, ending in totally over-the-top Queenstown.

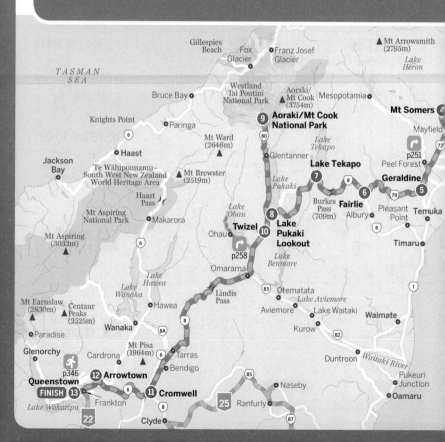

① Christchurch

Among many silver linings salvaged from Canterbury's devastating earthquakes is the surge of creativity and colour that has sprung up in the cracks. Just as well, for in the immediate aftermath of the February 2011 quake a major emergency response centre was housed in the city's much-loved art gallery, before that building itself was closed for repair. **Christchurch Art Gallery** (☎03-941 7300; www. christchurchartgallery.org.nz; cnr Montreal St & Worcester Blvd; ⏰10am-5pm Thu-Tue, to 9pm Wed) has re-emerged stronger than ever to occupy pride of place in the city's cultural scene, presenting a broad but primarily NZ-focused range of exhibitions.

But don't stop there. Take a walking tour (p286) to explore the bustling streets beyond the gallery, fizzing with upbeat inventiveness captured in colourful street art, pocket parks, up-cycled sculpture, and pop-up performance spaces. Shipping-container cafes and other temporary enterprises lend even more blink-and-you'll-miss-it dynamism.

Starting from the ground up after the earthquakes, the **Gap Filler** folks fill the city's empty spaces with fun times and eye-candy. Gaps open up and get filled, so check out the **Gap Map** on the website (www.gapfiller.org.nz).

✕ 🛏 p260

The Drive » From Christchurch drive 47km west on SH73 through the Canterbury Plains to Darfield. Continue west, this time on SH77 (aka Route 72), signposted for Mt Hutt, for the remaining 41km to Rakaia Gorge, the Southern Alps looming ever-larger through the windscreen.

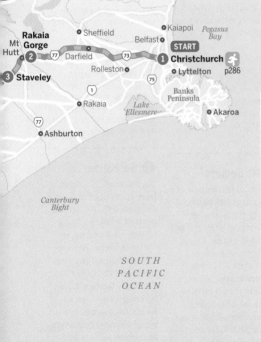

LINK YOUR TRIP

22 Milford Sound Majesty

Take in jaw-dropping lake, mountain and forest scenes virtually all the way from Queenstown to Milford Sound – the jewel in NZ tourism's crown.

25 Otago Heritage Trail

Drive 30km on SH8, from Cromwell to Alexandra, to experience more of Otago's flinty history and big-sky scenes.

Classic Trip

2 Rakaia Gorge

The Rakaia is one of NZ's most voluminous braided rivers, fed by the rains and melting snows of the Southern Alps where it starts out deep and swift. On its 150km journey to the Pacific coast it gradually widens and separates into strands over a gravel bed. At Rakaia Gorge, milky-blue waters are confined to a narrow chasm, crossed by twin bridges along SH72.

A car park alongside the bridge is the starting point for the well-graded **Rakaia Gorge Walkway** (www.doc.govt.nz; Rakaia Gorge Bridge, SH72), which traverses the river's terraces upstream into the upper gorge. Highlights of this half-day outing include native forest, old coal mines and the historic ferryman's cottage – along with various picnic spots – but the grand finale is the view at the walkway's end.

A speedier, more exhilarating alternative is to take a whizz through the gorge on the **Discovery Jet** (021 538 386, 0800 538 2628; www.discoveryjet.co.nz; Rakaia Gorge Bridge, SH72; adult/child $99/75), based downstream of the bridge. Its blood-pumping, 45-minute ride serves up all the obligatory twists, turns and 360-degree spins.

The Drive » After crossing the twin bridges, continue along SH72 with the alps to your right and classic patchwork fields and hedgerows to your left. The Staveley Store is 25km from the gorge.

3 Staveley Store

Situated in the middle of the Canterbury countryside, with just an old community hall and a clutch of houses for company, the cute little **Staveley Store** (03-303 0859; 2 Burgess Rd, Staveley; 9am-4.30pm) sells cheese rolls, sausage rolls, salad rolls and basic groceries including delicious home-made preserves. A scoop of ice cream – savoured out front in the sun – is hard to beat.

The Drive » A further 9km southwest on SH72 is the village of Mt Somers, on the cusp of the Southern Alps and Canterbury Plains.

4 Mt Somers

The small settlement of Mt Somers sits on the edge of the Southern Alps, beneath the mountain of the same name. The biggest drawcard to the area is the **Mt Somers track** (26km), a two-day tramp circling the mountain, linking the popular picnic spots of Sharplin Falls and Woolshed Creek.

The track's western end can be explored from Woolshed Creek, 13km up Ashburton Gorge Rd. A great five-hour return walk climbs to the abandoned **Blackburn Coal Mine** and along a ridge to the roaring **Wooolshed Creek Canyon**, with excellent views at Trig R along the way. You can return to the start the same way or via the Mt Somers and Rhyolite Ridge tracks.

In the forest, keep an ear out for the melodious bellbird (korimako), and an eye out for the teeny rifleman (tītipounamu), NZ's smallest bird. Above the bushline you may even be lucky enough to spot the super-swift NZ falcon (kārearea).

p260

The Drive » Drive south on SH72 for 50km to sweet Geraldine, along darn-near perfectly straight roads through classic Canterbury pastoral and agrarian landscapes.

5 Geraldine

Consummately Canterbury in its dedication to English-style gardening, pretty Geraldine has a village vibe and an active arts scene. Be sure to duck behind the war memorial on Talbot St to the **River Garden Walk**, where green-fingered locals have gone completely bonkers planting abundant azaleas and rhododendrons – utterly splendid in spring. Information about trails in **Talbot Forest**, on the town fringe, is available from the **visitor information centre** (☎03-693 1101; www.southcanterbury.org.nz; 38 Waihi Tce; ⏰8am-5.30pm).

Long overdue to be lauded 'Cheese & Pickle Capital of NZ', Geraldine is a boon to picnickers and other nibblers, boasting a terrific butchery and numerous artisan producers in Four Peaks Plaza. To cut to the cheesy chase, check out Talbot Forest Cheese (p283) before making a beeline for the delicious preserves at Barker's (p283). On summer Saturdays, the town kicks into foodie gear with a **farmers' market** (St Mary's Church car park; ⏰9am-12.30pm Sat Oct-Apr).

✗ ⫧ p260

The Drive » Drive 46km west on SH79 through increasingly hilly terrain as it heads to rural Fairlie and the junction with SH8.

- - - - - - - - - - - - - -

❻ Fairlie

Proclaimed 'Gateway to the Mackenzie', in reality tree-lined Fairlie feels a world away from the tussocky Mackenzie Country lying beyond over Burkes Pass. But this little town dishes up a double-whammy of Kiwiana that makes a pit stop pretty much compulsory.

First, there's the meat pie. This Kiwi icon has fuelled many a NZ road trip, but in truth most are not worth the calories. **Fairlie Bakehouse** (www.liebers.co.nz; 74 Main St; pies $5-7; ⏰7.30am-4.30pm; ☏) produces notable exceptions. The salmon and bacon pie is the stuff of legend, but any other option will do, even the vegetarian. Next to the

DETOUR: PEEL FOREST

Start: ❺ Geraldine

Tucked away between the foothills of the Southern Alps and the Rangitata River, Peel Forest is a small but significant remnant of indigenous podocarp (coniferous) forest, lined with various walking trails. Many of the totara, kahikatea and matai trees here are hundreds of years old and are home to an abundance of birdlife including riflemen (tītipounamu), wood pigeons (kereru), bellbirds (korimako), fantails (pīwakawaka) and grey warblers. A cafe, a DOC camping ground and other accommodation options encourage an overnight stay.

Continuing inland from the forest, a quiet, country road leads to Mesopotamia, the run of English writer Samuel Butler in the 1860s. It also passes the tour base of **Rangitata Rafts** (☎0800 251 251; www.rafts.co.nz; Rangitata Gorge Rd; ⏰Sep-May), which runs one of the most exhilarating rafting trips in NZ. The three-hour adventure begins in the stupendously beautiful Rangitata River valley before heading into the maelstrom of the gorge's Grade V rapids ($210, minimum age 15).

If the thought of white water leaves you cold, another way of soaking up the magnificent scenery is in the saddle with **Peel Forest Horse Trekking** (☎03-696 3703; www.peelforesthorsetrekking.co.nz; 1hr/2hr/half-day/full day $55/110/180/360). Trips through lush forest, up the flanks of Mt Peel and along the Rangitata River range from one-hour jaunts through to multiday expeditions.

To reach Peel Forest, turn off SH72 on to Peel Forest Road at Arundel, around 15km north of Geraldine. It's 8km off the highway.

⫧ p260

Classic Trip

DAVID WALL / ALAMY STOCK PHOTO ©

DANITA DELIMONT / GETTY IMAGES ©

WHY THIS IS A CLASSIC TRIP
LEE SLATER,
WRITER

Basically, I love mountain scenery and this trip has it in spades. As soon as you leave Christchurch's city limits, you're heading for the hills, and the further you travel inland the loftier and more impressive they become. Throw in super-starry night skies, surreal blue lakes, world-class wineries, and adrenaline-fuelled Queenstown at the trip's denouement, and you've got yourself one eye-popping adventure.

Top: Ohau skifield, Ruataniwha Conservation Park
Left: Cows grazing at the foot of Mt Somers, near Staveley
Right: Bungy jumping from Kawarau Bridge, near Queenstown

pastry warmer, American doughnuts and raspberry cheesecake elbow their way in among Kiwi classics such as custard squares and cream buns.

Instead of driving off on a full stomach, head to **Fairlie Heritage Museum** (www.fairlieheritagemuseum.co.nz; 49 Mt Cook Rd; adult/child $6/free; ⊙9.30am-5pm), a somewhat dusty window into Canterbury's old ways, complete with farm machinery, model aeroplanes, dodgy dioramas and random ephemera. Highlights include a homespun gyrocopter, an historic cottage, and a new automotive wing featuring mint-condition tractors.

The Drive » SH8 leads over the relatively low Burkes Pass (709m), up through sheep-peppered high country. After the pass you will round Dog Kennel Corner into the expanse of the Mackenzie Country, a land of golden tussock and surreal turquoise lakes, the star of which is Lake Tekapo. The total driving distance is 43km.

- - - - - - - - - -

TRIP HIGHLIGHT

❼ Lake Tekapo

The expansive basin before you, from which the scenic peaks of Aoraki/Mt Cook National Park escalate, was named the Mackenzie Country after the legendary rustler James 'Jock' McKenzie, who ran his stolen flocks in this then-uninhabited region in the 1840s.

When he was finally caught, other settlers realised the potential of the land and followed in his footsteps.

One of the area's few settlements, Lake Tekapo township was born of a hydropower scheme completed in 1953. Facing out across the opalescent, turquoise lake to a vast alpine backdrop, it's no wonder it has proven a hit with passing travellers.

The prime disgorging point for tour buses is the **Church of the Good Shepherd**, the interdenominational lakeside church built of stone and oak in 1935. A picture window behind the altar frames a distractingly divine view of lake and mountain majesty. Come early in the morning or late afternoon to avoid the peace-shattering masses, and snap your obligatory photo.

🍴 🛏 p260

The Drive » Drive southwest over the Mary Range on SH8. On a fine day the views north will be dominated by NZ's highest peak, Aoraki/Mt Cook. After 47km you will reach the lookout at the foot of Lake Pukaki.

❽ Lake Pukaki Lookout

The largest of the Mackenzie's three alpine lakes, Pukaki is a vast jewel of totally surreal colour. At the southern end of the lake, just off the highway, Lake Pukaki Lookout is a well-signed and perennially popular spot affording picture-perfect views across the lake's waters all the way up to Aoraki/Mt Cook and its surrounding peaks.

Beside the lookout, the **Lake Pukaki Visitor Centre** (www.mtcooka-lpinesalmon.com; SH8; ⏰8.30am-6pm) is actually an outpost of Mt Cook Alpine Salmon, the highest salmon farm on the planet, which operates in a hydropower canal system some distance away. If you fancy some sashimi or a smoked morsel for supper, this is your chance – think of it as an edible souvenir (so much better than a fridge magnet, don't you think?).

The Drive » Drive west for 2km along the base of Lake

AORAKI MACKENZIE DARK SKY RESERVE

If you think the Mackenzie Country is dashing during the day, just wait until you see it – or rather the skies above, to be precise – at night.

On cloud-free nights, prepare to be blown away by the brilliance of stars. So exceptional are the viewing conditions here that, in 2012, the Aoraki Mackenzie area was declared an **International Dark Sky Reserve**, one of only 10 in the world. If you check out the street lights in Lake Tekapo township you'll notice that they cannily shine down and not up, keeping light pollution to a minimum.

By rugging up in a jumper and finding a grassy knoll, you can stargaze easily and for free. But for truly out-of-this-world views of the Milky Way, globular clusters, nebulae, planets and the ever-popular craters of the moon, go on a tour (adult/child $145/80) with **Earth & Sky** (☎03-680 6960; www.earthandsky.co.nz; SH8) up to the University of Canterbury's observatory on the summit of Mt John, alongside Lake Tekapo.

As well as getting the chance to look through a powerful telescope, you can find out exactly what's going on inside those shiny, silver-domed buildings. There may also be some good astronomical gags and the odd boffin with long hair. Book ahead, especially if the weather forecast is looking good.

Pukaki then turn right up SH80, signposted for Aoraki/Mt Cook. This 55km drive, sidling alongside the lake with NZ's loftiest peaks looming ever larger, is totally distracting; pull over at designated lookouts to take it all in.

TRIP HIGHLIGHT

9 Aoraki/Mt Cook National Park

The 700-sq-km Aoraki/Mt Cook National Park forms part of the **Te Wāhipounamu–South West New Zealand World Heritage Area**, along with Fiordland, Aspiring and Westland Tai Poutini National Parks.

The national park is super-peaky. Nineteen of NZ's 23 mountains over 3000m high are found within its boundaries, and more than one-third of its area is permanently blanketed in snow and glacial ice. It is also, of course, home to the nation's tallest mountain – **Aoraki/Mt Cook** (3754m).

A series of vista-filled short walks can be enjoyed in conditions both claggy and clear. The most popular are the **Hooker Valley**, **Kea Point** and **Sealy Tarns** tracks, all starting from Mt Cook Village.

In the heart of the village, the **DOC Visitor Centre** (www.doc.govt.nz; ☎03-435 1186; 8.30am-4.30pm, to 5pm Oct-Apr) is arguably the best in the country. Not only does it dispatch vital informa-tion on hiking routes and weather conditions, it also houses extensive displays on the park's natural and human his-tory. Most local activities, including scenic flights, can be booked here.

🛏 p261

The Drive » Drive back down SH80 to the junction with SH8, then turn right and continue for 9km to Twizel. The total distance from Mt Cook Village to Twizel is 64km and the trip should take just under an hour.

- - - - - - - - - - - -

10 Twizel

Pronounced 'Twy-zel' but teased with 'Twizzel' and even 'Twizzlesticks' by outsiders, the little town of Twizel gets the last laugh. Built in 1968 to service construction of the nearby hydro-electric power station, it was slated for oblitera-tion in 1984 when the project was complete. But there was no way the locals were upping their twizzlesticks and relin-quishing their relaxed, mountain-country life-style, so Twizel resolutely stayed put.

Today the town is thriving with a mod-est boom in holiday homes and recognition from travellers that – as plain-Jane as it is – it's actually in the middle of everything and has al-most all one might need (within reason). Stock up, sup a craft beer or two at **Shawty's** (☎03-435 3155; www.shawtys.co.nz; 4 Market Pl; brunch $12-20, dinner

---

ELECTRIC-BLUE VIEWS

The **Waitaki Hydro Scheme** encompasses seven hydro lakes, including mighty Lake Tekapo and Lake Pukaki, as well as several smaller ones within the Mackenzie Country and adjacent Waitaki Valley.

Imbuing the landscape with considerable colour and texture, the scheme's lakes and canals brim with surreal blue waters contrasting starkly with the surrounding golden tussock and flinty grey ranges, while eight powerhouses and dams lend industrial elegance. Some of the power stations also double as mind-boggling lookout points, especially **Tekapo B** above Lake Pukaki (reached via Hayman then Tekapo Canal roads, off SH8, 18km from Twizel).

So, what gives these lakes and canals their blazing turquoise colour? The answer: tiny particles of rock – known as 'glacial flour' or 'rock flour' – ground down by glacial erosion and washed into the lakes. This sediment gives the water a milky quality and refracts the sunlight beaming down, hence the distinctive brilliant blue hue. Photoshop? Who needs it!

Classic Trip

PIYAPHON PHEMTAWEEPON / GETTY IMAGES ©

Lake Tekapo Lupin in flower on the lakeshore

257

Classic Trip

$29-34; ⊙8.30am-3pm Mon & Tue, to late Wed-Sun Apr-Oct, to late daily Nov-Mar; 🛜🅿), and plan an adventure such as tramping in Ruataniwha Conservation Park or cycling along the Alps 2 Ocean Cycle Trail (p268).

 p261

The Drive >> The scenic splendour continues as SH8 cuts through the Mackenzie Country flats to the small town of Omarama, and over Lindis Pass Alpine Hwy. Stop at the pass to eye the smooth, grey pyramidal hills softened with fluffy, golden tussock. Drive down through the Morven Hills and into Central Otago. This 140km drive should take around two hours.

---

⑪ Cromwell

Cromwell's historic town centre was flooded when the Clyde Dam was completed in 1992, erasing 280 homes, six farms and 17 orchards. Fortunately, many historic buildings were disassembled and rebuilt in the pedestrianised **Heritage Precinct** (www.cromwellheritage precinct.co.nz) at the southern end of Lake Dunstan. While some have been set up as period pieces – featuring stables and suchlike – others house cafes, galleries and charming little shops. In summer the town plays host to an excellent weekly **farmers market** (www.cromwell heritageprecinct.co.nz; ⊙9am-1pm Sun Nov-Feb), a great place to wrap your lips around the region's abundant produce.

Surrounded by orchards, Cromwell's speciality is luscious fruit celebrated in the South Island's most ridiculous 'big thing' – a gaudy sculpture of giant fruit alongside the highway. Other fruitful places for exploration are the local vineyards. Just south of Cromwell is one of Cen-

---

↱ DETOUR:
RUATANIWHA CONSERVATION PARK

Start: ⑩ Twizel

Taking in a large swathe of wilderness between Lake Pukaki and Lake Ohau, this 368-sq-km protected area includes the rugged Ben Ohau Range along with the Dobson, Hopkins, Huxley, Temple and Maitland valleys. It offers plenty of tramping and mountain biking opportunities, as detailed in DOC's *Ruataniwha Conservation Park* pamphlet (www.doc.govt.nz), with several day options close to Twizel.

Even if you're not keen on activity, it's well worth driving to **Lake Ohau**. Long-standing **Lake Ohau Lodge** (📞03-438 9885; www.ohau.co.nz; Lake Ohau Rd; s $144-200, d $159-220) – idyllically sited on the western shore, 42km from Twizel – is a welcoming establishment offering food, wine and panoramic views from the sunny deck. Consider an overnight stay if you have an addictive personality. Come winter, the lodge is packed with snow bunnies in raucous après-ski mode after hitting the slopes of **Ohau ski field** (p282).

Lake Ohau and its legendary lodge can also be reached by bicycle from Twizel on the Alps 2 Ocean Cycle Trail. One of the best day trips on the whole 300km trail, this mostly easy 38km section is a great way to survey these grand surroundings. Super-keen riders can return the same way, although the **Jollie Biker** (p268) and **Cycle Journeys** (p268) can provide transfers as well as bikes.

tral Otago's finest wine-growing subregions – Bannockburn (p307). Of the dozen or so wineries open to the public, Mt Difficulty (p308) is a consistent big-hitter with its plummy pinot noir and terrific terrace restaurant overlooking the Cromwell Basin.

✖ 🛏 p261

The Drive » This 48km drive along SH6 to Arrowtown through the Kawarau Gorge is packed full of dramatic mountain scenery. At Kawarau Bridge, the site of the first commercial bungy jump, pause to spectate or take the leap yourself. *Boing!* The turn off for Arrowtown is 6km after the bridge.

- - - - - - - - - - - - - -

TRIP HIGHLIGHT

⑫ Arrowtown

Quaint Arrowtown sprang up in the 1860s following the discovery of gold glistening in the Arrow River. Today its pretty, tree-lined avenues retain more than 60 of their original gold-rush buildings, but the only bling being flaunted these days are the credit cards being waved in the array of chichi shops.

Instead of joining the bonanza of daytime tourists, consider using Arrowtown as a base for exploring Queenstown and the wider region. That way you can enjoy its history, charm and excellent restaurants when the tour buses have decamped back to Queenstown.

The **Lakes District Museum & Gallery** (www. museumqueenstown.com; 49 Buckingham St; adult/ child $10/3; ⊙8.30am-5pm) is another good reason to stay. It's an excellent introduction to the area's colourful gold-rush history, and considerably caters for children by way of the Museum Fun Pack ($5) which includes activity sheets, museum treasure hunts, green-stone and a few flecks of gold. Jackpot!

✖ 🛏 p261

The Drive » Drive south past Lake Hayes back on to SH6 and then west towards Queenstown, with views of the Remarkables peaks rising dramatically on your left. Once past the airport, the road runs beside Lake Wakatipu for the remaining 8km into the centre of Queenstown, for a total hop of just 21km.

- - - - - - - - - - - - - -

TRIP HIGHLIGHT

⑬ Queenstown

Framed by the jagged peaks of the Remarka-bles and meandering coves of Lake Wakatipu, Queenstown is a right show-off. Looking like a small town but display-ing the energy of a small city, it wears its 'Global Adventure Capital' badge proudly, and most visitors take the time to do crazy things here that they've never done before.

One of the most fa-mous of these ridiculous feats is bungy jumping, pioneered by AJ Hackett. The original bungy base still operates from Kawarau Bridge, but you can take the leap much closer to town at the **Ledge** (☏0800 286 4958; www.bungy.co.nz; adult/child $195/145) – a 47m-high leap from high on the slopes of Ben Lomond. The bungy platform is located atop the Skyline Gondola. This iconic Queenstown lookout point is home to a cafe and restaurant, a paragliding launchpad, and the outrageously fun luge. You can take in the gondola as part of a great walking tour (p346).

✖ 🛏 p261

Eating & Sleeping

Christchurch ❶

✖ King of Snake   Asian $$$

(☏03-365 7363; www.kingofsnake.co.nz; 145
Victoria St; mains $27-43; ☺11am-late Mon-Fri,
4pm-late Sat & Sun) Dark wood, gold tiles and
purple skull-patterned wallpaper fill this hip
restaurant and cocktail bar with just the right
amount of sinister opulence. The exciting menu
gainfully plunders the cuisines of Asia – from
India to Korea – to delicious, if pricey, effect.

🛏 Eliza's Manor   Hotel $$$

(☏03-366 8584, 0800 366 859; www.elizas.
co.nz; 82 Bealey Ave; r $245-345; 🅿🛜) An
infestation of teddy bears has done little to dint
the heritage appeal of this large 1861 mansion.
Wisteria curls around weatherboards, while
inside the rooms are spacious and frilly.

🛏 Pomeroy's on Kilmore   B&B $$

(☏03-374 3532; www.pomeroysonkilmore.
co.nz; 282 Kilmore St; r $145-195; 🅿🛜) Even if
this cute wooden house wasn't the sister and
neighbour of Christchurch's best craft-beer
pub, it would still be one of our favourites.
Three of the five elegantly furnished, en suite
rooms open on to a sunny garden. Rates include
breakfast at Little Pom's (p245) cafe.

For more places to eat and stay in Christchurch
see pages 171, 227, 235, 245, and 284.

Mt Somers ❹

🛏 Stronechrubie   Motel $$

(☏03-303 9814; www.stronechrubie.co.nz; cnr
Hoods Rd & SH72; d $120-160; 🛜) Comfortable
chalets overlooking bird-filled gardens range
in size from studio to two-bedroom, but it's the
food that's the draw here. Enjoy a more formal
meal in the lauded, long-standing restaurant
(mains $34 to $38; serves dinner Wednesday
through Sunday and lunch Sunday). Or head to

the flash new bar and bistro (open 5.30pm to
late Thursday to Saturday) for modern, tapas-
style fare alongside lovely wines and craft beer.

Geraldine ❺

✖ Verde   Cafe $

(☏03-693 9616; 45 Talbot St; mains $11-18;
☺9am-4pm; 🖉) Down the lane beside the old
post office and set in beautiful gardens, this
excellent cafe is easily the best of Geraldine's
eateries. Shame that it's not open for dinner.

🛏 Scenic Route Motor Lodge   Motel $$

(☏03-693 9700; www.motelscenicroute.co.nz;
28 Waihi Tce; d $135-155; 🛜) There's a vaguely
heritage feel to this stone and timber motel,
but the modern units have double-glazing, flat-
screen TVs and larger studios have spa baths.

For more places to eat and stay in Geraldine
see p285.

Peel Forest

🛏 Peel Forest Lodge   Lodge $$$

(☏03-696 3703; www.peelforestlodge.co.nz; 96
Brake Rd; d $380, additional adult/child $40/20;
🛜) This beautiful log cabin hidden in the forest
has four rooms sleeping eight people. It only
takes one booking at a time, so you and your
posse will have the place to yourself. It's fully
self-contained, but meals can be arranged,
as can horse treks, rafting trips and other
explorations of this fascinating area.

Lake Tekapo ❼

✖ Astro Café   Cafe $

(Mt John University Observatory; mains $7-12;
☺9am-5pm) This glass-walled pavilion atop Mt
John has spectacular 360-degree views across
the entire Mackenzie Basin. Tuck into bagels
with local salmon, or fresh ham-off-the-bone
sandwiches; the coffee and cake are good, too.

Lake Tekapo Lodge
B&B $$$

(☏03-680 6566; www.laketekapolodge.co.nz; 24 Aorangi Cres; r $300-450; 🛜) This fabulously designed, luxurious B&B is filled to the brim with covetable contemporary Kiwi art, and boasts painterly views of the lake and mountains from the sumptuous rooms and lounge. Fine-dining evening meals by arrangement.

For more places to eat and stay in Lake Tekapo see p285.

Aoraki/Mt Cook National Park ⑨

Aoraki/Mt Cook Alpine Lodge
Lodge $$

(☏03-435 1860; www.aorakialpinelodge.co.nz; Bowen Dr; d $169-240; 🛜) This lovely modern lodge has en suite rooms, including some suitable for families and two with kitchenettes; most have views. The huge lounge and kitchen area also has a superb mountain outlook, as does the barbecue area – a rather inspiring spot to sizzle your dinner.

For more places to eat and stay at Aoraki/Mt Cook National Park see p269

Twizel ⑩

Poppies Cafe
Cafe $$

(☏03-435 0848; www.poppiescafe.com; 1 Benmore Pl; brunch $10-23, dinner $26-36; ⏱10am-3pm & 5.30-9pm; 🛜) This well-run crowd-pleaser serves up eggy breakfasts, burger and salad lunches, and the likes of lamb curry and excellent pizzas ($22 to $24) come evening. Craft beer encourages a wee sup and snack, if you're not going the whole hog. It's located in the southeast of town just off SH8.

For more places to eat and stay in Twizel see p269

Cromwell ⑪

Armando's Kitchen
Cafe $$

(☏03-445 0303; 71 Melmore Tce; mains $10-22; ⏱10am-3pm Sat-Thu, to 9pm Fri, extended hours in summer) Cromwell's heritage precinct is best enjoyed from the veranda of Armando's Kitchen, with an espresso or gourmet ice cream in hand. The homemade pasta, pizza and cakes are all excellent, and the breakfasts are legendary. On Friday nights it opens late for pizza and drinks.

Burn Cottage Retreat
B&B, Cottage $$$

(☏03-445 3050; www.burncottageretreat.co.nz; 168 Burn Cottage Rd; r/cottages $200/225; 🛜) Set among walnut trees and gardens 3km northwest of Cromwell, this peaceful retreat has three luxurious, self-contained cottages with classy decor, spacious kitchens and modern bathrooms. B&B accommodation is available in the main house.

Arrowtown ⑫

La Rumbla
Tapas $$

(☏03-442 0509; www.facebook.com/larumbla. arrowtown; 54 Buckingham St; tapas $11-22; ⏱4pm-midnight Tue-Sun) Tucked behind the post office, this little gem does a brilliant job of bringing the bold flavours and late-dining habits of Spain to sleepy little Arrowtown. Local produce is showcased in tasty bites such as lamb meatballs and Southland suede croquettes. The decor is a little uninspired but there's some serious NZ art on the walls.

Arrowtown Lodge
B&B $$

(☏03-442 1101; www.arrowtownlodge.co.nz; 7 Anglesea St; r/cottage $195/395; 🛜) From the outside, the guest rooms look like heritage cottages, but inside they're cosy and modern, with en suite bathrooms. Each has a private entrance from the pretty gardens. A continental breakfast is provided.

For more places to eat and stay in Arrowtown see p313.

Queenstown ⑬

Dairy
Boutique Hotel $$$

(☏03-442 5164; www.thedairy.co.nz; 10 Isle St; s/d from $435/465; 🅿🛜) Once a corner store, the Dairy is now a luxury B&B with 13 rooms packed with classy touches such as designer bed linen, silk cushions and luxurious mohair rugs. Rates include cooked breakfasts and freshly baked afternoon teas.

For more places to eat and stay in Queenstown see pages 285, 303 and 313.

Lake Ohau Cycle from the foot of the Southern Alps to the Pacific Ocean

Alps to Ocean

20

Popularised by an epic new cycle trail, this awe-inspiring route from the Southern Alps to the Pacific coast is destined to become one of the South Island's signature drives.

TRIP HIGHLIGHTS

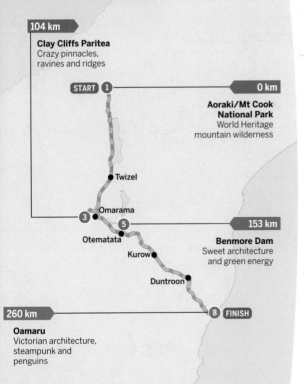

104 km

Clay Cliffs Paritea
Crazy pinnacles, ravines and ridges

START **1** — **0 km**

Aoraki/Mt Cook National Park
World Heritage mountain wilderness

● Twizel

3 ● Omarama

5

Otematata

Kurow ●

153 km

Benmore Dam
Sweet architecture and green energy

Duntroon ●

8 **FINISH**

260 km

Oamaru
Victorian architecture, steampunk and penguins

3–4 DAYS
260KM /
162 MILES

GREAT FOR...

BEST TIME TO GO

Spring and summer if you want to tramp or swim in the lakes

📷 ESSENTIAL PHOTO

The pointy end of Aoraki/Mt Cook from the Hooker Valley

☑ BEST FOR CYCLING

Swap the car for a bike on the Alps 2 Ocean Cycle Trail

20 Alps to Ocean

New Zealand's highest mountain – Aoraki/ Mt Cook – may be the geographical pinnacle of this memorable trip, but when it comes to eye-popping highlights it's merely the tip of the iceberg. Amid expansive landscapes lined with glacier-carved valleys, turquoise lakes, tussock-covered highlands and broad, braided rivers are several friendly towns and a series of fascinating hydropower structures.

TRIP HIGHLIGHT

❶ Aoraki/Mt Cook National Park

Aoraki/Mt Cook National Park's peaks are among NZ's grandest, with 19 numbering in the country's 23 over 3000m. It should come as no surprise, then, that NZ's greatest adventurer, Sir Edmund Hillary, honed his craft here, ascending Aoraki/Mt Cook – Australasia's highest mountain – in 1948.

The 3754m 'cloud piercer' (as it's known in

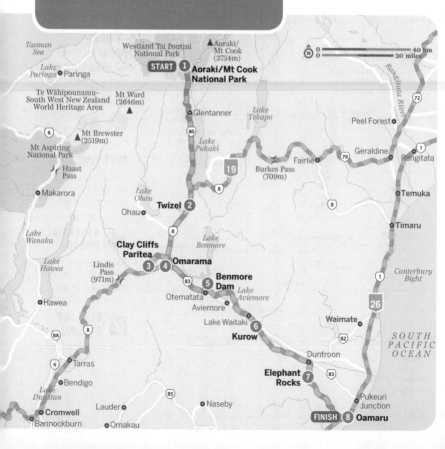

Māori) was actually at least 10m higher when Sir Ed climbed it, but in 1991 the summit collapsed sending 12 million cu metres of rock cascading down the mountain. Discover more of the national park's fascinating stories at DOC's splendid Aoraki/Mt Cook National Park Visitor Centre (p255).

A couple of minutes' walk away inside the huge Hermitage Hotel, the **Sir Edmund Hillary Alpine Centre** (www. hermitage.co.nz; The Hermitage, Terrace Rd; adult/child $20/10; ⏱7am-8.30pm Oct-Mar, 8am-7pm Apr-Sep) pays fitting tribute through various displays, while a series of movies screened throughout the day includes the rousing *Mt Cook Magic 3D* – a must-

LINK YOUR TRIP

19 Inland Scenic Route

At Aoraki/Mt Cook or Twizel, join this classic drive through the big-sky landscapes of the central South Island.

26 East Coast Express

From Oamaru, experience the East Coast's wildlife, ocean scenes and rural charm, plus rejuvenating Christchurch.

see if inclement weather means you can't see the mountain for real.

 p269

The Drive » Drive for 55km south on SH80, sidling alongside Lake Pukaki, pausing at lookout points to appreciate the colourful landscape. At the junction with SH8 turn right; it's 9km to Twizel.

- - - - - - - - - - - - - - -

② Twizel

Built in 1968 to temporarily house workers on the nearby hydropower scheme, Twizel has survived way past its use-by date thanks to locals who refused to leave their little slice of paradise. They were certainly on to something, for the Mackenzie Country is now one of NZ's most celebrated landscapes, with Twizel sitting pretty in the thick of it.

As well as being the primary hub for two-wheeled tours on the **Alps 2 Ocean Cycle Trail**, it's also a handy take-off point for scenic flights over **Aoraki/Mt Cook National Park**. **Helicopter Line** (☏03-435 0370; www.helicopter.co.nz; Pukaki Airport, Harry Wigley Dr), operating from Pukaki Airport 3km north of town, and Glentanner Park on SH80, offers a variety of options from 25 minutes to an hour, with the wow-factor rising in parallel with trip prices. All but the shortest

aerial adventures feature a snow landing.

 p269

The Drive » SH8 heads south through mountain surrounds. After 25km, turn right into Quailburn Rd and continue for 4km to the sign for Cathedral Cliffs, located at the end of an 11km private, unsealed road.

- - - - - - - - - - - - - - -

TRIP HIGHLIGHT

③ Clay Cliffs Paritea

Don't be put off by the name. In fact if we had our way they'd be renamed the Tectonic Towers, but perhaps that would blow their cover.

About as 'hidden gem' as you can get in an area rife with nosy tourists, these eerie pinnacles, ravines and ridges have been shaped by around two million years of erosion along the active Ostler fault. But you don't have to be a geology geek to appreciate their wacky lamellar form and aggregate tectonicity. Short trails lead around and between the forms so you can snap them from various angles.

The cliffs are on private land; be sure to pay the modest entrance fee ($5 per car) at Omarama Hot Tubs (p266).

The Drive » Return to SH8 via Quailburn Rd, and turn right towards Omarama, 5km away. The total distance is around 20km.

RAMIRO TORRENTS / GETTY IMAGES ©

④ Omarama

This quiet little town lies at a significant junction on the Inland Scenic Route between Christ-church and Queenstown, while SH83 funnels travellers down the Waitaki Valley towards the Pacific Ocean.

Omarama's summer thermals and alpine scenery have made it a world-renowned gliding base; **Glide Omarama** (☎03-438 9555; www.glideomarama.com) offers lessons and soaring scenic flights rang-ing from 30 minutes ($345) to 2½ hours ($745). The town's huge, pollution-free skies also encourage stargazing, particularly from the private, wood-fired hot tubs at **Omarama Hot Tubs** (☎03-438 9703; www.hottubsomarama. co.nz; 29 Omarama Ave/ SH8; per 1/2/3/4-person tub $52/90/114/136, pod $75/140/180/200; ☺11am-late). Choose between a 90-minute soak or a two-hour session in a 'wellness pod', which includes a sauna.

The Drive » Drive southwest along SH83 through the upper Waitaki Valley for 24km to Otematata, passing Lake Benmore which can be admired from Sailors Cutting. At Otematata, follow the signpost left to Benmore Dam, 5km away.

TRIP HIGHLIGHT

⑤ Benmore Dam

Benmore is the first of three hydro lakes in the upper Waitaki Valley, and the largest artificial lake in NZ. Benmore Dam, at its southern end, is a beauty. Completed and filled in 1965, it's the largest earth dam in the land and holds back enough water to power around 298,000 homes. Its concrete penstocks, pipes and flow ways add industrial elegance to the surrounding golden hills and pretty waters.

The road across the dam not only enables you to snap it from every highly Instagrammable angle, but also provides

Mt Cook

access to the scenic north-bank road that winds around the next arrestingly blue stretch of water, Lake Aviemore.

The Drive » After crossing the dam, drive for 23km along Te Akatarawa Rd until you reach Aviemore Dam. A refreshing dip may be had along the way. Cross the dam and follow SH83 down the Waitaki Valley to Kurow, 15km away.

❻ Kurow

One of the most appealing stops along the Waitaki Valley is tiny, lost-in-time Kurow, home town of All Black hero Richie McCaw.

The town also boasts champion wines. Housed in the old post office, **Vintner's Drop** (☏03-436 0545; www.ostlerwine.co.nz; 45 Bledisloe St; ⏱noon-5pm Thu-Sun Nov-Mar) is the tasting room for Ostler Vineyards, one of just a few Waitaki winemaking pioneers. They may have a long way to go to achieve the reputation enjoyed by their colleagues over in Central Otago, but some wonderful drops are produced from the tricky but propitious local terroir,

THE ALTERNATIVE ALPS 2 OCEAN

One of the best Great Rides within the **New Zealand Cycle Trail** (www.nzcycletrail.com), the 'A2O' serves up epic vistas from the foot of the Southern Alps all the way to the Pacific Ocean at Oamaru. In fact, the off-road trail parallels this road trip for much of the way.

Off-the-bike activities include wine tasting, scenic flights and soaking in al fresco hot tubs, and while the whole trail takes four to six days to complete, it can readily be sliced into shorter sections. Twizel is an excellent base for day trips, such as the five-to-six-hour big-sky ride from Tekapo to Twizel, or from Twizel out to the lodge at remote Lake Ohau for lunch or dinner.

Down-home hospitality, along with bike hire and shuttle companies such as Twizel-based **Cycle Journeys** (www.cyclejourneys.co.nz; ☎03-435 0578) and **Jollie Biker** (www.thejolliebiker.co.nz; ☎03-435 0517), make for easy logistics and maximum enjoyment. The A2O website (www.alps2ocean.com) has details; the trail is also showcased in Lonely Planet's *Epic Rides* book.

such as Ostler's velvety Caroline's pinot noir and lingering Lakeside riesling.

The Drive » Drive southeast on SH83 until you reach Livingstone–Duntroon Rd, just past teeny weeny Duntroon. Turn right, drive for 4km, then turn left into Island Cliff–Duntroon Rd. Elephant Rocks are 1km on the right, 29km from Kurow.

- - - - - - - - - - - -

❼ Elephant Rocks

Pop the trunk, pocket some peanuts, and wander into a geological wonderland you'll never forget – a series of huge limestone boulders lying like oddly cast, oversized knucklebones on a lush green paddock nibbled neatly by sheep. Such is the fantastical nature of this bizarre landscape that it appeared as Aslan's Camp in the *Narnia* movies.

These rock stars started life at the bottom of the ocean more than 24 million years ago. Originally formed from the skeletal remains of marine organisms compressed into limestone, they were thrust upwards and sculpted by wind, rain and rivers. Enjoy your peanut picnic in the warm cradle of a boulder. It may even bring on a wee nana nap.

The Drive » Continue southwest along Island Cliff–

Duntroon Rd, which becomes Tokarahi–Ngapara Rd and then Weston–Ngapara Rd, for a meandering 40km drive through rolling, pastoral landscapes to Oamaru. The Tokarahi Homestead & Farm, 9km south of Elephant Rocks, is a charming place to stay, if you're not pushing through to the coast.

- - - - - - - - - - - -

TRIP HIGHLIGHT

❽ Oamaru

Nothing moves very fast in Oamaru. Tourists saunter, locals linger and penguins waddle. Even its recently resurrected heritage transport – penny-farthings and steam trains – reflect an unhurried pace and a wellspring of eccentricity bubbling under the surface.

Most travellers come here for the little tykes of the **Blue Penguin Colony** (☎03-433 1195; www.penguins.co.nz; 2 Waterfront Rd; ⏰10am until 2hr after sunset), which surf in and wade ashore to their nests in an old stone quarry near the waterfront. General admission (adult/child $28/14) provides a good view of the action but the premium stand ($40/20), accessed by a boardwalk through the nesting area, will get you closer. You'll see the most penguins (up to 250) in November and December. From March to August there may be only 10 to 50 birds.

✕ 🛏 p269

Eating & Sleeping

Aoraki/Mt Cook National Park ❶

✕ Old Mountaineers' Cafe
Cafe $$

(www.mtcook.com; Bowen Dr; breakfast $10-15, lunch $14-26, dinner $18-35; ⊙10am-9pm daily Nov-Apr, Tue-Sun May & Jul-Oct; 🛜) Encouraging lingering with books, memorabilia and mountain views through picture windows, the village's best eatery also supports local and organic suppliers through a menu sporting salmon and bacon pies, cooked breakfasts, burgers and pizza.

🛏 Mt Cook YHA
Hostel $

(📞03-435 1820; www.yha.co.nz; 4 Bowen Dr; dm/d $38/137; 🛜) Handsomely decked out in pine, this excellent hostel has a free sauna, a drying room, log fires and DVDs. Rooms are clean and warm, although some are a tight squeeze (particularly the twin bunk rooms).

For more places to eat and stay in Aoraki/Mt Cook National Park see p261.

Twizel ❷

✕ High Country Salmon
Seafood $$

(📞0800 400 385; www.highcountrysalmonfarm.co.nz; SH8; ⊙8.30am-6pm) The glacial waters of this floating fish farm, 3km from Twizel, produce mighty delicious fish, available as fresh whole fillets and smoked portions. Our pick is the hot-smoked, flaked into hot pasta with a dash of cream.

🛏 Omahau Downs
Lodge, Cottage $$

(📞03-435 0199; www.omahau.co.nz; SH8; s $115, d $135-165, cottages $125-225; ⊙closed Jun-Aug; 🛜) This farmstead, 2km north of Twizel, has two cosy, self-contained cottages (one sleeping up to six), and a lodge with sparkling, modern rooms and a deck looking out at the Ben Ohau Range.

🛏 Heartland Lodge
B&B, Apartment $$$

(📞03-435 0008; www.heartland-lodge.co.nz; 19 North West Arch; apt $170, s $240-280, d $280-

320; 🛜) Built on the leafy outskirts of town, this elegant modern house offers spacious, en suite rooms upstairs and comfortable, convivial communal space on the ground floor. Friendly hosts prepare a cooked breakfast using organic, local produce where possible. The adjacent 'retreat' apartment (sleeping up to six) has its own kitchenette; breakfast not provided.

For more places to eat and stay in Twizel see p261.

Tokorahi

🛏 Tokarahi Homestead & Farm
B&B, Cabins $$

(📞03-431 2055; www.homestead.co.nz; 47 Dip Hill Rd, Tokarahi; d B&B/cabin $180/130; 🛜📶) Join the owners at the grand, renovated 1878 homestead, or stay down the road in super-cute cabins upcycled in admirable style using materials from the old farmhouse. Evening meals and lunches by arrangement. From Duntroon, drive down Livingstone-Duntroon Rd (which turns into Tokarahi-Duntroon Rd) for 12km and then turn right into Dip Hill Rd.

Oamaru ❽

✕ Northstar
Modern NZ $$

(📞03-437 1190; www.northstarmotel.co.nz; 495a Thames Hwy; mains lunch $19-23, dinner $30-34; ⊙noon-3pm & 6-9pm) Surprisingly upmarket for a restaurant attached to an SH1 motel, Northstar is the first choice for Oamaruvians with something to celebrate. Expect robust bistro fare with a touch of contemporary flair. The bar is popular, too.

🛏 Highfield Mews
Motel $$

(📞03-434 3437; www.highfieldmews.co.nz; 244 Thames St; units from $170; @🛜) Motels have come a long away from the gloomy concrete-block constructions of the 1960s and '70s, as this new build attests. The units are basically smart apartments, with kitchens, desks, stereos, tiled bathrooms and outdoor furniture.

Classic Trip

Southern Alps Circuit

21

See a stack of the South's top sights on this trip along ceaselessly scenic alpine, coastal, lakeland and rural highways, dotted with towns ranging from rustic Ross to racy Queenstown.

TRIP HIGHLIGHTS

148 km

Arthur's Pass National Park
Rugged mountains, braided rivers and great walks, both short and epic

406 km

Fox Glacier
Scenic flights and hikes amid the glaciers and NZ's highest peaks

Hokitika

2

Christchurch
START / FINISH

5

Haast

12

Geraldine

8

Queenstown

1104 km

Lake Tekapo
Surreal blue lake and astronomically good night skies

Wanaka
Sublime lakeside gateway to Mt Aspiring National Park

670 km

12–14 DAYS
1379KM /
857 MILES

GREAT FOR...

BEST TIME TO GO

This is a stunner all year round

ESSENTIAL PHOTO

Lake Tekapo and the Mackenzie Country from Mt John's summit

☑ BEST FOR MOUNTAIN SCENERY

An aerial sightseeing trip around Aoraki/ Mt Cook

Classic Trip

21 Southern Alps Circuit

Nothing defines the South Island like the Southern Alps, the 500km-long series of ranges stretching from Nelson Lakes to Fiordland. This trip offers the chance to admire a vast swathe of them from all manner of angles on such quintessential New Zealand experiences as glacier ice hikes, scenic flights, cross-country bike rides and nature walks – or just staring out the car window, if you prefer.

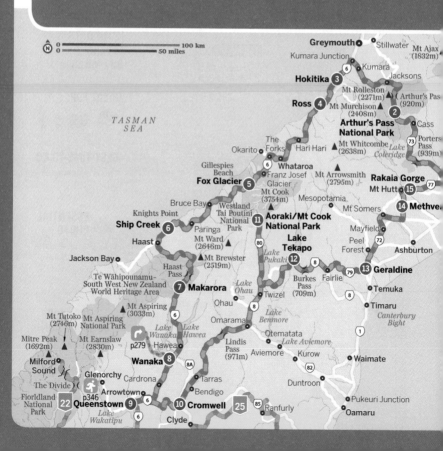

TASMAN SEA

Greymouth • Stillwater Mt Ajax (1832m)
Kumara Junction • Kumara
Hokitika **3** • Jacksons
Mt Rolleston (2271m) Arthur's Pass (920m)
Ross **4** Mt Murchison (2408m) **2**
Mt Whitcombe (2638m) **Arthur's Pass National Park** Cass
Okarito • The Forks • Hari Hari Lake Coleridge Porters Pass (939m)
Gillespies Beach Whataroa **73**
Fox Glacier Franz Josef Glacier Mt Arrowsmith (2795m) **Rakaia Gorge**
Bruce Bay Mt Cook (3754m) Mesopotamia Mt Hutt **15** **77**
Knights Point Westland Tai Poutini National Park **Aoraki/Mt Cook National Park** **11** Mt Somers **14** **Methven**
Ship Creek **6** Paringa Mayfield
Haast Mt Ward (2646m) **Lake Tekapo** **12** Peel Forest **72** Ashburton
Jackson Bay • Mt Brewster (2519m) Lake Pukaki Burkes Pass (709m) **8** **13** **Geraldine**
Haast Pass **80** **8** Fairlie **79**
Te Wāhipounamu– South West New Zealand World Heritage Area **7** **Makarora** Lake Ohau Twizel Temuka **8**
Mt Aspiring (3033m) Ohau **8** Timaru
Mt Tutoko (2746m) Mt Aspiring National Park Lake Wanaka Lake Hawea Omarama Lake Benmore Canterbury Bight
Mitre Peak (1692m) Mt Earnslaw (2830m) p279 Hawea Lindis Pass (971m) Otematata Lake Aviemore
Milford Sound Glenorchy Cardrona **8** **8A** Aviemore Kurow • Waimate
The Divide p346 Arrowtown Tarras **82** Duntroon
Fiordland National Park **22** **Queenstown** **9** Bendigo **1**
Lake Wakatipu **6** **10** **Cromwell** **25** **85** Ranfurly Pukeuri Junction
Clyde Oamaru

0 —— 100 km
0 —— 50 miles

➊ Christchurch

Nowhere in NZ is changing as fast as postearthquake Christchurch, and visiting the country's second-largest city during its rebuilding phase is both interesting and inspiring. What's more, the majority of Christchurch's prequake attractions are open for business, including the must-visit Canterbury Museum (p286). Not only does it provide a well-rounded introduction to the city and region, it's also particularly strong on the natural history of wider NZ.

Christchurch has been long been a regular departure point for travellers to Antarctica. Near the airport (and serviced by a free shuttle from the central city), the **International Antarctic Centre** (☎0508 736 4846; www.iceberg.co.nz; 38 Orchard Rd, Christchurch Airport; adult/child $39/19; ◷9am-5.30pm) offers visitors the opportunity to learn about the icy continent, see live penguins, and experience -18°C wind chill in the storm chamber.

 p284

The Drive ≫ Head out of the city limits on SH73, which strikes out across Canterbury Plains and heads into the Southern Alps. The Big Ben, Torlesse and Craigieburn Ranges are but a prelude to the mega-peaks of Arthur's Pass National Park, around two hours (148km) from Christchurch.

TRIP HIGHLIGHT

➋ Arthur's Pass National Park

Straddling the Southern Alps, Arthur's Pass National Park encompasses a seriously rugged landscape, riven with deep valleys and ranging in altitude from 245m at the Taramakau River to 2408m at the top of Mt Murchison. It's popular with alpinists and backcountry trampers, but its dramatic wilderness can readily be appreciated on brief forays close to the highway.

There are multiple walking options from the village, including one of the best day hikes in the country. The strenuous climb up **Avalanche Peak** (www.doc. govt.nz; 7km; six-to-eight hours return) should only be attempted in fine weather by fit, well-equipped and experienced walkers. Those who do make the effort, however, will be rewarded with

SOUTH
PACIFIC
OCEAN

🔗 LINK YOUR TRIP

22 **Milford Sound Majesty**

Lakes, mountains and waterfalls decorate this super-scenic drive from Queenstown to Milford Sound via Te Anau.

25 **Otago Heritage Trail**

Drive 24km south on SH8 from Cromwell to Clyde for a history-laden circuit around Central Otago and to the Pacific coast.

Classic Trip

staggering views of the surrounding mountains, valleys and hanging glaciers.

The village itself, home to a permanent population of around 60, sports a couple of cafes and the **Arthur's Pass Visitor Centre** (📞 03-318 9211; www.doc.govt.nz; 80 Main Rd; ⏰ 8.30pm-4.30pm). Pop in here for walking track information and local weather forecasts.

The Drive ›› Continue west on SH73. Beyond the actual pass (920m), craggy mountain vistas give way to rural scenes as the highway winds down to meet SH6, the West Coast Rd. At Kumara Junction head south to Hokitika, 22km away for a total of 100km (around 90 minutes) driving.

- - - - - - - - -

③ Hokitika

Just one of scores of West Coast towns founded on gold, Hokitika boasts an admirable array of historic buildings, including the 1908 Carnegie Building housing Hokitika Museum (p211). An exem-

MĀORI GREENSTONE ROUTES

The South Island is known in Māori as Te Waipounamu – the waters of greenstone – which gives some idea of the stone's importance during the early days of Aotearoa's settlement. *Pounamu* (greenstone) is nephrite jade, bowenite or serpentinite, prized for its toughness and beauty and used to make weaponry, tools and jewellery.

Pounamu comes from only one place in New Zealand – the western side of the Southern Alps, particularly from rivers around Hokitika. It was the search for *pounamu* that saw Māori, from around AD 1300, forge routes from the more populated east coast through river valleys and over mountain passes. These were incredibly intrepid journeys through wild terrain made all the more frightening by NZ's volatile maritime climate. The navigational and survival skills of these Māori explorers were a boon for pioneering Europeans who relied heavily on their guidance when surveying the south during the 19th century.

Arthur's, Haast and Lewis Passes, Buller Gorge and the Milford Hwy – all were once single-track pathways followed by Māori greenstone gatherers. Others – such as Mackinnon Pass (on the Milford Track) and Harper Pass – have remained passable only on foot.

plary provincial museum and easily the best on the Coast, its wide-ranging displays cover such topics as the gold rushes, the region's natural and social history, and traditional Māori use of *pounamu*.

Hokitika today is a stronghold of this indigenous and highly prized stone, judiciously gathered from nearby rivers. It is fashioned into pendants and other personal treasures by master carvers who jostle for position alongside jewellers, glass-blowers and various other craftspeople. Art-lovers will find the town a delight.

Keep your fingers crossed for a clear evening, because five minutes' walk from the town centre is **Sunset Point** – a primo place to watch the light fade with a feed of fish and chips, seagulls circling, and big Tasman Sea waves crashing on the driftwood-strewn shore.

🍴 🛏 p284

The Drive ›› Just south of Hokitika are a couple of scenic walks – the historic Mananui Tramline, which has outstanding historical information panels, and the commercial Treetop Walkway, a canopy-level construction built from steel. The rest of the 27km drive to Ross cuts inland through a mixture of pasture and patches of forest.

④ Ross

Ross was the scene of a major kerfuffle in 1907 when NZ's largest gold nugget (the 2.772kg 'Honourable Roddy') was unearthed. The **Ross Goldfields Heritage Centre** (www.ross.org.nz; 4 Aylmer St; ⊙9am-4pm Dec-Mar, to 2pm Apr-Nov) displays a replica Roddy, along with a scale model of the town in its glittering years. Starting near the museum, the **Water Race Walk** (one hour return) passes old gold diggings, caves, tunnels and a cemetery.

Apparently there's still gold in them thar hills, so you might like to try a spot of gold panning in Jones Creek. The $10 pan hire fee is a small outlay for the chance to find Roddy's great, great grandnuggets, don't you think?

Okay, maybe not. You could just spend the tenner on a pint at the **Empire Hotel** (✆03-755 4005; 19 Aylmer St). Established in 1866 and one of the West Coast's hidden gems, the bar (and many of its patrons) are testament to a bygone era. Breathe in the authenticity, along with a whiff of woodsmoke, over a beer and an honest meal.

The Drive » The 131km, two-hour drive south to Fox Glacier meanders inland crossing numerous mighty West Coast river systems, cutting through dense rainforest and passing tranquil lakes. The 30-minute section between Franz Josef Glacier and Fox Glacier townships will blow your socks off (if it's not raining…).

TRIP HIGHLIGHT

⑤ Fox Glacier

Fox Glacier is the smaller and quieter of the twin glacier townships, and is set in more rural surrounds. While you should linger in both if your itinerary allows, Fox is our pick of the two.

Fox's glacier viewing options are remarkably similar to those of Franz. Scenic helicopter flights are offered by a raft of operators touting for business on the main road. There is also a choice of independent or guided walks up into the glacier valley, as well as glacier hikes with Fox Glacier Guiding (p216).

For a unique perspective of the glaciers, consider leaping out of a perfectly good plane above them. **Skydive Fox Glacier** (✆0800 751 0080, 03-751 0080; www.skydivefox.co.nz; Fox Glacier Airfield, SH6) offer tandem jumps from 13,000ft and 16,500ft. If you want to strike skydiving off your bucket list, you'd be hard pushed to find a more dramatic setting for it.

✗ ⊨ p284

The Drive » Allow 90 minutes to reach Ship Creek, 103km away along a scenic stretch of highway chopped through lowland forest and occasional pasture with intermittent views seaward. Stop at Knights Point, 5km south of Lake Moeraki, a spectacular lookout commemorating the opening of this stretch of highway in 1965.

---

⑥ Ship Creek

For a taste of the wilderness that qualifies the Haast region for inclusion in Te Wāhipounamu–South West New Zealand World Heritage Area, you can't go past Ship Creek. Well, you can, but you shouldn't.

The car park alongside the highway is

✓ **TOP TIP: PESKY SANDFLIES**

You will encounter sandflies on the West Coast. While they don't carry diseases they are a pain in the bum, face, arm, leg, ankle or whatever else is exposed. Your best deterrent is to cover up, although effective DEET-free products such as Okarito Sandfly Repellent are also readily available. Thankfully sandflies do go to bed after dark, allowing you some respite!

Classic Trip

MARCO SIMONI / ROBERTHARDING / GETTY IMAGES ©

WHY THIS IS A CLASSIC TRIP
SARAH BENNETT, WRITER

This loop is the premier NZ road trip – the first I suggest to anyone exploring for a couple of weeks or more. There are endless reasons why – especially when you factor in dozens of possible detours – but it's the chance to penetrate deep into the mountains via Arthur's and Haast Passes that makes it so memorable. Incredibly dramatic in themselves, they also gate-keep the mind-bendingly different landscapes either side of the alps.

Top: Hot-air balloon near Methven
Left: Tourists on Fox Glacier
Right: Blue Pools, near Makarora

DANITA DELIMONT / GETTY IMAGES ©

the trailhead for two fascinating walks. We suggest starting with **Kahikatea Swamp Forest Walk**, a 20-minute amble through a weird bog, before heading on to the beach for the **Dune Lake Walk.** This salty, sandy amble is supposed to take half an hour but may well suck you into a vortex of beach-combing, wave-watching, seabird-spotting and perhaps even a spot of tree-hugging in the primeval forest around the reedy lake.

The Drive » SH7 sticks close to the coast before crossing the Haast River on NZ's longest single-lane bridge. At Haast Junction, around half an hour from Ship Creek, take SH6 to Haast township – a chance to stock up on food and fuel – before continuing on towards Haast Pass. This 97km leg will take just under two hours.

- - - - - - - - - -

❼ Makarora

The first sign of life after crossing Haast Pass into Central Otago, middle-of-nowhere Makarora survives as a road-trip stop and a base for adventure into Siberia.

No, not that Siberia. We're talking about the remote wilderness valley within **Mt Aspiring National Park,** reached on one of the South Island's signature adventure tours – the **Siberia Experience** (📞03-443 4385; www.siberiaexperience. co.nz; adult/child $355/287).

Classic Trip

This thrill-seeking extravaganza combines a 25-minute scenic small-plane flight, a three-hour tramp through the remote mountain valley and a half-hour jetboat trip down the Wilkin and Makarora Rivers. There may be better ways to spend four hours, but it's tough to think of any.

This terrific valley can also be reached on the **Gillespie Pass Circuit** (www.doc.govt. nz), a magnificent 58km, three- to four-day loop for experienced, well-equipped hikers. The side trip to Crucible Lake is one of our favourite day tramps.

The Drive » Boom! Classic Central Otago scenery – wide, open, and framed by schist peaks – welcomes you as SH6 snakes away from Makarora and sidles along the convoluted edges of Lake Wanaka and Lake Hawea. This glorious, 64km drive to Wanaka takes around an hour.

- - - - - - - - - - -
TRIP HIGHLIGHT

8 Wanaka

While certainly more laid-back than its amped-up sibling, Queenstown, Wanaka is not a sleepy hamlet any more. Its lakeside setting is utterly sublime, its streets less cluttered and clogged with traffic. Combine this

with a critical mass of shops, restaurants and bars, and you've got an arguably more charming (and slightly cheaper) rival.

There's also an endless array of adrenalising and inspiring outdoor activities. Wanaka is the gateway to Mt Aspiring National Park, as well as Cardrona and Treble Cone ski resorts. Closer to town, however, are heaps of easier and more accessible adventures; see DOC's *Wanaka Outdoor Pursuits* pamphlet for a comprehensive run-down.

A classic walkway hoofs it up to the summit of **Mt Iron** (527m, 1½ hours return), revealing panoramic views of Lake Wanaka and its mind-boggling surrounds. To get out on the lake, just jump right in wearing your underpants – or your swimsuit, obviously, if you have one – or head out for a paddle with **Wanaka Kayaks** (📞0800 926 925; www.wanakakayaks. co.nz; Ardmore St; ⏰9am-6pm Oct-Easter), located on the waterfront.

✕ 🛏 p284

The Drive » Head over to Queenstown via the well-signposted Crown Range, NZ's highest sealed road at 1121m. Pull over at designated lookout points to admire the view on the way down to the Wakatipu Basin, and at the junction with SH6 head right towards Queenstown. This 68km drive will take just over an hour.

9 Queenstown

New Zealand's premier resort town is an extravaganza of shopping, dining and tour booking offices, packaged up together in the midst of inspiring mountain surrounds. If you're looking to let your hair down and tick some big stuff off your bucket list, Queenstown's a beaut place to do it.

Ease your way into it on a walking tour (p346), taking in major sites such as **Skyline Gondola** and **Steamer Wharf**, and following **Queenstown Gardens'** lakeshore path, revealing ever-changing panoramas of Lake Wakatipu and the Remarkables. Add to this backdrop the region's other mountain ranges, tumbling rivers, hidden canyons and rolling high country, and it's not hard to see why Queenstown is the king of outdoor adventure.

The options are mind-boggling, so allow us to suggest one of the classics – a blast on the **Shotover Jet** (📞03-442 8570; www.shotoverjet. com; Gorge Rd, Arthurs Point; adult/child $135/75). Quite likely to be the most hair-raising boat ride of your life, this trip through a rocky canyon features famous 360-degree spins that may well blow your toupee clean off.

✕ 🛏 p285

The Drive >> This dramatic 60km drive through the Kawarau Gorge will take around an hour. Drive on SH6A out of Queenstown past the airport and then onwards beyond Lake Hayes and the turn-off for Arrowtown. There are numerous temptations on the way to Cromwell including Gibbston Valley wineries and the original AJ Hackett bungy jump.

- - - - - - - - - - - - - -

⑩ Cromwell

The hot, dry, highly mineral soils around Cromwell account for town's claim to fame as a fruit bowl – as celebrated in the giant, gaudy fruit sculpture that greets visitors as they arrive.

Among many luscious specimens are the grapes grown around **Bannockburn**, Central Otago's finest wine-growing sub-region, just south Cromwell (p307). A dozen or so wineries are open to the public, with several offering notable dining. **Carrick** (☏03-445 3480; www.carrick.co.nz; Cairnmuir Rd , Bannockburn; ⊙11am-5pm) is up there with the best, with an art-filled restaurant opening out on to a terrace and lush lawns, and a willow-framed view of the Carrick mountains. Their platters are a pleasurable complement to the wine range which includes an intense, spicy pinot noir – their flagship drop – as well as a rich, toasty chardonnay and citrusy aromatic varietals.

Designated drivers can blow off some steam at the **Highlands Motorsport Park** (☏03-445 4052; www.highlands.co.nz; cnr SH6 & Sandflat Rd; ⊙10am-5pm), a first-rate 4km racing circuit offering an array of high-octane experiences. Budding speed freaks can start out on the go-karts

➡ DETOUR: MT ASPIRING NATIONAL PARK

Start: ❽ Wanaka

Verdant valleys, alpine meadows, unspoiled rivers, craggy mountains and more than 100 glaciers make Mt Aspiring National Park an outdoor enthusiast's paradise. Protected as a national park in 1964, and now part of **Te Wāhipounamu–South West New Zealand World Heritage Area**, the park blankets 3555 sq km along the Southern Alps. Lording it over all is colossal Tititea/Mt Aspiring (3033m), the highest peak outside the Aoraki/Mt Cook area.

While the southern end of the national park near Glenorchy includes better-known tramps such as the Routeburn and Greenstone & Caples tracks, the Wanaka gateway offers an easier way in via Raspberry Creek, at the end of Mt Aspiring Rd, 50km from town – much of it along the lake shore. Well worth the drive in itself, even if you don't fancy tramping, the road is unsealed for 30km and involves nine ford crossings; it's usually fine in a 2WD, except in very wet conditions.

A good option for intermediate hikers, taking three to four hours return, **Rob Roy Glacier Track** is a chance to see glaciers, waterfalls and a swing bridge, among other landmarks. The **West Matukituki Valley Track**, meanwhile, heads up to historic Aspiring Hut, popular with overnight walkers. Sound tempting? Check out DOC's *Matukituki Valley Tracks* brochure (www.doc.govt.nz). Check in with **Tititea Mt Aspiring National Park Visitor Centre** (☏03-443 7660; www.doc.govt. nz; cnr Ardmore & Ballantyne Sts; ⊙8.30am-5pm daily Nov-Apr, Mon-Sat May-Oct) in Wanaka if the weather looks remotely dubious – even these lower-altitude tracks can be troublesome.

TOTAJLA / GETTY IMAGES ©

before taking a 200km/h ride in the Highlands Taxi, then completing three laps of the circuit as a passenger in a Porsche GT, or behind the wheel of a V8 muscle car.

The Drive » From Cromwell cross the bridge over Lake Dunstan and drive north on SH8 along the lake, through Tarras, and on to Lindis Pass before passing into Mackenzie

Country. Around 9km after Twizel is the turn-off for Aoraki/Mt Cook on SH80. This 204km journey should take less than three hours.

TRIP HIGHLIGHT

⑪ Aoraki/Mt Cook National Park

The spectacular 700-sq-km Aoraki/Mt Cook National Park, along with Fiordland, Aspiring

and Westland National Parks, forms part of the Te Wāhipounamu–South West New Zealand World Heritage Area, which extends from Westland's Cook River down to Fiordland. Fenced in by the Southern Alps and the Two Thumb, Liebig and Ben Ohau Ranges, more than one-third of the national park has a

Rakaia Gorge

blanket of permanent snow and glacial ice.

The highest *maunga* (mountain) in the park is mighty **Aoraki/Mt Cook** – at 3754m it's the tallest peak in Australasia. Among the region's other many great peaks are Sefton, Tasman, Silberhorn, Malte Brun, La Perouse, Hicks, De la Beche, Douglas and the Minarets.

Unless you're an able alpinist, the best way to view this mountain majesty is on a scenic flight. **Helicopter Line** (📞 03-435 1801; www.heli-copter.co.nz; Glentanner Park, Mt Cook Rd) at **Glentanner Park** and **Mount Cook Ski Planes** (📞 03-430 8026; www.mtcookskiplanes. com; Mt Cook Airport) at Mt Cook Airport will buzz you around the peaks on

a variety of trips; all but the shortest include a landing in the snow.

The Drive ≫ Return along SH80, pausing at lookout points along the 55km stretch to soak up more of the mesmerising lake and mountain scenery. At the junction with SH8 turn left and drive a further 47km northeast over the Mary Range to Lake Tekapo.

Classic Trip

- - - - - - - - - - -

12 Lake Tekapo

The mountain-ringed basin known as the Mac-kenzie Country – lined with surreal blue hydro lakes and canals, surrounded by golden tussock – is one of the South Island's most celebrated landscapes. Towards its northern boundary is Lake Tekapo township, born of a hydropower scheme completed in 1953, and today pretty much a compulsory stopping point for the passing traveller.

Perched on the shore of the opalescent, turquoise lake, with a backdrop of the snow-capped Southern Alps, it's no wonder the Church of the Good Shepherd is one of NZ's most photographed buildings. Built of stone and oak in 1935, it features a picture window that frames a distractingly divine view of lake and mountain majesty. Arrive early morning or late afternoon if you want to avoid the crowds.

The view is indeed divine, but still no match for the epic, 360-degree panorama from the top of **Mt John** (1029m). A winding but well-sealed road leads to the summit, home to astronomical observatories and fabulous Astro Café (p260). You can also reach the sum-

GETTING ON THE PISTE

The South Island is an essential southern-hemisphere destination for snow bunnies, with downhill skiing, cross-country (Nordic) skiing and snowboarding all passionately pursued. NZ's ski season is generally June through September, though it varies considerably from one resort to another, and can run as late as October.

NZ's ski fields come in all shapes and sizes. Some people like to be near Queenstown's party scene, others prefer the quality high-altitude runs on Mt Hutt or less-stressed and cheaper club-skiing areas. These are some of our favourite South Island skiing and snowboarding spots:

Treble Cone (☏03-443 1406, snow-phone 03-443 7444; www.treblecone.com; daily lift pass adult/child $106/52) The highest and largest of the southern lakes ski areas is in a spectacular location 26km from Wanaka, with steep slopes suitable for intermediate to advanced skiers (and a rather professional vibe). There are also halfpipes and a terrain park for boarders.

Coronet Peak (☏03-442 4620; www.nzski.com; Coronet Peak Rd; daily lift pass adult/child $104/59) At the Queenstown region's oldest ski field, snow-making and treeless slopes provide excellent skiing and snowboarding for all levels. There's night skiing Friday and Saturday.

Cardrona (☏03-443 8880, snow phone 03-443 7007; www.cardrona.com; Cardrona Skifield Access Rd; day pass adult/child $101/52; ⊙9am-4pm Jul-Sep) Around 34km from Wanaka, with several high-capacity chairlifts, beginners tows and Parks 'n' Pipes for the freestylers.

Mt Hutt (☏03-302 8811; www.nzski.com; day lift passes adult/child $98/56; ⊙9am-4pm) One of the highest ski areas in the southern hemisphere, located close to Methven. There are plenty of beginner, intermediate and advanced slopes.

Ohau (☏03-438 9885; www.ohau.co.nz; daily lift passes adult/child $83/34) This commercial ski area is on Mt Sutton, 42km from Twizel. There are plenty of intermediate and advanced runs, excellent snowboarding, two terrain parks and Lake Ohau Lodge.

mit via the circuit track
(2½ hours return).

✕ 🛏 p285

The Drive » Climb away
from the lake on SH8 over
the relatively low Burkes Pass
(709m) and on to the rural town
of Fairlie, home of super-fine
pies. From here, drive on SH79
through flatter but still rolling
countryside to Geraldine, the
cheese and pickle capital of New
Zealand. Total distance is 89km.

⑬ Geraldine

With a touch of quaint
English village about it,
Geraldine is a pleasant
place to break a journey
amid the rural Canter-
bury Plains.

On the town's north-
western fringe, **Talbot
Forest Scenic Reserve**
(www.doc.govt.nz; Tripp
St) is a good place to
stretch your legs and hug
some magnificent trees,
including lofty kahikatea
(white pine) and a mas-
sive totara estimated to
be around 800 years old.

The forest lends
its name to one of
Geraldine's signature
attractions, Talbot Forest
Cheese (p251). You'll
find it in the Four Peaks
Plaza alongside Barker's
(p251), the pickle-makers
that will complete your
ploughman's lunch.

🛏 p285

The Drive » Drive north on
SH72, crossing the braided
Rangitata River after 6km, then
passing through flat, irrigated
pastoral land along Roman-
straight roads. Continue on
SH72 as it traces around the
eastern edge of the mountains.
Turn right on to SH77, 72km
from Geraldine, and drive the
last 10km to Methven.

⑭ Methven

Methven is busiest in
winter, when it fills up
with snow bunnies head-
ing to nearby Mt Hutt ski
field. At other times tum-
bleweeds don't quite blow
down the main street –
much to the disappoint-
ment of the wannabe
gunslingers arriving
for the raucous October
rodeo. Over summer it's
a low-key and affordable
base for explorations into
the spectacular mountain
foothills.

The town itself can be
explored on a heritage
trail and the **Methven
Walk/Cycleway**. Maps
for these are available
from the **i-SITE** (📞03-302
8955; www.methvenmthutt.
co.nz; 160 Main St; ⏰9.30am-
5pm daily Jul-Sep, 9am-5pm
Mon-Fri, 10am-3pm Sat & Sun
Oct-Jun; 📶), which can
also provide information
about other activities in
the area including horse
riding, hot-air balloon

trips and jetboat trips on
the nearby Rakaia Gorge.

✕ p285

The Drive » Drive north on
Mt Hutt Station Rd and then
turn right on to SH72, passing
through Mt Hutt village before
reaching the beautifully blue
and braided river at Rakaia
Gorge, 16km from Methven.

⑮ Rakaia Gorge

One of NZ's most volumi-
nous braided rivers, the
Rakaia starts out deep
and swift in the moun-
tains before gradually
widening and separating
into strands over a gravel
bed. The half-day **Rakaia
Gorge Walkway** is a good
opportunity to survey the
river's milky blue waters
and take in other sites
including the historic
ferryman's cottage and
old coal mines.

The Drive » Drive east on
SH72 (aka Route 77) for 41km to
Darfield, leaving the mountains
in the rear-view mirror as you
reach the patchwork Canterbury
Plains. Continue east on
SH73, until the outskirts of
Christchurch, then follow signs
for the city centre. Total distance
is 88km.

Classic Trip

Eating & Sleeping

Christchurch ❶

✖ Fiddlesticks
Modern NZ **$$**

(📞03-365 0533; www.fiddlesticksbar.co.nz; 48 Worcester Blvd; lunch $25-40, dinner $24-48; ⏰8am-late Mon-Fri, 9am-late Sat & Sun) Sidle into slick Fiddlesticks and seat yourself in either the more formal dining room or the glassed-in patio attached to the curvy cocktail bar. Food ranges from soups and beautifully presented salads to fluffy gnocchi and Angus steaks.

🛏 Classic Villa
B&B **$$$**

(📞03-377 7905; www.theclassicvilla.co.nz; 17 Worcester Blvd; s $199, d $299-409, ste $499; 🅿🛜) Pretty in pink, this 1897 house is one of Christchurch's most elegant accommodation options. Rooms are trimmed with antiques and Turkish rugs, and the Mediterranean-style breakfast is a shared social occasion.

For more places to eat and stay in Christchurch see pages 171, 227, 235, 245 and 260.

Hokitika ❸

✖ Fat Pipi Pizza
Pizza **$$**

(89 Revell St; pizzas $20-30; ⏰12-2.30pm Wed-Sun, 5-9pm daily; 🍴) Vegetarians, carnivores and everyone in between will be salivating for the pizza (including a whitebait version) made with love right before your eyes. Lovely cakes, honey buns and Benger juices, too. Best enjoyed in the garden bar – one of the town's (in fact the West Coast's) best dining spots.

🛏 Shining Star
Holiday Park, Motel **$$**

(📞03-755 8921; 16 Richards Dr; sites unpowered/powered $32/40, d $115-199; 🛜) Attractive and versatile beachside spot with everything from camping to classy self-contained seafront units. Kids will love the menagerie, including pigs and alpacas straight from Dr Doolittle's appointment book. Parents might prefer the spa or sauna.

For more places to eat and stay in Hokitika see p219.

Fox Glacier ❺

✖ Last Kitchen
Cafe **$$**

(📞03-751 0058; cnr Sullivan Rd & SH6; lunch $10-20, dinner $24-32; ⏰11.30am-late) Making the most of its sunny corner location with outside tables, the Last Kitchen is a good option, serving contemporary fare, such as haloumi salad, pistachio-crusted lamb and genuinely gourmet burgers. It also satisfies for coffee and a wine later in the day.

🛏 Reflection Lodge
B&B **$$$**

(📞03-751 0707; www.reflectionlodge.co.nz; 141 Cook Flat Rd; d $210; 🛜) The gregarious hosts of this ski-lodge-style B&B go the extra mile to make your stay a memorable one. Blooming gardens complete with alpine views and a Monet-like pond seal the deal.

For more places to eat and stay in Fox Glacier see p219.

Wanaka ❽

✖ Francesca's Italian Kitchen
Italian **$$**

(📞03-443 5599; www.fransitalian.co.nz; 93 Ardmore St; mains $20-26; ⏰noon-3pm & 5pm-late) Ebullient expat Francesca has brought the big flavours and easy conviviality of an authentic Italian family trattoria to Wanaka in the form of this stylish and perennially busy eatery. Even simple things such as pizza, pasta and polenta chips are exceptional. She also runs a pizza cart on Brownston St, opposite Cinema Paradiso.

🛏 Alpine View Lodge B&B $$

(📞 03-443 7111; www.alpineviewlodge.co.nz; 23 Studholme Rd South; d from $180, cottage $285; 🛜) In a peaceful, rural setting on the edge of town, this excellent lodge has three B&B rooms, one of which has its own, private, bush-lined deck. Little extras include homemade shortbread in the rooms and a hot tub. Alternatively, you can opt for the fully self-contained two-bedroom cottage, which opens onto the garden.

For more places to eat and stay in Wanaka see p313.

Queenstown ⑨

🍴 Fergbaker Bakery $

(42 Shotover St; items $5-9; ⏱6.30am-4.30am) Fergburger's sweeter sister bakes all manner of tempting treats – and although most things look tasty with 3am beer goggles on, it withstands the daylight test admirably. Goodies include meat pies, filled rolls, danish pastries and banoffee tarts. If you're after gelato, call into Mrs Ferg next door.

🍴 Madam Woo Malaysian $$

(📞 03-442 9200; www.madamwoo.co.nz; 5 The Mall; mains $16-32; ⏱noon-late; 🍴) Wooing customers with a playful take on Chinese and Malay hawker food, the Madame serves up lots of tasty snacks for sharing (wontons, steamed dumplings, greasy filled-roti rolls), alongside larger dishes (beef rendang, duck salad, sambal prawns). Kids and distracted adults alike can have fun colouring in the menu.

🛏 Lomond Lodge Motel $$

(📞 03-442 7375; www.lomondlodge.com; 33 Man St; d $145-169; 🅿🛜) A makeover has modernised this midrange motel's decor. Share your on-the-road stories with fellow travellers around the garden barbecue or in the guest kitchen, although all rooms also have their own fridges and microwaves. It's worth paying extra for a lake view.

For more places to eat and stay in Queenstown see pages 261, 303 and 313.

Lake Tekapo ⑫

🍴 Kohan Japanese $$

(📞 03-680 6688; www.kohannz.com; SH8; dishes $8-20, mains $19-30; ⏱11am-2pm daily, 6-9pm Mon-Sat) With all the aesthetic charm of an office cafeteria, this is still one of Tekapo's best dining options, both for its distracting lake views, and its authentic Japanese food including fresh-as-a-daisy salmon sashimi. Leave room for the handmade green-tea ice cream.

🛏 Tekapo Motels & Holiday Park Holiday Park, Motel $

(📞 03-680 6825; www.laketekapo-accommodation.co.nz; 2 Lakeside Dr; sites $34-44, dm $30-32, d $90-110; 🛜) Supremely situated on terraced, lakefront grounds, this place has something for everyone. Backpackers get the cosy, log-cabin-style lodge, while others can enjoy cute Kiwi 'baches', basic cabins, and smart en suite units with particularly good views. Campervaners and tenters are spoilt for choice, and share the fantastic new amenities block.

For more places to eat and stay in Lake Tekapo see p261.

Geraldine ⑬

🛏 Geraldine Kiwi Holiday Park Holiday Park, Motel $

(📞 03-693 8147; www.geraldineholidaypark.co.nz; 39 Hislop St; sites $34-39, d $52-135; @🛜) This top-notch holiday park is set amid well-established parkland, two minutes' walk from the high street. Tidy accommodation ranges from budget cabins to plusher motel units, plus there's a TV room and playground.

For more places to eat and stay in Geraldine see p260.

Methven ⑭

🍴 Dubliner Restaurant $$

(www.dubliner.co.nz; 116 Main St; meals $26-34; ⏱4pm-late) This authentically Irish bar and restaurant is housed in Methven's lovingly restored old post office. Great food includes pizza, Irish stew and other hearty fare suitable for washing down with a pint of craft beer.

STRETCH YOUR LEGS
CHRISTCHURCH

Start/Finish Canterbury Museum

Distance 4.25km

Duration 3–4 hours

Flat as a pancake, Christchurch is easy to explore on foot. The city is still in recovery and rebuild mode, so there's always something new and interesting to look at, including fantastic street art filling the gaps where buildings used to be.

Take this walk on Trips

Canterbury Museum

Park your car on Rolleston Ave, handy to the excellent Canterbury Museum (www.canterburymuseum.com; ☎03-366 5000;Rolleston Ave; ⊘9am-5pm). The reproduction of Fred & Myrtle's gloriously kitsch Paua Shell House embraces Kiwiana at its best, and kids will enjoy the interactive displays in the Discovery Centre. Free, hour-long guided tours commence at 3.30pm on Tuesdays and Thursdays.

The Walk » Walk east along Worcester Blvd, crossing the Avon River on 1885 Italianate Worcester bridge. Head northeast along the river path, past the former Municipal Chambers.

Kate Sheppard Memorial

Beside the Avon River is the Kate Sheppard National Memorial sculpture, unveiled in 1993 to celebrate the centenary of women's suffrage in NZ. This pioneering lady spearheaded the campaign that enabled women over 21 to vote – NZ was the first self-governing country in the world to allow it.

The Walk » Walk east along Armagh St, skirting rejuvenated Victoria Square. Turn right on to pedestrianised (except for trams!) New Regent St.

New Regent Street

A forerunner to the modern mall, this pretty little stretch of pastel Spanish Mission–style shops was described as NZ's most beautiful street when it was completed in 1932. Fully restored postearthquake, **New Regent St** (www.newregentstreet.co.nz) is once again a delightful place to stroll and peruse the tiny galleries, gift shops and cafes.

The Walk » At the bottom of New Regent St, cross Gloucester St and continue south through the Cathedral Junction tram depot. Turn right on Worcester St to reach Cathedral Sq.

Cathedral Square

Christchurch's city square stands largely flattened and forlorn amid the surrounding rebuild, with the remains of ChristChurch Cathedral emblematic of the loss. The February 2011 earthquake

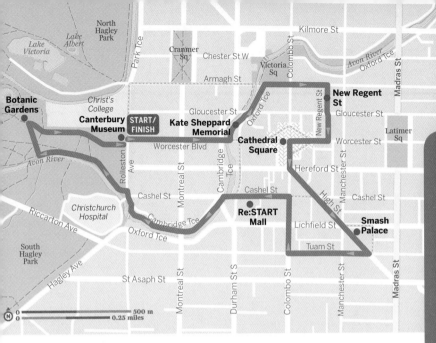

brought down the 63m-high spire, while subsequent earthquakes destroyed the prized stained-glass rose window. Other heritage buildings around the square were also badly damaged, but one modern landmark left unscathed is the 18m-high metal sculpture *Chalice*, designed by Neil Dawson.

The Walk ≫ Walk south along Colombo St until Hereford St then southeast along High St – another badly damaged area finding its feet via some edgy businesses and great drinking establishments.

Smash Palace

Part grease-monkey garage, part trailer-trash park and part proto-hipster hang-out – complete with a psychedelic school bus, edible garden and blooming roses – **Smash Palace** (☏03-366 5369; www.thesmashpalace.co.nz; 172 High St; ⏰4pm-late Mon-Fri, 12pm-late Sat & Sun) is one helluva beer garden.

The Walk ≫ Head west on Tuam St, passing legendary movie house, Alice In Videoland, then north on Colombo. Turn left at Cashel St.

Re:START Mall

With cafes, food trucks, shops and people-watching galore, the Re:START Mall's labyrinth of shipping containers is a pleasant place to hang out. Within the tailback of food trucks, our favourite is **Dimitris** (☏03-377 7110; Re:START Mall, Cashel St; souvlaki $11-16; ⏰11am-4pm; 🖊), deservedly famous for its tasty souvlaki.

The Walk ≫ Back on Cashel St, head west over the restored Bridge of Remembrance then along the Avon River before being spat out in the Botanic Gardens.

Botanic Gardens

Strolling through these blissful 30 riverside hectares of arboreal and floral splendour is a consummate Christchurch experience. There are thematic gardens to explore, lawns to sprawl on, and a playground adjacent to the cafe and visitor centre, 500m west of this walking tour's starting and finishing point, the Canterbury Museum.

Queenstown & the South Trips

DISCOVER THE LANDSCAPES THAT LURE IN TRAVELLERS FROM THE WORLD OVER – the mountains, fiords, lakes and coastlines of New Zealand's deep south.

The centre of the action is NZ's year-round adventure capital, Queenstown, with more direct flights making it an increasingly popular starting point for driving tours. It's a striking gateway to many of NZ's pin-up places, from the golden-hued schist country of Central Otago, to the deep green, ancient forests of Stewart Island. In between is Fiordland National Park – one of the world's great remaining wildernesses and home to Milford Sound – and coastal highway so spectacular yet so quiet you can only be at the very edge of civilisation.

Queenstown View over Lake Wakatipu from the Skyline Gondola (Trips 19, 21, 22 & 23)

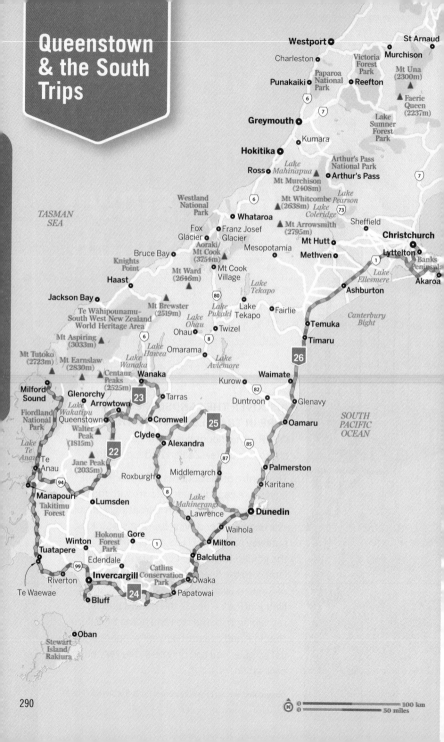

Queenstown & the South Trips

TASMAN SEA

Westport
St Arnaud
Charleston
Murchison
Victoria Forest Park
Mt Una (2300m)
Punakaiki
Reefton
Faerie Queen (2237m)
Greymouth
Lake Sumner Forest Park
Kumara
Hokitika
Arthur's Pass National Park
Ross
Lake Mahinapua
Mt Murchison (2408m)
Arthur's Pass
Westland National Park
Mt Whitcombe (2638m)
Lake Pearson
Whataroa
Lake Coleridge
Sheffield
Franz Josef Glacier
Mt Arrowsmith (2795m)
Fox Glacier
Mesopotamia
Mt Hutt
Christchurch
Bruce Bay
Aoraki/Mt Cook (3754m)
Lyttelton
Methven
Banks Peninsula
Knights Point
Mt Cook Village
Akaroa
Haast
Mt Ward (2646m)
Lake Tekapo
Ashburton
Lake Ellesmere
Jackson Bay
Mt Brewster (2519m)
Lake Pukaki
Lake Tekapo
Fairlie
Canterbury Bight
Te Wāhipounamu–South West New Zealand World Heritage Area
Lake Ohau
Temuka
Mt Aspiring (3033m)
Ohau
Twizel
Timaru
Omarama
Lake Hawea
Lake Aviemore
Mt Tutoko (2723m)
Mt Earnslaw (2830m)
Lake Wanaka
26
Centaur Peaks (2525m)
Wanaka
Waimate
Milford Sound
Glenorchy
23
Tarras
Kurow
Fiordland National Park
Lake Wakatipu
Arrowtown
Glenavy
SOUTH PACIFIC OCEAN
Queenstown
Cromwell
Duntroon
Lake Te Anau
Walter Peak (1815m)
22
Clyde
25
Oamaru
Te Anau
Jane Peak (2035m)
Alexandra
85
Roxburgh
Middlemarch
87
Palmerston
Manapouri
Lumsden
Karitane
Takitimu Forest
8
Lake Mahinerangi
94
Lawrence
Dunedin
Hokonui Forest Park
Gore
Waihola
Winton
1
Milton
Tuatapere
Edendale
Balclutha
99
Riverton
Catlins Conservation Park
Invercargill
Owaka
24
Te Waewae
Bluff
Papatowai

Oban

Stewart Island/Rakiura

0   100 km
0   50 miles

Matukituki River near Wanaka

✓ DON'T MISS

Bendigo
Wind up into the
Dunstan Range to
ramble around rusty
gold-mining relics and
stone huts on
Trip 23

**Mt Aspiring
National Park**
Penetrate World
Heritage wilderness on a
day walk on Trip 23

Moeraki Boulders
The aliens landed
and left behind their
concrete cocoons. See
for yourself on
Trip 26

Lost Gypsy Gallery
Get your ribs tickled by a
bamboozling collection
of up-cycled curios on
Trip 24

Ulva Island
See, hear and be
beguiled by the feathery
flocks on this remote
jewel of an island on
Trip 24

Milford Sound Majesty

22

Explore two totally different Southern Lakes resorts – thrilling Queenstown and tranquil Te Anau – before following New Zealand's premier wilderness highway to majestic Milford Sound.

TRIP HIGHLIGHTS

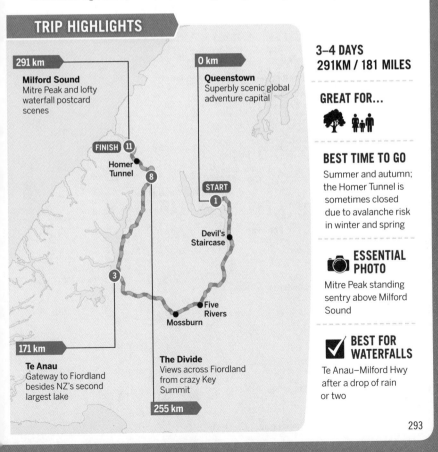

291 km

Milford Sound
Mitre Peak and lofty waterfall postcard scenes

FINISH 11

Homer Tunnel

8

0 km

Queenstown
Superbly scenic global adventure capital

START
1

Devil's Staircase

3

Five Rivers

Mossburn

171 km

Te Anau
Gateway to Fiordland besides NZ's second largest lake

The Divide
Views across Fiordland from crazy Key Summit

255 km

3–4 DAYS
291KM / 181 MILES

GREAT FOR...

BEST TIME TO GO

Summer and autumn; the Homer Tunnel is sometimes closed due to avalanche risk in winter and spring

ESSENTIAL PHOTO

Mitre Peak standing sentry above Milford Sound

BEST FOR WATERFALLS

Te Anau–Milford Hwy after a drop of rain or two

22 Milford Sound Majesty

A well-beaten path this may well be, but its bookends are nothing short of sublime – Queenstown, buzzing with adrenaline and fueled up on fabulous food and wine; and at the other end Milford Sound, NZ's most famous sight. In between is a series of eye-popping, often untouched wilderness landscapes, with the lovely lakeside town of Te Anau a handy base for exploring them.

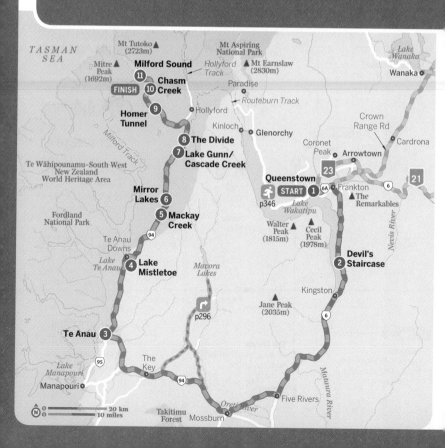

TASMAN SEA

Mt Tutoko ▲ (2723m)

Mitre ▲ Peak (1692m)

Milford Sound

⑪

⑩ **Chasm Creek**

FINISH

Mt Aspiring National Park

Hollyford Track

▲ Mt Earnslaw (2830m)

Lake Wanaka

Wanaka

Paradise

Homer Tunnel

⑨

Routeburn Track

Hollyford

Kinloch

Glenorchy

Crown Range Rd

Cardrona

Milford Track

⑧ **The Divide**

⑦ **Lake Gunn/ Cascade Creek**

Coronet Peak ▲

Arrowtown

21

Te Wāhipounamu–South West New Zealand World Heritage Area

Mirror Lakes ⑥

Queenstown

START ①

p346

⑥A Frankton

▲ The Remarkables

6

⑤ **Mackay Creek**

Lake Wakatipu

23

Fiordland National Park

94

Walter Peak ▲ (1815m)

Cecil Peak ▲ (1978m)

Nevis River

Te Anau Downs

Lake Te Anau

④ **Lake Mistletoe**

Mavora Lakes

② **Devil's Staircase**

Kingston

p296

Jane Peak ▲ (2035m)

6

Te Anau ③

95

The Key

94

Matukituki River

Lake Manapouri

Manapouri

Takitimu Forest

Mossburn

Oreti River

Five Rivers

Mataura River

0 — 20 km
0 — 10 miles

❶ Queenstown

A small town with a big attitude, Queenstown is synonymous with the outdoors, and often crazy adventures such as bungy jumping, skydiving and jetboating. Then there's the other Queenstown – the one with the cosmopolitan restaurant and arts scene, excellent vineyards and five world-class golf courses. For the best of both worlds, it's hard to beat.

If that weren't enough, Queenstown goes for gold with an utterly sublime setting along the meandering shore of Lake Wakatipu, framed by the jagged peaks of the Remarkables. To soak up the town's scenery,

LINK YOUR TRIP

21 Southern Alps Circuit

From Queenstown, embark on this granddaddy of road trips taking in the best of the South Island's mountain scenery.

23 Central Otago Explorer

Queenstown is the start of a tour around this bountiful region's highlights.

stroll along Steamer Wharf to **Queenstown Gardens** (Park St), the leafy peninsula just five minutes' walk away. The lakeside track affords ever-changing panoramas of the lake and surrounds, while its interior sports lush lawns, fine trees, rose gardens and occasional curiosities, including the fun and free **frisbee golf course** (www. queenstowndiscgolf.co.nz; Queenstown Gardens).

 p303

The Drive » Head east along SH6A to Frankton, then turn onto SH6 south signposted for Te Anau. Skirting past the Kelvin Peninsula at the foot of the Remarkables, the road then follows the eastern shore of Lake Wakatipu with stunning alpine views either side of the highway. The distance from Queenstown to the Devil's Staircase is 35km.

❷ Devil's Staircase

The views along the shores of Lake Wakatipu, NZ's longest and third-largest lake, are distractingly beautiful, with the Remarkables and Hector ranges rising to the east, Cecil Peak and the Fyfe Mountains to the west, and the deep blue lake in between.

This is a winding drive ripe for rubbernecking, so keep your eyes on the road and your hands upon the wheel. Look out for the well-signposted Devil's Staircase, the aptly named lookout

point that punctuates a tortuous section of road that winds up, over and around the lake edge. Pull over, jump out, breathe in that clear mountain air and revel in the amazing views.

The Drive » Continue along SH6. The topography flattens as you approach Five Rivers, 58km from the Devil's Staircase. Turn right for Mossburn and the junction with SH94. Turn right and drive 60km northwest to Te Anau. At the Key, 34km from Mossburn, the Fiordland mountains appear for the first time. This 136km drive should take around two hours.

❸ Te Anau

Peaceful, lakeside Te Anau township is the main gateway to Fiordland National Park and ever-popular Milford Sound, as well as a pleasant place to while away a few days. It's large enough to have a smattering of good eateries and places to stay, but it's much easier on the liver and wallet than attention-grabbing Queenstown.

The lake, NZ's second largest, was gouged out by a huge glacier and has several arms that extend into the mountainous, forested western shore. Hidden away on this side, accessible only by boat, are the **Te Anau Glowworm Caves**, which first surfaced in Māori legend and were subsequently

'rediscovered' in 1948. The 200m-long cave system is a magical wonderland of strange rock forms, whirlpools, and waterfalls. The glittering pièce de résistance is the glowworm grotto in its inner reaches. **Real Journeys** (www.realjourneys.co.nz; ☎0800 656 501; 85 Lakefront Dr; ⏰7.30am-8.30pm Sep-May, 8am-7pm Jun-Aug) runs 2¼-hour guided tours, reaching the heart of the caves

via a lake cruise, walkway and a short underground boat ride.

✗ ⛺p303

**The Drive ›› ** Follow the signs to one of NZ's most scenic drives – the Te Anau–Milford Hwy, which traces the lake edge for most of the way to the Lake Mistletoe car park (28km).

- - - - - - - - - - - - - -

④ Lake Mistletoe

It's an easy amble through manuka (tea tree) scrub and regenerating mountain beech forest to this compact and serene glacial lake. Beside the lake, an excel-

lent place for a picnic, there are great views of the mountain ranges that make up some of the vast Fiordland National Park.

On the lake and among the surrounding rushes and flax you're likely to see resident scaup (ducks), and if you look really carefully you may spot native frogs hopping about. The frogs (known to Māori as pepeketua) are of the genus *Leiopelma*, a primitive group of amphibians that have hardly changed over millions of years.

DETOUR: MAVORA LAKES

Start: ❸ Te Anau

Mavora Lakes Conservation Park (www.doc.govt.nz; Centre Hill Rd), in the Snowdon State Forest, lies within the Te Wāhipounamu–South West New Zealand World Heritage Area. As the crow flies the park is relatively close to the tourist honey-pots of Queenstown, Te Anau and the Milford Rd, but a slow, gravel road and spartan facilities (long-drop toilets, water supply and fire-pits) mean that only the eager venture in.

The heart of the park is the sublime Mavora Lakes camping area, huge golden meadows sitting alongside two lakes – North and South Mavora – fringed by forest and towered over by the impressive Thomson and Livingstone Mountains with peaks rising to more than 1600m. Cloaked in beech, the valley walls pitch steeply skyward, terminating in ranges of rocky peaks that contrast starkly against the undulating blanket of golden grassland on the valley floor.

If you're camping or in a campervan, this is a tranquil place to stay, although it can get busy during the school summer holidays (December to January).

Those short on time can still savour its serenity on a 2½-hour walk that circumnavigates the smaller South Mavora Lake. On the western edge of the lake the track passes through mature beech forest, while on the other side it traverses large grassy flats. There are two scenic, springy swing bridges to cross, views galore and squadrons of birds – from honking flocks of waterfowl in the marsh to tiny rifleman and robins flitting through the forest.

Reach Mavora Lakes via Centre Hill Rd, 14km west of Mossburn on SH94. From there, it's another 38km, heading north along a mostly unsealed road, to South Mavora Lake.

CRUISING THE SOUND

There's no getting around it: no visit to Fiordland is complete without a trip to Milford Sound (Piopiotahi), the first sight of which will likely knock your socks off (if the drive there hasn't already). Sheer rocky cliffs rise out of still, dark waters, and forests clinging to the slopes sometimes relinquish their hold, causing a 'tree avalanche' into the drink. The spectacular, photogenic 1692m-high **Mitre Peak/ Rahotu** rises dead ahead – its image has dominated NZ tourism brochures since year dot and is one of few vistas truly worthy of the word 'iconic'.

A postcard will never do it justice, and a big downpour will only add to the drama. The average annual rainfall of 7m is more than enough to fuel cascading waterfalls and add a shimmering moody mist to the scene, while the freshwater sitting atop warmer seawater replicates deep-ocean conditions, encouraging the activity of marine life such as dolphins, seals and penguins.

A cruise is Milford Sound's most accessible experience, as evident from the armada of companies berthed at the waterfront cruise terminal. Each company claims to be quieter, smaller, bigger, cheaper, or in some way preferable to the rest. What really makes a difference is the timing of the cruise. Most bus tours aim for 1pm sailings, so if you avoid that time of day there will be fewer people on the boat, fewer boats on the water and fewer buses on the road. With some companies you get a better price on cruises outside rush hour, too. If you're particularly keen on wildlife, ask whether there will be a nature guide on board.

The Drive » Continue north on SH94 for around 1km before cutting inland at Te Anau Downs and heading up the Eglinton Valley. After another 21km you will reach Mackay Creek.

❺ Mackay Creek

One of many well-signposted spots to pull over and soak up the Milford Rd's majesty, Mackay Creek offers an escape from the sweet but somewhat claustrophobic confines of the beech forest to the open surrounds of the Eglinton Valley.

There's little here except for basic camping, picnic benches, and the wonderfully expansive views of the valley and vertiginous Earl Mountains, which provide a taste of what's to come. The creek is particularly photogenic in late spring when the lupins lining its banks are gloriously in bloom. Take care when pulling off or turning back on to the highway, as visibility is poor.

All the viewpoints and nature walks lining the Te Anau–Milford Hwy are detailed in DOC's *Fiordland National Park Day Walks* brochure, available online (www.doc.govt.nz) or from the Fiordland National Park Visitor Centre in Te Anau.

The Drive » Drive for 7km along the Eglinton River valley flats and through beech forest until you see the DOC sign for Mirror Lakes.

❻ Mirror Lakes

The boardwalk at Mirror Lakes takes you through beech forest and wetlands, and on a calm day the lakes reflect the Earl Mountains across the valley and the harakeke (flax) that fringes the water. Head here early in the morning for your best chance of seeing double. If, however, your arrival coincides with a tour bus, be prepared for a swarm of snappy happy tourists as multitudinous as the sandflies.

The lakes area is also a good place to spot bird life, such as scaup, South Island kaka, ruru (morepork) and robins. Also keep an eye and ear out

Classic Trip

WHY THIS IS A CLASSIC TRIP
LEE SLATER, WRITER

I must have seen Milford Sound and the Eglinton Valley in online articles and glossy magazines a thousand times, and visited on at least a dozen occasions. And yet I'm still blown away by its World Heritage grandeur. My ideal Milford Sound trip involves sunny, blue skies on the way there, followed by torrential rain fuelling the lofty waterfalls and raging rivers.

Top: Campsite at Mavora Lakes
Left: Mackay Falls on the Milford Track
Right: Entrance to Te Anau Glowworm Caves

S. PORTEROJ / GETTY IMAGES ©

for the endangered mo-hua (yellowhead), with its colourful plumage and machine-gun-like chitter-chatter. In 2015 the valley's mohua population was bolstered by the relocation of 80 birds from a predator-free island sanctuary in Dusky Sounds, testament to the dedication of local conservationists.

The Drive ›› Continue driving north mainly through red beech forest, with occasional glimpses of the valley and mountains. It's a 20-minute, 19km drive from Mirror Lakes to Lake Gunn.

➐ Lake Gunn/ Cascade Creek

The area around Cascade Creek and Lake Gunn, known to Māori as O Ta-para, was a regular stop-over for parties heading to Anita Bay in search of *pounamu* (greenstone). The **Lake Gunn Nature Walk** (45 minutes return) loops through tall red beech forest ringing with birdsong, with side trails leading to peaceful lakeside beaches.

The Drive ›› From Lake Gunn/ Cascade Creek, continue driving north for 7km to the Divide. You'll pass the smaller Lake Fergus and Lake Lochie along the way.

TRIP HIGHLIGHT

➑ The Divide

Stunted silver beech predominates as you make your way up to the

harsher environs of the Divide, the lowest east–west pass in the Southern Alps. The car park and shelter here serve hikers on the Routeburn, and Greenstone & Caples Tracks, both of which head off from this point.

A marvelous two-hour return walk can be had along the start of the Routeburn, ascending (in gut-busting fashion) through beech forest to the alpine tussockland of **Key Summit**. The nature walk around the boggy tops, festooned with mountain flax, snow totara and Dr Seuss–esque *dracophyllum*, is a great excuse to linger, while on a good day the 360-degree panorama encompasses the Hollyford, Eglinton and Greenstone valleys, and Lake Marian basin with pyramidal Mt Christina (2474m). The view is truly worth the effort, but in anything less than clear weather, don't even go there.

The Drive » From the Divide, SH94 snakes west, passing Marian Corner where safety gates will be closed if there is a risk of avalanche further along. The road then passes Camera Flat and climbs through the cascade-tastic upper Hollyford Valley to the Homer Tunnel. It's 16km from the Divide to the tunnel entrance.

❾ Homer Tunnel

Framed by a spectacular, high-walled, ice-carved amphitheatre, the 1270m-long Homer Tunnel is the only vehicular access point for Milford Sound.

Begun as a relief project in the 1930s' Depression and finally opened to motor traffic in 1954, the tunnel is one way, with in-flows controlled by traffic lights. During the summer months, this can mean delays of up to 20 minutes while you wait for the lights to turn green, but when immersed in such a spectacular environment, who cares?

Dark, rough-hewn and dripping with water, the

FIORDLAND NATIONAL PARK

Fiordland National Park is arguably NZ's finest outdoor treasure. At 12,607 sq km it is the country's largest national park, making up half of the Te Wāhipounamu–South West New Zealand World Heritage Area, and one of the largest in the world. You don't have to look too hard to see why it buddies up with the Egyptian pyramids and the Grand Canyon on the World Heritage list.

It is jagged and mountainous, densely forested and cut through by numerous deeply recessed sounds (technically fiords) that reach inland like crooked fingers from the Tasman Sea. Indeed, one of the first impressions visitors gain of the park is of the almost overpowering steepness of the mountains, an impression accentuated by the fact that the mountains are usually separated only by narrow valleys. Formed during the glacial periods of the last ice age, its peaks are very hard and have eroded slowly, compared to the mountains of Mt Aspiring and Arthur's Pass, which are softer. Gentle topography this is not. It is raw and hard-core all the way.

High annual rainfall – delivered across the Tasman Sea – results in super-lush vegetation. Inland forests feature red, silver and mountain beech, while coastal forest is dominated by podocarp species such as matai, rimu, and totara as well as the red-bloomed southern rata. Fiordland is well known to bird-watchers as the home of the endangered takahe, but more commonly spotted are kereru (NZ pigeons), riflemen, tomtits, fantails, bush robins, tui, bellbirds and kaka, as well as kea and rock wrens in alpine areas. If you wander around at night you might occasionally hear a kiwi.

It's around 85 million years since the snippet of land that became NZ split off from Gondwanaland; Fiordland makes it seem like just yesterday.

**TOP TIP:
MILFORD MAYHEM**

To evade Milford's crowds, leave Te Anau early (by 8am) or later in the morning (11am) to avoid the tour buses heading for midday cruises. Be sure to fill up with petrol in Te Anau, and note that chains must be carried on icy or avalanche-risk days from May to November.

tunnel emerges at the other end at the head of the spectacular **Cleddau Valley**. Any spare 'wows' might pop out about now. Kea (alpine parrots) loiter in gangs around the tunnel entrance looking to mug tourists for scraps of food, but don't feed them as it's bad for their health.

The Drive » From the parking area on the Milford Sound side of the Homer Tunnel to Chasm Creek it's a 9km drive. If it's wet or has been raining, waterfalls cascading down the Cleddau Valley walls resemble brooding skies streaked with bolts of lightning.

- - - - - - - - - - - - -

⑩ Chasm Creek

The **Chasm Creek Walk** is an easy 20-minute return walk from the car park and well worth a stop come rain or shine. The forest-cloaked Cleddau River plunges through scooped-out boulders in a narrow chasm, creating deep falls and a natural rock bridge. The power of the surging waters is awe-inspiring and more than a little frightening. A quick dip is definitely off the cards. Along the way, look out for glimps-

es of Mt Tutoko (2723m), Fiordland's highest peak, above the beech forest.

The Drive » The final 10km to Milford Sound continues down the Cleddau Valley, passing the Tutoko River suspension bridge at around the halfway point.

- - - - - - - - - - - - -

TRIP HIGHLIGHT

⑪ Milford Sound

Sydney Opera House, Big Ben, the Eiffel Tower – Milford Sound is up there with the best of them, which explains why it receives about half a million visitors each year, many of them crammed into the peak months (January and February). Some 14,000 arrive on foot via the Milford Track, which ends at the sound. Many more drive from Te Anau, but most arrive via the multitude of bus tours. But don't worry: out on the water all this humanity seems tiny compared to nature's vastness.

And getting out on the water is a must. Fortunately there are cruises galore, but kayak trips offer an even more mind-blowing perspective of this monumental landscape. Te Anau–based **Rosco's Milford Kayaks** (☎03-249 8500, 0800 476 726; www.roscosmilfordkayaks. com; 72 Town Centre, Te Anau; trips $99-199; ☺Nov-Apr) offers guided, tandem-kayak trips including the 'Morning Glory' ($199), a challenging paddle the full length of the fiord to Anita Bay, and the less strenuous 'Stirling Sunriser' ($195), which ventures beneath the 151m-high **Stirling Falls**.

Although Milford Sound is best appreciated from the water or air, killer views of Mitre Peak can still be enjoyed on the 30-minute interpretive **Foreshore Walk**.

🛏 p303

Eating & Sleeping

Queenstown ❶

✖ Bespoke Kitchen   Cafe $$

(📞03-409 0552; www.facebook.com/
Bespokekitchenqueenstown; 9 Isle St; mains
$11-19; ⏰7.30am-5pm; 📶) Occupying a light-
filled corner site between the town centre and
the gondola, Bespoke delivers everything you'd
expect of a smart Kiwi cafe. There's a good
selection of counter food, beautifully presented
cooked options, free wi-fi and, of course, great
coffee.

✖ Blue Kanu   Modern NZ $$

(📞03-442 6060; www.bluekanu.co.nz;
16 Church St; mains $27-39; ⏰4pm-late)
Disproving the rule that all tiki houses are
inherently tacky, Blue Kanu somehow manages
to be not just tasteful but stylish. The menu
meshes robust Māori, Pasifika and Asian
flavours with local ingredients to come up with
an exotic blend of delicious dishes, designed to
be shared. The service is excellent too.

✖ Vudu Cafe & Larder   Cafe $$

(📞03-441 8370; www.vudu.co.nz; 16 Rees St;
mains $14-20; ⏰7.30am-6pm) Excellent home-
style baking combines with great coffee and
tasty cooked breakfasts at this cosmopolitan
cafe. Admire the huge photo of a much less
populated Queenstown from an inside table,
or head through to the rear garden for lake and
mountain views.

🛏 Creeksyde Queenstown
Holiday Park & Motels   Holiday Park $$

(📞03-442 9447; www.camp.co.nz; 54 Robins
Rd; site $55, d without bathroom $81, unit from
$138; 🅿 @ 📶) In a garden setting, this pretty
and extremely well-kept holiday park has
accommodation ranging from small tent sites to
fully self-contained motel units. Quirky touches
include oddball sculptures and an ablutions
block disguised as a medieval oast house.

For more places to eat and stay in Queenstown
see pages 261, 285 and 313.

Te Anau ❸

✖ Miles Better Pies   Fast Food $

(📞03-249 9044; www.milesbetterpies.co.nz;
19 Town Centre; pies $5-6.50; ⏰6am-3pm) The
bumper selection includes venison, lamb and
mint, and fruit pies. There are a few pavement
tables, but sitting and munching beside the lake
is nicer.

✖ Redcliff Cafe   Modern NZ $$$

(📞03-249 7431; www.theredcliff.co.nz; 12
Mokonui St; mains $38-42; ⏰4-10pm) Housed in
a replica settler's cottage, relaxed Redcliff offers
generous fine-dining in a convivial atmosphere
backed by sharp service. The predominantly
locally sourced food is truly terrific: try the wild
venison or hare. Kick off or wind it up with a
drink in the rustic front bar, which often hosts
live music.

🛏 Te Anau Top 10   Holiday Park $

(📞0800 249 746, 03-249 7462; www.
teanautop10.co.nz; 128 Te Anau Tce; sites from
$44, unit from $129, without bathroom from $77;
@ 📶) Near the town and lake, this excellent,
compact holiday park has private sites, a
playground, lake-facing hot tubs, bike hire, a
barbecue area and modern kitchen facilities.
The motels units are very good indeed and there
are well-priced cabins for those not bothered by
communal bathrooms.

For more places to eat and stay in Te Anau see
p326.

Milford Sound ⓫

🛏 Milford Sound Lodge   Lodge $$$

(📞03-249 8071; www.milfordlodge.com; SH94;
sites from $25, dm/d without bathroom $35/99,
chalets $345-395; 📶) Alongside the Cleddau
River, 1.5km from the Milford hub, this simple
but comfortable lodge has a down-to-earth,
active vibe. Travellers and trampers commune
in the lounge or on-site Pio Pio Cafe, which
provides meals, wine and espresso. Luxurious
chalets enjoy an absolute riverside location.
Booking ahead is strongly recommended.

Bannockburn One of Central Otago's finest wine-growing subregions

Central Otago Explorer

23

Indulge in an extravaganza of food, wine, outdoor activities and charming heritage sites along this loop through majestic mountain landscapes around Queenstown.

TRIP HIGHLIGHTS

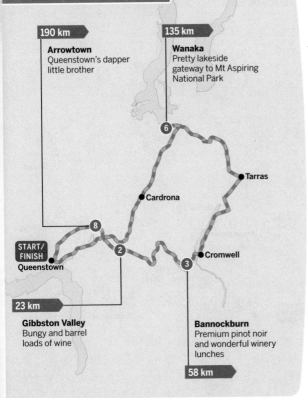

190 km

Arrowtown
Queenstown's dapper little brother

135 km

Wanaka
Pretty lakeside gateway to Mt Aspiring National Park

START/FINISH
Queenstown

23 km

Gibbston Valley
Bungy and barrel loads of wine

Bannockburn
Premium pinot noir and wonderful winery lunches

58 km

Cardrona
Tarras
Cromwell

2–4 DAYS
210KM / 130 MILES

GREAT FOR...

BEST TIME TO GO

All year, but winter snows sometimes close the Crown Range Rd

ESSENTIAL PHOTO

Wakatipu Basin from the Crown Range Rd

BEST FOR FOODIES

Amisfield, often voted New Zealand's top winery restaurant

23 Central Otago Explorer

Welcome to one of New Zealand's most popular outdoor playgrounds, vaunted for adrenalised pursuits such as skiing, hiking, mountain biking and skydiving taking place in sublime alpine surrounds. Central Otago also drips with gold-rush history, brims with world-class wineries and boasts the energetic resort, Queenstown. This relatively short tour packs a helluva punch, but you'll want to stretch it out to take it all in.

1 Queenstown

Queenstown is the vortex of a whirl of wild adventures taking place in its inspiring mountain surrounds. If you're looking for some high speed, free fall, dizzying spins and head rushes, this racy resort is just the ticket.

The town, however, has a quieter side. Stop and smell the roses, play some frisbee golf, and wander the lake-shore path as it reveals ever-changing panoramas of Lake Wakatipu and the Remarkables, as you'll

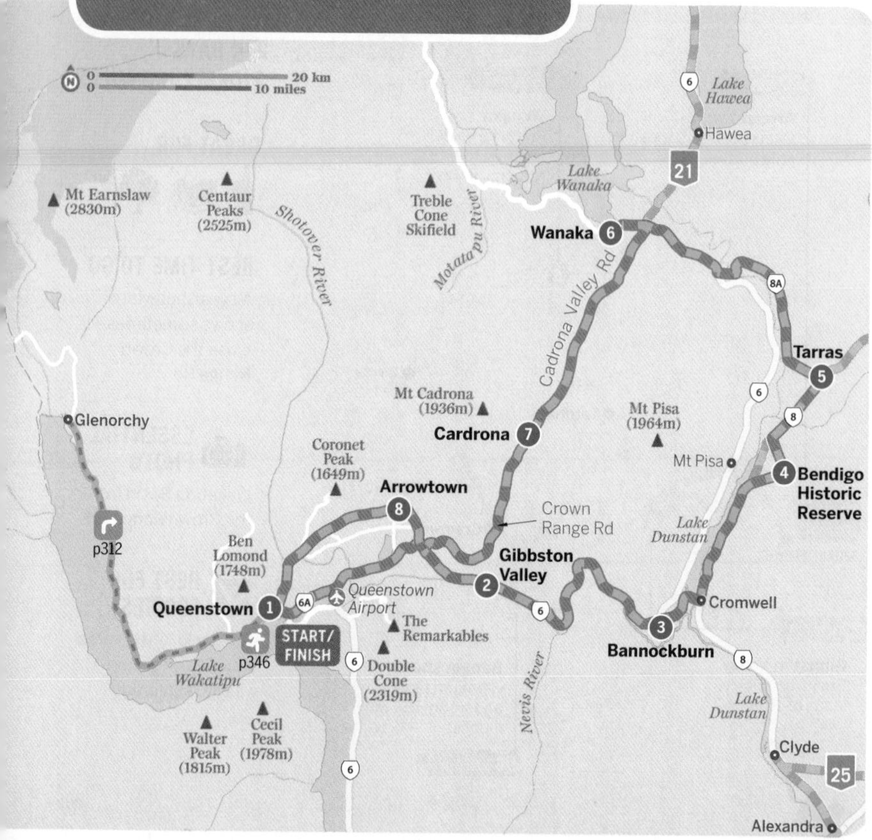

0 20 km
0 10 miles
Lake Hawea
Hawea
Lake Wanaka
Mt Earnslaw (2830m)
Centaur Peaks (2525m)
Shotover River
Treble Cone Skifield
Motatapu River
Wanaka 6
8A
Cadrona Valley Rd
Tarras 5
Mt Cadrona (1936m)
Mt Pisa (1964m)
Glenorchy
Cardrona 7
Coronet Peak (1649m)
Mt Pisa
4 Bendigo Historic Reserve
Arrowtown 8
Crown Range Rd
Lake Dunstan
p312
Ben Lomond (1748m)
Gibbston Valley
2
Queenstown 1
6A
Queenstown Airport
The Remarkables
Cromwell
3
START/ FINISH
p346
Bannockburn
Lake Wakatipu
Double Cone (2319m)
Nevis River
Cecil Peak (1978m)
Walter Peak (1815m)
Clyde
25
Alexandra

see on the walking tour (p346), which takes in the relaxing environs of Queenstown Gardens. Beyond the gardens, the path continues to Frankton and beyond, as part of the **Queenstown Trail** (www.queenstown-trail.co.nz), best explored by bicycle – hire one from **Outside Sports** (☎03-441 0074; www.outsidesports.co.nz; 9 Shotover St; ⊙8.30am-8pm) in the centre of town.

Come evening, head to Queentown's cosmopolitan restaurants and bars, lingering over fine local food and world-class wine. Evenings are also a good time to head up the iconic Skyline Gondola (p347), when the crowds have thinned and the city lights twinkle in the lively streets below.

LINK YOUR TRIP

21 Southern Alps Circuit

See some of the South Island's best mountain scenery by hopping on this circuit at Queenstown or Wanaka.

25 Otago Heritage Trail

Keep mining for gold history and gorgeous Otago scenery by jumping on this loop at Clyde, 24km from Cromwell.

 p313

The Drive » State Hwy 6 heads northeast out of town, past pretty Lake Hayes to Arrow Junction, where you should stay on the highway signposted to Cromwell. It's less than half an hour (23km) to Kawarau Bridge, gateway to Gibbston Valley.

- - - - - - - - - - -

TRIP HIGHLIGHT

❷ Gibbston Valley

Travellers through Gibbston Valley may find themselves immediately arrested by the sight of **AJ Hackett's Bungy** (www.bungy.co.nz), which greets them at the valley's western entrance. Historic Kawarau Bridge is the world's first bungy jump site, and therefore a fitting place to take the 43m plunge. Should that escapade not appear on your hit-list, perhaps just pull in for a coffee and watch others do it – the best free entertainment in town.

The stunning, schist-lined valley is one of Central Otago's main wine subregions, accounting for around 20% of grape plantings. Get into the groove at **Gibbston Valley** (☎03-442 6910; www.gibbstonvalley.com; 1820 Gibbston Hwy (SH6), Gibbston; tastings $5-12, tour incl tastings $15; ⊙10am-5pm), less than a kilometre from Kawarau Bridge, where you can taste both wine and cheese, take an informative tour into a wine cave, and hire bikes to pedal around the win-

eries along the **Gibbston River Trail**.

Whether travelling by car, bike or on foot, don't miss **Peregrine** (☎03-442 4000; www.peregrinewines.co.nz; 2127 Gibbston Hwy (SH6), Gibbston; ⊙10am-5pm), one of Gibbston's top wineries, producing excellent sauvignon blanc, pinot gris, riesling and, of course, pinot noir. Also impressive is the winery's architecture – a bunker-like building with a roof reminiscent of a falcon's wing in flight.

The Drive » SH6 snakes through Kawarau River gorge with its schist outcrops and wild briar rose. After around 20 minutes, it emerges into the dry, lumpy landscape of Cromwell Basin. Pearson Rd is well-signposted to your right; follow it to Bannockburn Rd and turn right where you will see signposts for various wineries. This drive will take around 30 minutes in total (35km).

- - - - - - - - - - -

TRIP HIGHLIGHT

❸ Bannockburn

Two-thirds of Central Otago's grapes are grown within Cromwell Basin, but of the many subregions here, none is more famous than Bannockburn. Lying in the rain-shadow of the Carrick Range, its highly variable terroir lends itself to numerous varietals including riesling, chardonnay and pinot gris. Pinot noir, however, is king of the castle, with Bannockburn lauded as one of the best places

outside of Burgundy for cultivating this notoriously fickle grape.

As detailed on the widely available *Central Otago Wine Map* (www.cowa.org.nz), a dozen or so wineries are open to the public, all within a very short drive. The pick of the crop is **Mt Difficulty** (☎03-445 3445; www.mtdifficulty.co.nz; 73 Felton Rd, Bannockburn; mains $30-35; ⊙tastings 10.30am-4.30pm, restaurant noon-4pm), whose genesis dates back to the early 1990s when five growers collaborated to produce wine from the promising but unproven Central Otago region. Not only does it offer the chance to taste various wines at its welcoming cellar door, its spectacular perch overlooking the Cromwell Basin encourages a very long lunch. Sharp and modern with scrumptious fare and alfresco dining on the terrace, it will pay to book a table and sort out well in advance who's responsible for driving.

The Drive » Head to Cromwell on Bannockburn Rd, following it for 7km all the way to the intersection with SH8B. Head right to cross Lake Dunstan – formed when the mighty Clutha River was dammed in the early 1990s – then turn left and follow SH8 as it skirts along the lake edge. The Loop Rd to Bendigo Historic Reserve is signposted 15km from Cromwell at Crippletown, from where it's another 5km to the entrance, around 35 minutes from Bannockburn.

Wakatipu Basin, near Queenstown

CENTRAL OTAGO WINE

Central Otago's wild landscapes make up the world's southernmost wine region and NZ's highest, ranging between 200m and 450m above sea level. Vineyards are spread throughout the deep valleys and basins of six subregions – **Gibbston**, **Bannockburn**, **Cromwell Basin**, **Wanaka**, **Bendigo** and **Alexandra**. In all, Central Otago boasts nearly 6% of the country's grape growing area (although its wine output is less than 3%).

The industry is reasonably young, with the few vines planted back in 1864 an early forerunner of an industry that has only burgeoned since the mid-1990s. The scene remains largely in the hands of friendly boutique enterprises, and winemakers still experimenting with terroir not yet fully understood. But don't let this fool you into thinking that their wines are in any way substandard. Diminutive Otago may lack history and might, but an intoxicating number of its wines are world-class.

Soils are wide-ranging but predominantly glacial, with a high mineral content, while various microclimates share a common theme of hot days, cold nights and low rainfall. These conditions have proven excellent for aromatics, particularly riesling and pinot gris, but Central Otago's hero is pinot noir, the best of which give Burgundian reds a run for their money. This varietal accounts for more than 75% of the region's plantings.

It would take a good two days' touring to get a comprehensive taste of the terroir, with around 30 wineries regularly open to visitors, and many more by appointment. If you're short on time you could focus on the Gibbston Valley (with cycle touring a possibility), but a much broader picture is revealed around Cromwell and Bannockburn, beyond the gates of the dramatic Kawarau Gorge.

Download the wine-touring maps from the **Central Otago Winegrowers Association** (www.cowa.org.nz) to plan your vinophilic odyssey.

④ Bendigo Historic Reserve

Located high in the Dunstan Range, **Bendigo** (www.doc.govt.nz) is just one of 20 or so significant goldfield sites within Otago, a region originally settled during the 1860s rushes. Gold was first discovered in Bendigo in 1862, mined from alluvial gravels. These easy pickings soon ran out, forcing hundreds of miners into the hard task of extracting the gold from quartz reefs. Relics from this era include mine shafts and tunnels, machinery, dams and water races, as well as the crumbled stone remnants of Crippletown, Logantown and Welshtown where the miners lived.

From the Loop Rd turn-off, a winding gravel road leads to two car parks. From the upper car park, a fruitful wander can be had around the ruins of Welshtown, Logantown and the aurora stamping battery where quartz was crushed. If your will and the weather permit it, consider the five-hour **Kanuka Loop Track** punctuated by relics, craggy rocks and regenerating kanuka forest, as well as offering totally mind-boggling views over Lake Dunstan and the Upper Clutha Valley.

The Drive » From the reserve's lower car park, continue north along Bendigo Loop Rd, which rejoins SH8 several kilometres from where you headed in. Turn right to continue on SH8 7km through farmland to the Wanaka–Lindis Pass junction. The road to Wanaka leads west, but it's worth driving the extra 1.5km north on SH8 to Tarras, 20 minutes (15km) from Bendigo.

- - - - - - - - - - - - - -

⑤ Tarras

An endearing stopping point on the Inland Scenic Route, tiny Tarras is a one-horse town in the middle of merino-sheep country. This makes it the perfect place to buy possibly the finest woollen garments known to humankind. Enjoy a cuppa at the country store, then peruse its divine merchandise (don't miss the 'merinomink', wool mixed with snuggly possum fur). While you're here, be sure to ask about Shrek and find out exactly what ovine roguery is required to become NZ's most famous sheep.

The Drive » Return the way you came, back to the junction, and take SH8A signposted to Wanaka. The highway heads up the mountain-lined valley of the mighty Clutha River/Mata-au, which it eventually crosses to join SH6 heading to Wanaka. The 35km journey will take around 30 minutes.

TRIP HIGHLIGHT

⑥ Wanaka

What a peach! An enviable lakeside setting amid a sublime alpine landscape would be reason enough to linger in Queenstown's smaller twin. However, its outdoor adventure scene – although decidedly less flashy than over the hill – offers more than enough

buzz and fun, plus there's easily enough shopping, dining and nightlife to satisfy the town types.

As well as being the gateway to nearby **Mt Aspiring National Park** (and two ski resorts, in the winter), there are numerous walks and cycle rides closer to town; see DOC's *Wanaka Outdoor Pursuits* pamphlet (www.doc.govt.nz) for a comprehensive rundown.

Among many family-friendly urban attractions is the **National Transport & Toy Museum** (☎03-443 8765; www.nttmuseumwanaka.co.nz; 891 Wanaka Luggate Hwy/SH6; adult/child $17/5; ⊙8.30am-5pm; 🅿), where small armies of Smurfs, Star Wars figurines and Barbie dolls share billing with dozens of classic cars and a mysteriously acquired MiG jet fighter. In all there are around 30,000 items filling four giant hangers, so there's bound to be at least one or two that usher you back down memory lane.

✕ 🛏 p313

The Drive » Follow the well-signposted Cardrona Valley Rd up the pretty Cardrona Valley. It's a 20-minute drive to reach the Cardrona Hotel, 24km from Wanaka.

- - - - - - - - - - - - - -

⑦ Cardrona Hotel

The cute hamlet of Cardrona reached its zenith in the 1870s at the height of the gold rush when

its population numbered over a thousand. Now it's a sleepy little place that wakes up with a jolt for the ski season.

The heart of the village is the **Cardrona Hotel** (☎03-443 8153; www.cardronahotel.co.nz; 2310 Cardrona Valley Rd; r $185; 🛜), an icon not just of the village but of the nation, partly due to its appearance in an incredibly manly beer commercial back in the day. Dating back to 1863, it seriously hits its straps après-ski, but its atmospheric interior, good restaurant (breakfast $14 to $20, mains $26 to $34) and garden bar make it a worthy stop all year round.

The Drive » Follow Crown Range Rd, which tops out in tussock-covered style at 1121m, making it NZ's highest sealed road. Pull over at designated lookout points to admire the view on the way down to the Wakatipu Basin, and once at the junction follow SH6 right for a few kilometres to Arrow Junction. Take the right towards Arrowtown, along McDonnell Rd, 31km (around 40 minutes) from the Cardrona Hotel.

- - - - - - - - - - - - - -

TRIP HIGHLIGHT

⑧ Arrowtown

Established in the 1860s following the discovery of gold glistering in the Arrow River, Arrowtown's pretty, tree-lined avenues retain more than 60 buildings dating back to those glory days. The Lakes District

DETOUR: GLENORCHY

Start: ❶ Queenstown

Set in achingly beautiful surroundings, postage-stamp-sized Glenorchy is the perfect low-key antidote to Queenstown.

The 45-minute drive to reach it from Queenstown, along Lake Wakatipu's northern shoreline, is an absolute doozy. The further you go, the more gob-smacking the vistas become, as the jagged peaks of the Humboldt and Forbes mountains reveal themselves.

At Glenorchy itself, an expanding array of adventure operators can get you active on the lake and in nearby mountain valleys by kayak, horse, helicopter or jetboat. If you prefer to strike out on two legs, the mountainous region at the northern end of Lake Wakatipu is also the setting for some of the South Island's finest hikes, including the **Routeburn** and **Greenstone & Caples Tracks** (www.doc.govt.nz).

Those with sturdy wheels can explore the superb valleys north of Glenorchy. **Paradise** lies 15km northwest of town, just before the start of the Dart Track. Keep your expectations low: Paradise is just a paddock, but the gravel road there runs through beautiful farmland fringed by majestic mountains. You might recognise it from the *Lord of the Rings* movies as the approach to both Isengard and Lothlórien.

Glenorchy-based **Dart River Wilderness Jet** (☎03-442 9992; www.dartriver.co.nz; 45 Mull St; adult/child $229/129; ☺departs 9am & 1pm) runs one of NZ's most memorable boat trips into the heart of this spectacular wilderness. As well as some high-octane zipping along this beautiful braided river, there's a short walk through pristine beech forest and epic views of **Mt Earnslaw/Pikirakatahi**. Also on offer are jetboat rides combined with a thrilling river descent in an inflatable three-seater 'funyak'.

Museum & Gallery (p259) provides a comprehensive introduction to the area's colourful history, while just down the road you can see where Chinese diggers lived and worked along the Arrow River. NZ's best example of an early **Chinese settlement**, it features interpretation panels as well as restored huts and shops that make the story more tangible. Subjected to significant racism, the Chinese often had little choice but to rework old tailings rather than seek new claims.

Arrowtown makes a great base for exploring the Wakatipu Basin, especially if Queenstown's buzz might blow your circuits. One of Central Otago's signature wineries, in fact, is just 8km from town and can be reached by bicycle on the **Arrow River Bridges Trail**, part of the **Queenstown Trail** (www.queenstowntrail.co.nz).

As famous for its superb dining as it is for its wines, **Amisfield** (☎03-442 0556; www.amisfield.co.nz; 10 Lake Hayes Rd; mains $38-45; ☺tasting 10am-6pm, restaurant 11.30am-8pm) is a must-visit for the travelling gastronome.

✕ 🛏 p313

The Drive » Take the alternative route back to Queenstown, via Malaghans Rd, a 20km journey taking around 20 minutes.

Eating & Sleeping

Queenstown ❶

✕ Halo   Cafe $$

(☎03-441 1411; www.haloforbiddenbite.co.nz;
Camp St; brunch $13-22, dinner $19-28; ☺7am-
9pm; ☎) This stylish, sunny place effortlessly
blurs the line between breakfast, lunch and
dinner. The breakfast burrito will set you up for
a day's adventuring. There's plenty of outdoor
seating.

✕ Rata   Modern NZ $$$

(☎03-442 9393; www.ratadining.co.nz; 43
Ballarat St; mains $36-42, 2-/3-course lunch
$28/38; ☺noon-11pm) After gaining Michelin
stars for restaurants in London, New York and
LA, chef-owner Josh Emett has brought his
exceptional but surprisingly unflashy cooking
back home in the form of this upmarket but
informal back-lane eatery. Native bush, edging
the windows and in a large-scale photographic
mural, sets the scene for a short menu
showcasing the best seasonal NZ produce.

⌂ Queenstown Top 10
Holiday Park   Holiday Park $

(☎03-442 9306; www.qtowntop10.co.nz;
70 Arthurs Point Rd, Arthurs Point; sites $48,
units with/without bathroom from $95/85;
P☎) High above the Shotover River, this
relatively small, family-friendly park with
excellent motel units is 10 minutes' drive from
the hustle and bustle of Queenstown. Fall out
of your campervan straight onto the famous
Shotover Jet.

⌂ Eichardt's Private
Hotel   Boutique Hotel $$$

(☎03-441 0450; www.eichardts.com; 1-3 Marine
Pde; apt/ste from $1300/1750; ☎) Dating from
1867, this restored hotel enjoys an absolute
lakefront location. Each of the five giant suites
has a fireplace, king-sized bed, heated floor,
lake-sized bath tub and views. Four nearby
apartments are equally luxurious.

For more places to eat and stay in Queenstown
see pages 261, 285 and 303.

Wanaka ❻

✕ Kai Whakapai   Cafe $$

(☎03-443 7795; cnr Helwick & Ardmore Sts;
brunch $13-19, dinner $19-23; ☺7am-11pm; ☻)
An absolute Wanaka institution, Kai (the Māori
word for 'food') is the place to be for a liquid
sundowner accompanied by a massive filled
baguette or pizza. Locally brewed craft beers
are on tap and there are Central Otago wines
as well.

⌂ Criffel Peak View   B&B $$

(☎03-443 5511; www.criffelpeakview.co.nz; 98
Hedditch St; s/d/apt from $135/160/270; ☎)
Situated in a quiet cul-de-sac, this excellent
B&B has three rooms sharing a large lounge
with a log fire and a sunny wisteria-draped
deck. The charming hostesses live in a separate
house behind, which has a self-contained two-
bedroom apartment attached.

For more places to eat and stay in Wanaka see
p285.

Arrowtown ❽

✕ Provisions   Cafe $$

(☎03-445 4048; www.provisions.co.nz; 65
Buckingham St; mains $8.50-24; ☺8.30am-
5pm; ☎) One of Arrowtown's oldest cottages
is now a cute cafe surrounded by fragrant
gardens. Pop in for breakfast or a coffee and
don't leave town without trying one of their
deservedly famous sticky buns. They bake
everything on site, including bread and bagels.

⌂ Millbrook   Resort $$$

(☎03-441 7000; www.millbrook.co.nz;
Malaghans Rd; r from $212; @☎≋) Just
outside Arrowtown, this enormous resort is a
town unto itself. Cosy private villas have every
luxury and there's a top-class golf course right
at your front door. At the end of the day, take
your pick from four restaurants, or relax at
the **spa** (☎03-441 7017; www.millbrook.co.nz;
Malaghans Rd; treatments from $79).

For more places to eat and stay in Arrowtown
see p261.

Southern Scenic Route

24

Take the long way round New Zealand's southern extremities, from Fiordland National Park, through pretty countryside, and along raw coastlines with wildlife and weird land forms.

TRIP HIGHLIGHTS

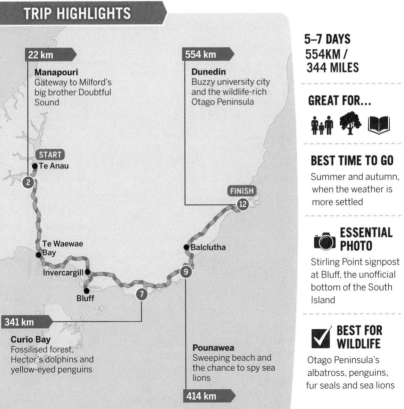

22 km

Manapouri
Gateway to Milford's big brother Doubtful Sound

554 km

Dunedin
Buzzy university city and the wildlife-rich Otago Peninsula

START
● Te Anau
2

FINISH
12

Te Waewae Bay
● Balclutha

● Invercargill
9

● Bluff
7

341 km

Curio Bay
Fossilised forest, Hector's dolphins and yellow-eyed penguins

Pounawea
Sweeping beach and the chance to spy sea lions

414 km

5–7 DAYS
**554KM /
344 MILES**

GREAT FOR...

BEST TIME TO GO

Summer and autumn, when the weather is more settled

ESSENTIAL PHOTO

Stirling Point signpost at Bluff, the unofficial bottom of the South Island

BEST FOR WILDLIFE

Otago Peninsula's albatross, penguins, fur seals and sea lions

Classic Trip

24 Southern Scenic Route

This long, u-shaped noodle around NZ's deep south takes travellers from the Fiordland's deep forest, lakes and Doubtful Sound, to the wildlife-rich Otago Peninsula. Unforgettable coastal landmarks include lonely beaches, cliffs, sea caves and other salt-crusted oddities, but there's plenty of pretty countryside inland, too. The trip to Stewart Island makes for the ultimate detour.

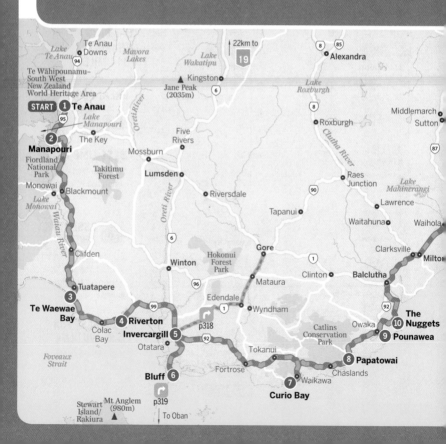

1 Te Anau

Lake Te Anau is NZ's second largest lake, bound by the Takitimu Mountains to the south, the Livingstone Mountains to the east, and rugged Fiordland peaks to the north and west. Gouged out by a huge glacier, it has several arms that extend into the mountainous, forested western shore. The lake's deepest point is 417m, about twice the depth of Loch Ness.

At its southern end is Te Anau township, Fiordland National Park's low-key but likeable hub. As well as the main base for national park tramps and trips to Milford Sound (p302), it's a great launch pad for aerial adventures, too. Get a bird's-eye view of the lake, Kepler Mountains and the town's rural surrounds on a 30-minute chopper flight ($240) with **Southern Lakes Helicopters** (📞 03-249 7167; www.southernlakes helicopters.co.nz; Lakefront Dr), or take off on longer trips over Doubtful, Dusky and Milford sounds (from $685).

✕🍴 p326

The Drive » Head 22km south on SH95 to Manapouri with the low pastoral hills of the Ramparts to the left and the forested foothills of the Kepler Mountains on your right. As you approach Lake Manapouri prepare yourself for another Fiordland 'wow' moment as the lake, its many islands and wild mountain backdrop come into view.

2 Manapouri

In 1969, Lake Manapouri was the focus of NZ's first major environmental campaign when hydroelectric dam plans proposed raising the lake level by 30m. A whopping 17% of voting-age citizens signed a petition against the idea, an action that also contributed to the downfall of the government at the following election. The West Arm power station was eventually built without any change to the lake level.

The remote power station can be seen on cruises to Doubtful Sound, departing from Manapouri. At three times the length and 10 times the area of Milford, and much, much less visited, Doubtful Sound is a must-see if you have the time and money. The day-long 'wilderness cruise' (adult/child from $250/65) run by Real Journeys (p296) includes

LINK YOUR TRIP

19 Inland Scenic Route

Pick up this classic trip at Queenstown, 171km northeast of Te Anau, and drive it in reverse.

26 East Coast Express

From Dunedin, continue up the east coast for a good slice of New Zealand history, plenty of seaside fun and some great food.

a three-hour cruise aboard a modern catamaran with a specialist nature guide. Intrepid travellers can head out with **Adventure Kayak & Cruise** (☎0800 324 966, 03-249 6626; www.fiordland-adventure.co.nz; 33 Waiau St; ◷Oct-Apr) for the ultimate self-powered expedition.

Few visitors actually linger in the town, which is a shame as it has many merits including a backdrop to rival Te Anau.

The Drive » Drive 5km east and then head south through rural Southland. At the 90km mark you will reach Te Waewae Bay having passed through Clifden (where the road becomes SH99) with its Victorian suspension bridge.

- - - - - - - - -

❸ Te Waewae Bay

This long, moody, windswept stretch of beach sets a steely glare towards Antarctica. It's particularly impressive if you're travelling from the east as it provides a first glimpse of the snow-capped Southern Alps descending into the sea, framing the western end of the bay.

Stop at the spectacular lookout at **McCracken's Rest** and keep an eye out for the Hector's dolphins and southern right whales that are occasionally sighted here. Just past Orepuki is the turnoff for **Monkey Island**, a grassy islet just metres offshore and accessible at low tide.

The Drive » Follow SH99 along the coast then cut across

DETOUR: GORE

Start: ❺ Invercargill

Around 66km (roughly an hour's drive) northeast of Invercargill, the rural town of Gore is the proud 'home of country music' in NZ, with the annual **Gold Guitar Week** (www.goldguitars.co.nz; ◷late May-early Jun) ensuring the town musters a buzz at least 10 days per year. For the other 355 days, good reasons to stop include an outstanding art gallery, a neat little museum and the chance to fly in vintage planes.

Housed in the century-old former public library, **Eastern Southland Gallery** (☎03-208 9907; www.esgallery.co.nz; 14 Hokonui Dr; ◷10am-4.30pm Mon-Fri, 1-4pm Sat & Sun) – aka the 'Goreggenheim' – houses a hefty collection of NZ art, including many works by Ralph Hotere. The also-amazing John Money Collection combines indigenous folk art from West Africa and Australia with works by esteemed NZ artist Rita Angus.

Across the road from the gallery, the **Hokonui Heritage Centre** (☎03-208 7032; 16 Hokonui Dr; ◷8.30am-5pm Mon-Sat, 1-4pm Sun) incorporates the town's visitor centre, the Gore Historical Museum and the **Hokonui Moonshine Museum** (☎03-208 9907; www.hokonuiwhiskey.com; 16 Hokonui Dr; adult/child $5/free; ◷8.30am-5pm Mon-Sat, 1-4pm Sun). Together they celebrate the town's proud and intoxicating history of fishing, farming and illegal distilleries. Admission to the Moonshine Museum includes a wee dram of the local liquid gold.

Wannabe WWI flying aces should buzz over to **Croydon Aircraft Company** (☎03-208 9755; www.croydonaircraft.com; 1558 Waimea Hwy, SH94; 10/30min flight $95/220; ◷9.30am-4.30pm Mon-Fri Nov-Mar, 11am-3pm Mon-Fri Apr-Oct), 16km northwest of Gore on SH94. These aerophiles are world-famous for restoring vintage aircraft and also offer flights in a two-seater 1930s Tiger Moth biplane.

DETOUR:
STEWART ISLAND/RAKIURA

Start: ❻ Bluff

Travellers who make the effort to reach NZ's 'third island' are rewarded with a warm welcome from both the local kiwi and the local Kiwis. A bushy island, 85% of which is designated **Rakiura National Park**, it is arguably the best place to spy the country's shy, feathered icon in the wild. With an estimated population of 20,000 they outnumber the locals by approximately 50 to one.

Stewart Island/Rakiura is a bird sanctuary of international repute, and even the most amateur of spotters are likely to be distracted by the constant – and utterly glorious – squawking, singing and flitting of feathery flocks. Guided by expert naturalists, **Ulva's Guided Walks** (☎03-219 1216; www.ulva.co.nz) offers excellent half-day tours ($125; transport included) exploring **Ulva Island** in Paterson Inlet. If you're a mad-keen twitcher, look for the *Birding Bonanza* trip ($395) on its website.

Add in a hike or kayak trip around the island's staggeringly lovely coast, and you've got a good reason to stay overnight. This will not only allow you to mix and mingle with the affable locals over a beer at the legendary local pub (NZ's southernmost), but you may also get to know why Stewart Island's Māori name, Rakiura, translates as 'land of glowing skies'.

✕ ⊨ p326

---

the headland to Colac Bay, and on to Riverton, 40km distant.

- - - - - - - - - - - - -

❹ Riverton

Quiet little Riverton (known to Māori as Aparima) is worth a stop for lunch and a wander around the museum. Also, if frigid swimming takes your fancy, the long, broad sands of Taramea Bay are good for a bracing dip.

Te Hikoi Southern Journey (☎03-234 8260; www.tehikoi.co.nz; 172 Palmerston St; adult/child $6/free; ⊙10am-4pm) is a fantastic little museum relaying local stories in clever and inspiring ways. Highlights include a fascinating 16-minute film

about sealer Jack Price and his Māori wife who were stranded on the Solander Islands, south of Fiordland. Oh, if only all small-town museums could be this good!

✕ p326

The Drive » Drive east on SH99 over the flat agricultural terrain of southern Southland until you reach the junction with SH6 at Lorneville, 33km from Riverton. Turn right onto SH6 and follow the dead-straight road to Invercargill, 8km away. Invercargill's suburban sprawl starts around 5km north of the city centre.

- - - - - - - - - - - - -

❺ Invercargill

This flat and somewhat featureless town tends to inspire ambivalence in its

visitors (except for Keith Richards, who famously dubbed it the 'arsehole of the world' during the Rolling Stones' 1965 visit), yet it satisfies all key requirements as a pit stop between the Catlins, Stewart Island/Rakiura and Fiordland. Moreover, it sports some handsome buildings, a notable craft brewery and an excellent museum.

Housed in a big white pyramid (a low-rent Louvre?), **Southland Museum & Art Gallery** (☎03-219 9069; www.southland museum.com; Queens Park, 108 Gala St; ⊙9am-5pm Mon-Fri, 10am-5pm Sat & Sun) is Invercargill's cultural hub with permanent displays on the region's

Classic Trip

WHY THIS IS A CLASSIC TRIP
SARAH BENNETT,
WRITER

Travel major highways between Christchurch and Queenstown and you could be forgiven for thinking that there's no such thing as 'off the beaten track' in these parts. Venture further south, however, and remote detours can be a daily occurrence. During peak season this highway's pretty quiet, but deviate down back roads to experience an inspiring sense of solitude and surprises even we can't anticipate. The deep south has a life all of its own.

Top: Curio Bay, the Catlins
Left: Yellow-eyed penguins, Otago Peninsula
Right: Mrs Clark's Cafe, Riverton

natural and human history, recounting plenty of salty tales around maritime exploits, in particular. Be sure to check out the museum's indubitable rock stars, the tuatara – unique lizard-like reptiles, unchanged for 220 million years. If the glacially paced 115-years-old-and-counting patriarch Henry is any example, they're not planning to do much for the next 220 million years either. Feeding time is 4pm on Fridays.

✕ ⊨ p326

The Drive » The drive south to Bluff and Stirling Point is 30km. Head south on SH1 skirting around the New River Estuary to the west and then Bluff Harbour to the east. Across the harbour you'll see Tiwai Point, the site of an aluminium smelter – NZ's largest single consumer of electricity.

----

6 Bluff

Windswept and more than a little bleak, Bluff is Invercargill's port. The main reason folk come here is to catch the ferry to Stewart Island/ Rakiura or to pose for a photo beside the **Stirling Point** signpost, to show that you've reached the furthest southern reaches of NZ. Sorry to disappoint you, but you haven't. Despite the oft-quoted phrase 'from Cape Reinga to Bluff' and the fact that SH1 terminates at Stirling

Classic Trip

Point, the South Island's southernmost point is Slope Point in the Catlins with Stewart Island/Rakiura and remote dots of rock lying even further south. But let's not let the facts get in the way of a good story, or photo...

Bluff Hill (Motupōhue) is another reason to visit. Accessed on foot from Stirling Point, or via Flagstaff Rd in the middle of town, this wind-ravaged reserve boasts awesome views across Foveaux Strait to Stewart Island/Rakiura. If the wind isn't threatening to sweep you off your feet, follow the spiraling path up to the lookout.

The Drive » Drive back to Invercargill, then head east on Gorge Rd–Invercargill Hwy to Fortrose, 46km away. Continue east on SH92 for 31km then turn right towards Waikawa. Drive south for 12km, through Niagara (note the cafe) to Waikawa, then

on to Curio Bay, 118km in all from Stirling Point.

TRIP HIGHLIGHT

❼ Curio Bay

Named after a 19th-century whaling captain, the Catlins coast is a beguiling blend of fecund farmland, native forest, lonely lighthouses, empty beaches and wildlife-spotting opportunities. On a clear summer's day it's a beauty to behold. In the face of an Antarctic southerly, it's an entirely different story. Good luck.

The beachy settlement of Curio Bay attracts a deluge of sunseekers in the summer months but is a sleepy hamlet at other times. Most of its accommodation lines up along **Porpoise Bay**, a glorious stretch of sand conducive to swimming. Blue penguins nest in the dunes and in summer Hector's dolphins come here to rear their young.

Curio Bay itself lies just around the southern headland on a more rugged stretch of coast. It's famous for its fossilised Jurassic-age trees, which are visible for four hours either side of low tide. Yellow-eyed penguins waddle ashore here an hour or so before sunset. Do the right thing and keep your distance.

The Drive » Drive north for 12km back to the junction with SH92, turn right and head east through the forested foothills of the Maclennan Range to Papatowai. The total distance is 43km. The long solitary sweep of Tautuku Bay, just shy of Papatowai, is worth a quick stop and a leg-stretch.

❽ Papatowai

Nestled near the mouth of the Tahakopa River, the leafy village of Papatowai has perhaps a few dozen regular inhabitants but swells with holidaymakers in summer, who are mainly drawn by the languid vibe, good bush walks and pretty picnic spot at the river mouth.

One of the best reasons to stop here is the **Lost Gypsy Gallery** (☏03-415 8908; www.thelostgypsy.com; 2532 Papatowai Hwy; admission $5; ⊙10am-5pm Thu-Tue, closed May-Sep; 🛜). Fashioned from re-maindered bits and bobs, artist Blair Sommerville's and friends' intricately crafted automata are wonderfully irreverent. The bamboozling collection in the bus (free entry) is a teaser for the

TOP TIP:
A CATLINS CAPER

Many of the Catlins' splendid, often strange surprises – such as **Waipapa Point**, **Slope Point** and **Purakaunui Bay** – await discovery down back roads, dead-end roads, gravel roads and other roads-less-travelled. If you have the time, it's definitely worth tracking them down with a copy of the local touring map (www.catlins.org.nz).

DETOUR:
OTAGO PENINSULA

DETOUR: OTAGO PENINSULA

Start: 12 Dunedin

Right on Dunedin's doorstep, the Otago Peninsula is a hot spot for wildlife-watching, with species including fur seals, sea lions, albatross, penguins and a fleet of other seabirds. The rugged headland also boasts walking trails, beaches and interesting historical sites.

Twitchers of any persuasion won't want to miss Taiaroa Head, the world's only mainland royal albatross colony, accessible on guided tours run by **Royal Albatross Centre** (03-478 0499; www.albatross.org.nz; Taiaroa Head; 11.30am-dusk Oct-Apr, 10.15am-dusk May-Sep). The birds are present throughout the year, but the best time to see them is from December to March, when one parent is constantly guarding the young while the other delivers food. Watching these clumsy giants coming in to land is pretty hilarious.

Another rewarding way to encounter the peninsula's critters is with **Nature's Wonders Naturally** (03-478 1150; www.natureswonders.co.nz; Taiaroa Head; adult/child $59/45; tours from 10.15am). The tours along the beautiful beaches of a coastal sheep farm allow a chance to see yellow-eyed penguins and NZ fur seals, blissfully unfazed by the 'go-anywhere' Argo vehicles.

carnival of creations through the gate (young children not allowed, sorry...). The buzz, bong and bright lights of the organ are bound to tickle your ribs.

The Drive » Drive north and then northeast for 26km along SH92 through forest and farmland to Owaka. Worthy stops en route (but off the main road) include McLean Falls, Matai Falls, Purakaunui Falls and Jack's Blowhole. Owaka provides a chance to stock up on petrol and groceries before you turn right and follow the signs for Pounawea, 4km away.

TRIP HIGHLIGHT

9 Pounawea

Pounawea, a beautiful hamlet on the edge of the **Catlins River Estuary**, is a delightful place

to linger for a night or two, with accommodation there as well as at Newhaven, just across the inlet. Look out for the daft-looking royal spoonbill and listen to the roar of the waves coming over the bar.

Within walking distance of Newhaven car park, **Surat Bay** is a serene spot, notable for the sea lions that laze around between here and **Cannibal Bay**. Give them a wide birth (that's the sea lions and any cannibals, of course).

The Drive » Return to Owaka and then drive 7km north on SH92 to Ahuriri Flat. Turn right here, signposted for Kaka Point, and drive 8km to Molyneux Bay. Turn right and drive along the coast on the windy and

sometimes steep and narrow road to the Nugget Point car park, 6km away. Total driving distance is 25km.

10 The Nuggets

The biggest attraction at the northern end of the Catlins is **Nugget Point/Tokatā**. This is the king of the region's viewpoints, made all the more interesting by the wave-thrashed cliffs and the toothy islets known as the Nuggets protruding from the surf. Seals and sea lions can often be spotted lolling about below and there's also plenty of bird life, such as soaring shearwaters and spoonbills huddling in the lea of the breeze. A 900m walk leads from

the car park to the light-house on the point itself.

Just shy of the Nugget Point car park is **Roaring Bay**, where a well-placed hide allows you to spot yellow-eyed penguins (hōiho) coming ashore (best two hours before sunset). Obey all signs: as you can see, this is a pretty precarious existence.

The Drive » Drive north along the coast through Kaka Point to the junction with SH1. Turn right and drive 81km northeast on SH1 through the rural Otago towns of Balclutha and Milton to the Dunedin suburb of Burnside. Turn right into Stevenson Rd, then Emerson St, then Blackhead Rd; Tunnel Beach Rd will be on your left. Total distance is 107km.

⑪ Tunnel Beach

A short but steep track accesses a dramatic, rocky stretch of coast where the wild Pacific has carved sea stacks, arches and unusual formations out of the limestone. The beach takes its name from a hand-hewn stone tunnel at the bottom of the track, which civic father John Cargill had built to give his family access to secluded beach-side picnic spots.

The ocean may look inviting but strong cur-rents make swimming here dangerous. The track crosses private land and is closed for lambing between August and November. There are, however, dozens of other satisfying walks detailed in the *Dunedin Walks* brochure (www.dunedin.govt.nz).

The Drive » Return back to SH1 and head east following the signs for Dunedin city centre. Out of peak times, this 8km drive through the western suburbs and central Dunedin should take around 15 minutes.

TRIP HIGHLIGHT

⑫ Dunedin

Known as the 'Edin-burgh of the South' due to its settlement by two shiploads of Scots in 1848, Dunedin is an atmospheric place to while away a few days. There's plenty to admire architecturally, includ-ing classic weatherboard villas peppering the hillsides, and various Victorian buildings punctuating the city centre. One of these, the striking bluestone rail-way station, claims to be NZ's most photographed building.

Two worthy museums admirably present the region's backstory, but if you're feeling arty, **Dunedin Public Art Gal-lery** (✆03-474 3240; www.dunedin.art.museum; 30 The Octagon; ◷10am-5pm; 🖥) is one of NZ's best. Its airy exhibition spaces principally present im-portant works from the nation's back catalogue, but plenty of floor space is also set aside for con-temporary shows.

Dunedin

The gallery is a stalwart proponent of the edgy creativity typifying this little city, to which its large university-student population undoubtedly contributes. Their patronage also underpins a solid offering of espresso bars, cheap ethnic restaurants, bars and music venues, all part of the diverse hospitality scene that runs the full gamut. If you like eating, drinking and live music, Dunedin will do for you.

✕ 🛏 p327

Eating & Sleeping

Te Anau ①

✗ Sandfly Cafe   Cafe $

(☏03-249 9529; 9 The Lane; mains $7-20; ◷7am-4.30pm; ☏) Clocking the most local votes for the town's best espresso, simple but satisfying Sandfly is a top spot to enjoy an all-day breakfast, soup, sandwich or sweet treat, while listening to cruisy music or sunning yourself on the lawn.

⇌ Te Anau Lakeview Kiwi
Holiday Park & Motels   Holiday Park $

(☏0800 483 262, 03-249 7457; www.teanauholidaypark.co.nz; 77 Manapouri–Te Anau Hwy; sites from $21, dm/s/d without bathroom $29/40/72, units with/without bathroom from $179/72; @☏) This 9-hectare grassy lakeside holiday park has plenty of space to pitch your tent or park your van in. It also has a wide range of accommodation from basic dorms through to tidy cabins and the rather swanky Marakura deluxe motels with enviable lake and mountain views. Friendly staff will hook you up with local activities and transport.

For more places to eat and stay in Te Anau see p303.

Riverton ④

✗ Mrs Clark's Cafe   Cafe $$

(☏03-234 8600; 108 Palmerston St; meals $12-24; ◷8am-3pm Sun-Thu, to 8pm Fri & Sat; ☏) Housed in an insanely turquoise building that has been various forms of eatery since 1891, Mrs Clark's serves thoroughly contemporary and delicious day-time food (beaut baking!), ace espresso, craft beer, and pizza on Friday and Saturday evenings.

Invercargill ⑤

✗ Batch   Cafe $$

(☏03-214 6357; 173 Spey St; meals $13-20; ◷7am-4.30pm; ☏) Large, shared tables, a relaxed beachy ambience, and top-notch coffee and smoothies add up to this cafe being widely regarded as Southland's best. Delicious counter food includes bagels, sumptuously filled rolls, banoffee brioches, brownies and cakes that are little works of art. A smallish wine and beer list partners healthy lunch options. In summer, it stays open until 8pm on Fridays.

⇌ Tower Lodge Motel   Motel $$

(☏03-217 6729; www.towerlodgemotel.co.nz; 119 Queens Dr; unit from $130; ☏) Right opposite Invercargill's oddly ornate Victorian water tower, this older motel has been made over with new carpets, fresh decor and a mushroom colour scheme. Even the studio units are spacious and some of the one-bedrooms have spa baths.

Stewart Island

South Sea Hotel   Pub $$

(☏03-219 1059; www.stewart-island.co.nz; 26 Elgin Tce, Oban; ◷7am-9pm; ☏) Welcome to one of New Zealand's classic pubs, complete with stellar cod and chips, beer by the quart, a reliable cafe (mains $15 to $33) and plenty of friendly banter in the public bar. Great at any time of day (or night), try to wash up for the Sunday night quiz – an unforgettable slice of island life. Basic rooms are available too.

⇌ Observation Rock Lodge   B&B $$$

(☏03-219 1444; www.observationrocklodge.co.nz; 7 Leonard St, Oban; r $395; ☏) Secluded in bird-filled bush and angled for sea, sunset and aurora views, Annett and Phil's lodge has three stylish, luxurious rooms with private decks and a shared lounge. Guided activities, a sauna, a hot tub and Annett's gourmet dinners are included in the deluxe package ($780) or by arrangement as additions to the standard B&B rate.

Niagara

✕ Niagara Falls   Cafe $$

(📞03-246 8577; www.niagarafallscafe.co.nz; 256 Niagara–Waikawa Rd, Niagara; mains $14-22; ⏰11am-late Dec-Mar, 11am-4pm Thu-Mon Apr-Nov; 📶) Located in a Victorian schoolhouse, this is a decent spot to linger over coffee and a scone, or to tuck into homemade meals. Tasty lamb burgers are sandwiched into freshly baked bread, and there's blue cod, chowder and decadent chocolate brownies. Relax in the grassy garden with a local craft beer or a glass of wine.

Owaka

🛏 Newhaven Holiday Park   Holiday Park $

(📞03-415 8834; www.newhavenholiday.com; 324 Newhaven Rd, Owaka; sites from $32, units from $100, without bathroom from $66; 📶) Sitting on the estuary edge at the gateway to the Surat Bay beach walk, this excellent little holiday park has good communal facilities, cheerful cabins and three self-contained units. When we last sneaked around, not only were we serenaded by a bellbird but we swear the toilets smelt of cinnamon.

Dunedin ⑫

✕ No 7 Balmac   Cafe $$

(📞03-464 0064; www.no7balmac.co.nz; 7 Balmacewen Rd, Maori Hill; mains brunch $14-25, dinner $29-37; ⏰7am-late Mon-Fri, 8.30am-late Sat, 8.30am-5pm Sun; 📶) We wouldn't recommend walking to this sophisticated cafe at the top of Maori Hill but luckily it's well worth the price of a cab. The fancy cafe fare stretches to the likes of venison loin and dry-aged beef. If you're on a diet, avoid eye contact with the sweets cabinet.

✕ Plato   Modern NZ $$$

(📞03-477 4235; www.platocafe.co.nz; 2 Birch St; mains lunch $19-24, dinner $34-36; ⏰noon-2pm Wed-Sun, 6pm-late daily) The kooky decor (including collections of toys and beer tankards) gives little indication of the seriously good food on offer at this relaxed eatery by the harbour. Fresh fish and shellfish feature prominently in a lengthy menu full of international flavours and subtle smoky elements. Servings are enormous.

🛏 858 George St   Motel $$

(📞03-474 0047; www.858georgestreetmotel.co.nz; 858 George St, North Dunedin; units from $150; 🅿️📶) Cleverly designed to blend harmoniously with the neighbourhood's two-storey Victorian houses, this top-quality motel complex has units ranging in size from studios to two bedrooms. Studios are fitted with microwaves, fridges, toasters and kettles, while the larger units also have stove tops or full ovens.

🛏 Bluestone on George   Apartment $$$

(📞03-477 9201; www.bluestonedunedin.co.nz; 571 George St, North Dunedin; apt from $225; 🅿️@📶) If you're expecting an imposing old bluestone building, think again: this four-storey block couldn't be more contemporary. The elegant studio units are decked out in muted tones, with kitchenettes, laundry facilities and decks or tiny balconies. There's also a small gym and a guest lounge.

For more places to eat and stay in Dunedin see pages 336 and 345.

Otago Heritage Trail

25

Follow the trails of gold-miners and historic railways on this journey through inland Otago's rocky gorges and broad, big-sky plains.

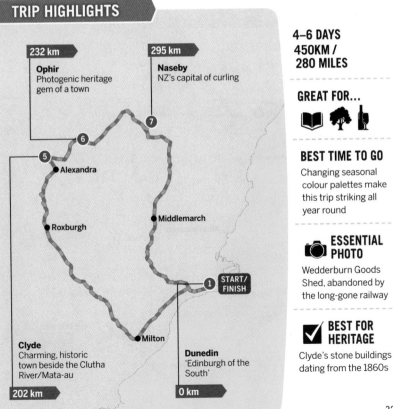

232 km

Ophir
Photogenic heritage gem of a town

295 km

Naseby
NZ's capital of curling

● Alexandra

● Roxburgh

● Middlemarch

① **START/ FINISH**

● Milton

Clyde
Charming, historic town beside the Clutha River/Mata-au

202 km

Dunedin
'Edinburgh of the South'

0 km

**4–6 DAYS
450KM /
280 MILES**

GREAT FOR...

BEST TIME TO GO

Changing seasonal colour palettes make this trip striking all year round

ESSENTIAL PHOTO

Wedderburn Goods Shed, abandoned by the long-gone railway

BEST FOR HERITAGE

Clyde's stone buildings dating from the 1860s

329

25 Otago Heritage Trail

It was the discovery of gold in the 1860s that led to settlement of the rugged and remote Otago region. Today, the old miners' trails and an abandoned railway lead visitors on a fascinating voyage of discovery across one of the country's most beloved landscapes, taking in more stone buildings, sluicings, viaducts and goods sheds than you can shake a spade at.

TRIP HIGHLIGHT

❶ Dunedin

Settled by Scots in 1848, Dunedin is immensely proud of its heritage, never missing an opportunity to break out the haggis and bagpipes on civic occasions.

Dunedin even has its own tartan, but such Scottishness makes up only part of the city's cultural tapestry, as stitched together tidily at **Toitū Otago Settlers Museum** (☏ 03-477 5052; www.toituosm.com; 31 Queens

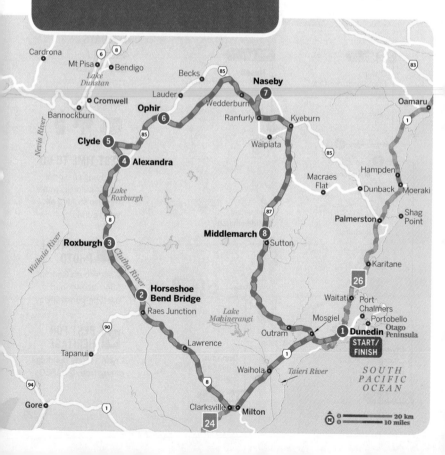

Gardens; 10am-5pm;). Interactive and engrossing, it features a Māori section, an awesome car collection and a room devoted to a seminal New Zealand music production company, Flying Nun Records. Inside the Victorian portrait gallery, a host of early settlers stare out from behind whiskers and lace.

For more in that genteel vein, visit **Olveston** (03-477 3320; www. olveston.co.nz; 42 Royal Tce, Roslyn; adult/child $20/11; tours 9.30am, 10.45am, noon, 1.30pm, 2.45pm & 4pm), a spectacular 1906 mansion providing a wonderful window into Dunedin's past. Formerly home to the Theomin family, Olveston's grand interiors feature works by major NZ artists

LINK YOUR TRIP

24 Southern Scenic Route

Head south from Dunedin to explore the wild, crazy Catlins coast, Stewart Island and the pretty, rural Southland.

26 East Coast Express

Head north from Dunedin to experience the east coast's wildlife, ocean scenes, rural charm and rejuvenating Christchurch.

Charles Goldie and Frances Hodgkins. Entry is via fascinating guided tours, so it pays to book ahead.

Another must for heritage buffs is Dunedin's striking Victorian bluestone **railway station** (22 Anzac Ave). Claiming to be NZ's most photographed building, it features mosaic-tile floors and glorious stained-glass windows.

p336

The Drive » Head South on SH1. Around 57km along, just after Milton, turn right onto SH8 and follow it inland towards Lawrence – the scene of NZ's first gold rush in 1861. Continue to Raes Junction, after which it's around 10km to the Horseshoe Bend Bridge car park. Total journey time is around 90 minutes (127km).

- - - - - - - - - - - -

❷ Horseshoe Bend Bridge

This historically significant bridge was built in 1913 to replace a 'wire and chair' arrangement used to ferry early settlers over the Clutha River/Mata-au – NZ's second-longest river. What a prospect! The mighty river's swift, swirling waters can be admired on the **Horseshoe Bend Track**, taking around 45 minutes each way.

Beyond the handsome timber bridge, it's another 15 minutes or so to the **Lonely Graves**, one of

the area's more poignant gold-rush relics. Sitting side by side in a fenced plot, their tale tells of the discovery of the body of a young man. Unable to be identified, the body was said to have been buried by a certain William Rigney in the company of other concerned citizens, and marked with the words 'Somebody's Darling Lies Buried Here'. When Rigney himself died in 1912, he was buried alongside.

The Drive » Following the banks of the Clutha River/Mata-au, continue north on SH8 for 25km to Roxburgh.

- - - - - - - - - - - -

❸ Roxburgh

Surrounded by apple, apricot and other sweet-smelling orchards, the rural village of Roxburgh is a core member of Central Otago's fruit-growing set. The main attraction for passing travellers is a cycle ride along the **Roxburgh Gorge** or **Clutha Gold Trails** (www.clutha gold.co.nz); these trails follow the ever-changing, highly scenic banks of the mighty Clutha River and Lake Roxburgh, which pools against one of the river's dams. The twin trails offer a chance to survey many historic gold-mining relics, including water races and rock bivvies; the fragrance of wild thyme introduced by Chinese miners is often pervasive.

COLIN MONTEATH / ALAMY STOCK PHOTO ©

Trail Journeys (☏03-449 2150; www.trailjourneys.co.nz; 16 Springvale Rd; ⏰tours Sep-Apr) can provide bike hire and transport.

But hang on, slam on the anchors! Roxburgh has another major attraction – **Jimmy's Pies** (☏03-446 9012; www.jimmyspies.co.nz; 143 Scotland St; pies $4-6.50; ⏰7.30am-5pm Mon-Fri), **world-famous in New Zealand since**

way back in 1959. These buttery, calorific treats are best piping hot straight out of the oven. An apricot and chicken pie will give you a taste of the terroir.

The Drive » SH8 winds along rugged, rock-strewn hills above the Clutha River, passing a scattering of tiny towns, many of which date from the gold rushes. In season, roadside fruit stalls sell just-picked stone

fruit, cherries and berries. It's 42km/30 minutes to Alexandra.

- - - - - - - - - -

④ Alexandra

Unless you've come especially for the Easter Bunny Hunt or the springtime Blossom Festival and NZ Merino Shearing Championships, the main reason to visit unassuming Alexandra is mountain biking. The

Ophir Historic bridge across the Manuherikia River

major settlement along the **Central Otago Rail Trail** – NZ's original off-road cycling epic – it offers more eating and sleeping options than the rest of the one-horse (or fewer) towns on that route. It's also the predominant starting point of the aforementioned **Roxburgh Gorge Trail** (www.cluthagold.co.nz), some of the craziest bits of which can be explored on foot from the old Alexandra Bridge.

There is, however, a rather spectacular walk around **Flat Top Hill Conservation Area** (www.doc.govt.nz), 6km south of town (on the SH8 road to Roxburgh). A 40-minute loop features information panels explaining the significance of this 'block mountain' and its threatened eco-systems. There are also vast, panoramic views from the high points.

Alex, as it's known to the locals, marks the southeastern corner of the acclaimed Central Otago wine region. Of the dozen wineries in the immediate vicinity, only a handful are open for tastings. These are detailed on the *Central*

Otago Wine Map, available from **Alexandra i-SITE** (☎03-262 7999; www.centralotagonz.com; 21 Centennial Ave; ⏰9am-5pm; 🛜).

✕ 🛏 p336

The Drive » Follow signs along SH8 – which vaguely parallels the Clutha River/Mata-au – to Clyde, 8km away.

TRIP HIGHLIGHT

5 Clyde

Considerably more charming than his buddy Alex, 8km down the road, Clyde looks more like a 19th-century gold-rush film set than a real town. Set on the banks of the emerald-green **Clutha River/Mata-au**, Clyde retains a friendly, small-town feel, even when holidaymakers flood in during the peak summer season. Pick up a copy of *Walk Around Historic Clyde* from the Alexandra i-SITE to explore.

A popular amble is the **Alexandra–Clyde 150th Anniversary Walk**, a fairly flat, one-way (three-hour) riverside trail with ample resting spots and shade. The walkway also doubles as the western end (and most popular starting point) for the Otago Central Rail Trail.

✕ 🛏 p336

The Drive » Head back to SH8, and if you are happy to cut the corner and skip Alex, take Springvale Rd heading east from town. At Springvale, around 11km from Clyde, head northeast on SH85 for 17km to the Ophir turn-off. It's another 1.5km or so to the town.

TRIP HIGHLIGHT

6 Ophir

Ophir (population 58) is one of Central Otago's true heritage gems. Gold was discovered here in 1863 and the town swiftly formed, adopting the name of the biblical place where King Solomon sourced his gold. By 1875, the population hit over 1000 but when the gold disappeared, so did the people. Ophir's fate was sealed when the railway bypassed it in 1904, leaving its main street trapped in time.

The most photogenic of Ophir's many heritage buildings is the still-functioning 1886 post office. At the far end of the town, the sealed road

OTAGO CENTRAL RAIL TRAIL

The trailblazer for a growing series of off-road recreation trails located all around New Zealand, the Otago Central Rail Trail follows a 150km stretch of the original railway line that once linked the inland goldfield towns with Dunedin from the early 20th century through to the 1990s.

Running between Clyde and Middlemarch – thus paralleling part of this road trip – it offers opportunities to get out of your vehicle, don the walking shoes or hire a bike, and explore a historic route complete with old rail bridges, viaducts and tunnels. It sports excellent facilities (toilets, shelters and information), few hills, a smooth surface, gob-smacking scenery and profound remoteness in places, and attracts well over 25,000 visitors annually; March is the busiest time.

The entire trail takes approximately four to five days to complete by bike (or a week on foot), and can be ridden in either direction. It is, however, easy to tailor day trips of various lengths, with plenty of bike hire and shuttle services available. Good bases for riding the trail include Clyde, Alexandra, Ranfurly and Middlemarch, with others such as Naseby and St Bathans easy detours off the trail.

In person, any of the area's i-SITEs can provide advice on ride options, accommodation and all-important refreshment stops. Comprehensive planning information is available at www.otagocentralrailtrail.co.nz and www.otagorailtrail.co.nz.

ends at the 1870s **Dan O'Connell Bridge** across the scenic Manuherikia River. Single lane and built of schist and timber, it's a classic Central Otago suspension bridge, and a handsome specimen at that.

📖 p337

The Drive » Follow Ida Valley–Omakau Rd, which parallels the Central Otago Rail Trail for part of the way. Turn right at the SH85 junction. Five minutes along, stop to photograph Wedderburn Goods Shed before completing the 16km leg to the Ranfurly–Naseby Rd turn-off to Naseby, 63km (50 minutes) from Ophir.

TRIP HIGHLIGHT

7 Naseby

Cute as a button, surrounded by forest and dotted with old stone buildings, Naseby (www.nasebyinfo.org.nz) is the kind of small settlement where life moves slowly. But typical of Central Otago's townships, these streets once ran hot with gold fever.

Naseby was once home to 4000 or so miners. After the rushes the town was all but forgotten, leaving its 19th-century streetscape virtually intact. Heritage lovers will adore the village's old-world architecture, brought to life in the heritage trail map – *A Walk Through History* – available from the **information centre** (📞03-444 9961; www.nasebyinfo.org.nz; Old Post Office, Derwent St; ⊙9am-1pm Tue-Thu, 10am-4pm Fri-Mon, reduced hours in winter).

The **Maniototo Museum** (📞03-444 9937; www.maniototomuseums.org.nz; cnr Leven & Earne Sts, Naseby; entry by donation; ⊙10am-3pm Nov-Apr) provides greater background.

As well as heritage charm, Naseby also boasts pleasant walking and cycling trails in the surrounding forest. But why would you take a walk when you could curl? Yes, that's right. Naseby is home to NZ's only year-round curling rink, so if you've always fancied giving it a whirl – that gentle skidding of stones across the ice, the furious sweeping of brooms – then slide on over to **Maniototo Curling International** (📞03-444 9878; www.curling.co.nz; 1057 Channel Rd; per 90min adult/child $30/12; ⊙10am-5pm May-Oct, 9am-7.30pm Nov-Apr).

📖 p337

The Drive » Return to SH85 the way you came in. At the junction, follow SH85 left to reach Kyeburn, then turn right onto SH87 to reach Middlemarch, 75km (around an hour) from Naseby.

8 Middlemarch

With the Rock & Pillar Range as an impressive backdrop, the small town of Middlemarch (www.middlemarch.co.nz) is famous in NZ for its Singles Ball (held across Easter in odd-numbered years), where southern men gather to entice city gals to the country life.

Like its sibling towns throughout Central Otago, Middlemarch has many charming heritage buildings, including the railway station built when the Otago Central line reached town in 1891. Today Middlemarch is the eastern end of the Otago Central Rail Trail; with two large cycle-hire companies on the main street, this is a great spot to get out for a ride.

Heading south, though, the trains still rumble on under the banner of **Taieri Gorge Railway** (📞03-477 4449; www.dunedinrailways.co.nz; ⊙Sun May-Sep, Fri & Sun Oct-Apr). Travelling between Dunedin and Middlemarch the highly scenic journey takes in narrow tunnels, deep gorges, winding tracks, rugged canyons and viaduct crossings. It's six hours' return from Middlemarch ($113), although most trips end at Pukerangi Station, 20km further south ($91, four hours return).

🍴 p337

The Drive » Continue south on SH87 for 65km until you reach SH1, which you should follow the final 15km into central Dunedin. The journey time is just over an hour (80km).

Eating & Sleeping

Dunedin ❶

✕ Bracken   Modern NZ $$$

(☏03-477 9779; www.brackenrestaurant.co.nz;
95 Filleul St; 5/7/9-course menu $79/99/120;
☺5.30-11pm Tue-Sat) Bracken's tasting menus
offer a succession of pretty little plates bursting
with flavour. While the dishes are intricate,
nothing's overly gimmicky, and the setting, in
an old wooden house, is classy without being
too formal.

🛏 Argoed   B&B $$

(☏03-474 1639; www.argoed.co.nz; 504 Queens
Dr, Belleknowes; s/d from $150/190; 🅿🖧)
Roses and rhododendrons encircle this gracious
two-storey wooden villa, built in the 1880s. Each
of the three charmingly old-fashioned bedrooms
has its own bathroom but only one is en suite.
Guests can relax in the conservatory or tinkle
the ivories of the grand piano in the lounge.

For more places to eat and stay in Dunedin see
pages 327 and 345.

Alexandra ❹

✕ Courthouse Cafe & Larder   Cafe $

(☏03-448 7818; www.packingshedcompany.
com; 8 Centennial Ave; mains $10-20;
☺8am-4pm) Floral wallpaper and bright
vinyl tablecloths help to dispel any lingering
austerity from this stone courthouse building,
dating from 1878 and surrounded by lawns.
The counter groans under the weight of an
extraordinary array of baked goods (macadamia
custard croissants, gooey doughnuts, slices,
cakes), which compete with a menu full of
interesting dishes (beef-cheek burgers, pulled-
pork sliders, eggy breakfasts).

🛏 Asure Avenue Motel   Motel $$

(☏03-448 6919; www.avenue-motel.co.nz; 117
Centennial Ave; unit from $135; 🖧) If you're after
a clean, modern motel unit with a kitchenette
or a full kitchen, this is the pick of the bunch.
There's nothing remarkable about the decor or
setting but the rooms are comfortable and well
maintained.

🛏 Speargrass Inn   Historic Hotel $$

(☏03-449 2192; www.speargrassinn.co.nz;
1300 Fruitlands-Roxburgh Rd/SH8, Fruitlands; r
$180; ☺cafe 8.30am-4pm Mon-Thu, 8.30am-
9pm Fri-Sun, closed Tue & Wed May-Sep; 🖧) On
the road to Roxburgh 13km south of Alexandra,
the historic Speargrass Inn has three handsome
rooms in a block out the back, set in attractive
gardens. The original 1869 building houses
a charming cafe. It's a good place to stop for
coffee and cake or a more substantial meal.

Clyde ❺

✕ Oliver's   Modern NZ $$

(☏03-449 2805; www.oliverscentralotago.co.nz;
34 Sunderland St; mains lunch $18-26, dinner
$30-39; ☺11.30am-2.30pm & 5.30-9.30pm)
Housed in a gold-rush-era general store,
this wonderful complex incorporates a craft
brewery (the Victoria Store Brewery), bar and
deli-cafe within its venerable stone walls. The
restaurant shifts gears from on-trend cafe fare
at lunchtime (tuna sliders, pulled pork belly etc)
to a bistro showcasing the best local, seasonal
produce in the evenings (venison noisette, lamb
rump, salmon).

✕ Post Office Cafe & Bar   Cafe $$

(www.postofficecafeclyde.co.nz; 2 Blyth St;
mains $13-30; ☺10am-9pm; 🖧) Clyde's 1899
post office houses a popular restaurant famous
for its garden tables and hearty food. There
are loads of nooks and crannies conducive to
newspaper perusing.

🛏 Postmaster's House   B&B $$

(☏03-449 2488; www.postofficecafeclyde.
co.nz; 4 Blyth St; d with/without bathroom
$125/95) Antique furnishings are dotted around
the large and lovely rooms in this pretty stone
cottage. Two of the three rooms share an en
suite bathroom; the third has its own.

Ophir ⑥

⌂ Pitches Store   B&B $$$
(☏03-447 3240; www.pitches-store.co.nz; 45
Swindon St, Ophir; r $280; ⊘ restaurant 10am-
late daily Nov-Apr, 10am-3pm Mon, Sun & Thu,
10am-late Fri & Sat May & Aug-Oct) Formerly a
general store and butcher, this heritage building
has been sensitively transformed into six
elegant guest rooms and a humdinger of a cafe/
restaurant (brunch from $13 to $19, dinner from
$33 to $37). Exposed stone walls may speak
of the past but the menu offers contemporary
country cooking.

Naseby ⑦

⌂ Royal Hotel   Pub $
(☏03-444 9990; www.naseby.co.nz; 1 Earne St;
dm $40, r with/without bathroom $110/80; ☜)
The better of the town's historic pubs, the 1863
Royal Hotel sports the royal coat of arms and
what just might be NZ's most rustic garden bar.
Rooms are simple but spotless.

⌂ Old Doctor's Residence   B&B $$$
(☏03-444 9775; www.olddoctorsresidence.
co.nz; 58 Derwent St; r/ste $295/345; ☜) Old
doctors take note: this is how to reside! Sitting
behind a pretty garden, this gorgeous 1870s
house offers two luxurious guest rooms and a
lounge where wine and nibbles are served of an
evening. The suite has a sitting room and an en
suite bathroom (with a fabulous make-up desk).
The smaller room's bathroom is accessed from
the corridor.

Ranfurly

⌂ Peter's Farm Lodge   Lodge $
(☏03-444 9811; www.petersfarm.co.nz; 113
Tregonning Rd, Waipiata; per person $55) Set on
a sheep farm 13km south of Ranfurly, this rustic
1882 farmhouse offers comfy beds, hearty
barbecue dinners ($25) and free pick-ups from
the Rail Trail. Kayaks, fishing rods and gold
pans are all available, so it's worth staying a
couple of nights. Further beds are available in
neighbouring Tregonnings Cottage (1882).

⌂ Hawkdun Lodge   Motel $$
(☏03-444 9750; www.hawkdunlodge.co.nz;
1 Bute St; s/d from $113/150; ☜) This smart
boutique motel is the best option in the town
centre by far. Each unit has a kitchenette with
a microwave, but travelling chefs can flex their
skills in the guest kitchen and on the barbecue.
Rates include a continental breakfast.

Middlemarch ⑧

✕ Kissing Gate Cafe   Cafe $
(☏03-464 3224; 2 Swansea St; mains $7-18;
⊘8.30am-4pm; ☜) Sit out under the fruit trees
in the pretty garden of this cute little wooden
cottage and tuck into a cooked breakfast, fancy
meat pie, zingy salad or some home baking.
Nana-chic at its best.

Moeraki Stone spheres scatter the wind-sculpted beach

East Coast Express

26

Turn a straightforward drive up State Hwy 1 into a journey of surprises on small detours to see steampunk inventions, alien beach boulders and New Zealand's most arty garden.

482 km

Lyttelton
Post-quake vibrancy on Christchurch's doorstep

402 km

Akaroa
Banks Peninsula's Gallic-flavoured hub

FINISH Christchurch

6

● Rakaia

5

● Ashburton

3

● Moeraki

116 km

Oamaru
Celebrate the past and future in NZ's coolest town

0 km

1

START

Dunedin
Buzzy university city with proud Scottish heritage

**5–7 DAYS
495KM /
363 MILES**

GREAT FOR...

BEST TIME TO GO

Spring and autumn for abundant wildlife and fewer crowds

ESSENTIAL PHOTO

Upcycled industrial detritus at Oamaru's Steampunk HQ

BEST FOR DOLPHINS

Swim with the world's smallest and rarest dolphin in Akaroa Harbour

East Coast Express

The West Coast Rd and Inland Scenic Route may hoover up most of the tourist traffic heading north and south, but this road still claims the crown of 'State Hwy 1'. Typical of NZ, though, it's mostly little more than a quiet country road, dotted with sweet-as towns and peppered with detours to surprising places such as Oamaru's Victorian Precinct, and experiences such as swimming with dolphins in Akaroa.

▲ Mt Arrowsmit (2795m)

Lake Heron

Mesopotamia

Lake Tekapo

Peel Forest

Lake Tekapo (8)

Geraldine

Burkes Pass (709m)

Fairlie (79)

Temuka (8)

Timaru ❹

(1)

Waimate (82)

Waitaki River

Takiroa
Duntroon

Glenavy (83)

Pukeuri Junction

Weston ❸ **Oamaru**

(85)

Hampden

❷ **Moeraki**

Palmerston

Shag Point

Karitane

(1)

Port Chalmers

❶ **Dunedin**
START

(24)

- - - - - - - - - - - - - -

TRIP HIGHLIGHT

❶ Dunedin

Dunedin is synonymous with the students who attend the country's oldest university. Swelling the city's population during term time, they inject an energy and edgy creativity that gives the city's Victorian streetscapes and cultural scene some zing.

Settled by two shiploads of Scots in the mid-19th century, Dunedin is also defined by its Scottishness, and remains immensely proud of its heritage. Indeed, Dunedin's name is derived from the Gaelic

name for Edinburgh: *Dùn Èideann*.

The region's broader, multicultural backstory is presented in conventional but satisfying style at **Otago Museum** (☏03-474 7474; www.otagomuseum. nz; 419 Great King St, North Dunedin; ◷10am-5pm), the centerpiece of which is *Southern Land, Southern People* showcasing Otago's past and present, from geology and dinosaurs to the modern day. The Tāngata Whenua Māori gallery houses an impressive *waka taua* (war canoe), wonderfully worn old carvings, and *pounamu* (greenstone) weapons, tools and jewellery.

✕ 🛏 p345

The Drive » Drive north on SH1, over the Silverpeaks Range and back down to Blueskin Bay. SH1 then tracks mainly inland, passing through rural Palmerston before continuing along the coast. After 74km, turn right and drive 2km along Hillgrove-Moeraki Rd to Moeraki village.

- - - - - - - - - -

Moeraki

The name Moeraki means 'a place to sleep by day', which should give you some clue as to the pace of life in this little fishing village – one of the first European settlements in NZ.

There are two major attractions here; the first is NZ's most famous seafood restaurant, **Fleur's Place** (☎03-439 4480; www.fleursplace.com; Old Jetty, 169 Haven St; mains $35-44; ☺10.30am-late Wed-Sun). Down by the wharf, it

LINK YOUR TRIP

11 **Kaikoura Coast**
Head up from Christchurch through wine country and New Zealand's marine-life mecca to the ferry port town of Picton.

24 **Southern Scenic Route**
Dunedin bookends this classic U-shaped coastal and countryside route through to Fiordland and Te Anau.

 0 — 50 km
0 — 25 miles

341

has a rumble-tumble look about it, but inside you can tuck into fresh shellfish, tender muttonbird and other recently landed ocean bounty.

Just north on SH1 is the turn-off to **Moeraki Boulders** (Te Kaihinaki), a collection of large spherical boulders scattered along a beautiful stretch of beach (best viewed at low tide; also accessible via a 45-minute beach walk from the village). Heading north along the beach, the **Kaiks Wildlife Trail** leads to a cute wooden lighthouse, with the chance of spotting yellow-eyed penguins and fur seals.

p345

The Drive » Return to SH1 and head north for 40km to Oamaru, driving through relatively flat pastoral land, a journey of just over 30 minutes.

- - - - - - - - - -

TRIP HIGHLIGHT

3 Oamaru

In recent decades Oamaru's canny creative types have cottoned on to the uniqueness of their surviving Victorian streetscapes, unlocking the town's potential for extreme kookiness.

Down by the harbour, the **Victorian Precinct** is a treasure trove of once-neglected buildings now filled with offbeat galleries, fascinating shops, hip venues and even an 'urban winery'.

Most visible are the steampunks, their aesthetic boldly celebrating the past and the future with an ethos of 'tomorrow as it used to be'. Inside **Steampunk HQ** (027 778 6547; www. steampunkoamaru.co.nz; 1 Itchen St; adult/child $10/2; 10am-5pm), imaginatively upcycled ancient machines wheeze and splutter, and the industrial detritus of the last century or so is repurposed and reimagined to creepy effect.

The Drive » Drive northeast on SH1. Just before Waitaki Bridge, around 19km from Oamaru, is one of NZ's best restaurants. Continue north through primarily agricultural land all the way to Timaru, 86km from Oamaru.

- - - - - - - - - -

4 Timaru

Highway travellers could be forgiven for thinking that this small port city is merely a handy stop for food and fuel. Not so. Straying into town reveals a remarkably intact Edwardian centre with some good dining and interesting shopping, not to mention a clutch of cultural attractions and lovely parks.

Fronting the town, expansive **Caroline Bay Park** ranges over an Edwardian-style garden under the Bay Hill cliff, then across broad lawns to low sand dunes and the beach itself. As well as a playground, skate

park, sound shell and ice-cream kiosk, it boasts the triumphant **Trevor Griffiths Rose Garden**, particularly aromatic in the late afternoon sun.

Eager aesthetes may wish to make the pilgrimage to the **Aigantighe Art Gallery** (www.timaru. govt.nz/art-gallery; 49 Wai-iti Rd; 10am-4pm Tue-Fri, noon-4pm Sat & Sun), one of the South Island's finest public galleries, with a notable collection of NZ and European art.

The Drive » Stay on SH1 north to the Canterbury Plains, crossing NZ's longest bridge at Rakaia. At Burnham, 135km from Timaru, turn off SH1 and drive through Lincoln to Tai

Oamaru Steampunk HQ

Tapu, turning right on to SH75 towards Akaroa on the Banks Peninsula via a winding drive. It'll take three hours to drive this 200km leg.

TRIP HIGHLIGHT

5 Akaroa

Charming Akaroa ('Long Harbour' in Māori) on the Banks Peninsula, was the site of the country's first French settlement. It strives to recreate the feel of a sleepy, French provincial village, down to the names of its streets and houses, but its peacefulness is periodically shattered by hordes descending from gargantuan cruise ships. Seek refuge in the old churches, gardens and cemeteries that lend Akaroa its character.

Hands down the most beautiful spot in Akaroa is the **Giant's House** (www.thegiantshouse.co.nz; 68 Rue Balguerie; adult/child $20/10; ⏲12-5pm Jan-Apr, 2-4pm May-Dec), an 1880 residence once occupied by Akaroa's first bank manager but now the labour of love of artist Josie Martin. Her whimsical combination of sculpture and mosaics cascades down a hillside garden, echoing Gaudí and Miró in its intricate collages.

🍴 🛏 p345

The Drive » Follow SH75 for 54km back around Akaroa Harbour and over to Little River. Turn right into Gebbies Pass Rd, and drive 9km to Teddington beside Lyttelton Harbour. Turn left to meander along the harbourside for 17km to Lyttelton town. Total distance is 80km.

TRIP HIGHLIGHT

6 Lyttelton

Badly damaged during the 2010 and 2011 earthquakes, the port town of Lyttelton has re-emerged as one of Christchurch's most vibrant communities, one with an obsession with its stomach.

Time your visit to coincide with the **Lyttelton Farmers' Market** (www.lyttelton.net.nz; London St; ⊙10am-1pm Sat), a smorgasbord of local produce, artisan goodies and high-quality food.

The tiny town has a more than respectable selection of bars and eateries, too, some of which have risen from the rubble in admirable fashion. One example is **Lyttelton Coffee Company** (☎03-328 8096; www.lytteltoncoffee.co.nz; 29 London St; meals $11-23; ⊙7am-4pm Mon-Fri, 8am-4pm Sat & Sun; 🖉 📶), a cafe serving wholesome food in an atmospheric environment featuring edgy artwork, occasional music and harbour views from the back deck.

✗ p345

The Drive » Drive through the 2km Lyttelton road tunnel, NZ's longest, and continue northwest on SH74 following signs for Christchurch city centre. Out of peak times, this 13km journey should take around 20 minutes.

- - - - - - - - - - - - - -

❼ Christchurch

Re-emerging amid a major rebuild, post-quake Christchurch emits a crazy, occasionally chaotic but undeniably exciting vibe. To see how far it has come, visit **Quake City** (www.quakecity.co.nz; 99 Cashel St; adult/child $20/free; ⊙10am-5pm). Conveniently located in the groovy Re:START (p287) shopping precinct, this compact museum retells stories through photography and various artefacts, including bits that have fallen off the cathedral, but most affecting is

the film featuring locals recounting their own experiences.

The suburb of Woolston, on the way between Lyttelton and the Christchurch CBD, is home to the **Tannery** (www.thetannery.co.nz; 3 Garlands Rd, Woolston; ⊙10am-5pm Mon-Wed, Fri & Sat, to 8pm Thu). A fine restoration job has seen this historic factory converted into a boutique but unpretentious shopping centre, complete with an art-house cinema and eateries. The hub of the complex is the **Brewery** (www.casselsbrewery.co.nz; 3 Garlands Rd, Woolston; ⊙7am-late), a notable gastropub featuring hand-pulled craft beers, wood-fired pizza, live music and a pleasant courtyard.

🛏 p345

BANKS PENINSULA

Gorgeous Banks Peninsula (Horomaka) was formed by two giant volcanic eruptions about eight million years ago; the volcanoes are long extinct and have since been eroded by the elements. Harbours and bays radiate out from the peninsula's centre, giving it an unusual cogwheel shape. Akaroa – its main township – is popular with visitors, including many who now arrive on large cruise ships.

The must-do is the absurdly beautiful drive along **Summit Road**, around the edge of one of the original craters. It's also worth exploring the little bays that dot the peninsula's perimeter, accessible via steep and winding routes spidering off the Summit Rd – perfectly fine for driving but take your time.

The waters around Banks Peninsula are home to one of the smallest and rarest dolphin species, the Hector's dolphin, found only in NZ waters. Tours (September to May) with **Black Cat Cruises** (☎03-304 7641; www.blackcat.co.nz; Main Wharf; nature cruises adult/child $74/30, dolphin swims adult/child $155/120) provide good odds for striking the dolphin-swim off your bucket list: a 98% chance of spotting them and over 80% success rate of actually swimming with them. All activities involving marine mammals such as dolphins are highly regulated and monitored by the Department of Conservation. Other wildlife tours from Akaroa offer the chance to see white-flippered penguins, orca, seals and other critters.

Eating & Sleeping

Dunedin ❶

✗ Starfish   Cafe $$

(☎03-455 5940; www.starfishcafe.co.nz; 7/240 Forbury Rd, St Clair; mains brunch $14-20, dinner $20-30; ⊙7am-5pm Sun-Tue, to late Wed-Sat) Starfish is the coolest creature in the growing restaurant scene at St Clair Beach. Pop out on a weekday to score an outside table, and tuck into gourmet pizza and wine. Dinners are big and robust (steak, fish and chips, pulled-pork sliders), and there's a good selection of craft beer.

⫚ Majestic Mansions   Apartment $$

(☎03-456 5000; www.st-clair.co.nz; 15 Bedford St, St Clair; apt from $140; P 🛜) One street back from St Clair beach, this venerable 1920s apartment block has been thoroughly renovated, keeping the layout of the original little flats but sprucing them up with feature wallpaper and smart furnishings. Each has kitchen and laundry facilities.

For more places to eat and stay in Dunedin see pages 327 and 345.

Moeraki ❷

⫚ Riverside Haven Lodge & Holiday Park   Hostel $

(☎03-439 5830; www.riversidehaven.nz; 2328 Herbert Hampden Rd/SH1, Waianakarua; sites/ dm $12/31, s/d without bathroom $50/75, d with bathroom $85; 🛜) Nestled in a loop of the Waianakarua River, 12km north of the Moeraki turnoff, this pretty farm offers both bucolic camping sites and a colourful lodge with a sunny communal lounge. Kids will love the playground and highland cattle; parents will love the spa and peaceful vibe.

Waitaki Bridge

✗ Riverstone Kitchen   Modern NZ $$

(☎03-431 3505; www.riverstonekitchen.co.nz; 1431 SH1, Waitaki Bridge; breakfast $16-18, lunch $20-32, dinner $32-35; ⊙9am-5pm Thu-Mon, 6pm-late Thu-Sun) A riverstone fireplace and polished concrete floors set the scene for a menu that's modern without being overworked. Much of the produce is from the extensive on-site kitchen gardens (take a look, they're impressive), topped up with locally sourced venison, pork, salmon and beef. It's a smashing brunch option, with excellent coffee and legendary truffled scrambled eggs.

Banks Peninsula

✗ Hilltop Tavern   Pub Food $$

(☎03-325 1005; www.thehilltop.co.nz; 5207 Christchurch-Akaroa Rd; pizzas $24-26, mains $23-30; ⊙10am-late, reduced hours in winter) Killer views, craft beer, proper wood-fired pizzas and a pool table. Occasional live music seals the deal for locals and visitors alike at this historic pub. Enjoy grandstand views of Akaroa harbour backdropped by the peninsula.

⫚ Coombe Farm   B&B $$

(☎03-304 7239; www.coombefarm.co.nz; 18 Old Le Bons Track, Takamatua Valley; d $170-190; 🛜) Choose between the private and romantic Shepherd's Hut – complete with an outdoor bath – and the historic farmhouse lovingly restored in shades of Laura Ashley. After breakfast you can take a walk to the waterfall with Ned, the friendly dog.

Lyttelton ❻

✗ Roots   Modern NZ $$$

(☎03-328 7658; www.rootsrestaurant.co.nz; 8 London St; 5-/8-/12-course degustation excl wine $90/125/185; ⊙11.30am-2pm Fri & Sat, 5.30pm-late Tue-Sat) Let chef/owner Giulio Sturla take you on a magical mystery tour via degustation menus championing all things local and seasonal. Individual dishes are revealed and described as they arrive at the table, and can be accompanied by carefully curated wine matches, should you choose to splurge.

Christchurch ❼

For places to eat and stay in Christchurch see pages 171, 225, 235, 245, 260 and 284.

STRETCH
YOUR LEGS
QUEENSTOWN

Start/Finish Queenstown Recreation Ground

Distance 4.5km

Duration Three hours

Soak up Queenstown's buzzy cosmopolitan vibe and sublime lakeside setting. Be bamboozled by the mountain views and take stock with a coffee, wine or beer in its surfeit of quality cafes and bars.

Take this walk on Trips

Queenstown Recreation Ground

Park in the car park on Memorial St, then linger in the park to watch any tandem paragliders dropping in from the top of the Gondola. Tempted? You'll get your chance at the end of this walking tour.

The Walk » Head down Camp St and turn right into Shotover St. Squeeze past Fergburger's queue and turn left down Rees St.

Vudu Cafe & Larder

Fortify yourself at Vudu Cafe & Larder (p303) with great coffee, sticky buns or a tasty cooked breakfast while admiring the huge photo of a much less populated Queenstown, or head to the rear garden for lake and mountain views.

The Walk » At Eichardt's Hotel turn left into the Mall, then right down the alleyway by Ballarat Bar leading to Searle Lane (a late-night hot spot). Keep going to Church St and turn left.

St Peter's Anglican Church

Admire this pretty wood-beamed stone church (1932) with its colourful stained glass, gilded organ, and an eagle-shaped cedar lectern carved in 1874 by Ah Tong, a Chinese immigrant.

The Walk » Turn right into Camp St, walk to the end, then over the creek. Stay on the footpath as far as the four-way intersection then head down Park St to Queenstown Gardens.

Queenstown Gardens

Set on a little tongue of land, this pretty park was founded in 1876 by promenading Victorians. Various pathways make for a decent stroll, although many folk just come here to laze around and smell the roses. Active types should head for the frisbee golf course or ice-skating rink.

The Walk » Cut through the ice rink car park and wander downhill to the Lakeside Path. Follow it in a clockwise direction, resting at a bench at the end of the peninsula.

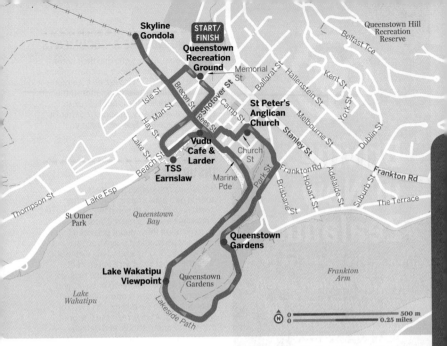

Lake Wakatipu Viewpoint

Soak up the majestic views across Lake Wakatipu to Cecil and Walter Peaks. There were four paddle steamers and 30 other craft plying these waters during the gold rushes; today the peace is broken occasionally by jetboats and the tooting of the TSS *Earnslaw* steamer.

The Walk » Continue along the path back to town and follow the pedestrianised waterfront path to Steamer Wharf.

TSS Earnslaw

More than a century old, the steamship TSS *Earnslaw* was once the lake's major means of transport. Now its puffs of black smoke seem a little incongruous in such a pristine setting. Climb aboard for the 1½-hour Lake Wakatipu tour or the 3½-hour excursion to the high-country Walter Peak Farm for sheepdog and shearing demonstrations.

The Walk » Behind the wharf building, follow the road around into Shotover St and continue to Brecon St. Turn left and head up the steps,

crossing Man St to follow the masses up to the Skyline Gondola.

Skyline Gondola

See Queenstown from on high at the top of the **Skyline Gondola** (☎03-441 0101; www.skyline.co.nz; Brecon St; adult/child return $32/20; ⊙9am-late), also home to an array of activities including paragliding, mountain biking, bungy jumping and the outrageously fun luge. There are also some great and very scenic walking trails that can be accessed from the top, including a loop track through the Douglas firs (30 minutes return). The energetic (or frugal) can forgo the gondola and hike to the top on the **Tiki Trail** and then continue on the **Ben Lomond Track**.

The Walk » Return back down Brecon St and turn left into Isle St. At the bottom turn right into Camp St to return to the Recreation Ground car park.

Driving in New Zealand

New Zealand crams diversity into its island borders, and road journeys seamlessly combine ocean-fringed coastal roads, soaring alpine peaks and impressive glaciers.

Driving Fast Facts

➡ **Right or left?** Drive on the left

➡ **Manual or automatic?** Mostly automatic

➡ **Legal driving age** 18

➡ **Top speed limit** 100km/h

➡ **Best bumper sticker** 'Sweet as bro'

DRIVING LICENCE & DOCUMENTS

International visitors can use their home country driving licence, or an International Driving Permit (IDP) issued by their home country's automobile association. If their home country licence is not in English, they must also carry an approved translation of the licence. See www.nzta.govt.nz/driver-licences.

INSURANCE

Rental car companies include basic insurance in hire agreements, but it's often worth paying an additional fee – usually on a per day basis – to reduce your excess. This will bring the amount you need to pay in case of an accident down from around $1500 or $2000 to around $200 or $300. Note that most insurance agreements won't cover the cost of damage to glass (including the windscreen) or tyres, and insurance coverage is often invalidated on beaches and certain rough (4WD) unsealed roads. Always read the fine print, ask pertinent questions, and definitely refrain from driving a rental car along Ninety Mile Beach, Northland.

HIRING A CAR

Hiring a vehicle is very popular in NZ, and the country is perfect for self-drive adventures. Most – but not all – rental car companies require drivers to be at least 21 years old. The main companies are all represented; the following are good-value independent operators with national networks.

Ace Rental Cars (☑09-303 3112, ☑0800 502 277; www.acerentalcars.co.nz)

Apex Rentals (☑03-363 3000, ☑0800 500 660; www.apexrentals.co.nz)

Go Rentals (☑09-974 1598, ☑0800 467 368; www.gorentals.co.nz)

Also very popular is renting a campervan and taking advantage of the Department of Conservation (DOC)'s network of campsites. The following are three well-regarded local companies.

Apollo (☑09-889 2976, ☑0800 113 131; www.apollocamper.co.nz)

Jucy (☑09-929 2462, ☑0800 399 736; www.jucy.co.nz)

Maui (☎09-255 3910, ☎0800 688 558; www.maui.co.nz)

Another option is to contact **Transfercar** (☎09-630 7533; www.transfercar.co.nz), one-way relocation specialists for car rental.

BUYING A VEHICLE IN NEW ZEALAND

Buying a car then selling it at the end of your travels can be one of the cheapest ways to see NZ.

➡ Auckland is the easiest place to buy a car, followed by Christchurch. **Turners Auctions** (www.turners.co.nz) is NZ's biggest car-auction operator, with 10 locations.

➡ Make sure your prospective vehicle has a **Warrant of Fitness** (WoF) and registration valid for a reasonable period: see the **New Zealand Transport Agency** website (www.nzta.govt.nz) for details.

➡ Buyers should take out third-party insurance, covering the cost of repairs to another vehicle resulting from an accident that is your fault: try the **Automobile Association** (AA; ☎0800 500 444; www.aa.co.nz/travel).

➡ To have a car inspected before you purchase it (around $150), see **Vehicle Inspection New Zealand** (VINZ; ☎09-573 3230, ☎0800 468 469; www.vinz.co.nz) or the AA.

➡ To establish if there's anything dodgy about the car (eg stolen, outstanding debts), try the AA's **LemonCheck** (☎09-420 3090, ☎0800 536 662; www.lemoncheck.co.nz) service.

BRINGING YOUR OWN VEHICLE

As NZ is an island nation, it is extremely rare for travellers to bring their own vehicle to the country. One exception where it could be financially worthwhile is for Australian visitors who are planning on travelling in their own campervan or caravan. Search for 'Importing a Vehicle Temporarily' on www.nzta.govt.nz.

MAPS

➡ Excellent national and regional maps published by the **New Zealand Automobile Association** (www.aa.co.nz) are available

Road Trip Websites

AUTOMOBILE ASSOCIATIONS
New Zealand Automobile Association (www.aa.co.nz/travel) Provides emergency breakdown services, maps and accommodation guides.

CONDITIONS & TRAFFIC
New Zealand Transport Agency (www.nzta.govt.nz/traffic) Advice on road works, road closures and potential delays.

ROAD RULES
Drive Safe (www.drivesafe.org.nz) A simplified version of NZ's road rules, with the information of most interest to international visitors.

New Zealand Transport Agency (www.nzta.govt.nz) Search for 'Road Code' for the full version of NZ's road rules.

free of charge at regional i-SITEs (tourist information centres) and at main international airports. Also free and available at i-SITEs are regional maps and guides published by **Jasons** (www.jasons.co.nz).

➡ More detailed maps including street and topographic information are published by **Land Information New Zealand** (LINZ; www.linz.govt.nz).

➡ The Automobile Association also has a good online **Travel Time and Distance Calculator** to plan driving routes around NZ.

ROADS & CONDITIONS

➡ Kiwi traffic is usually pretty light, but it's easy to get stuck behind a slow-moving truck or a line of campervans. Be patient.

➡ One-way bridges, winding routes and unsealed gravel roads all require a more cautious driving approach.

➡ Carry tyre chains with you if you're travelling in alpine areas or over high passes during autumn and winter.

➡ If you stop for a photo, pull well over to the left and ensure your vehicle is not in the way of traffic.

Road Distances (km)

	Auckland	Cape Reinga	Hamilton	Napier	New Plymouth	Paihia	Rotorua	Taupo	Tauranga	Thames	Waitomo Caves
Cape Reinga	430										
Hamilton	125	555									
Napier	420	860	300								
New Plymouth	360	790	240	410							
Paihia	225	220	340	645	590						
Rotorua	235	670	110	220	300	460					
Taupo	280	720	155	140	300	505	80				
Tauranga	210	635	110	300	330	435	85	155			
Thames	115	540	110	360	340	345	170	210	115		
Waitomo Caves	200	620	75	300	180	420	165	170	150	175	
Wellington	640	1080	520	320	350	860	450	375	530	590	460

➡ Distances on the map can be deceptive as narrow roads are often slower going than expected. Allow enough time for travel, and in more remote areas, ask at local petrol stations about the road ahead.

➡ Animal hazards often include farmers moving herds of cows or flocks of sheep. Slow your vehicle to a crawl – you may need to stop altogether – and patiently let the animals move around your car.

➡ Because of Auckland's geographic location, squeezed into a narrow coastal isthmus, rush hour motorway traffic from 7am to 9am and 4pm to 7pm can be very slow. If possible, try and avoid heading north or south out of the city around these times.

ROAD RULES

The full version of New Zealand's road code can be found on www.nzta.govt.nz, but here are the basics:

➡ Drive on the left, overtake on the right.

➡ Safety belts (seat belts) must be worn by the driver and all passengers. Younger children must be secured in an approved child seat (these can be rented from rental-car companies).

➡ Motorcyclists and their passengers must always wear helmets.

➡ When entering a roundabout (traffic circle), always give way to the right.

➡ Come to a complete halt at STOP signs.

➡ The speed limit is 100km/h on motorways and the open road, and usually 50km/h in towns and cities. Always drive to the conditions and reduce speed if it is raining, windy or icy.

➡ For drivers over 20 years of age, the legal alcohol limit is 50mg of alcohol per 100ml of blood. This equates to around one to two standard drinks, but as different people process alcohol differently it is recommended that drivers should not drink at all. In NZ, drivers under the age of 20 cannot legally drink any alcohol if they are planning on driving.

➡ Driving under the influence of drugs is strictly illegal.

PARKING

Finding a car park definitely gets easier – and substantially cheaper – out of Auckland, but locations around key attractions

Road Distances (km), South Island

	Blenheim	Christchurch	Dunedin	Franz Josef Glacier	Greymouth	Invercargill	Kaikoura	Milford Sound	Nelson	Picton	Queenstown	Te Anau
Christchurch	310											
Dunedin	665	360										
Franz Josef Glacier	500	390	560									
Greymouth	330	250	550	180								
Invercargill	870	570	210	530	710							
Kaikoura	130	185	535	540	330	745						
Milford Sound	1060	760	410	630	805	275	930					
Nelson	115	425	775	470	290	990	245	1100				
Picton	30	340	690	530	355	900	160	1090	120			
Queenstown	785	480	285	355	530	190	660	290	820	815		
Te Anau	945	640	295	515	690	160	815	120	980	975	170	
Timaru	465	165	200	490	350	410	340	605	580	495	330	490

definitely get very busy during peak periods.

➡ In city centres, most on-street parking is by 'pay and display' tickets available from on-street machines.

➡ Timing for paid parking is usually from 9am to 6pm Monday to Saturday with free parking on Sundays. This does vary in larger urban centres, however, so always check times carefully.

➡ Cash is needed for machines in provincial towns, but most city machines can also be paid by credit card or by smartphone.

➡ Most expensive is central Auckland, with costs up to $6 per hour from Monday to Friday. Prices are usually cheaper on weekends.

➡ See www.wilsonparking.co.nz for locations of paid multistorey and underground car parks in Auckland, Hamilton, Wellington, Christchurch, Queenstown, Invercargill and Dunedin.

➡ Yellow lines along the edge of the road indicate a nonparking area, and drivers should also be aware of 'loading zones' which can only be used by commercial vehicles for short time periods.

➡ Clamping of vehicles is not very common in NZ, but council parking wardens and tow-truck drivers strictly enforce local parking rules –

tow-away warnings should definitely be taken seriously.

FUEL

➡ Fuel is readily available throughout the country.

➡ See www.aa.co.nz/cars/motoring-blog/petrolwatch for current petrol and diesel prices.

➡ Fuel prices are generally cheaper in cities than in provincial areas.

➡ Most supermarkets offer fuel discount vouchers with shopping purchases over $40; check your docket.

SAFETY

➡ Driving in NZ is generally a hassle-free experience, but it is not unknown for rental cars and campervans to be targeted by opportunistic thieves.

➡ Always keep baggage and valuables locked in the back of the vehicle, out of sight. When parking in unattended car parks in popular tourist spots, consider carrying passports, money and other valuable items with you while you are away from your vehicle.

➡ If you have just arrived in the country after a long international flight, it is strongly recommended that you have a re-energising overnight stay in your city of arrival before getting behind the wheel on NZ roads.

➡ **DriveSafe** (www.drivesafe.org.nz) is an excellent online resource – published in English, French, German and Chinese – for international drivers on NZ roads.

DOC CAMPSITES & FREEDOM CAMPING

A great option for campervan travellers are the 250-plus vehicle-accessible 'Conservation Campsites' run by the Department of Conservation (www.doc.govt.nz). Fees range from free (basic toilets and fresh water) to $15 per adult (flush toilets and showers). Pick up brochures detailing every campsite from DOC offices and i-SITEs or see online.

New Zealand is so photogenic, it's often tempting to just pull off the road and camp for the night, but there are strict guidelines for 'freedom camping'. See www.camping.org.nz for more freedom-camping tips.

➡ Never assume it's OK to camp somewhere: always ask a local or check with the local i-SITE, DOC office or commercial camping ground.

➡ If you are freedom camping, treat the area with respect and do not leave any litter.

➡ If your chosen campsite doesn't have toilet facilities and neither does your campervan, it's illegal for you to sleep there (your campervan must also have an on-board grey-water storage system).

➡ Legislation allows for $200 instant fines for camping in prohibited areas or improper disposal of waste (in cases where dumping waste could damage the environment, fees are up to $10,000).

RADIO

New Zealand is well-covered by radio, and national station networks can be listened to on different frequencies around the country. Check each network's website for the relevant frequency in various areas of the country.

Driving Problem-Buster

What should I do if my car breaks down? Call the service number of your car-hire company and a local garage will be contacted. If you're travelling in your own vehicle, join the New Zealand Automobile Association; they can attend to breakdowns day and night. Another option is Motoring 24-7 (www.roadside-assistance.co.nz).

What if I have an accident? Exchange basic information with the other party (name, insurance details, driving licence number). No discussion of liability needs to take place at the scene. It's a good idea to photograph the scene of the accident noting key details. Call the police (☑111) if necessary.

What should I do if I get stopped by the police? They will want to see your driving licence, and a valid form of ID if you are visiting from overseas. Breath testing is mandatory in NZ.

What if I can't find anywhere to stay? Try to book ahead during busy periods. Local i-SITEs can often help with last-minute accommodation bookings.

Will I need to pay tolls in advance? New Zealand has three toll roads: the Northern Gateway Toll Road north of Auckland, and the Tauranga Eastern Link Toll Road and the Takitimu Drive Toll Road, both in Tauranga. Tolls are specific to a vehicle's registration number and can be paid online at www.nzta.govt.nz or at Caltex and BP service stations. Tolls can be paid either prior to travel, or within five days of travelling on a specific toll road.

Cruising Cook Strait

On a clear day, sailing into Wellington Harbour, or into Picton in the Marlborough Sounds, is magical. Cook Strait can be rough, but the big ferries handle it well, and distractions include cafes, bars and cinemas. Booking online is easiest; sailings can usually be booked up to a couple of days in advance. Exceptions are during school and public holidays, and from late December to the end of January. There are two ferry options:

Bluebridge Ferries (☏04-471 6188, 0800 844 844; www.bluebridge.co.nz; 50 Waterloo Quay) Crossing takes 3½ hours; up to four sailings in each direction daily. Bluebridge is based at Waterloo Quay, opposite Wellington train station.

Interislander (☏04-498 3302, 0800 802 802; www.interislander.co.nz; Aotea Quay) Crossings take three hours, 10 minutes; up to five sailings in each direction daily. Interislander is about 2km northeast of Wellington's centre at Aotea Quay.

Car-hire companies allow you to pickup/drop off vehicles at ferry terminals. If you arrive outside business hours, arrangements can be made to collect your vehicle from the terminal car park. In some cases, it may suit the hire company for you to take your rental car with you on the ferry – eg for relocations etc – so ask them to advise what will be the best deal.

Radio New Zealand National (www.radionz.co.nz/national) News-oriented station with excellent coverage of local issues, arts and culture.

Newstalk ZB (www.newstalkzb.co.nz) Talkback station where the issues of the day are discussed passionately.

Radio Sport (www.radiosport.co.nz) Understand the difference between the All Blacks, Black Caps and Silver Ferns (respectively NZ's national rugby, cricket and netball teams).

Hauraki (www.hauraki.co.nz) Iconic rock music station with a quintessentially irreverent Kiwi tone.

BEHIND THE SCENES

SEND US YOUR FEEDBACK

We love to hear from travellers – your comments help make our books better. We read every word, and we guarantee that your feedback goes straight to the authors. Visit **lonelyplanet. com/contact** to submit your updates and suggestions.

Note: We may edit, reproduce and incorporate your comments in Lonely Planet products such as guidebooks, websites and digital products, so let us know if you don't want your comments reproduced or your name acknowledged. For a copy of our privacy policy visit lonelyplanet.com/privacy.

ACKNOWLEDGMENTS

Climate map data adapted from Peel MC, Finlayson BL & McMahon TA (2007) 'Updated World Map of the Köppen-Geiger Climate Classification', *Hydrology and Earth System Sciences*, 11, 163344.

Front cover photographs: (top) Piha Beach and Lion Rock at sunset, Travelscape Images/Alamy©; (left) Vintage Dodge car, A Demotes/Corbis©; (right) Road sign in front of Mt Ruapehu, Tim90/ Shutterstock©

Back cover photograph: Beach at Mahia Peninsula, Doug Pearson/AWL©

WRITER THANKS

BRETT ATKINSON

Cheers to the chefs and craft brewers of NZ for on the road sustenance, and to Carol for support on island, capital city and Hobbit-inspired getaways. Sarah Bennett and Lee Slater were brilliant co-authors, and thanks to Tasmin Waby at Lonely Planet for the opportunity to explore my Kiwi backyard.

SARAH BENNETT & LEE SLATER

Thanks to everyone who helped us find the South Island's best trips, particularly DOC and i-SITE staff, and travellers, as well the kindly folks who let us park up and put our flagon in the fridge. Thanks also to our fellow author, Brett Atkinson, and Tasmin Waby for paving the way.

THIS BOOK

This 1st edition of *New Zealand's Best Trips* was researched and written by Brett Atkinson, Sarah Bennett and Lee Slater. This guidebook was produced by the following:

Destination Editor Tasmin Waby
Coordinating Editor Gemma Graham
Product Editor Tracy Whitmey
Senior Cartographer Diana Von Holdt
Book Designer Cam Ashley
Assisting Editors Imogen Bannister, Michelle Bennett, Bruce Evans, Jodie Martire, Monique Perrin, Jeanette Wall
Assisting Cartographers Corey Hutchison, Julie Sheridan
Cover Researcher Naomi Parker
Thanks to Jennifer Carey, David Carroll, Daniel Corbett, Peter Dragicevich, Lauren Keith, Catherine Naghten, Charles Rawlings-Way, Angela Tinson, Tony Wheeler.

OUR STORY

A beat-up old car, a few dollars in the pocket and a sense of adventure. In 1972 that's all Tony and Maureen Wheeler needed for the trip of a lifetime – across Europe and Asia overland to Australia. It took several months, and at the end – broke but inspired – they sat at their kitchen table writing and stapling together their first travel guide, *Across Asia on the Cheap*. Within a week they'd sold 1500 copies. Lonely Planet was born.

Today, Lonely Planet has offices in Dublin, Franklin, Melbourne, London, Oakland, Beijing and Delhi, with more than 600 staff and writers. We share Tony's belief that 'a great guidebook should do three things: inform, educate and amuse'.

INDEX

OUR WRITERS

BRETT ATKINSON

Born in Rotorua, and now resident in Auckland, Brett Atkinson has been tripping around New Zealand for most of his life. For this 1st edition of *New Zealand's Best Trips*, he ventured to sleepy harbours in Northland, negotiated coastal roads around Coromandel, and quaffed the best of Wellington craft beer. Together with his wife, Carol, he's explored many countries independently behind the wheel of a car.

My Favourite Trip `1` **Northland & the Bay of Islands** I love this area's diversity, especially the differences between the east and west coasts. It's also a poignant journey packed with many family memories.

SARAH BENNETT

Sarah grew up in Marlborough, but her life-long love affair with Wellington has left her loyalties divided between North and South. What is constant is her obsession with NZ road trips, which keeps her and husband, Lee, on the road in their little campervan for around four months each year. Their mountain bikes always come with them, as do hiking boots, a hot water bottle and the laptop (of course) because it's not always sunshine and wine.

My Favourite Trip `15` **The West Coast Road** because few things make me happier than unspoilt New Zealand wilderness.

Read more about Sarah at: https://auth. lonelyplanet.com/profiles/sarahbennett39

LEE SLATER

Lee embarked on his first NZ road trip just after moving there from the UK in 1999. What soon became blindingly obvious was the difference between the two country's roads. Swapping 20-mile traffic jams on multi-laned highways for empty, winding roads cut through some of the world's most impressive scenery has been a tough job. Upgrading from pup tent to campervan with his beau, Sarah Bennett, has softened the blow somewhat.

My Favourite Trip `19` **Inland Scenic Route** because it's filled with the things that make me sing: mountains, lakes and Central Otago pinot noir.

Read more about Lee at: https://auth. lonelyplanet. com/profiles/leeslater41

Published by Lonely Planet Publications Pty Ltd
ABN 36 005 607 983
1st edition – Sep 2016
ISBN 978 1 78657 025 3
© Lonely Planet 2016   Photographs © as indicated 2016
10 9 8 7 6 5 4 3 2
Printed in Malaysia

Although the authors and Lonely Planet have taken all reasonable care in preparing this book, we make no warranty about the accuracy or completeness of its content and, to the maximum extent permitted, disclaim all liability arising from its use.